Brief Review in Global Studies

Robert Feeney
Maureen Kovalesky
James Barry

Prentice Hall

Needham, Massachusetts Upper Saddle River, New Jersey

CREDITS

Illustrations Boston Graphics, Inc.
Cover Design Hannus Design Associates

ISBN 0-13-435905-4

1 2 3 4 5 6 7 8 9 02 01 00 99 98

Table of Contents

Pretest: Regents Examination—January 1990 1
Answers to the Pretest 13
Test-Taking Strategies: What You Need to Know to Pass the Regents Exam 14
Key Social Studies Vocabulary to Know 28
Key Geography Terms to Know 30
Key English Vocabulary to Know 31

UNIT 1 The Geographic Setting 32

Section 1 Africa 33
Section 2 India/South Asia 39
Section 3 Southeast Asia 43
Section 4 China 46
Section 5 Japan 49
Section 6 Latin America 52
Section 7 The Middle East 58
Section 8 Western Europe 63
Section 9 Northern Eurasia and Eastern Europe 67

UNIT 2 Global History 74

Section 1 Africa 75
Section 2 India/South Asia 81
Section 3 Southeast Asia 86
Section 4 China 92
Section 5 Japan 98
Section 6 Latin America 103
Section 7 The Middle East 115
Section 8 Western Europe 120
Section 9 Northern Eurasia and Eastern Europe 162

UNIT 3 Global Society 186

Section 1 Africa 187
Section 2 India/South Asia 191
Section 3 Southeast Asia 196
Section 4 China 198
Section 5 Japan 203
Section 6 Latin America 206
Section 7 The Middle East 210
Section 8 Western Europe 215
Section 9 Northern Eurasia and Eastern Europe 222

UNIT 4 Global Economics 236

Section 1 Africa 237
Section 2 India/South Asia 242
Section 3 Southeast Asia 245
Section 4 China 247
Section 5 Japan 251
Section 6 Latin America 255
Section 7 The Middle East 260
Section 8 Western Europe 264
Section 9 Northern Eurasia and Eastern Europe 271

UNIT 5 Global Politics 284

Section 1 Africa 285
Section 2 India/South Asia 290
Section 3 Southeast Asia 293
Section 4 China 296
Section 5 Japan 299
Section 6 Latin America 301
Section 7 The Middle East 306
Section 8 Western Europe 312
Section 9 Northern Eurasia and Eastern Europe 319

UNIT 6 The World Today 334

Regions Review Chart **346**

Chart: Nationalist Groups **348**

Chart: Nationalist Leaders **350**

Regents Examinations: 361
June 1998 362
June 1997 374
June 1996 387
June 1995 399

Glossary 408

Index 413

ABOUT THIS BOOK

This book is intended for you, the student, to help you to review the two-year Global Studies course. Throughout this book, the focus is on those facts that you need to know in order to succeed on the Regents Examination in Global Studies that you will be taking soon.

This book highlights the major ideas and themes that are stranded throughout the Global Studies curriculum. This approach will help you to understand more clearly what the nine regions have in common and what makes them different.

In this book, the 9th and 10th grade Global Studies curriculum is viewed from the perspectives of the social sciences contained in it. These include the geography, history, social life, economics, and political background of each of the nine global regions. As you review and study, the connections between regions will become clearer. The ''Making Connections'' column that appears on the syllabus review pages will also help you to tie facts together and to draw conclusions across the nine regions. You will be much more successful on the Regents exam if you can do this; the many cross-cultural questions require that you draw conclusions across the global regions.

The Pretest at the beginning of the book will provide you with some measure of your curriculum strengths and possible weaknesses. The Test-Taking Strategies section that follows provides you with instructions and hints for Regents success using examples from the Pretest.

This book contains many additional Regents questions for practice at the end of each unit. There are also four complete Regents exams at the conclusion of the book to provide complete test practice.

Review charts provide you with the opportunity to reinforce what you have learned as you bring the most important facts and themes together.

The goal of this book is to make your review of 5,000 years of global history more efficient and easier. Good luck on the Regents!

ABOUT THE AUTHORS

Robert Feeney is the District Coordinator of Social Studies for the William Floyd School District. He received his B.A. in Government and International Relations from the University of Notre Dame, and advanced degrees from S.U.N.Y. at Stony Brook and St. John's University. He is a member of the executive boards of the New York State Social Studies Supervisory Association and the Long Island Council for the Social Studies. He has served on Regents and RCT examination committees for the State Education Department. He has travelled throughout Europe, Asia, and Africa and is currently a trustee for the Middle Country School District.

Maureen Flanagan Kovalesky is a graduate of St. John's University. She holds a B.A. in Social Studies as well as an M.A. in International Relations and Comparative Government. Her teaching experience has centered on grades 9 and 10. Ms. Kovalesky has also contributed to several curriculum development projects in Global Studies. She is a teacher of Global Studies in the William Floyd School District.

James J. Barry is a teacher of Global Studies in the William Floyd School District. Born in Brooklyn, his Bachelor's degree is from the State University of New York, New Paltz (1968) and his Master's degree is from the University of California, Berkeley (1972). Mr. Barry has been employed by the United Nations and has traveled throughout Asia, the Soviet Union, and Western Europe.

The authors dedicate this book to their families and friends with appreciation for their love and support throughout the writing process: Robert Feeney to Roberta, Katie, and Christopher, with thanks to Karen Fitzer; Maureen Kovalesky to Paul, Sara, her parents, brothers and sisters; James Barry to Dawn and Jim.

Pretest

The following pretest is an actual New York State Regents Examination that was given in June of 1990. Taking this exam and checking your results will help you to identify your strengths and weaknesses. This process will help you to focus your review in Global Studies on those subject areas you need to study most.

On the day you take the Regents Examination, you will be filling in an Answer Sheet with your answers to Part I and writing your answers to Part II essay questions on separate sheets of paper. In this book, you will be circling the correct answers to Part I and answering essay questions on separate sheets of paper.

Complete this exam and then correct it, using the answers directly following it. As you proceed to read the Test-Taking Strategies section of this book, you will find even more information that will help you to succeed on the Regents Examination in Global Studies.

Part I (55 credits)

Answer all 48 questions in this part.

Directions (1–48): For each statement or question, write on the separate answer sheet the *number* of the word or expression that, of those given, best completes the statement or answers the question.

1 The geographic isolation of a people frequently reinforces
1 a traditional way of life
2 the development of scientific investigation
3 the need for higher education
4 a process of cultural diffusion

2 Nationalism is most likely to develop in an area that has
1 land suited to agriculture
2 adequate industry to supply consumer demands
3 a moderate climate with rivers for irrigation
4 common customs, language, and history

3 Which generalization about the geography of Latin America is accurate?
1 Geographic features prevented foreign imperialism.
2 Harsh climatic conditions have prevented the development of large-scale agriculture.
3 The lack of geographic barriers facilitated the development of transportation and communication systems.
4 Great variations in latitude and land forms resulted in a diversity of climates.

4 Which factor best accounts for the existence of cash-crop production as the major form of agriculture in many Central American nations today?
1 demand of world markets for such crops
2 lack of modern agricultural technology
3 inadequate supply of water and other natural resources
4 peasant ownership of most farmlands

5 Which has been an important factor that has discouraged investment in the economic development of many Latin American nations?
1 lack of natural resources
2 history of colonial dependence
3 declining birth rate
4 political instability

6 Which statement best describes the Roman Catholic Church in most Latin American countries in the 1980's?
1 The activities of the Church are controlled by the national governments.
2 The Church has confined its activities to religious issues.
3 The Church has become active in social and human rights issues.
4 Most people see the Church as having little influence in daily life.

7 The major goal of the Organization of American States (OAS) is to
1 develop trade between Europe and the nations of Latin America
2 provide a peaceful way to settle disputes in the Western Hemisphere
3 encourage political, economic, and social changes in Latin America
4 promote United States investment in South America

8 Which statement best describes the effects of the geography of Africa?
1 Geography has encouraged physical mobility throughout Africa.
2 The geography of Africa has hindered economic development.
3 The geography of Africa has stimulated political and cultural unity.
4 The geography of Africa has resulted in most African countries having similar economic and social systems.

9 A major result of the development of civilization in ancient Egypt was the
1 conquest and settlement of Western Europe by the Egyptian Empire
2 establishment of a democratic system of government in Egypt
3 establishment of trade routes between Egypt and other kingdoms
4 decline of agriculture as an important occupation in Egypt

Base your answer to question 10 on the table below and on your knowledge of social studies.

MINERAL RESOURCES - REPUBLIC OF SOUTH AFRICA
(Averages, in percent, 1981-84)

	Industrial diamond stones	Platinum group metals	Chromium	Vanadium	Manganese	Uranium	Gold
Share of U.S. imports originating in South Africa	67	67	56	38	33	24	n.a.
South Africa's share of world reserves	7	81	84	47	71	14	55.1
South Africa's share of world production	14.8	43.2	n.a.	42.2	14.7	14.8	47.0

Sources: U.S. Department of Commerce; U.S. Bureau of Mines; Organization for Economic Cooperation and Development

10 Which is the most valid statement about the Republic of South Africa that can be made based on the information in the table?
1 Most of South Africa's trade is with other African countries.
2 Trade with the United States is not important to South Africa.
3 South Africa is the single most important producer of manganese in the world.
4 The export of mineral resources is an important part of the economy of South Africa.

---

11 During the 1950's and 1960's, the history of most African countries was characterized by
1 colonization by imperialist nations
2 the achievement of political independence
3 a sharp decrease in the birth rate
4 the development of economic self-sufficiency

12 The term "Pan-Africanism" can best be defined as a movement whose purpose is to
1 promote African unity
2 support cultural diversity
3 encourage European investment in Africa
4 advocate a return to colonial conditions

13 A valid statement concerning the caste system in India is that it has
1 been weakened by urbanization
2 been reinforced by aid from the United States
3 been strengthened by government legislation
4 become a cohesive force for national unity

14 The government of Great Britain built railroads, schools, and irrigation systems in colonial India primarily to
1 prepare India for independence
2 strengthen its political and economic control in India
3 secure favorable trading arrangements with different Indian leaders
4 help India maintain its traditional cultural systems

15 Which generalization best explains the creation of the nations of India and Pakistan in 1947?
1 Armed conflict is necessary for independence movements to succeed.
2 Religious conflicts may have a strong influence on political events.
3 Industrialization needs to reach a high level before a nation can become independent.
4 Similar geographical and historical conditions may promote unity between nations.

Base your answer to question 16 on the cartoon below and on your knowledge of social studies.

Now, remove that and fix this one.

IBH Publishing Company, Bombay.

16 The cartoon illustrates India's problems with
1 an inadequate transportation system
2 inefficient government agencies
3 conflict between religious groups
4 the monsoon cycle

17 In traditional Chinese culture, which philosophy had the greatest influence on the development of social order and political organization?
1 Taoism
2 Shintoism
3 Confucianism
4 Marxism

18 Which statement best describes the status of women in most traditional Asian societies?
1 Women were encouraged to obtain an education.
2 Women were expected to run for political office.
3 Women were expected to dedicate their lives to their families.
4 Women were encouraged to work outside the home.

19 The Boxer Rebellion of the early 20th century was an attempt to
1 eliminate poverty among the Chinese peasants
2 bring Western-style democracy to China
3 restore trade between China and European nations
4 remove foreign influences from China

20 Which statement about the economy of China in the 1980's is most accurate?
1 China surpassed the Soviet Union in steel production.
2 China's economy slowed down because of a lack of natural resources.
3 China increased its industrial capacity and foreign trade.
4 China's economy suffered from overproduction of consumer goods.

21 In Japan, a major economic problem has been the lack of
1 natural resources
2 investment capital
3 skilled labor
4 experienced management

Base your answers to questions 22 and 23 on the cartoon below and on your knowledge of social studies.

"Don't worry, I'll only use it if I fall behind."

22 What is the main idea of the cartoon?
1 The Japanese should trade only with the United States.
2 The United States has threatened to use tariffs to protect its industries from Japanese competition.
3 Sports competition between the United States and Japan can have an effect on reducing tariffs.
4 United States tariffs have hurt post-war Japanese economic development.

23 Which situation led to the idea presented in the cartoon?
1 the unfavorable United States balance of trade with Japan
2 the superior quality of goods made in the United States
3 takeover of Japanese businesses by Americans
4 the Japanese defeat in World War II

24 Which geographic feature has been most responsible for the population distribution in the Middle East?
1 abundance of oil deposits
2 location of water
3 presence of high plateaus
4 availability of natural harbors

25 Which has been a serious problem for many nations of the Middle East since World War II?
1 renewed colonial conquest by Europeans
2 cutbacks in foreign aid from the United States
3 increased world demand for oil
4 conflicts between traditionalists and modernists

26 The primary goal of the Palestine Liberation Organization (PLO) has been to
1 establish a home state for Palestinian Arabs
2 eliminate communist influence in the Arab nations
3 bring about a peaceful settlement of the conflicts between Egypt and Palestinian Arabs
4 control the Organization of Petroleum Exporting Countries (OPEC)

27 In most of the oil-rich Arab nations, the wealth generated by oil has affected the way of life in that
1 most people have adopted a Western lifestyle and given up their traditional ways
2 oil money has been used by the religious institutions, but not for educational and health facilities
3 technological modernization has occurred, but traditional laws and customs continue
4 women have been given political and social rights equal to those of men

28 Which statement best explains why many Jews left Russia during the late 1800's?
1 There was tremendous overcrowding in the regions of Russia where most of the Jews lived.
2 The Jews experienced many forms of discrimination and persecution.
3 The climate of Western Europe was better suited to the Jews' tradition of farming.
4 The Jews were forced to work in Russian factories.

29 The political reorganization of Russia after the Communist Revolution of 1917 resulted in
1 the establishment of a two-party political system
2 increased political power for ethnic minorities
3 a limited monarchy with the Czar as a figurehead
4 a federation of socialist republics

30 The events that took place in Hungary in the 1950's and in Czechoslovakia in the 1960's demonstrated the Soviet Union's
1 support of nationalism among satellite nations
2 influence on the economies of developing nations
3 determination to maintain political control over Eastern Europe at that time
4 attempts to promote its artistic and literary achievements in Western Europe

31 During the 1980's in the Soviet Union, a major element of the economic policy of *perestroika* was
1 increased collectivization of farms
2 more reliance on local and regional decision-making
3 the expanded use of national five-year plans
4 an emphasis on the redistribution of wealth

32 "All things were under its domain . . . its power was such that no one could hope to escape its scrutiny."

Which European institution during the Middle Ages is best described by this statement?
1 the guild
2 knighthood
3 the Church
4 the nation-state

33 Which was a major result of the Reformation?
1 New Christian denominations emerged.
2 Religious teachings were no longer allowed in the universities.
3 The Crusades were organized.
4 The power of the Pope was strengthened.

34 Karl Marx believed that a proletarian revolution was more likely to occur as a society became more
1 religious
2 militarized
3 industrialized
4 democratic

Base your answers to questions 35 and 36 on the maps below and on your knowledge of social studies.

EUROPE BEFORE AND AFTER WORLD WAR I

Europe Before World War I

Europe After World War I

35 The boundaries of which two countries were most changed by World War I?
1 France and Italy
2 Germany and Belgium
3 Austria-Hungary and Russia
4 Greece and Bulgaria

36 Which is the most valid conclusion that can be drawn from a study of these maps?
1 European boundaries more closely reflected ethnic patterns after World War I.
2 Communist expansion into Eastern Europe began in 1919.
3 The end of World War I brought the need for military alliances.
4 The new boundaries resulted in an end to ethnic conflicts in Europe.

37 Which was a result of the Industrial Revolution in England during the 19th century?
1 The number of farmers increased as the demand for wool in the textile industry rose.
2 Democratic principles were weakened as the power of the working class increased.
3 Workers became more secure in their jobs and less dependent on employers.
4 The structure of society changed to include a growing middle class.

38 The major factor that enabled Western Europe to dominate large parts of Asia and Africa in the 19th and early 20th centuries was the
1 technological and military superiority of European nations
2 acceptance of Christianity by many Asians and Africans
3 desire of Asians and Africans for European raw materials
4 refusal of Asians and Africans to fight against European imperialism

☞ GO RIGHT ON TO THE NEXT PAGE.

39 Global problems of uneven economic development, environmental pollution, and hunger reflect the need for
1 a return to policies of economic nationalism
2 increased military spending by all nations
3 a reduction in foreign aid provided by industrialized nations
4 increased international cooperation

40 Eighteenth-century Russia and nineteenth-century Japan were similar in that both countries
1 began the process of modernization after a long period of isolation
2 developed democratic governments after years under absolute monarchies
3 refused to accept Western technological ideas
4 adopted socialist economic systems after capitalism had failed

41 The French Revolution of 1789 and the Cuban Revolution of 1959 were similar in that both were caused primarily by the
1 desire of the people to be free from foreign rule
2 pressure of religious leaders for government reform
3 failure of the government to meet the needs of the people
4 ambition of the upper class to attain wealth and property

42 A major cause of the continued conflicts in Northern Ireland and Lebanon has been
1 opposing dynastic claims
2 religious differences
3 interference from the superpowers
4 industrial rivalry

43 Which statement is most characteristic of totalitarian governments?
1 Local media report a variety of opinions concerning government policies.
2 The judiciary is independent of the executive branch of government.
3 Human rights are constitutionally guaranteed for all people.
4 Loyalty is measured by the extent to which a person agrees with government policy.

44 Feudalism in Western Europe was similar to feudalism in Japan in that
1 power was based on class relationships
2 the national government controlled the nobility
3 social mobility was easily achieved
4 most of the people lived in cities

Base your answers to questions 45 and 46 on the passage below and on your knowledge of social studies.

> "... But there come some occasions ... when he considers certain laws to be so unjust as to render obedience to them a dishonor. He then openly and civilly breaks them and quietly suffers the penalty for their breach. ..."

45 This passage supports the use of
1 military force
2 civil disobedience
3 appeasement
4 retaliation

46 Which leader based his actions on the philosophy expressed in this passage?
1 Vladimir I. Lenin
2 Simón Bolívar
3 Yasir Arafat
4 Mohandas K. Gandhi

---

47 Which was characteristic of France under Napoleon's rule and Germany under Hitler's rule?
1 Democratic ideas and diversity were encouraged.
2 Authoritarian control and a strong sense of nationalism prevailed.
3 Peaceful relations with neighboring countries were fostered.
4 Artistic and literary freedom flourished.

48 The best example of nationalism is
1 the people of India demanding independence from Great Britain
2 a medieval lord raising an army to protect his manor
3 the peacekeeping forces of the United Nations patrolling in Lebanon
4 Spain deciding to join the North Atlantic Treaty Organization (NATO)

Answers to the following questions are to be written on paper provided by the school.

STUDENTS PLEASE NOTE:

In developing your answers to Part II, be sure to

(1) include specific factual information and evidence whenever possible
(2) keep to the questions asked; do not go off on tangents
(3) avoid overgeneralizations or sweeping statements without sufficient proof; do not overstate your case
(4) keep these general definitions in mind:

(a) discuss means "to make observations about something using facts, reasoning, and argument; to present in some detail"
(b) describe means "to illustrate something in words or tell about it"
(c) show means "to point out; to set forth clearly a position or idea by stating it and giving data which support it"
(d) explain means "to make plain or understandable; to give reasons for or causes of; to show the logical development or relationships of"

Part II

ANSWER THREE QUESTIONS FROM THIS PART. [45]

1 Many problems of regions and nations of the world are related to geography.

Geographic Characteristics
Climate
Location
Mountains
Lack of natural barriers
Scarcity of water
Scarcity of mineral resources

Select *three* geographic characteristics from the list and for *each* characteristic:

- Discuss how that characteristic has created a problem for a specific region or nation selected from Africa, Asia, Europe, the Middle East, or Latin America [You must use a different region or nation for each characteristic discussed.]
- Explain an action the region or nation has taken to adapt to or modify the effect of the geographic characteristic [5,5,5]

☞ GO RIGHT ON TO THE NEXT PAGE.

2 Throughout history, the lives of people have been shaped by the forms of government under which they live.

Forms of Government

Nazi totalitarianism
Communist totalitarianism
Constitutional democracy
Absolute monarchy

Select *one* of the forms of government from the list.

a Discuss *two* factors that led to the establishment of this form of government in a specific nation. [You may *not* select the United States for your answer.] [6]

b Describe *two* ways the lives of the people in the nation identified in part *a* were affected following the establishment of this form of government. [4]

c Discuss the extent to which this form of government improved or hindered the political, economic, or social development of the nation. [5]

3 A strong leader acts decisively not only to influence events within his or her nation but also to influence relations with other nations.

Leaders

Corazón Aquino
Peter the Great
Ayatollah Khomeini
Deng Xiaoping
Fidel Castro
Napoleon Bonaparte
Indira Gandhi
Jomo Kenyatta

Select *three* leaders listed and for *each* leader:

- Identify the nation in which the leader acted
- Discuss *one* domestic policy or *one* foreign policy of the leader
- Discuss a method used by the leader to put his or her policies into effect [5,5,5]

4 Since World War II, the 20th century has been a period of increased interdependence. International organizations reflect this interdependence.

International Organizations

European Economic Community (EEC)
North Atlantic Treaty Organization (NATO)
Warsaw Pact
Organization of Petroleum Exporting Countries (OPEC)
United Nations
Organization of African Unity (OAU)

Select *three* of the organizations listed and for *each* organization:

- Describe the organization
- Identify a major goal of the organization
- Discuss a problem faced by the organization in attempting to achieve this goal [5,5,5]

5 Throughout history, both men and women have had an impact on their times. They have played various roles.

Roles

Scientist
Political reformer
Social reformer
Writer
Revolutionary

a Select *two* roles from the list and for *each* role selected, identify *one* man or woman who played the role in a specific African, Asian, Latin American, Middle Eastern, or European nation. [You must identify a different person for each role.] [5]

b Describe an action, discovery, or work of *each* individual identified in part *a*, and discuss the individual's impact on the political, economic, or social development of his or her nation or society. [10]

☞ GO RIGHT ON TO THE NEXT PAGE.

6 Throughout history, great civilizations have existed in different areas of the world.

Civilizations

Ancient Mesopotamia
Ancient Africa
Golden Age of Athens
Golden Age of China
Ancient Latin American Empires
Golden Age of Muslim Culture

Select *three* of the civilizations listed and discuss *two* specific characteristics or achievements of each civilization. [5,5,5]

7 Nations and regions often adopt ideas and practices from other parts of the world. The nations listed below have experienced cultural diffusion.

Japan from China
Mexico from Spain
Rome from Greece
Europe from Africa
Russia from the Byzantine Empire
Southeast Asia from India

Select *three* of the examples listed and for *each* example:

- Describe one idea or practice that was acquired by the first nation or region from the second
- Discuss the effect of the idea or practice on the nation or region that adopted it [5,5,5]

PRETEST ANSWERS

Part I (55 credits)

1. **1**	13. **1**	25. **4**	37. **4**
2. **4**	14. **2**	26. **1**	38. **1**
3. **4**	15. **2**	27. **3**	39. **4**
4. **1**	16. **4**	28. **2**	40. **1**
5. **4**	17. **3**	29. **4**	41. **3**
6. **3**	18. **3**	30. **3**	42. **2**
7. **2**	19. **4**	31. **2**	43. **4**
8. **2**	20. **3**	32. **3**	44. **1**
9. **3**	21. **1**	33. **1**	45. **2**
10. **4**	22. **2**	34. **3**	46. **4**
11. **2**	23. **1**	35. **3**	47. **2**
12. **1**	24. **2**	36. **1**	48. **1**

Part II (45 credits)

Refer to the Test-Taking Strategies section that follows for review of how to best organize and answer essay questions. Instruction is given on blocking essays, and specific essays from the Pretest are used as examples.

Test-Taking Strategies

This section provides strategies for success on both parts of the Regents Examination in Global Studies. Examples will be used from the June 1990 Regents Pretest you have just taken.

The multiple-choice strategies will help you toward earning all of the possible 55 points for Part 1 of the exam. The essay strategies include actual blockings for each of the seven essays on the Pretest. These blockings help you to learn how to organize complete essay answers so you can earn all of the possible 45 points for Part II.

Within this section there are also analyses of past Regents Examinations that will indicate the number of times that specific topic has been tested in past Regents.

Finally, there are lists of Key Social Studies Vocabulary, Key Geography Terms, and Key English Vocabulary with definitions. Be sure to know the meanings of all of these terms that are frequently used in the exam questions.

Multiple Choice Analysis of Regents Examinations

Now that you have had the experience of taking the Pretest in Global Studies and determined the areas that you are strongest in, and those that you need to concentrate on, review the following charts to see the general pattern of questions from each region that have appeared on the Regents examinations. The breakdown of the questions into specific areas is sometimes difficult, as the questions often tend to cover more than one region. Note that the test always starts by asking you to respond to general social science type of questions. The numbers of questions on each of the regions in the Global Studies curriculum generally follows a pattern as you will see. Two trends are worth paying attention to at this point. The first is that the number of questions on Western Europe have experienced a decline.

The second is that the amount of data-based questions (charts, graphs, cartoons, etc.) have increased. Be aware that the number of data-based questions on the following charts include those associated with a specific region or area; thus, the total number of questions on each test will be greater than the usual 48 questions per test. The following charts are in order by region as tested on each examination.

Global Studies Regents Analysis: Multiple-Choice by Region

June '90

Area	# of Questions
Social Science	4
Latin America	5
Africa	5
India	6
China	4
Japan	3
Middle East	4
Soviet Union	4
Western Europe	10
Cross Cultural	6

Data Based: –1 chart (Africa)
1 cartoon (India)
2 cartoons (Japan)
2 maps (Europe)
2 passages (India)

June '91

Area	# of Questions
Social Science	6
Latin America	5
Africa	5
India/South Asia	3
Southeast Asia	1
China	2
Japan	4
Middle East	4
Western Europe	12
Soviet Union/Eastern Europe	6
Cross-Cultured	4

Data-Based: –2 cartoons (South Africa)
1 cartoon (Western Europe)
1 cartoon (China)
1 poem (Western Europe)
1 flyer (Western Europe)
1 quote (Soviet Union)
1 quote (Middle East)

June '92

Area	# of Questions
Social Science	2
Middle East	6
India/South Asia	4
China	4
Japan	3
Africa	5
Latin America	4
Western Europe	6
Russia/Soviet Union	6
Cross-Cultured	6

Data-Based: –1 chart (South Asia)
1 graph (Latin America)
2 cartoons (Communism)

June '93

Area	# of Questions
Social Science	4
Africa	4
India/South Asia	3
China	5
Japan	3
Middle East	3
Latin America	7
Western Europe	6
Soviet Union	2
Cross-Cultural	11

June '94

Area	# of Questions
Social Studies	6
Africa	4
Latin America	5
India	3
Southeast Asia	1
China	2
Japan	2
Middle East	4
Western Europe	9
Soviet Union/Eastern Europe	5
Cross-Cultured	6

Data Based: –1 chart (Middle East)
1 cartoon (Eastern Europe)
1 cartoon (Bangladesh)
1 quotation (nationalism)

Social Science and Cross-Cultural Questions

Two areas that you should examine more closely are the social science questions, and those that are cross-cultural and topical. The social science questions that have been asked have to do with concepts, such as, culture, cultural diffusion, feudalism, capitalism, and, especially, ***nationalism*** and ***totalitarianism***. As with most of the multiple-choice questions, you are asked to give ***the best example of***, answer ***how it developed or can develop***, or to describe a ***characteristic*** (a quality) ***of a particular*** political system.

The cross-cultural questions ask you to respond to several historical situations or people, and to make a deduction that is ***valid*** (true) about all of them. So, for example, you might be asked to identify a similarity between Christianity and Islam (a belief in one god), or a ***characteristic*** of feudalism that was found in Western Europe and in Japan (provided a system of order and stability). In most cases you must describe what the items mentioned have in common, and if you can identify one of the items listed and select an accurate choice related to this item (if you can't figure out the answer), then you stand a pretty good chance of answering the question correctly. For instance, read the following question.

> Czar Peter the Great of 18th-century Russia and Shah Mohammed Reza Pahlavi of 20th-century Iran were similar in that both leaders
> 1. established democratic institutions in their nations.
> 2. converted their nations to Christianity.
> 3. introduced Western ideas and technology into their nations.
> 4. expanded political and human rights in their nations.

Choice #1 is unlikely since you know that the Czars of Russia had absolute power, and were not supporters of democracy. *Choice #2* is, also, not a possibility, because if you weren't sure of the religion in Russia, then the fact that Iran is a Middle Eastern country would most probably mean that it is a country practicing Islam; that would rule out this answer. *Choice #4* is more than likely not a correct answer, because the nature of the role of a Czar in Russian history did not show concern for individuals' rights, just as it didn't for democratic institutions. If you knew about the Shah of Iran's use of the secret police, the Savak, to repress people's rights, this would also help you to eliminate this response. The correct answer is *Choice #3*, and, again, if you were able to analyze each of the other choices, and to remember something about Peter's program of Westernization for Russia, then you would choose the right answer. If you couldn't remember anything about Peter the Great, but did about the Iranian Revolution of 1979, you would recall that the Shah of Iran's government was overthrown by the fundamentalists (Shiite Moslems) of Ayatollah Khomeini, because he introduced too many Western ideas and customs into the Islamic country of Iran.

Multiple-Choice Strategies

1. Read the entire question and *all* of the choices carefully.
2. Look for the *key* vocabulary word that tells you *what* you should be looking for in this question.
3. Eliminate those choices that don't appear to be true, and cross them out in the test booklet.
4. If you're given a cross-cultural and topical question, and you're only able to identify a characteristic or similarity of *one* of them, make your selection accordingly.

Examine the following question by using the above mentioned strategies.

> A problem that faced the Austro-Hungarian Empire, the Ottoman Empire, and the Soviet Union was the
> 1. effect of urbanization on a rural population.
> 2. monopoly of the traditional church.
> 3. inability to produce modern weapons.
> 4. tension between many different ethnic groups.

Choice #1– If you couldn't recall anything about the Austro-Hungarian Empire or the Ottoman Empire, remember that urbanization (the movement of large numbers of people from rural villages to cities) is a post-World War II phenomenon, and in the Soviet Union under the Communist government, the movement of people from one area to another was tightly controlled, so this choice cannot be true. *Choice #2*, the monopoly of the traditional church, wouldn't be accurate simply based upon the historical restriction of religious practices in the Soviet Union. *Choice #3*, the inability to produce modern weapons, clearly is false based upon the Soviet Union's historical military capabilities. Thus, *Choice #4*, the tension between many different ethnic groups, must be the correct response. You can see how you can eliminate incorrect answers by using some logic, even if you were unaware of the problems that faced the Austro-Hungarian Empire or the Ottoman Empire, and if you didn't know about the disturbances that took place in the Baltic States and other republics within the Soviet Union. The same problem facing the Soviet Union must be true for *all three* examples.

The most frequent phrases used in multiple-choice questions appear on the list below. Examples are given and correct answers are indicated with asterisks.

1. *Which is a characteristic of*? This means what is a quality or trait of something or someone on the exam.

Which was a characteristic of feudalism in both medieval Europe and Japan?
1 The middle class acquired more power than any other class did.
2 Political power was held by a strong centralized government.
3 The army encouraged strong nationalistic feelings among the people.
*4 All the people knew their roles in a rigid class system.

Which is a characteristic of a feudal society?
1 rapid social change
2 high literacy rates
3 industrial-based economy
*4 rigid class structure

2. What is a *valid generalization*? This asks you to identify which broad statement is true.

What is the most valid generalization about the Crusades?
1 The Crusades strengthened the power of the serfs in Europe.
*2 The Crusades increased trade between Europe and Asia.
3 The Crusades brought European influence to Africa.
4 The Crusades supported the idea of religious tolerance.

3. Which *statement best describes*?
Which *best accounts for*?
Which is the *most accurate statement*?
These phrases ask you to identify which answer choice is the best and most accurate. Read *all* choices; don't stop at the first one with *some* truth to it.

Which statement best describes conditions in Japan today?
1 Japan has become an urban society that has adopted Western values in nearly every aspect of life.
2 Japan has continued to rely on China and Korea for its cultural values and technological development.
3 Japan has remained a primarily agrarian society with an emphasis on maintaining traditional values.
*4 Japan has adopted modern technological advances, while maintaining aspects of the traditional culture.

What factor *best* accounts for the existence of cash-crop production as the major form of agriculture in many Central American nations today?
*1 demand of world markets for such crops
2 lack of modern agricultural technology
3 inadequate supply of water and other natural resources
4 peasant ownership of most farmlands

4. What is the *main idea/reason*?

What is the *main* reason for the international importance of the countries in the Middle East today?

1 They have made innovative political and social reforms.
2 They have superior weapons capability.
*3 They are strategically located and have important natural resources.
4 They have an advanced level of scientific and industrial development.

Data-Based Questions

In these types of questions (cartoons, graphs, reading passages, etc.) you are generally asked two questions. In the first you are required to identify the main idea, and in the second, you are asked to draw a valid conclusion based upon the information being provided to you. You must be careful to look over the entire data that is given to you, and try to first decide *what it tells you* before you begin answering the questions!

Data-Based Questions The most common phrases are:

What *best accounts for*?
Which is a *valid conclusion*?
The *main idea*?
Which is an *accurate statement*?
Which statement is *best supported by the data*?
Which situation *most likely accounts for*?

Cartoons

In cartoon analysis make sure that you can identify the key figures and understand their problem or reaction to the specific situation that is illustrated.

The crisis illustrated in the cartoon involves the

1 internal problems in the Philippines.
2 border conflicts between Honduras and Nicaragua.
*3 conflict between Israel and its Arab neighbors.
4 flight of Afghan refugees into Pakistan.

Shanks in The Buffalo Evening News

The main idea of the cartoon is that the crisis will

1 be confined to the Middle East.
2 be controlled by Western democracies.
3 totally destroy the Islamic religion.
*4 eventually affect the entire world.

This cartoon requires that you are able to identify the countries in the Middle East that are behind this crisis; namely, Israel and its Arab neighbors. The main idea of the cartoon is clearly that the entire world will be eventually affected by the crisis.

Graphs/Charts

Review all graphs and charts before answering questions related to them. Be sure you understand the Keys and the general trends indicated.

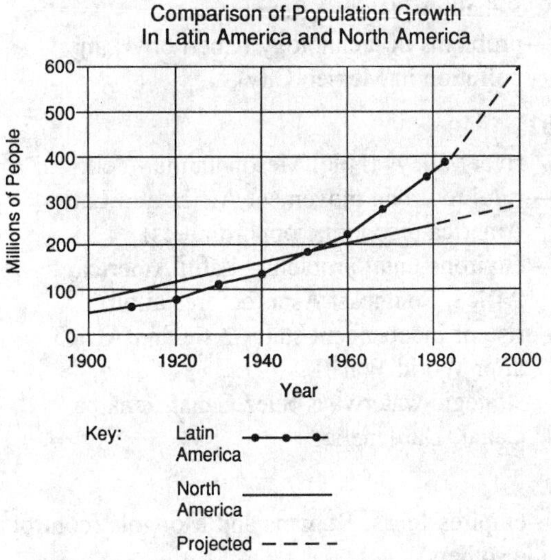

Based on the information in the graph, which is a valid conclusion about the populations of Latin America and North America?

1 There has always been a large difference in the population growth of Latin America and North America.

*2 By the year 2000, the population of Latin America is expected to be approximately twice that of North America.

3 In 1900, the number of people in Latin America was equal to the number of people in North America.

4 In the early 1980s, the difference in population between the two regions was about 300 million.

Which best accounts for the situation shown in the graph?

1 decline in the standard of living in North America

2 growing trade surplus of most Latin American nations

*3 improved nutrition and medical care in Latin American nations

4 increased death rate in North America due to contagious diseases

Global Studies Regents Analysis

Social Science Questions

June '90

nationalism (best example of)
totalitarianism (characteristic of)
geographical isolation (reinforces)
nationalism (most likely to develop)

Cross-Cultural/Topical Questions

—Global problems (reflect the need to cooperate)

—18th-century Russia & 19th-century Japan (similar)

—French Revolution & Cuban Revolution (similar)

—Northern Ireland & Lebanon (conflicts over religion)

—Feudalism under Napoleon and Germany under Hitler (characteristic of)

Social Science Questions		Cross-Cultural/Topical Questions
	June '91	
traditional societies cultural diffusion (rock music) traditional societies (family values) industrialization (need for capital) democracy (generalization) archeology (earliest humans)		—terrorism (Sikh Separatists/PLO) —developing countries (foreign debt) —resisting foreigners (Sepoy Meeting, Boxer Rebellion, Islamic Revolution) —problems of technology (Chernobyl, air pollution in Mexico City)
	June '92	
nationalism (quote) urbanization (weakened traditional value) feudalism (characteristics of)		—river valleys (Nile, Mesopotamia, Yellow) —rural to urban movement-Africa and Latin America (economic opportunities) —environmental problem—Latin/America, Africa, Southeast Asia (deforestation) —rise of independent states-Asia and Africa after World War II —strategic waterways-Suez Canal-Panama Canal, Dardanelles
	June '93	
nationalism (best defined as) interdependence (diffusion of items) nonalignment (in Africa and Asia during the Cold War)		—empires-Incas, Romans and Mongols (control of others) —China and Japan similar until the 1500s —Holocaust and Khmer Rouge (similar) —destructions of rainforests in Brazil and Africa (concern over) —Green Revolution in Mexico and India (result of) —Peter the Great (Russia) and Meiji Restoration (Japan)-similar —Mao Zedong and Fidel Castro (similar) —Notre Dame Cathedral, Dome of the Rock, Great Pyramid (reflect religious beliefs) —Suez Canal, Strait of Hormuz, and Strait of Gibraltar (control water routes)
	June '94	
sociologist (influence of Hinduism in India) cultural diffusion (spread of European languages) market economy (consumer controlled) writing systems/growth of cities (developed with complex institutions) imperialism (British, French, Spanish control over colonies) ethnocentrism (China's Middle Kingdom/European view of China as backward) nationalism (definition of)		—river valley civilizations-Nile, Tigris-Euphrates, Hwang Ho (transportation and communication) —Bolivar and Hidalgo inspired by revolutions (U.S. and France) —encomienda system (Latin America) and plantation system (Southeast Asia) similar in forced labor —Maya/Gupta/Songhai cultures (similar-great civilizations with no outside influence) —decline of Roman Empire and Manchu Dynasty (led to political chaos)

Essay Strategies

45 points of the Global Studies Regents examination consists of writing *three* 15 point essays. You have to choose three from a possible seven essays, and this section will help show you the pattern of topics that have appeared on the tests, as well as giving you some hints and strategies that you can use to achieve the maximum amount of points with your essays.

Global Studies Essay Topics

June '90

1. geographic problems
2. forms of government
3. nationalist leaders
4. international organizations
5. roles and impacts of individuals
6. great civilizations—achievements
7. cultural diffusion

June '91

1. important individuals
2. changes in traditional values
3. human rights
4. geography
5. areas of world conflict (cartoon)
6. revolutions
7. historical events

June '92

1. geographic influences
2. groups influencing events
3. changes influenced by women
4. religions
5. technological developments
6. historical events
7. human rights

June '93

1. groups achieving goals
2. nationalism/imperialism caused conflicts
3. leaders—ideas
4. world problems
5. geographic factors
6. human rights
7. historical events

June '94

1. geographic influences
2. human rights (cartoons)
3. important historical people
4. historical events
5. imperialism
6. world problems
7. decline of communism

After reviewing the chart on the essay topics for each of the exams that has been given, it should be clear to you that the topics you are asked to write about are truly global in nature. They are the most important themes and concepts that you have studied during the last two years. You will notice that on each exam the choices of the topics that you must select, such as leaders, political systems, religions, etc., provide you with a balanced choice of examples from both ninth and tenth grades. This fact should be an advantage to you, especially if you study the recurrent themes in Global Studies, which will be highlighted for you in the following chapters. The topics such as nationalism and nationalistic leaders, revolutions, religions, world problems, and the effects of a country's geography, are ones that have been repeatedly tested. In dedicating your study time for the essays, it is important that you concentrate on reviewing three to four likely topics that you can respond to on the exam. Preparation in essay topics, as those mentioned in the chart, is essential to your success on the test. Now, let's refer back to the essays on Part II of the June 1990 exam and use some strategies for better essay writing.

As is standard practice on each Regents exam, there are directions and definitions given in each exam booklet. **Read them carefully before you begin**! The instructions for Part II are as follows:

Answers to the following questions are to be written on paper provided by the school.

Students Please Note:

In developing your answers to Part II, be sure to
(1) include specific factual information and evidence whenever possible
(2) keep to the questions asked; avoid unnecessary detail
(3) avoid overgeneralizations or sweeping statements without sufficient proof; do not overstate your case
(4) keep these general definitions in mind:
(a) *discuss* means "to make observations about something using facts, reasoning, and argument; to present in some detail"
(b) *describe* means "to illustrate something in words or tell about it"
(c) *show* means "to point out; to set forth clearly a position or idea by stating it and giving data that support it"
(d) *explain* means "to make plain or understandable; to give reasons for or causes of; to show the logical development or relationship of"

Rules to Follow in Answering Essays:

1. It is extremely important to read through *all* of the seven essays before you begin answering them.
2. Check off the *three* or *four* that you feel most comfortable in answering at your first glance.
3. Pay attention to all of the important *word clues* that are given in each question.
4. The usual point breakdown of each essay is 5 points, 5 points, and 5 points, asking you to define, describe, or explain *three* examples of whatever concept that you are being asked about.
5. *Supporting information and examples are critical* in order for you to receive the most out of each of the 5 point parts that you are writing.

In giving
examples—give specific instances of the topic that you are answering
details— pieces of information that help describe something
facts— true statements that offer useful information
reasons— arguments that help persuade

When asked to
compare—give the similarities and resemblances
contrast— give the differences
define— explain what it is
illustrate—show

Blocking Method

For *each* essay that you do you must first draw a diagram or chart to decide what information you are being asked, what examples must be given, and how much of the essay you will be able to answer.

Now, refer back to each of the seven essay questions on the June 1990 Regents Examination Pretest as you study the following blockings for them.

JUNE 1990 REGENTS ESSAY BLOCKINGS

Essay #1

(A) Geographic Characteristics	(B) Region/Problem	(C) Action taken
Climate	India—monsoon	technology—built dams
Location	Netherlands—borders North Sea	technology—flood control systems
Mountains	Chile (Latin America)—isolation of its people	technology—planes, satellites, radios
Lack of Natural Barriers	Soviet Union—invaded by Napoleon/Hitler	technology—now a major military power
Scarcity of Water	Saudi Arabia (Middle East)—limits food growing; travel	technology—desalinization plants
Scarcity of Mineral Resources	Japan—must import most of its oil	technology—built super oil tankers

In this question you had to select *three* (3) characteristics, and pick a *different region/nation* for each geographical characteristic discussed. Label each of the three parts to the essay—A, B, C. The breakdown of scoring would be 5 points for each of the three chosen. When writing about an action taken, be sure to use common sense, if you can't recall a specific project done by a nation. When you are ready to put the information from the chart into essay form, it should be easy to select your three strongest parts of this question, and to use parts A, B, and C of each characteristic as your introduction, body, and conclusion for the three geographical factors that you have chosen to discuss. Organizing each essay that you do in this way will help you:

1. gather the pertinent information
2. *support it by example*
3. not leave out a necessary part that could cost you points.

Essay #2

(Select One)	(A) 2 Factors that led to it (6 pts.)	(B) 2 Ways lives affected	(C) Improved/ Hindered the nation
Nazi Totalitarianism (Germany)	Great Depression Treaty of Versailles Rise of Hitler as Chancellor	Holocaust Jobs created in rearmament of Germany	Genocide of the Jewish people
Communist Totalitarianism (Soviet Union)	Food shortages Overthrow of Czar Nicholas II	Famine New Economic Policy	Totalitarian state with no individual rights
Constitutional Democracy (France)	French Revolution Heavy taxation Squandering of $	Unemployment Food shortages	Did not last and led to Napoleon as leader
Absolute Monarchy (France)	Rise to power of Louis XIV with the death of his father, Louis XIII, and later of Cardinal Mazarin	Estates General never met Built the palace of Versailles	French pride and nationalism Heavy debt

Essay #3

(Select three Leaders)	(A) Nation (5 pts.)	(B) Domestic/ Foreign policy (5 pts.)	(C) Method used (5 pts.)
Corazon Aquino	Philippines	land reform	orderly transfer
Peter the Great	Russia	Westernization	force (men had to shave their beards)
Ayatollah Khomeini	Iran	seizure of the American Embassy and 59 Americans	force—kept them for 444 days
Deng Xiaoping	China	responsibility system Tiananmen Square (July '89)	government decree military force
Fidel Castro	Cuba	businesses nationalized/ collectivization of farms	government decree
Napoleon Bonaparte	France	Napoleonic Code of Laws	spread as his troops conquered Europe

Essay #4

(Select three) International organizations	**(A) Describe it (5 pts.)**	**(B) Major goal (5 pts.)**	**(C) Problem faced (5 pts.)**
European Economic Community (EEC)	organization of 12 countries in a Common Market	to lower trade barriers and increase trade	agreeing on common programs with all nations following the decision
North Atlantic Treaty Organization (NATO)	defense alliance of European nations and U.S. and Canada (12)	to protect member nations from attack	role of the alliance today with the change in Eastern Europe
Warsaw Pact	alliance of Soviet Union & Eastern European countries	mutual defense pact	role of the alliance today with the changes in Eastern Europe
Organization of Petroleum Exporting Countries (OPEC)	cartel of 13 oil-producing countries	attempts to control the production and price of oil	splits among the countries; declining price of oil
United Nations (UN)	organization formed after World War II—159 member nations	to preserve international peace	–financial –inability to settle military conflicts
Organization of African Unity (OAU)	union of all African nations (except the Rep. of South Africa)	to promote African unity and encourage cooperation and settle disputes	–countries unwilling to allow outside nations to assist in internal matters

Essay #5

(Select two) Roles	(A) (5 pts.) Identify person	(B) (5 pts.) Action taken	(C) (5 pts.) Impact on nation
Scientist	Marie Curie (France)	discovered radium	Radiation is a treatment in fighting diseases such as cancer.
Political Reformer	Mikhail Gorbachev (Soviet Union)	Glasnost	easing of restrictions on expression; may lead to political instability
Social Reformer	Peter the Great (Russia)	Westernization	Industrial progress made Russia a more modern and powerful nation.
Writer	Karl Marx (Germany)	*Communist Manifesto* (1848)	Russia became the first Communist nation in 1917.
Revolutionary	Mao Zedong (China)	Cultural Revolution (1966–69)	disrupted China's entire economic and political systems

Essay #6

(Select three) Civilizations (A)	2 Characteristics/Achievements (B/C) (5 pts.)
Ancient Mesopotamia	first to use the wheel; code of Hammurabi
Ancient Africa	Kingdom of Ghana; Timbuktu, center of trade (gold & iron) and learning
Golden Age of Athens	democracy; Olympic games
Golden Age of China	Tang and Sung dynasties—Confucianism; civil service tests
Ancient Latin American Empires	Mayan calendar; Incan road system (2,500 miles)
Golden Age of Muslim Culture	algebra; advanced system of medicine—hospitals and training

Essay #7

(Select three) Examples (A)	One Idea/Practice (B)	Effect (C) (5 pts.)
Japan from China	written language	adapted and in use
Mexico from Spain	Spanish	language spoken today
Rome from Greece	alphabet	adopted and modified it—formed the basis for many European languages
Europe from Africa	art	Spanish artist, Pablo Picasso, was heavily influenced by African art
Russia from Byzantine Empire	Cyrillic alphabet	used today
Southeast Asia from India	Buddhism	major religion found there today

Key Social Studies Vocabulary to Know

absolutism: the belief that monarchs hold supreme power and are responsible only to God

agrarian: pertaining to land and the agricultural interests of farmers

alliance: any union, coalition, or formal agreement between nations in their common interest

annexation: to add to existing possessions/ territory

apartheid: policy of racial segregation in the Republic of South Africa

appeasement: making concessions to an aggressor in order to preserve the peace

bourgeoisie: in Marxism, the social class opposed to the proletariat or working class

capitalist: a person who invests in business in order to make a profit

cash crops: a crop that can be sold on the world market for money

civil disobedience: refusal to comply with certain laws by means of passive resistance

coalition: temporary alliance between parties in government

colony: territory that an outside power controls directly

collectivization: a system in which the state owns and controls the means of production and distribution

command economy: state controlled economic system

culture: customs, ideas, and way of life of a group of people

cultural diffusion: when a custom or item of a culture moves from one part of the world to another

cultural diversity: variety of customs, ideas, and ways of living among the people within a region or nation

Crusades: series of wars launched by Christians against Muslims who controlled the Holy Lands

decentralization: to break down into smaller units

deforestation: to clear land of forests and trees

desertification: the spread of desert into semi-arid regions nearby

d'etente: easing of international tension between the Soviet Union and the United States

developed countries: countries who have established agriculture, industries, advanced technology, and strong education systems

developing countries: countries who have limited resources, and who face obstacles, such as, overpopulation, natural disasters, and indebtedness in achieving modern industrial economies

dynasty: ruling family that passes the right to rule from one member to another

federation: the joining together of two or more states into a union of confederacy

federal republic: a country that has a representative democracy with a centralized government

feudalism: system of rule by local lords who were bound to a king by ties of loyalty

genocide: the systematic extermination or destruction of an entire people or national group

glasnost: policy of openness domestically and towards the West initiated by Soviet leader Mikhail Gorbachev

Green Revolution: scientific efforts to increase the amount of food produced on the same amount of land

humanism: the intellectual and literary movement during the Renaissance characterized by an emphasis on human interests and a study of the Greek-Roman classics

imperialism: domination by one country of the political, economic, or cultural life of another country or region

industrialization: to establish large-scale industries

interdependence: countries in the world being dependent upon each other for various resources and products for their mutual benefit

isolationism: a policy of having little to do with foreign nations

laissez-faire: an economic system in which the government does not interfere with the economy

life expectancy: the probable length of life for an individual

literacy: the ability to read and write

illiteracy: inability to read and write

manorial: during the Middle Ages the system in which land, the manor, was administered by a lord

market economy: an economy based on the buying and selling of goods and services

materialism: the belief that the accumulation of possessions is what is necessary for a good life

mercantilism: economic theory that judged a nation's economic strength on the importation of gold and silver and the establishment of colonies to serve the needs of the mother country

militarized: to train, prepare, or equip for warfare

modernization: creation of a stable society capable of producing a high level of goods and services

monarchy: government headed by a king or queen

monsoon: seasonal wind that blows along the Asian coast of the Pacific and from the Indian Ocean. The summer monsoon brings heavy rains, and the winter monsoon brings hot, dry weather.

nationalism: feeling of pride and devotion to one's country

nativism: to favor people born in a particular country over those who live in that country but are foreign born.

natural resources: a source of wealth provided by nature, as forests, minerals, and water supply

Neolithic: the period of human culture characterized by the development of a system of settled agriculture

neutral: not taking the part of either side in a dispute

non-alignment: foreign policy of many developing countries to remain neutral with respect to the positions of the United States and the Soviet Union

pacifist: one who is opposed to war and serving in the military

Pan-Africanism: movement whose goal is to create a unified Africa politically and economically

per-capita: for each person

perestroika: plan for restructuring of the Soviet economy and society by Mikhail Gorbachev

polytheistic: belief in many gods

proletariat: in Marxism, the working class that rises up and overthrows the bourgeoisie

proliferation: to grow rapidly

quotas: a part or a share required for each person, group, or state

revolution: the overthrow or replacement of a government or political system

Russification: the policy of the czars to have the people they conquered be forced to learn the Russian language, culture, and convert to the Eastern Orthodox religion

self-sufficiency: able to support oneself without aid or cooperation from others

scarcity: inadequate supply

social mobility: the ability to move up or down in the social class system

socialism: economic and political system in which society as a whole, rather than private individuals, owns all property and operates all businesses

tariffs: to fix a price on imported or exported items

terrorism: unlawful acts of violence, such as bombings, hijackings, arson, etc. to publicize and achieve their causes

topography: the physical features of a region

totalitarianism: political system in which the government has a single-party dictatorship and controls every aspect of citizen's lives

tribalism: loyalty and devotion to one's tribe, as opposed to one's nation (nationalism)

universal suffrage: the right or privilege of voting extended to all

urbanization: movement of large numbers of people from rural villages to cities

westernization: adoption of western (European) ideas and customs by non-western nations

Key Geography Terms to Know

archipelago: a group or a chain of islands

arid: dry

climate: weather conditions of a region over a long period of time

geographic location: where a country is situated in relation to other places

irregular coastline: a coastline that has many natural harbors

isthmus: a narrow strip of land connecting two larger bodies of land

latitude: is the distance north or south as measured from the equator

longitude: is the distance east or west as measured from the Prime Meridian

monsoons: seasonal winds: if they blow from the sea they carry rain; if they blow from the land they bring dry air

natural barriers: land forms that help to isolate and/or protect an area

peninsula: an area of land surrounded on three sides by water

river valley: an area surrounding a river that is usually fertile and able to support a large population

strait: a narrow strip of water connecting two larger bodies of land

topography: the physical features (land surfaces) of a region

Key English Vocabulary to Know:

abundance: a large amount of something
acceptance: approval
accurate: correct; reliable
achievement: accomplishment
acquire: get; obtain
adherence: sticking to; following
adopt: to take up and practice as one's own
advocate: support
aggressive: forceful; self-assertive
availability: capability of being used
artistic: fond of or sensitive to art
centralized: concentrated at one point
characteristic: the distinctive quality of; typical
characterize: to describe by qualities
cohesive: joining or sticking together
conclusion: final decision
constitute: make up, compose
consumer: one of the buying public
cooperative: willing to act with others
decreasing: growing less or smaller
dependence: reliance; trust
discontent: dissatisfied
discourage: to hinder; lessen the confidence of
disorder: confusion
dissenter: one who disagrees
disunity: lack of agreement
diversity: difference; variety
domination: control; authority
eliminate: to get rid of
elite: a special group
emerge: to come forth from something
emphasize: to stress as important
enable: to make possible
encourage: to help or foster
endorsing: giving support to
establish: to set up on a lasting basis
equality: having the same rights
ethnic: belonging to a particular racial, or cultural group
evolve: to develop gradually
expansion: an increase in size
expenditure: expense; cost
facilitate: to make easier
factor: an element that produces a result
foster: to help along; promote the development of
hinder: to prevent from occurring
generalization: a broad application or statement
inadequate: insufficient
inspire: to move a person to a particular idea or feeling
instability: unreliability
integration: bringing together as a whole
internal: on the inside; interior
isolation: setting apart from the group
literary: characteristic of literature
maintain: to continue
migration: seasonal move from one region to another
mobility: ability to move easily from one thing to another
moderate: to keep within reasonable limits
mortality: frequency of death
partition: the act of dividing up or separating
persecution: maltreatment because of race, religion, or beliefs
philosophy: the general laws that provide a rational explanation of anything
postpone: to delay
predominate: to be superior in power or influence
prejudice: hatred or dislike for a particular group, race, religion, etc.
primarily: essentially; originally
productivity: tendency to increase in quantity or value
prohibit: to prevent; hinder
promote: to further; encourage
prosperity: material well-being
recognition: acknowledgment of a fact
reforms: changes for the better
regional: pertaining to a particular section or region
reinforced: strengthened
reliance: trust; dependence
renew: to restore; to begin again
restoring: bringing back to an original condition
restrict: to confine
retaliation: revenge
revival: a renewal of interest in
scrutiny: close examination of
secure: safe; guaranteed
seizure: taking possession of
specialize: to concentrate on one particular field
stability: permanence
stimulated: roused into quick action
superiority: surpassing in quality
suppress: to stop; put an end to by force
surpass: to go beyond; excel
theory: a plan or idea
tradition: custom/knowledge passed from one generation to the next
valid: acceptable; convincing
variations: differences; diversity

UNIT 1 The Geographic Setting

MAKING CONNECTIONS

As you review each unit, you will find additional information in this column: major ideas, connecting themes, and questions to reinforce your learning. These items are closely tied to the Regents examination. Read this material carefully, and jot down any other facts that you would like to remember in the column's blank spaces. Using this column will **add to your success on the Regents exam.**

Section 1 Africa

Section 2 India

Section 3 Southeast Asia

Section 4 China

Section 5 Japan

Section 6 Latin America

Section 7 The Middle East

Section 8 Western Europe

Section 9 Northern Eurasia and Eastern Europe

Each section of the Geography Unit contains comprehensive coverage of the major facts (location), topography (physical features), climate, natural resources, and major geographic themes you need to know to succeed on the Regents exam. Major ideas and concepts of each region are identified, making it easier to understand the connecting themes and the effects geography has had on the course of history.

Geography is the study of the earth—its people, their environment, and their resources. Within each Section, be aware of the five elements that make up the study of geography:

1. location (position on the earth's surface)
2. place (the physical and human characteristics of a location)
3. interaction (relationships between people and their environment)
4. movement (of ideas, products, people)
5. regions (physical and cultural characteristics)

SECTION 1 Geographic Setting: Africa

MAJOR FACTS

MAKING CONNECTIONS

Africa is the second largest continent in the world. (Only Asia is larger.) It is almost three times bigger than the United States. The 55 countries of Africa have a population of more than 700 million people.

Four major bodies of water border Africa. The Atlantic Ocean stretches along Africa's entire western coast. The Mediterranean Sea lies to the north, and the Red Sea and the Indian Ocean lie to the east. The waters of the Atlantic and Indian oceans come together at Africa's southern tip, the Cape of Good Hope.

TOPOGRAPHY

Deserts

Deserts make up about 40 percent of Africa's land surface.

THE SAHARA, NAMIB, AND KALAHARI The **Sahara** in North Africa is the largest desert in the world. It covers an area larger than the entire continental United States. The Sahara stretches about 3,200 miles (5,150 kilometers) from east to west and about 1,400 miles (2,250 kilometers) from north to south, occupying one-third of the continent. Sand dunes cover only about 20 percent of the Sahara. Most of the desert is rock and gravel. The Sahara has served as a barrier separating the peoples and cultures to the north and south of it.

Africa's other two deserts are the Namib and the Kalahari. The **Namib** lies along the continent's southwestern coast; the **Kalahari** covers the south-central portion.

DESERTIFICATION Expansion of Africa's deserts—a process known as **desertification**—has created a great problem for the continent. The hardest hit region is the **Sahel**, the area south of the Sahara. The Sahel includes parts of the nations of Mauritania, Mali, Niger, Chad, Sudan, and Ethiopia. These nations—as well as Senegal, Nigeria, and Burkina Faso—experienced droughts from 1963 to 1973 and throughout the 1980s. As more and more land turned into desert, millions of people suffered from malnutrition and starvation.

Key Concepts: Environment
Since the Iron Age, if not earlier, people have had a profound effect in shaping the natural environment, often harming the ecosystem and upsetting the balance of nature.

Geography of Africa

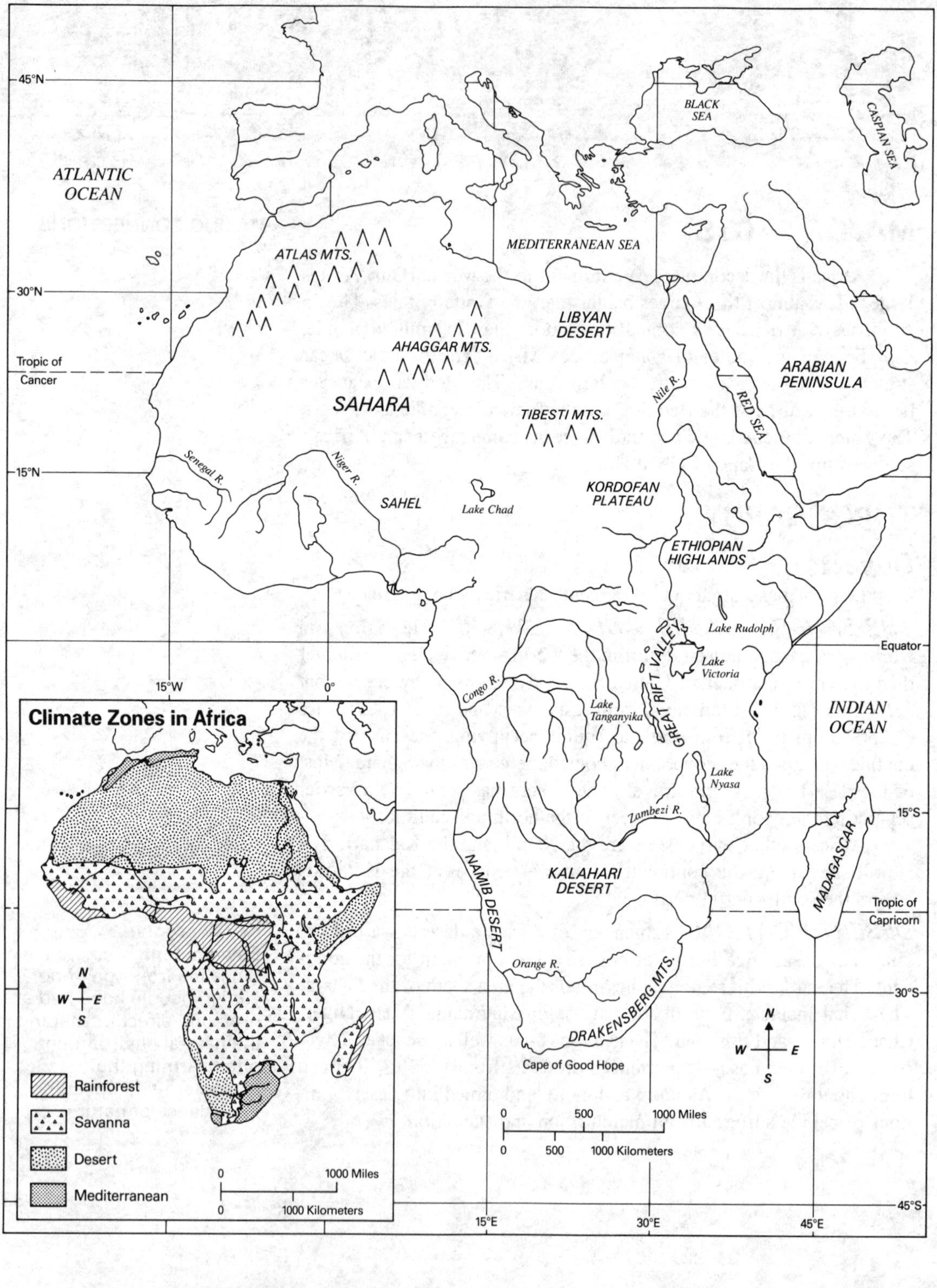
45°N
ATLANTIC OCEAN
BLACK SEA
CASPIAN SEA
MEDITERRANEAN SEA
ATLAS MTS.
30°N
LIBYAN DESERT
AHAGGAR MTS.
Tropic of Cancer
ARABIAN PENINSULA
Nile R.
RED SEA
SAHARA
TIBESTI MTS.
Senegal R.
Niger R.
15°N
KORDOFAN PLATEAU
SAHEL
Lake Chad
ETHIOPIAN HIGHLANDS
Lake Rudolph
GREAT RIFT VALLEY
Equator
Lake Victoria
15°W
0°
Congo R.
Lake Tanganyika
INDIAN OCEAN
Lake Nyasa
Zambezi R.
15°S
MADAGASCAR
NAMIB DESERT
KALAHARI DESERT
Tropic of Capricorn
Orange R.
DRAKENSBERG MTS.
30°S
N
W
E
S
Cape of Good Hope
0
500
1000 Miles
0
500
1000 Kilometers
45°S
15°E
30°E
45°E
Climate Zones in Africa
N
W
E
S
Rainforest
Savanna
Desert
Mediterranean
0
1000 Miles
0
1000 Kilometers

The Spreading Desert

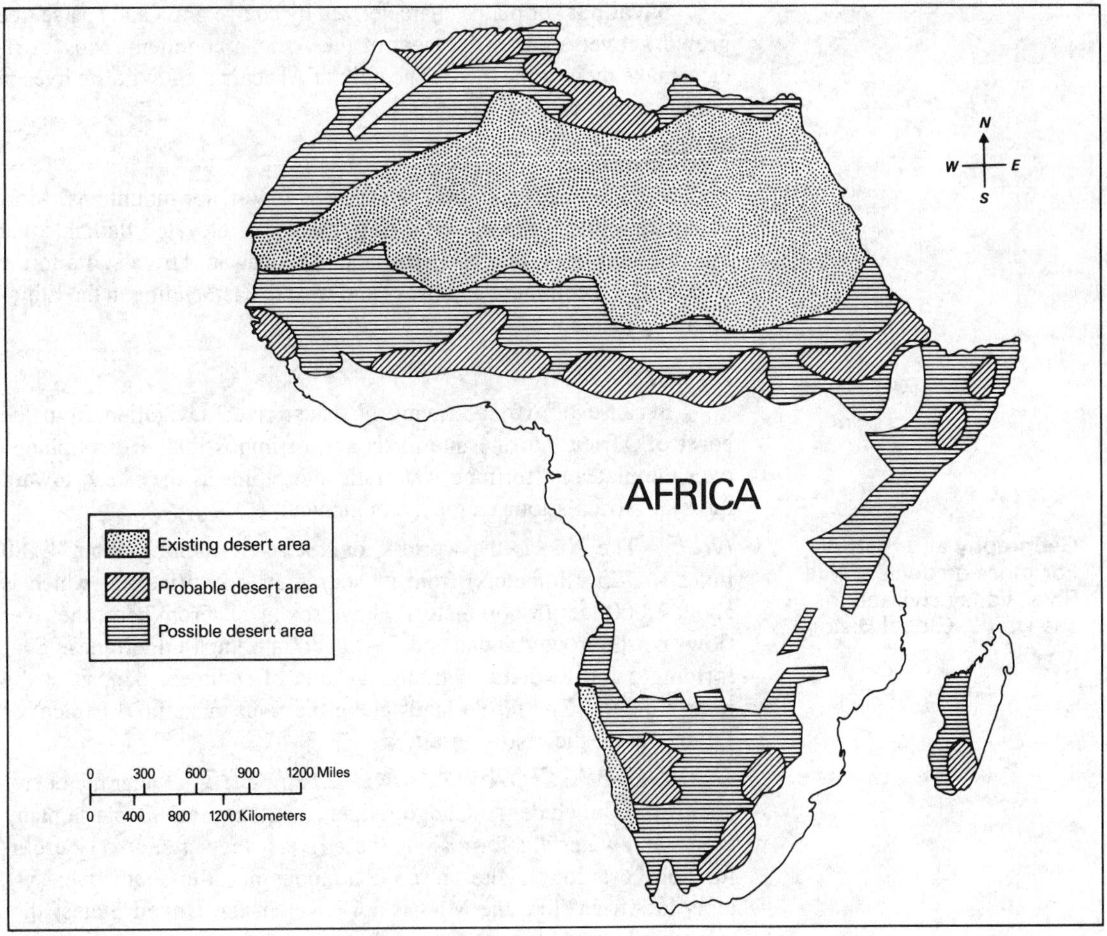

Causes of Desertification
• Overuse by farmers of semiarid land next to a desert to make up for low crop yields from poor soil • Overgrazing by cattle and goats • Overcutting of trees for firewood • *Result*: With no grass or tree roots to hold topsoil in place, it blows or washes away, and the desert advances
Solutions
• Crop rotation to prevent the soil from wearing out • Terracing to prevent rain from washing soil away • Tree belts to stop erosion and hold the soil in place

MAKING CONNECTIONS

Regents Tip Practice your data-based skills by answering the following question about the map:

The map indicates that the area most threatened by the spreading desert lies

a in central Africa.
b in southeastern Africa.
c directly adjacent to an existing desert area.
d along the coast.

MAKING CONNECTIONS

Savannas

Savannas, or plains characterized by coarse grass and sparse tree growth, cover about 50 percent of the African continent. Most Africans make their home there. The bulk of Africa's great wildlife lives in the savannas, too.

Plateaus

Unlike other continents, Africa has few major mountains. Most of Africa's interior is made up of **plateaus**, or elevated flatlands that fall off sharply on one end. The major plateau in Africa starts in the middle of the continent and rises from west to east, ending in the Ethiopian Highlands.

Rivers

Because of Africa's many plateaus, river navigation from the coast of Africa into the interior is almost impossible. Rivers plunge over the plateaus, forming waterfalls and rapids as they head toward the sea. Africa's four major rivers include:

Geography and History
For more on ancient Nile River Valley civilizations, see Unit 2, Global History.

NILE The **Nile** is the world's longest river, running about 4,180 miles (6,725 kilometers) from its source at Lake Victoria, which is about 4,000 feet (3,660 meters) above sea level. From here, the river flows north through Sudan and Egypt and into the Mediterranean Sea, forming a fertile **delta**, a triangular area of sediment deposit at the river's mouth. The fertile lands along the river make up 4 percent of Egypt's area; the rest is desert.

CONGO, NIGER, AND ZAMBEZI RIVERS Other major rivers in Africa include the **Congo, Niger,** and **Zambezi**. Because many rapids and waterfalls form along these rivers, they are not very useful for transportation. There are no continuous north-to-south river systems in Africa (like the Mississippi River in the United States) that might unify the African continent.

Coastline

Although Africa has an extensive coastline, much of it is smooth, or regular. Few natural harbors provide places for ships to anchor safely. Africa's lack of harbors has served as a barrier to trade throughout much of its history.

Geography and History
Archeologists have discovered the remains of the oldest humans in the Great Rift Valley, buried beneath ash and debris deposited over millions of years. The oldest skeleton has been found in Ethiopia. Archeologists believe it to be some 3 million years old.

The Great Rift Valley

The **Great Rift Valley** is a large canyon in eastern Africa, extending for almost 4,000 miles (6,437 kilometers) from Ethiopia in the north to Mozambique in the south. It has served as a natural barrier to communication and trade between African peoples living to the east and west of it. Many of Africa's lakes are in the Great Rift Valley, which acts as a basin to collect the rain that falls in the tropical zone along the Equator.

CLIMATE

Africa's climate varies greatly from north to south, but generally it includes four main climate types.

Savanna

The savanna climate is characterized by hot and rainy weather in the summer and hot and dry weather in the winter.

Tropical Rain Forests

The areas along the Equator in central and western Africa and in eastern Madagascar are hot and rainy year-round. This climate encourages the growth of dense forests. Many people think of Africa as a land of steamy, hot jungles. But only 8 percent of Africa is covered by tropical rain forests.

Desert

Africa's desert climate is hot and dry year-round. There is little or no vegetation in this climate zone.

Mediterranean Climate

The coastal areas in northwestern Africa and parts of South Africa have a **Mediterranean climate**—long, warm, dry summers and short, mild, rainy winters.

NATURAL RESOURCES

Africa has limited farmland but is rich in mineral and water resources.

Agricultural Resources

Though farmers in the tropical regions produce cash crops of peanuts, rubber, bananas, tea, coffee, and cotton, the soil in much of Africa is not good for agricultural use. Too much rain in some areas causes **leaching**, or the washing away of nutrients. In areas of too little rain, the nutrients decompose.

Water Resources

The many rapids and waterfalls in Africa provide a potential source of hydroelectric power. However, to date, only a few African nations have had the resources to create the technology to produce hydroelectricity. In addition, there is still a great need for water management in Africa. The rain forest areas have too much water, while the rest of Africa generally has too little.

MAKING CONNECTIONS

Key Concepts: Environment
There are few jungle environments in Africa. Nearly 40 percent of the continent consists of desert or dry steppe, with most of the remainder grassland, or open savanna.

Key Concepts: Diversity
The geographic diversity of Africa has significantly influenced the course of human development on the continent.

Regents Tip List several examples of geographic diversity in Africa. (An example has been listed.)
deserts vs. tropical rain forests

MAKING CONNECTIONS

MAJOR GEOGRAPHIC THEMES

1. The fertile soil along the Nile River encouraged the rise of one of the world's great early civilizations—Ancient Egypt.
2. Many geographic features within Africa have prevented contact, trade, and unity among African peoples throughout history.
3. Geographic factors have promoted **cultural diversity** on the continent of Africa.

Physical Features	Result
• The Sahara • Smooth coastline • Lack of continuous, navigable river systems • Great Rift Valley	More than 800 different languages are spoken in present-day Africa.

4. Africa's many raw materials and resources led European nations to divide and colonize the African continent in the nineteenth century.

Geography and History
For more on European division of Africa, see Unit 2, Global History.

SECTION 2 Geographic Setting: India

MAJOR FACTS

India lies on a **subcontinent**—a large area of land separated from the rest of a continent by a natural barrier. In the north, the Himalaya and Hindu Kush mountains separate the Indian subcontinent from the rest of Asia. (See the map, Asia: Physical.) Nations on the subcontinent include India, Pakistan, Bangladesh, Sri Lanka, Nepal, and Bhutan. India is the largest nation and forms a **peninsula**, or area surrounded on three sides by water. The Bay of Bengal lies to the east, the Arabian sea to the west, and the Indian Ocean to the south.

MAKING CONNECTIONS

Key Concepts: Culture
Topographically, the Indian subcontinent has natural barriers that separate it from the rest of Asia and have helped isolate it from other Asian cultures.

TOPOGRAPHY

India has a diverse landscape with several landforms that have helped isolate it from other Asian peoples.

Mountains

The Himalayan Mountains are the highest in the world. For thousands of years, they have helped to isolate India from its Asian neighbors and permitted the peoples of the subcontinent to develop their own unique cultures. The Himalayas include Mt. Everest, the world's highest peak. The subcontinent's other mountain ranges can be seen on the map, Asia: Physical.

Rivers

All of the major rivers on the Indian subcontinent flow out of the northern mountain ranges.

INDUS RIVER The Indus River lies in the west. It regularly overflows its banks and leaves rich deposits of silt. The ancient river valley civilization of the **Harappans** developed along the Indus River in what is now Pakistan. It lasted from approximately 2500 B.C. to 1500 B.C.

Geography and History
For more on ancient river valley civilizations in India, see Unit 2, Global History.

GANGES RIVER This river flows 1,500 miles (2,400 kilometers) from its source in the Himalayas to its ten mouths on the Bay of Bengal. It flows through the north-central portion of India and is sacred to Indians who follow the Hindu religion. The areas of greatest population density in India are along the Ganges and on the Ganges Plain.

Key Concepts: Diversity
The geographic diversity of the Indian subcontinent has led to an uneven distribution of people, with the highest population densities along rivers and low-lying coastal areas.

Asia: Physical

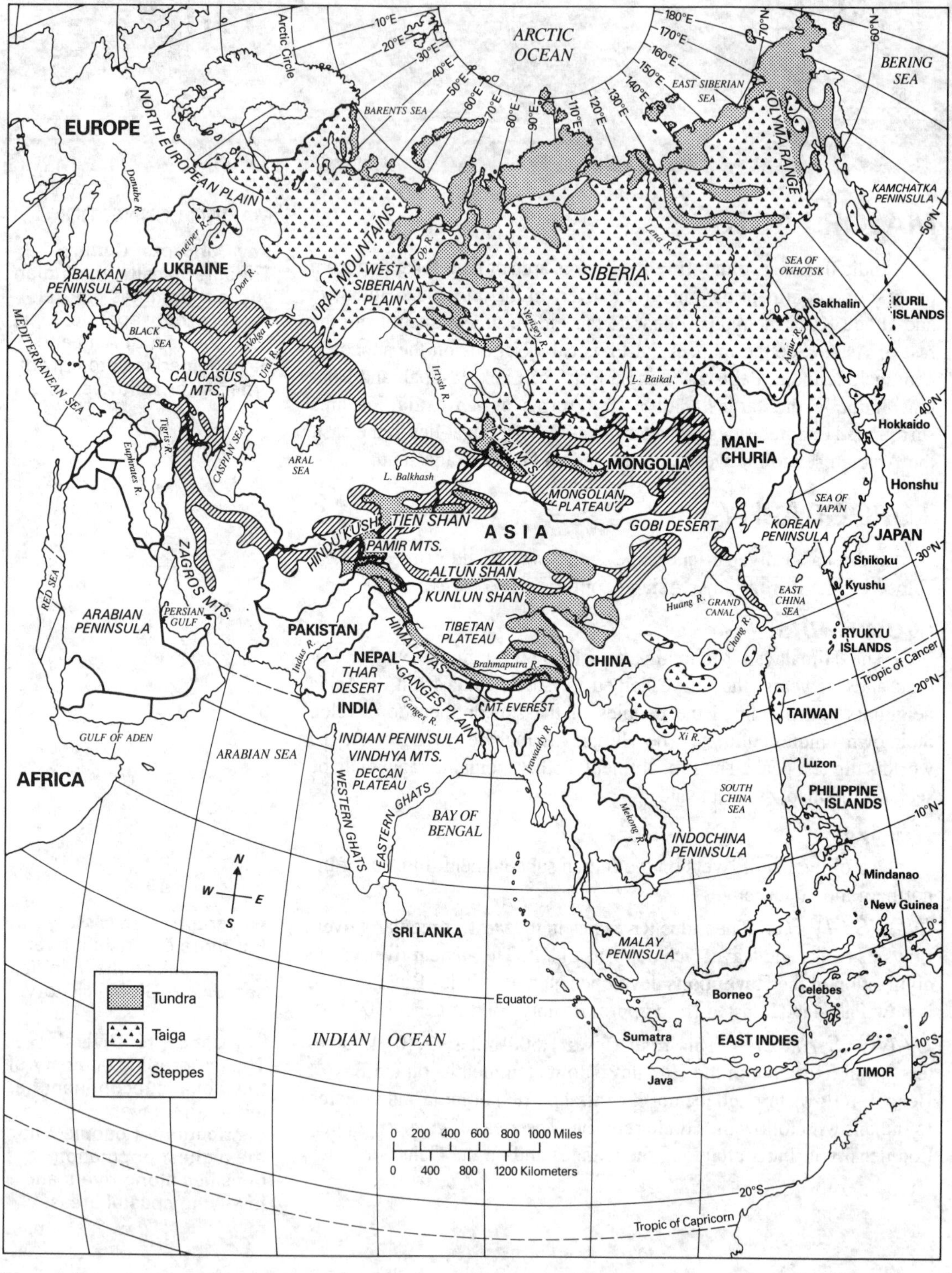
ARCTIC OCEAN
BERING SEA
EAST SIBERIAN SEA
BARENTS SEA
EUROPE
NORTH EUROPEAN PLAIN
URAL MOUNTAINS
WEST SIBERIAN PLAIN
SIBERIA
KOLYMA RANGE
KAMCHATKA PENINSULA
SEA OF OKHOTSK
Sakhalin
KURIL ISLANDS
UKRAINE
BALKAN PENINSULA
MEDITERRANEAN SEA
BLACK SEA
CAUCASUS MTS.
CASPIAN SEA
ARAL SEA
L. Balkhash
L. Baikal
ALTAI MTS.
MONGOLIA
MONGOLIAN PLATEAU
GOBI DESERT
MAN-CHURIA
Hokkaido
Honshu
SEA OF JAPAN
KOREAN PENINSULA
JAPAN
Shikoku
Kyushu
TIEN SHAN
ASIA
HINDU KUSH
PAMIR MTS.
ALTUN SHAN
KUNLUN SHAN
TIBETAN PLATEAU
HIMALAYAS
MT. EVEREST
ZAGROS MTS.
PERSIAN GULF
RED SEA
ARABIAN PENINSULA
PAKISTAN
NEPAL
THAR DESERT
INDIA
GANGES PLAIN
INDIAN PENINSULA
VINDHYA MTS.
DECCAN PLATEAU
WESTERN GHATS
EASTERN GHATS
GULF OF ADEN
ARABIAN SEA
AFRICA
BAY OF BENGAL
SRI LANKA
CHINA
GRAND CANAL
EAST CHINA SEA
RYUKYU ISLANDS
TAIWAN
SOUTH CHINA SEA
Luzon
PHILIPPINE ISLANDS
Mindanao
INDOCHINA PENINSULA
MALAY PENINSULA
New Guinea
Borneo
Celebes
Sumatra
EAST INDIES
Java
TIMOR
INDIAN OCEAN
Danube R.
Dneiper R.
Don R.
Volga R.
Ural R.
Ob R.
Yenisey R.
Irtysh R.
Lena R.
Amur R.
Huang R.
Chang R.
Xi R.
Mekong R.
Irawaddy R.
Brahmaputra R.
Ganges R.
Indus R.
Tigris R.
Euphrates R.
Arctic Circle
Tropic of Cancer
Equator
Tropic of Capricorn
10°E
20°E
30°E
40°E
50°E
60°E
70°E
80°E
90°E
110°E
120°E
130°E
140°E
150°E
160°E
170°E
180°E
70°N
60°N
50°N
40°N
30°N
20°N
10°N
0°
10°S
20°S
N
S
E
W
Tundra
Taiga
Steppes
0 200 400 600 800 1000 Miles
0 400 800 1200 Kilometers

BRAHMAPUTRA RIVER A third great Indian river, the Brahmaputra, is located in northeastern India and Bangladesh.

The Deccan Plateau

The Deccan Plateau is located in central India. It is bordered by mountain ranges—the Ghats—on India's eastern and western coasts. This plateau and the surrounding mountain ranges have separated the peoples of northern and southern India.

CLIMATE

Most of India has warm, dry winters and hot, wet summers. About 80 percent of India's rainfall comes during a five-month period.

Monsoons

The dominant climatic feature in India is the **monsoons**. These seasonal winds sweep across the Arabian Sea and Bay of Bengal in the spring, picking up water. As they head inland and run into the mountains, the winds drop their rains. The monsoon season lasts from June to October.

In the winter, from December through March, the monsoons reverse direction and head back to sea. As they sweep out of the north, the winds bring cool, dry air to much of India.

POPULATION

With more than 900 million people, India is the second most populated nation on earth. (China is first.)

Overpopulation

Overpopulation—there are more than a million births in India each month—has strained the region's limited natural resources. It has caused heavy dependence on the fertile lands along the banks of rivers. People also rely on the timely arrival of the summer monsoons, which are essential to avoid crop failures and famine.

Cultural Diversity

Because of India's topography, the Indian people have developed diverse cultures. India has 15 major languages, one of which is English, and over 800 dialects.

NATURAL RESOURCES

Mineral Resources

India is a leading producer of iron ore, steel, and manganese. India has a shortage of natural gas and petroleum and must import much of its energy resources.

MAKING CONNECTIONS

Geography and Society
Uneven seasonal distribution of rainfall affects the way of life on the Indian subcontinent.

Geography and History
The presence of English is the result of British rule over India. See Unit 2, Global History.

Key Concepts: Scarcity and Interdependence
The scarcity of natural gas and petroleum has caused interdependence between India and the oil-rich Middle East.

MAKING CONNECTIONS

Agricultural Resources

India's farmers produce many cash crops for export. These crops include tea (about 40 percent of the world's total), rice (about 25 percent of the world's total), sugar cane, wheat, cotton, and jute.

MAJOR GEOGRAPHIC THEMES

Geography and History Over the centuries, foreign invaders have occupied India, risking dangerous treks through the Khyber Pass in the northwestern mountains. These invaders have contributed to India's cultural diversity.

Regents Tip List ways in which topography and climate have helped shape human geography in India. (An example has been listed.)
Population has concentrated along the banks of rivers.

1. An ancient river valley civilization grew up along the Indus River—the Harappan civilization (2500 B.C.–1,500 B.C.). India is the second oldest continuous civilization on earth. (The Chinese civilization is first.)
2. Many geographic features have isolated India from its Asian neighbors. As a result, India has developed a unique culture over the last 5,000 years.

Physical Features	**Result**
(from north to south) • Himalaya Mountains • Eastern jungles • Thar Desert (west) • Ganges Plain • Vindhya Mountains • Deccan Plateau • Western/Eastern Ghats	All of these geographic features have isolated the Indian subcontinent from the rest of Asia.

3. Geographic factors have promoted **cultural diversity** within the Indian subcontinent. This cultural diversity has been influenced by historic factors as well.

SECTION 3

Geographic Setting: Southeast Asia

MAJOR FACTS

Southeast Asia lies between India and China. It is made up of two areas: (1) a peninsula, known as Indochina, that juts into the Indian Ocean and South China Sea and (2) several **archipelagos**, or large island chains, to the south and east of the peninsula. The nations that make up Indochina are Burma (Myanmar), Thailand, Cambodia (Kampuchea), Laos, Vietnam, part of Malaysia, and Singapore at the southernmost tip. The island nations include the rest of Malaysia, Brunei, Indonesia, and the Philippines.

MAKING CONNECTIONS

Key Concepts: Culture The location of Southeast Asia has exposed the region to the cultures of India and China.

TOPOGRAPHY

Mountains

Various mountain ranges separate Indochina from the rest of Asia. (See the map, Asia: Physical.) Several rugged mountain chains also cut through the narrow southern part of the peninsula. These ranges have promoted cultural diversity within the region.

Key Concepts: Diversity and Environment The topographic diversity of Southeast Asia has led people to adapt in varying ways to the differing environments.

Rivers

Most of the major rivers in Indochina have their source in the northern mountains, especially the Himalayas. The rivers form huge, flat deltas where they enter the sea.

MEKONG RIVER The Mekong is the longest river in Southeast Asia. It originates in Tibet and flows about 2,800 miles (4,500 kilometers) to the South China Sea. The Mekong passes through China and Laos, along the eastern border of Thailand, and into Cambodia and southern Vietnam.

IRRAWADDY AND SALWEEN RIVERS Two other great rivers in Southeast Asia are the Irrawaddy and the Salween. These rivers, which also start in Tibet, flow through Burma.

Regents Tip List topographic and climatic features that have influenced culture in Southeast Asia. (An example has been provided.)
Several rugged mountain chains run down the Southeast Asian peninsula.

River Valleys

Heavy rains in Southeast Asia cause river flooding, which deposits rich sediment along the region's broad, flat valleys. In addition, the major rivers have formed extensive deltas at their mouths. The

Southeast Asia: Political

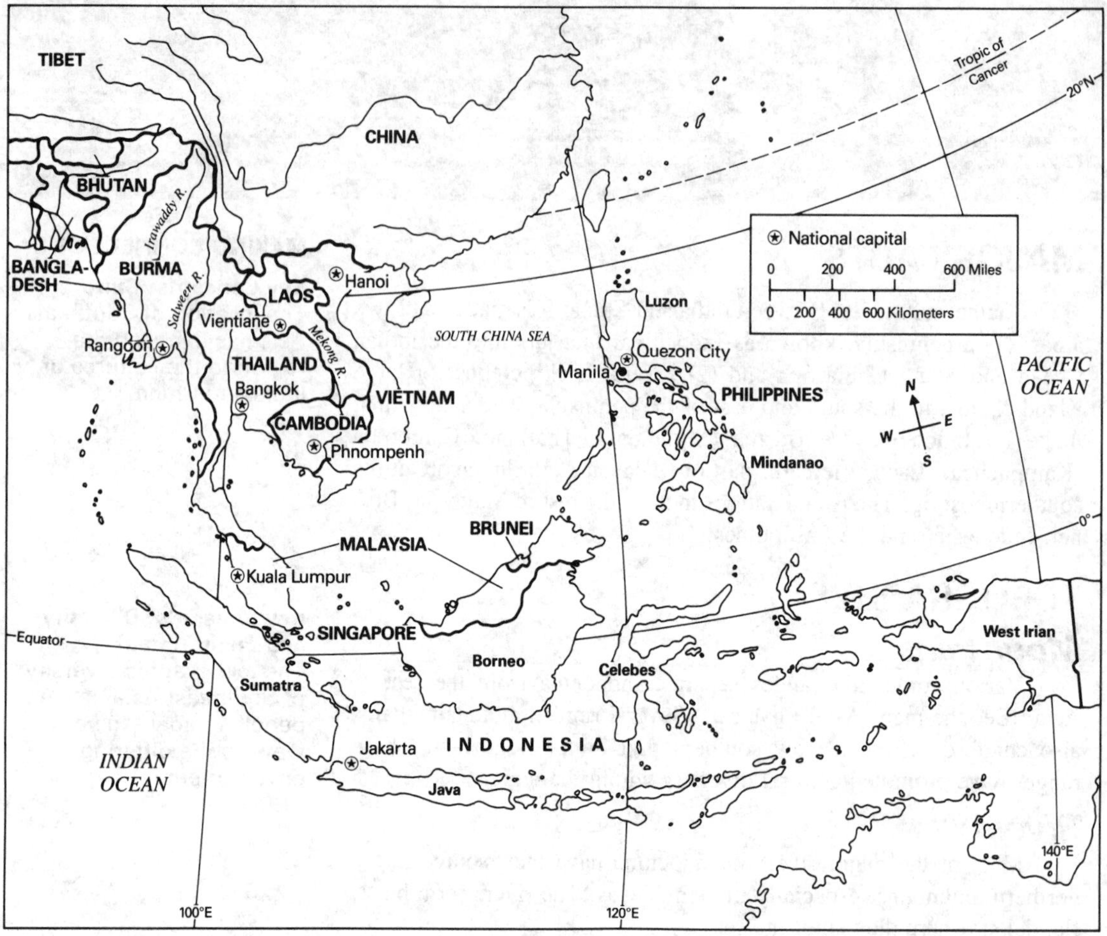

MAKING CONNECTIONS

Regents Tip Practice your data-based skills by answering the following question about the map:

Which geographic factor contributed most to Singapore's becoming an important commercial center?

a its distance from China
b its location along a strategic shipping route
c its status as an island nation
d its isolation from other Southeast Asian nations

Irrawaddy delta, for example, begins 150 miles (240 kilometers) from the sea. The sediment deposited by the rivers makes Indochina an important rice-growing region.

Volcanoes

Hundreds of volcanoes lie along the arc of island nations. Indonesia has more volcanoes than any other part of the world.

CLIMATE

Most of the countries in Southeast Asia lie close to the Equator and have **tropical climates**. High temperatures and humidity make the weather hot and muggy for much of the year.

Monsoons

As in India, the monsoons dominate the climate in Southeast Asia. Heavy rains fall from June to September in nations north of the Equator. Southeast Asia is one of the wettest regions on earth. Farmers depend on the rains for crops, but the downpours leach, or wash away, many minerals from the soil.

Tropical Rain Forests

Tropical rain forests cover large parts of Southeast Asia, where average rainfall is 80 inches (200 centimeters) per year and temperatures rarely fall below 65°F (18°C).

MAKING CONNECTIONS

Geography and Economics
The monsoons influence the type of agricultural products grown in Southeast Asia and have led farmers to rely on traditional farming methods.

NATURAL RESOURCES

Mineral Resources

Malaysia has one-third of the world's supply of tin and deposits of bauxite, important to the manufacture of aluminum. Indonesia and Thailand also have deposits of tin. Oil is found in Indonesia, Burma, Brunei, and Malaysia. The dense rain forests of Southeast Asia, however, hinder exploration. Therefore, the full extent of the region's mineral wealth remains unknown.

Agricultural Resources

Plantations in Malaysia produce most of the world's rubber. Other agricultural products of Southeast Asia include spices, tea, coffee, lumber, coconuts, and rice.

Geography and Culture
Examples of cultural diffusion from other regions include:

Religion: Buddhism, Hinduism, and Islam spread to Southeast Asia from India, China, and the Middle East.

Scholarship: Confucianism reached Southeast Asia from China.

Economics: Trade brought Southeast Asian people in contact with Arab, Indian, Chinese, and European merchants in search of spices and other goods.

MAJOR GEOGRAPHIC THEMES

1. The topography of Southeast Asia has isolated and separated peoples and nations and thus has promoted cultural diversity in the region.
2. The location of Southeast Asia has made it vulnerable to outside influences.
3. The valuable resources found in Southeast Asia have led imperialist nations to build colonies there.
4. The topography of Southeast Asia has resulted in a concentration of population in rural areas and a dependence on agriculture.

SECTION 4 Geographic Setting: China

MAKING CONNECTIONS

MAJOR FACTS

China is the largest country in Asia and the third largest country in the world. (Only Russia and Canada cover more territory.) With more than one billion people, China is the world's most populous nation.

China is bounded on the north by the Gobi Desert, on the east by the Pacific Ocean, on the west by the Himalaya and Tien Shan mountains, and on the south by jungles and the Himalaya Mountains. (See the map, Asia: Physical.)

TOPOGRAPHY

Key Concepts: Culture
Topography and drainage patterns in China influenced the distribution of population and the formation of culture.

The landforms along China's border have helped isolate it from other nations. Two-thirds of the area consists of mountains and deserts, which have affected the distribution of people. Nearly 96 percent of China's vast population live in the eastern part of the nation.

Mountains

The Himalayas form the southern and southwestern borders of China. Great ranges along China's borders include the Tien Shan, Altai, Kunlun Shan, and Altun Shan. The region of Tibet lies on a high plateau between the Kunlun Shan and the Himalayas. It has the highest elevation of any nation on earth. The Himalayas separate India and China (Asia's two largest nations) from each other.

Geography and History
China's earliest civilizations developed in the Chang, Huang, and Xi river valleys.

Rivers

Most of China's rivers start in the western mountains. They head east across China and empty into the Pacific Ocean. China's rivers have traditionally served as important waterways.

CHANG (YANGTZE) RIVER The Chang River flows through central China and is the nation's most important river system. Most of China's major industrial and agricultural centers have developed along the Chang.

HUANG (YELLOW) RIVER The Huang River runs through northern China. Flooding by the river has left fertile deposits of yellow soil, or **loess**, on the plains surrounding it. These deposits have raised the river's banks, forcing the Chinese to build dikes and canals to control its flooding. The many devastating floods along the Huang throughout Chinese history have earned it the name "River of Sorrows." Here the ancient Chinese river valley civilization developed around 3000 B.C.

XI (HSI) RIVER The third major river in China is the Xi, which flows through the south-central highlands. Its waters overflow during the summer monsoons, and farmers use them to produce two to three rice crops a year.

THE GRAND CANAL The Chinese have linked their natural waterways through a system of canals. The greatest of these is the Grand Canal, started almost 1,300 years ago. It connects the Huang and Chang rivers.

Deserts

Deserts lie in the north and west of China. The largest desert area is the Gobi Desert (See the map, Asia: Physical.) The Gobi extends from Mongolia into northern China. The Gobi has isolated China, but it did not prevent a series of invasions by the Mongols, who conquered China and ruled it at one point in its history.

CLIMATE

There are two main climate regions in China. Southern China is affected by the monsoons. It has hot, humid summers with heavy rains. Farmers in this region grow major crops of tea and rice. Mountains in central China block the rain-carrying monsoons from reaching farther inland. Therefore, northeastern China receives little rain. It has hot summers and cold winters. Here farmers produce wheat as their major crop.

NATURAL RESOURCES

Agricultural Resources

China is primarily an agricultural nation. However, only about 11 percent of China's land is suitable for farming. Most of it lies in a basin between the Chang, Huang, and Xi rivers. Here about 80 percent of China's population works at labor-intensive farming, or farming with little machinery. The major crop in southern China is rice. In the north, wheat, sorghum, millet, and soybeans are grown.

Mineral Resources

China has vast reserves of coal, iron ore, and uranium. Manchuria is especially rich in iron ore, which has led various nations, especially Japan, to seek its conquest throughout history.

MAKING CONNECTIONS

Regents Tip Describe the landscape in each of the following parts of China. (An example has been provided.)

East: Fertile farmland caused by river flooding.

West:

North:

South:

Geography and Economics Monsoons cause crop failures and food shortages in China when they fail to arrive on time or create unexpected flooding.

MAKING CONNECTIONS

Geography and History For more on the diffusion of Chinese culture, see Unit 2, Global History.

Regents Tip List topographic features that encouraged the rise of ethnocentrism in China. (An example has been listed.)
Gobi Desert

MAJOR GEOGRAPHIC THEMES

1. Physical features in China have helped it develop a unique culture little affected by outside influences.
2. The early development of a geographically isolated river valley civilization in China gave rise to **ethnocentrism**—the belief that one's culture is superior to all others. The Chinese believed their nation was the center of the world and called it the "Middle Kingdom." As Chinese culture—particularly Confucianism and the written language—spread to Korea, Vietnam, and Japan, this ethnocentric attitude continued.
3. China's topography limits its ability to grow food for the largest population on earth. The challenge of feeding the Chinese people has been a continuing issue in China's history.

SECTION 5 Geographic Setting: Japan

MAJOR FACTS

Japan is an archipelago, or chain of islands, located east of the Asian mainland. It comprises four main islands and more than 3,000 smaller islands. The four main islands include Honshu (the largest), Hokkaido, Shikoku, and Kyushu. Japan extends about 1,500 miles (2,400 kilometers) and is roughly the same size as California. Fewer than 30 million people live in California, while more than 123 million live in Japan. It is the most densely populated nation in the world with roughly 844 people per square mile.

TOPOGRAPHY

Japan's island location helped isolate it from the Asian continent and protect it from outside invasion. The Japanese developed a sense of cultural unity and distrust of foreign influences.

Mountains and Volcanoes

Mountains cover about 85 percent of Japan. To maximize the area available for farming, the Japanese use **terrace farming** by building step-like levels of gardens up hillsides.

About 200 volcanoes are found in Japan. The most famous of these is Mt. Fuji, which is not active. More than 1,500 tremors shake Japan each year, and earthquakes are not uncommon.

Rivers

Short, fast rivers flow out of the mountains and into the surrounding bodies of water. These rivers are not very useful for transportation, but the Japanese have harnessed them for irrigation and for generating hydroelectric power.

Coastline

The Japanese coastline is irregular, or jagged, and has many good harbors for trade. Its long coastline has made it easy for the Japanese to turn to the sea as a valuable resource. Japan is one of the leading fishing nations in the world, and fish is a mainstay of the Japanese diet. More than 75 percent of the Japanese population lives in cities along the coast.

MAKING CONNECTIONS

Key Concepts: Culture
Japan's island location has allowed it to borrow selectively from other cultures without being overwhelmed by them.

Key Concepts: Identity
Japan's distance from the Asian continent and its secure island boundaries permitted the Japanese to develop an independent cultural identity at a very early period.

Key Concepts: Environment
Natural hazards in Japan, such as volcanic eruptions and earthquakes, have given the Japanese a keen awareness of their environment.

Geography and Economics
Japan's mountainous topography and its status as an island nation have influenced the economic development of Japan as a nonagricultural nation.

MAKING CONNECTIONS

Regents Tip Practice your data-based skills by answering the following questions about the map:

Most of Japan lies south of which degree latitude?

Most of Japan lies east of which degree longitude?

Approximately how many miles of water separate Korea from Tokyo?

a 125 miles c 600 miles
b 250 miles d 1000 miles

Geography of Japan

CLIMATE

Like the United States, most of Japan lies in the temperate zone and has four seasons. Hot, humid summers prevail in much of the nation. Cold winds out of Siberia (in Russia) produce cold winters in the north, while winters in the south are milder. Monsoons sweep off the Pacific in the summer and drop heavy rains on Shikoku and Kyushu. No part of Japan, however, receives less than 40 inches (100 centimeters) of rain a year, and many areas get more than 100 inches (254 centimeters). This helps the Japanese to grow large crops of rice.

NATURAL RESOURCES

Mineral Resources

Japan lacks many mineral resources for industry. The islands have deposits of copper and coal, but not enough to meet Japan's needs. The nation must import 90 percent of its oil from the Middle East. This scarcity of minerals led Japan to become an imperial power in the late 1800s and first half of the 1900s. It sought to take over mineral-rich territories such as Manchuria. Japan's imperialism led it into military conflicts, including World War II.

HUMAN RESOURCES

Japan's most valuable resource has been its people and their ability to industrialize on a small area of land. A leading export of Japan is its technology, which has made it one of the world's leading economic powers.

MAJOR GEOGRAPHIC THEMES

1. The geographic isolation of Japan has produced cultural unity and a tightly knit society resistant to outside influence.
2. Japan's status as an island nation has helped it ward off foreign invasions. (Mongol invasions failed in 1274 and 1281.)
3. Japan's proximity to the Asian mainland has allowed the Japanese to **assimilate**, or adapt, certain Asian cultural ideas to fit their own culture. These ideas have been borrowed through the process of cultural diffusion.
4. A scarcity of mineral resources hindered Japanese efforts to industrialize. The Japanese sought to gain these resources through a policy of imperialism. Today Japan trades its technology for raw materials.

MAKING CONNECTIONS

Key Concepts: Scarcity
A scarcity of raw materials in Japan influenced its international relations in the late 1800s and first half of the 1900s.

Key Concepts: Technology and Environment
The Japanese have used technology to overcome problems posed by the physical environment, particularly a lack of natural resources.

Geography and History
For more on the development of Japanese imperialism, see Unit 2, Global History.

Geography and Economics
For more on Japan's position in the world economy, see Unit 4, Global Economics.

SECTION 6 Geographic Setting: Latin America

MAKING CONNECTIONS

Key Concepts: Diversity
There is enormous diversity within Latin America, and this includes cultural, physical, and climatic characteristics.

MAJOR FACTS

Latin America includes four distinct areas: Mexico (which forms part of North America), Central America (the nations south of Mexico and north of South America), South America, and numerous islands in the Caribbean. Find the nations in each of these regions on the map, Geographic Setting: The Americas. Five major bodies of water surround Latin America: the Gulf of California, the Gulf of Mexico, the Caribbean Sea, the Atlantic Ocean, and the Pacific Ocean.

TOPOGRAPHY

Latin America extends 7,000 miles (11,265 kilometers) from the northern border of Mexico to the southern tip of Chile. It includes a diverse landscape with many physical barriers that have hindered unity among its peoples.

Over the years, the topography of Latin America has encouraged the rise of **regionalism**, or loyalty to a specific locale or geographic area. Mountains and highlands have hindered trade and contact among people. In the past, the topography of Latin America has prevented communication and **cultural diffusion**, or the exchange of ideas. As a result, many regional differences have developed within Latin America.

Mountains and Highlands

THE ANDES MOUNTAINS The Andes run along the western coast of South America. They form the highest mountain range in the Western Hemisphere and the second highest mountain range in the world. (The Himalayas are higher.) The tremendous height of these mountains cuts off the eastern part of South America from the west coast.

HIGHLANDS In Mexico and Central America, highlands and plateaus cover much of the area. Several large expanses of highlands stretch across South America, too. These include the Guiana Highlands, Brazilian Highlands, and Patagonia (in Argentina). Many of the islands in the Caribbean are also quite rugged.

Geographic Setting: The Americas

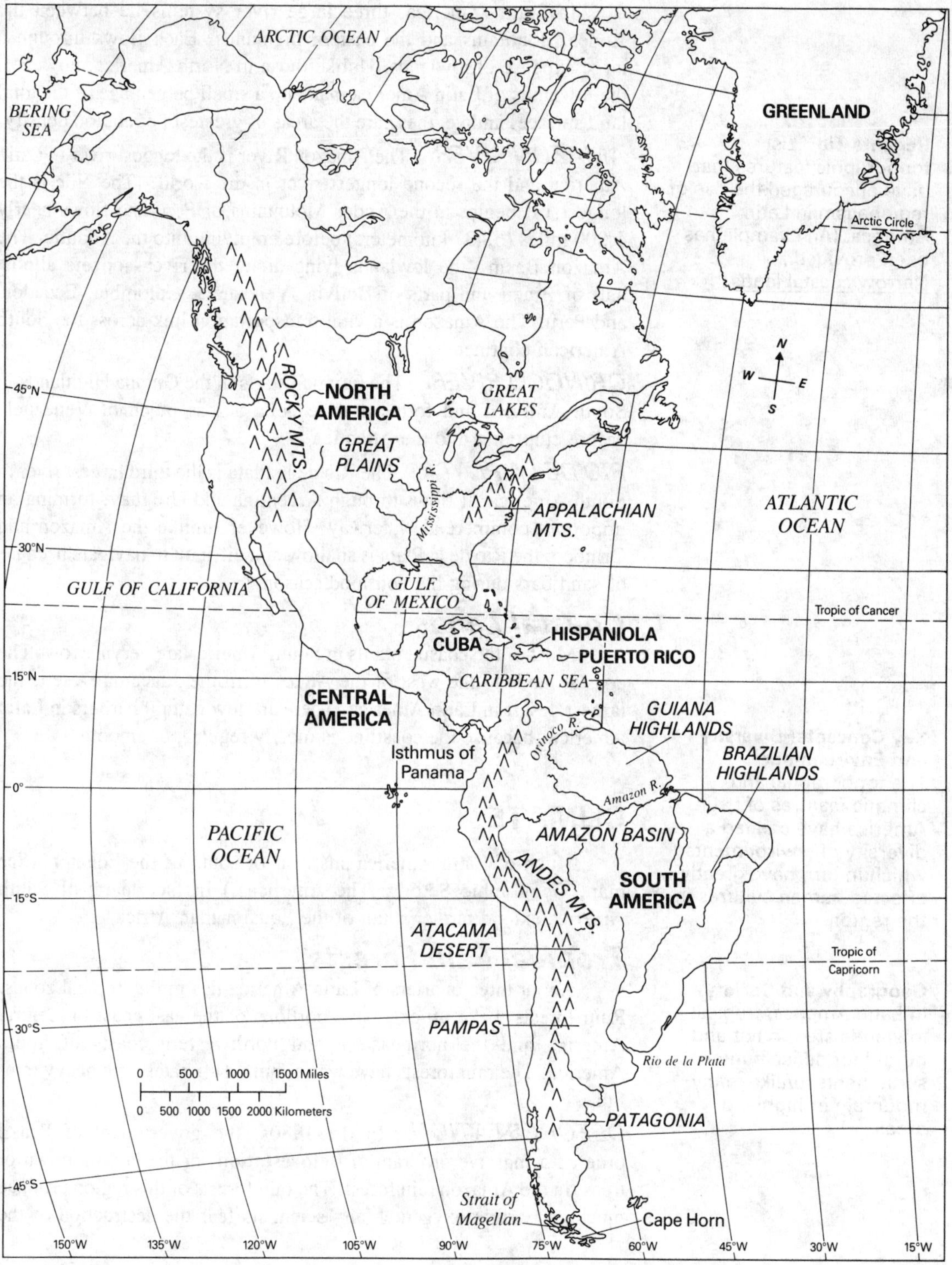
ARCTIC OCEAN
BERING SEA
GREENLAND
Arctic Circle
N
W
E
S
45°N
NORTH AMERICA
GREAT LAKES
ROCKY MTS.
GREAT PLAINS
Mississippi R.
APPALACHIAN MTS.
ATLANTIC OCEAN
30°N
GULF OF CALIFORNIA
GULF OF MEXICO
Tropic of Cancer
CUBA
HISPANIOLA
PUERTO RICO
15°N
CARIBBEAN SEA
CENTRAL AMERICA
GUIANA HIGHLANDS
Orinoco R.
Isthmus of Panama
BRAZILIAN HIGHLANDS
0°
Amazon R.
PACIFIC OCEAN
AMAZON BASIN
ANDES MTS.
SOUTH AMERICA
15°S
ATACAMA DESERT
Tropic of Capricorn
30°S
PAMPAS
Rio de la Plata
0 500 1000 1500 Miles
0 500 1000 1500 2000 Kilometers
PATAGONIA
45°S
Strait of Magellan
Cape Horn
150°W
135°W
120°W
105°W
90°W
75°W
60°W
45°W
30°W
15°W

MAKING CONNECTIONS

Regents Tip List topographic features that have encouraged the rise of regionalism in Latin America. (An example has been provided.)
Narrow coastal lands

Key Concepts: Diversity and Environment
The topographic and climatic features of Latin America have created a diversity of environments, which in turn have greatly affected human cultures in the region.

Geography and Society
In Latin America, tropical lowlands are too hot and humid for dense human settlements, unlike many mountain or highland areas.

Rivers

In South America, three large river systems lie between the Andes Mountains and the eastern highlands. Each flows through a large expanse of lowlands. Unlike those in North America, however, the lowlands of Latin America make up a small percentage of the total land surface, and yet these are the areas of greatest population density.

AMAZON RIVER The Amazon River is the longest river in Latin America and the second longest river in the world. (The Nile is the longest.) It begins in the Andes Mountains of Peru and flows nearly 4,000 miles (6,437 kilometers) before emptying into the Atlantic. The Amazon Basin—the lowlands lying along the river—covers almost half of Brazil and parts of Bolivia, Venezuela, Colombia, Ecuador, and Peru. The Amazon is a vital transportation link across the South American continent.

ORINOCO RIVER The Orinoco starts in the Guiana Highlands in South America and forms a wide delta across much of Venezuela before emptying into the Atlantic.

RIO DE LA PLATA The Rio de la Plata is the third largest river in South America. It flows through Argentina and Uruguay, forming an important commercial waterway. However, unlike the Amazon and Orinoco, the Rio de la Plata is shallow and difficult to navigate because of sand bars during the nonflood season.

Coastal Lands

Most of the coastal plains in South America are very narrow. The coastal lands to the west of the Andes form the Atacama Desert, the largest desert in Latin America. There are few natural harbors in Latin America, because the coastline is mostly regular, or smooth.

CLIMATE

Much of Latin America sits near or south of the Equator. (See map, Geographic Setting: The Americas.) In fact, parts of South America extend farther south of the Equator than Africa.

Tropical Rain Forests

About three quarters of Latin America lies in the tropical zones. Rain forests make up extensive portions of the east coast of Central America and the northeastern and northwestern coasts of South America. The rain forests have warm, humid climates with heavy rainfall.

DEFORESTATION In the 1980s, the government of Brazil ordered a massive program of **deforestation**, or the cutting down of trees, in the Amazon rain forest. The rain forests of this region produce much of Earth's oxygen. Many scientists fear the destruction of the

Destruction of Tropical Forests

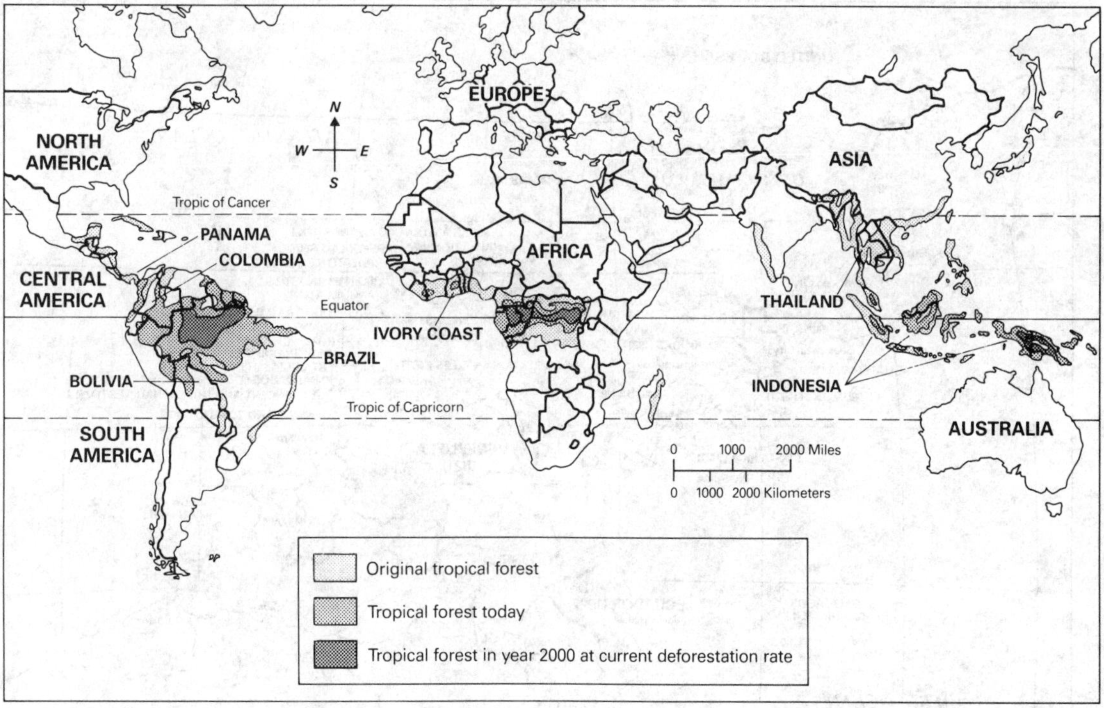

rain forests will lead to warming of Earth's climate and have disastrous effects.

Tropical Savannas

This climate zone is found in the northern and central portions of South America and several of the Caribbean islands. The tropical savannas have warm temperatures and alternate between wet and dry seasons.

Arid Lands

Parts of Latin America are arid, or dry. However, Latin America has a far smaller percentage of dry lands than Africa. Desert and dry lands occupy much of northern Mexico, the Pacific coast of South America, and the southern part of Argentina.

NATURAL RESOURCES

Agricultural Resources

The topography of Latin America makes farming difficult. Even so, the nations of Latin America are still largely agricultural. Ranchers raise cattle on the grasslands and savannas, and farmers grow crops on river lowlands and in the savannas.

MAKING CONNECTIONS

Regents Tip Practice your data-based skills by answering the following question about the map:

In which country is the greatest area of present-day tropical forest threatened with destruction?

a Ivory Coast
b Bolivia
c Brazil
d Thailand

Geography and Economics
For more on Latin American economic development, see Unit 2, Global History and Unit 4, Global Economics.

Latin America: Political

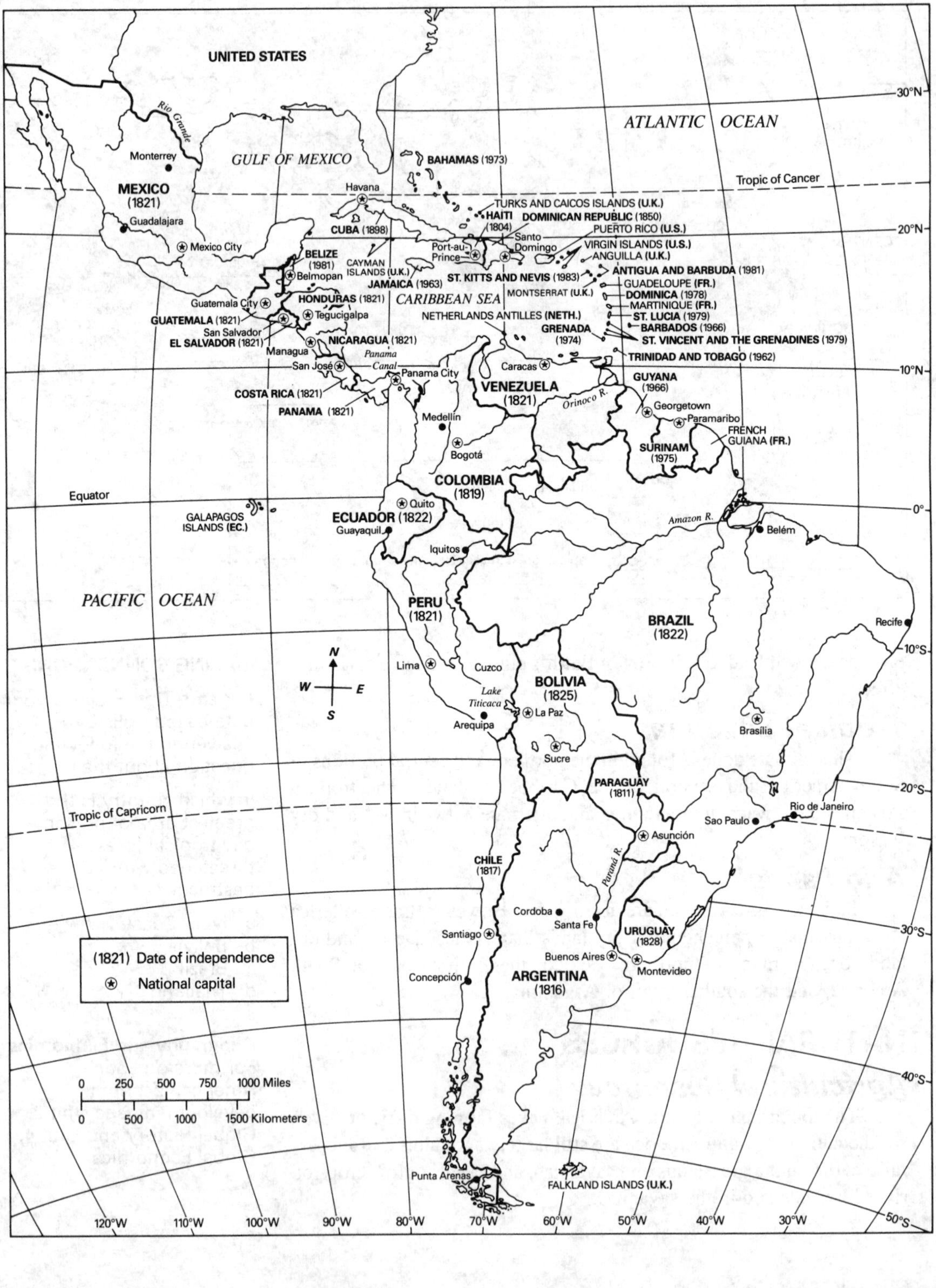
UNITED STATES
Rio Grande
ATLANTIC OCEAN
GULF OF MEXICO
Monterrey
MEXICO (1821)
Guadalajara
Mexico City
BAHAMAS (1973)
Tropic of Cancer
Havana
TURKS AND CAICOS ISLANDS (U.K.)
HAITI (1804)
DOMINICAN REPUBLIC (1850)
CUBA (1898)
PUERTO RICO (U.S.)
Santo Domingo
Port-au-Prince
VIRGIN ISLANDS (U.S.)
ANGUILLA (U.K.)
BELIZE (1981)
Belmopan
CAYMAN ISLANDS (U.K.)
JAMAICA (1963)
ST. KITTS AND NEVIS (1983)
ANTIGUA AND BARBUDA (1981)
GUADELOUPE (FR.)
MONTSERRAT (U.K.)
DOMINICA (1978)
MARTINIQUE (FR.)
ST. LUCIA (1979)
BARBADOS (1966)
ST. VINCENT AND THE GRENADINES (1979)
TRINIDAD AND TOBAGO (1962)
Guatemala City
HONDURAS (1821)
Tegucigalpa
CARIBBEAN SEA
NETHERLANDS ANTILLES (NETH.)
GRENADA (1974)
GUATEMALA (1821)
San Salvador
EL SALVADOR (1821)
Managua
NICARAGUA (1821)
Panama Canal
San José
Panama City
Caracas
COSTA RICA (1821)
PANAMA (1821)
VENEZUELA (1821)
Orinoco R.
GUYANA (1966)
Georgetown
Paramaribo
FRENCH GUIANA (FR.)
SURINAM (1975)
Medellín
Bogotá
COLOMBIA (1819)
Equator
GALAPAGOS ISLANDS (EC.)
Quito
ECUADOR (1822)
Guayaquil
Amazon R.
Belém
Iquitos
PACIFIC OCEAN
PERU (1821)
BRAZIL (1822)
Recife
N
W
E
S
Lima
Cuzco
Lake Titicaca
BOLIVIA (1825)
La Paz
Arequipa
Brasília
Sucre
PARAGUAY (1811)
Tropic of Capricorn
Rio de Janeiro
Sao Paulo
Asunción
CHILE (1817)
Paraná R.
Cordoba
Santa Fe
Santiago
URUGUAY (1828)
(1821) Date of independence
National capital
Buenos Aires
Montevideo
Concepción
ARGENTINA (1816)
0 250 500 750 1000 Miles
0 500 1000 1500 Kilometers
Punta Arenas
FALKLAND ISLANDS (U.K.)
30°N
20°N
10°N
0°
10°S
20°S
30°S
40°S
50°S
120°W
110°W
100°W
90°W
80°W
70°W
60°W
50°W
40°W
30°W

MAKING CONNECTIONS

Latin America produces one half of the world's coffee and bananas and one third of the world's sugar and cocoa. Overdependence on a single **cash crop**, or crop sold for a profit, has made many Latin American nations vulnerable to poor weather conditions or world price fluctuations.

Mineral Resources

Some Latin American nations have large mineral reserves. Oil is found in Mexico, Venezuela, and Colombia. Bolivia is the second largest producer of tin in the world. Chile is the world's largest exporter of copper. Mexico has large deposits of silver.

POPULATION

Overpopulation and rapid population growth threaten the economic development of Latin America. The total population of Latin America in 1990 was around 455 million people. Population is expected to top 787 million by the year 2025.

Geography and Society
For more on overpopulation in Latin America and elsewhere, see Unit 6, The World Today.

MAJOR GEOGRAPHIC THEMES

1. Geographic barriers, such as the Andes Mountains and Latin America's many highlands, have discouraged unity and encouraged the rise of regionalism.
2. Because of Latin America's varied landscape and climate, many diverse cultures have developed, often isolated from each other by geographic barriers.
3. Deforestation in parts of Latin America has created a problem for the global community.
4. Overpopulation and dependence on single cash crops are issues faced by most Latin American nations in the 1990s.

SECTION 7 Geographic Setting: The Middle East

MAKING CONNECTIONS

Regents Tip Describe how each of the following geographic factors influenced culture and history in the Middle East.
Location:

Lack of Natural Barriers:

Climate:

Geography and History For more on ancient river valley civilizations in the Middle East, see Unit 2, Global History.

MAJOR FACTS

The Middle East, including North Africa, lies at the junction of three continents—Europe, Africa, and Asia. Its strategic location has made it a center of trade throughout history and earned it the name "the crossroads of the world." The Middle East extends from Morocco in the west to Afghanistan in the east and from Turkey in the north to the Arabian Peninsula in the south. Its total area is twice the size of the United States.

TOPOGRAPHY

Deserts and plateaus make up much of the Middle East. There are also several fertile river valleys where some of the world's earliest civilizations arose.

Fertile Crescent

The core, or central area, of the Middle East is a fertile strip of land along the Tigris and Euphrates rivers. It extends in an arch from the Mediterranean Sea in the west to the Persian Gulf in the east. This curve of land is known as the **Fertile Crescent**.

A BREADBASKET IN THE DESERT Since ancient times, melting snows in nearby mountains have flooded the Tigris and Euphrates rivers each spring. The flooding deposits **silt**, or soil rich in minerals, on the surrounding plain. Though the flooding is unpredictable and sometimes causes destruction, it makes agriculture possible in a dry, desert region.

"CRADLE OF CIVILIZATION" The Fertile Crescent has sometimes been called the "Cradle of Civilization." There are no natural barriers in the Fertile Crescent. Over the centuries, a diversity of people have migrated across, settled in, or invaded the area. In ancient times, the Fertile Crescent was called **Mesopotamia**, or "land between two rivers." Here, three great river valley civilizations flourished between 3500 B.C. and 612 B.C. They were Sumer, Babylonia, and Assyria. The ancient Hebrews, or Jews, carved out a home in western Mesopotomia, too. Over the years, three great religions—Judaism, Christianity, and Islam—took root here.

Geography of the Ancient Middle East

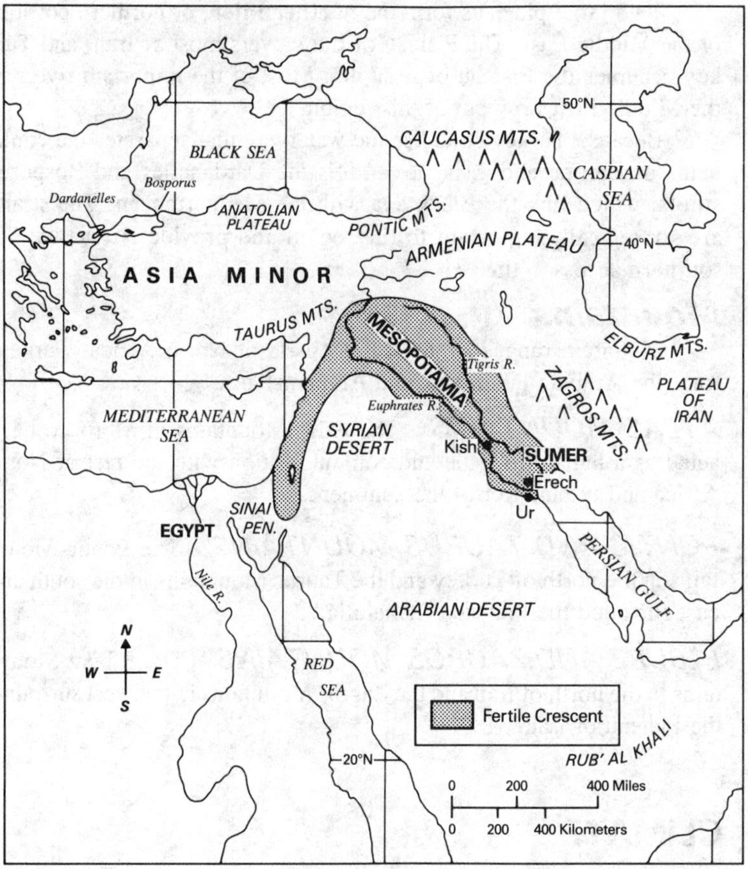

MAKING CONNECTIONS

Regents Tip Practice your data-based skills by answering the following question about the map:

Can you identify the two major river valley civilizations indicated on this historical map?

Nile River

The Nile River also flows through the Middle Eastern nations of Sudan and Egypt. Along its banks, the ancient river valley civilization of Egypt took shape.

Deserts

Two huge deserts occupy the Middle East: (1) the Sahara, in North Africa, separates the region from the rest of Africa, and (2) the Arabian Desert—which includes the Rub' al Khali, or Empty Quarter—covers most of the Arabian Peninsula. Together these two deserts account for more than 90 percent of the land surface in these two areas.

Arabian Peninsula

The Arabian Peninsula is surrounded by the Red Sea to the west, the Arabian Sea to the south, and the Persian Gulf to the east. The Suez Canal connects the Red Sea to the Mediterranean Sea, making the waterway a vital link between Europe and Asia.

MAKING CONNECTIONS

The Northern Tier

Two large plateaus form the **northern tier**, or northern portion, of the Middle East. The Plateau of Iran covers most of Iran, and Turkey occupies the Plateau of Anatolia. Most of the important rivers in the Middle East flow out of this region.

Because Turkey straddles the waterway that separates the continents of Europe and Asia, it controls the Dardanelles and Bosporus straits, which link the Black Sea with the Mediterranean. The straits are strategically important to the region and provide Russia with a southern access to the sea.

Mountains

Mountain ranges stretch across parts of North Africa, Turkey, Iran, the Arabian Peninsula, and Afghanistan.

ATLAS MOUNTAINS The Atlas Mountains in Morocco have acted as a barrier to trade and communication with the rest of North Africa and the interior of the continent.

PONTIC AND TAURUS MOUNTAINS The Pontic Mountains in the north of Turkey and the Taurus Mountains in the south and east surround the Plateau of Anatolia.

ELBURZ AND ZAGROS MOUNTAINS The Elburz Mountains in the north of Iran and the Zagros Mountains in the west surround the Plateau of Iran.

CLIMATE

The mountains along the coastal areas of the Middle East, such as the Atlas Mountains, prevent moisture-bearing clouds from reaching the interior. The region also lies near the Equator. Because of these two factors, the region has warm winters and hot summers. Rainfall is infrequent; three fourths of the region gets less than 10 inches (25 centimeters) of rain a year. When it does rain, flash flooding often occurs.

Key Concepts: Scarcity
The scarcity of water in the Middle East has concentrated population in those areas where irrigation is possible.

POPULATION

The Middle East is one of the driest areas in the world. This fact contributes to a great population imbalance. Most people live in the river valleys or along the coasts, where a Mediterranean climate prevails. Here there are hot, dry summers and cool, rainy winters suitable for growing grapes, olives, and citrus fruits. Rapid population growth in a land of deserts presents a continuing problem for the Middle East.

The Middle East and North Africa: Political

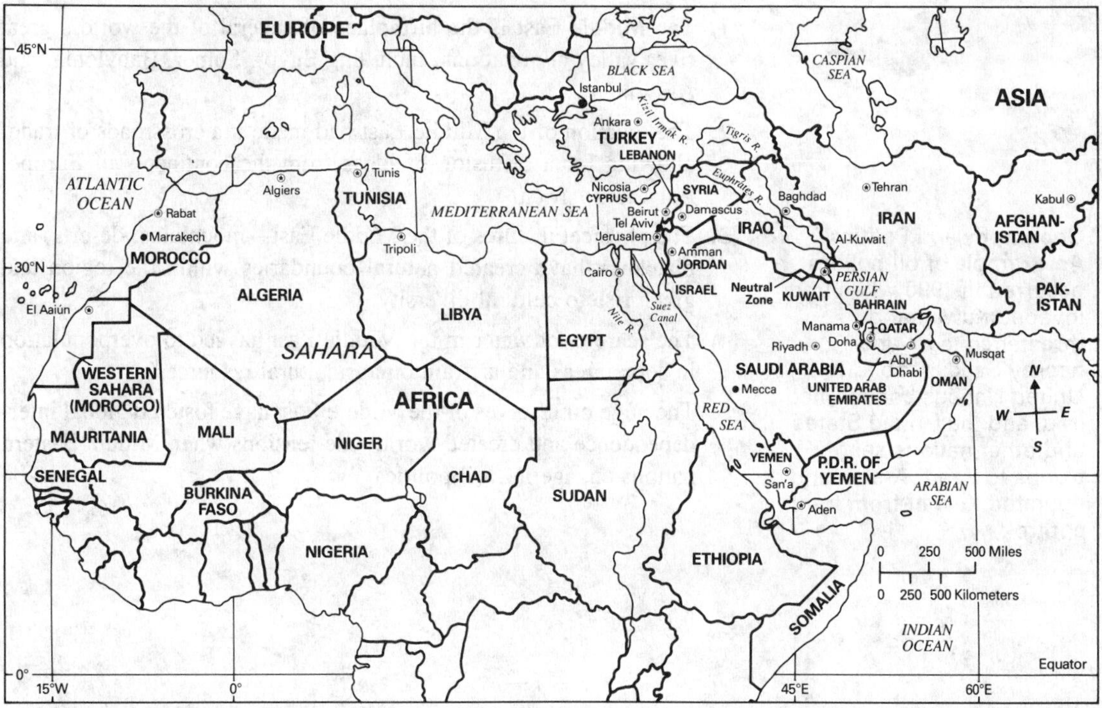

NATURAL RESOURCES

Mineral Resources

About 70 percent of the world's known oil reserves are found in certain countries of the Middle East, principally those along the Persian Gulf. These countries produce 50 percent of the world's current supply of oil.

Water Resources

The most precious resource in the Middle East is water. Only about 7 percent of the land can be farmed because of deserts and lack of rain.

Agricultural Resources

Wheat, barley, rice, and millet are grown on most land farmed in the Middle East. Israel exports Jaffa oranges, and Iraq is the world's leading producer of dates. Turkey exports nuts, figs, olives, and tobacco. Egypt exports cotton.

Overpopulation on farmland has contributed to smaller plots for each farmer. Most nations in the Middle East do not produce enough food to feed their people. The reliance on single cash crops in the Middle East has made the region dependent on world market prices.

MAKING CONNECTIONS

Regents Tip Practice your data-based skills by answering the following questions about the map:

Which Middle Eastern nation lies in North Africa?

a Turkey
b Israel
c Saudi Arabia
d Egypt

Which two nations border the Persian Gulf?

a Kuwait and Syria
b Egypt and Iraq
c Bahrain and Afghanistan
d Saudi Arabia and Iran

MAKING CONNECTIONS

MAJOR GEOGRAPHIC THEMES

1. The Middle East is the birthplace of several of the world's great river valley civilizations, including Egypt, Sumer, Babylonia, and Assyria.
2. The location of the Middle East had made it a crossroads of trade, allowing for a diffusion of ideas from the continents of Europe, Asia, and Africa.
3. The physical features of the Middle East—mountains, deserts, and plateaus—have created natural boundaries within the region and given rise to cultural diversity.
4. The scarcity of water in the Middle East has led to overpopulation in some areas and a strain on agricultural resources.
5. The huge oil reserves of the Middle East have fostered global interdependence and created worldwide tensions when Middle Eastern nations engage in "oil politics."

Geography and Politics
An example of oil politics occurred in 1990 when Iraq invaded Kuwait and threatened to invade nearby Saudi Arabia. The United Nations condemned Iraq, and the United States and other nations sent troops to Saudi Arabia and liberated Kuwait from Iraqi control.

SECTION 8 Geographic Setting: Western Europe

MAJOR FACTS

Europe is the second smallest continent in the world. (Only Australia is smaller.) It is bounded on the west by the Atlantic Ocean, on the south by the Mediterranean Sea, and on the north by the Arctic Ocean. The Ural and Caucasus mountains separate Europe from Asia in the east.

TOPOGRAPHY

Europe is really a peninsula located on a huge landmass called **Eurasia** (made up of the continents of Europe and Asia). Europe itself has been called a "peninsula of peninsulas," because it consists of so many peninsulas. Find some of these peninsulas on the map, Geographic Setting: Europe (p. 64).

Coastline

Europe has an irregular, or ragged, coastline with hundreds of excellent harbors and inlets. It has more miles of coastline than any other continent—50,000 miles (80,400 kilometers) total. No part of Western Europe is more than 300 miles (480 kilometers) from the sea. This geographic fact has helped Western European nations develop many trade and transportation links with the world.

Mountains

Many mountain ranges cross Western Europe. The Alps are the highest and run through Switzerland and Austria. In the past, they acted as a barrier to peoples along the Mediterranean Sea. Other important mountain ranges in Western Europe include the Pyrenees between Spain and France, the Apennines in Italy, and the Sierra Nevada in southern Spain.

Plains

Along the coasts and between the mountain ranges run flat, fertile plains. The most important plain in Western Europe is the North European Plain, extending from Great Britain in the west to Russia in the east. The greatest population density in Europe is found on the North European Plain. It is the site for most agriculture and many major industries. There are no natural barriers in this region to prevent invasion by outside forces.

MAKING CONNECTIONS

Key Concepts: Culture and Interdependence
Most of Western Europe has easy access to warm-water ports and many navigable rivers. These two factors have encouraged cultural diffusion and economic interdependence within the region.

Geography and History
The location of Europe has influenced its role in world affairs. From the 1600s to the mid-1900s, Europeans set out by sea to build worldwide empires. Western European nations held colonies on all the other continents. For more on European colonization, see Unit 2, Global History.

Geography and History
Napoleon marched into Russia across the North European Plain. During World War II, Hitler swept across the plain to invade both Eastern and Western Europe.

Geographic Setting: Europe

Lowlands

Some areas along the North Sea, especially in the Netherlands, lie below sea level. Systems of dikes and sea walls have allowed these lowlands to be reclaimed from the sea.

Rivers

Western Europe has many navigable rivers that have encouraged trade and linked the nations in the region.

DANUBE RIVER The longest river in Europe is the Danube, about 1,766 miles (2,840 kilometers) long. The Danube starts in Germany and flows east into the Black Sea.

RHINE RIVER The Rhine is one of the most important rivers for commerce. Its flows out of the Swiss Alps, across Germany and the Netherlands, and into the North Sea.

OTHER RIVERS Other important rivers in the region include the Seine and the Loire in France, the Po in Italy, the Elbe in Germany, and the Thames in England.

CLIMATE

Almost 50 percent of Western Europe lies at the same latitude as Canada, which is very cold. However, because the countries of Europe lie close to the sea, their climate is warmer and wetter than Canada's.

The Atlantic Drift

The warm-water Gulf Stream flows out of the Gulf of Mexico and Caribbean Sea and heads northeast across the Atlantic. These waters eventually wash the shores of Western Europe. Known as the Atlantic Drift, this current moderates the climate in Western Europe for most of the year. As a result, there are many warm-water, or ice-free, ports in Western Europe.

Mediterranean Climate

The climate south of the Alps is very different from that in the rest of Europe. In Spain, southern France, Italy, and Greece, summers are hot and dry. In winter, clouds off the Mediterranean Sea bring rain, but for most of the year, a subtropical climate prevails. Though this weather pattern has become known as a Mediterranean climate, it is found in other parts of the world, such as California and South Africa.

NATURAL RESOURCES

Mineral Resources

Most nations in Western Europe have plentiful reserves of the resources necessary for industry—particularly coal and iron ore. The Industrial Revolution began in this region. Although Norway and Great Britain produce oil, much of Western Europe relies on imports from the Middle East.

MAKING CONNECTIONS

Key Concepts: Environment and Technology
Europeans have used technology to reshape their physical environment. This is especially true in lowland areas such as the Netherlands.

Regents Tip Name some of the topographic features in Western Europe that have encouraged regional interdependence. Keep in mind features that might promote contact among peoples. (An example has been provided.)
North European Plain

History and Geography
The need for warm-water ports has been a recurring theme in Russian history and has led to conflicts with Western and Eastern European nations.

Geography and Economics
Despite a narrow resource base, Western Europe is a highly developed, technological region. Dependence on the resources of other areas, such as oil from the Middle East, affects economic and political decisions in Western Europe.

MAKING CONNECTIONS

Key Concepts: Technology
The application of modern technology has made Western European agriculture among the most productive in the world.

Agricultural Resources

Western Europe has only a small percentage of land suitable for farming. Nevertheless, its farms are some of the most efficient in the world. Western Europeans use technology and scientific farming methods to produce huge yields of grains, sugar beets, potatoes, and other crops. They produce food to feed themselves and for export.

Other Resources

Because Western European nations are surrounded by water, they have traditionally turned to the seas for a living, making fish an important economic item. So too are the products of Western European factories. Like Japan, Western European nations export their technological knowledge and equipment to the rest of the world.

MAJOR GEOGRAPHIC THEMES

1. Because Western Europeans live on a giant peninsula, they have traditionally reached out to the rest of the world for trade and conquest. By so doing, they have exchanged ideas with peoples around the globe.
2. The topography of Western Europe has created separate regions and encouraged the development of independent nations with their own cultures, languages, and beliefs.
3. The availability of many mineral resources and access to warm-water ports helped spawn the Industrial Revolution in Western Europe—an event that had worldwide impact.
4. Without natural geographic barriers, certain nations within Western Europe, such as France and Belgium, have been the targets of territorial expansion and warfare by other nations seeking more resources and land.

Key Concepts: Change
The Industrial Revolution brought radical change not only to the nations of Western Europe but to global society as a whole. For more on the Industrial Revolution, see Unit 2, Global History.

SECTION 9 Geographic Setting: Northern Eurasia and Eastern Europe

MAJOR FACTS

Northern Eurasia covers all of the area previously known as the Soviet Union. It includes the Commonwealth of Independent States—the independent nations of Russia, Ukraine, Moldova, Uzbekistan, Turkmenistan, Armenia, Azerbaijan, Kazakhstan, Georgia, Tajikistan, Kyrgyzstan, and Byelarus—and Latvia, Estonia, and Lithuania, independent nations that are not part of the commonwealth. More than three quarters of the region is occupied by Russia, the largest nation in the world. Russia is more than twice the size of the United States and spans two continents—25 percent of Russia lies in Eastern Europe and 75 percent lies in Asia.

Eastern Europe is a group of nations between Western Europe and Northern Eurasia. These nations, dominated by the Soviet Union after World War II, were for many years Soviet **satellites**, or nations controlled by an outside power. The Eastern European nations include Albania, Poland, Romania, Hungary, Bulgaria, the Czech Republic, Slovakia, and the parts of the former Yugoslavia: Serbia, Montenegro, Bosnia-Hercegovina, Croatia, and Slovenia. Another former Eastern European nation, East Germany, united with West Germany in 1990, as part of Eastern Europe's move away from Soviet domination and Communist rule.

MAKING CONNECTIONS

Key Concepts: Diversity
The region's size and location affect its topographic and climatic diversity.

Geography and Politics
For more on recent changes in Northern Eurasia and Eastern Europe, see Unit 5, Global Politics and Unit 6, The World Today.

TOPOGRAPHY

Northern Eurasia

Russia covers more than 6,500,000 square miles (16,250,000 square kilometers) and has a variety of landscapes. Despite its large size, much of Russia is in effect landlocked because its ports to the north are frozen much of the year. Throughout much of its history, therefore, the country has sought to conquer and control warm-water ports.

TUNDRA About 10 percent of Russia is located along the Arctic Circle. Here the ground is frozen all year, and little vegetation exists.

TAIGA This area spreads out just below the **permafrost**, or permanently frozen land, of the tundra. The taiga extends in a band of pine

Northern Eurasia: Political

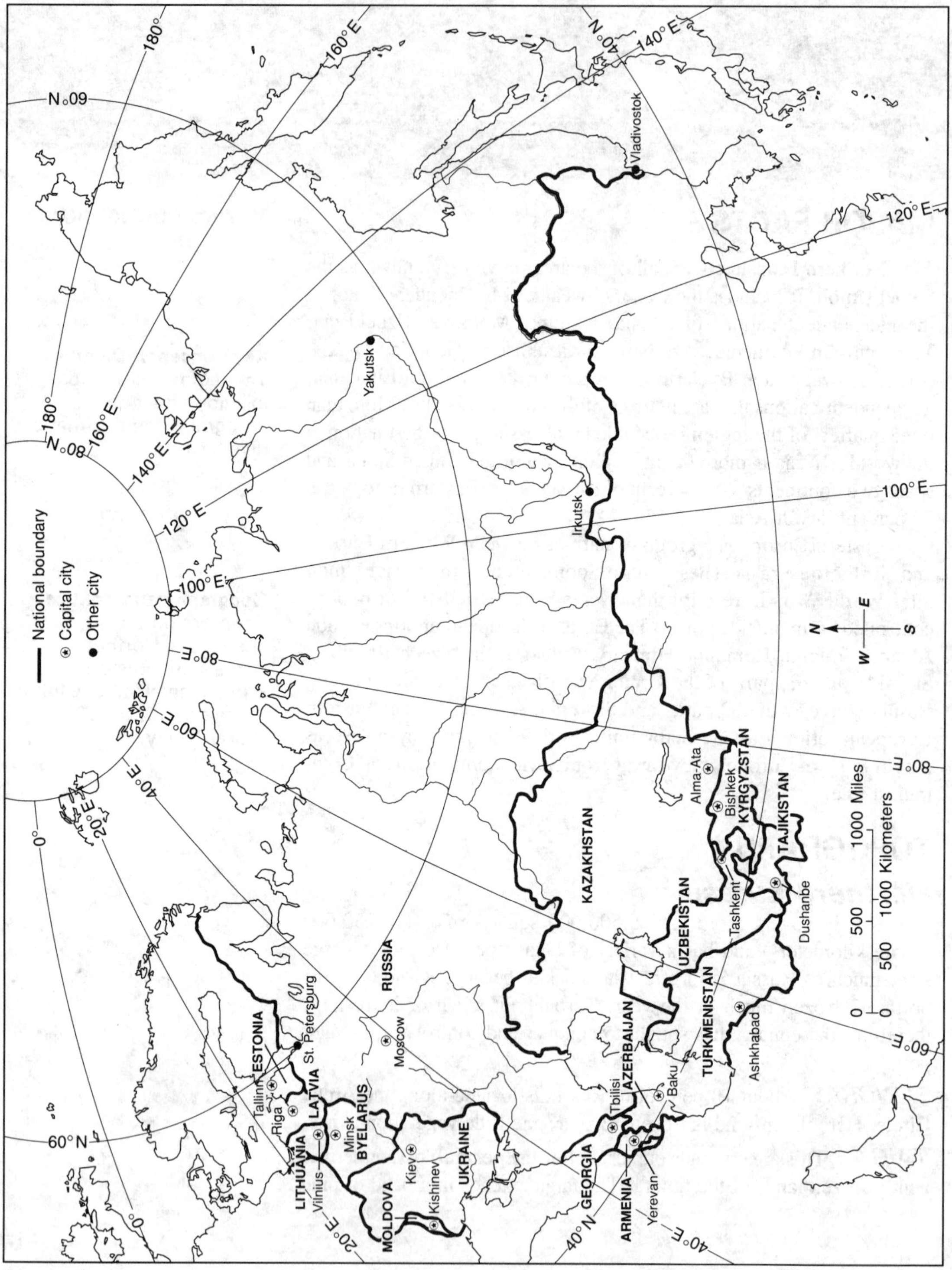

forests from Russia across Asia and is not well-suited for agriculture. Together, the tundra and taiga make up the area known as Siberia.

STEPPES South of the taiga lie vast plains known as steppes. These grasslands provide rich farmland and are called the "breadbasket of Russia." The Russian and West Siberian steppes are an extension of the North European Plain and run from Ukraine in the west to China in the east. The steppes cover about 50 percent of the land in Russia. This barrier-free corridor allows for easy passage across Russia. In the past, invaders have marched across the steppes to seek conquest.

DESERTS Deserts stretch south of the steppes from the Caspian Sea to the border of China.

RIVERS Northern Eurasia has many rivers, the longest of which is the Ob-Irtysh. Other important rivers include the Yenisey, Amur, Lena, Don, Dneiper, and Volga. In spite of their length—the Ob-Irtysh extends more than 3,400 miles (5,470 kilometers)—many of the rivers in Northern Eurasia have limited use, because they flow north into the Arctic Ocean and are frozen for many months of the year.

MOUNTAINS Several major mountain ranges separate the nations of Northern Eurasia from other nations. The Pamir Mountains separate Tajikistan from Iran and Afghanistan. The Caucasus Mountains help isolate Armenia and Azerbaijan from Turkey and northwestern Iran, and the Urals divide the European and Asian portions of Russia.

Eastern Europe

The North European Plain reaches into Eastern Europe. So does the Danube River, known as the Mississippi of Europe. The Danube flows more than 1,700 miles (2,735 kilometers) through the center of Eastern Europe into the Black Sea, forming the major commercial route for shipping. The Balkan Peninsula is surrounded by four seas—the Black, Adriatic, Mediterranean, and Aegean.

Several mountain ranges divide Eastern Europe and have encouraged cultural differences and diversity in languages. These ranges include the Carpathian Mountains, the Sudeten Mountains, and the Julian and Dinaric Alps.

Poland and Hungary lie largely on the North European Plain. With few natural boundaries, they have been subject to foreign invasions throughout their histories.

CLIMATE

Northern Eurasia

Russia has a varied climate to match its landscape. Temperatures range from the frigid subzero weather of the tundra to the warm climates of the Black Sea. Much of Russia lies at about the same latitude as Canada. However, Russia does not benefit from the Atlantic Drift

MAKING CONNECTIONS

Geography and History
In the 1200s, invading Mongols crossed the steppes from the east. In more recent times, Napolean's and Hitler's armies used the steppes to invade from the west. See Unit 2, Global History.

Key Concepts: Environment
Environmental and physical features have influenced the course of history of the peoples of Central Asia and Eastern Europe.

MAKING CONNECTIONS

Geography and Economics A resource-rich environment may help a nation become an economic power. However, the key to great economic power is the ability to use these resources to an advantage. In the former Soviet Union, climatic and political factors adversely affected economic development.

Regents Tip Name some of the geographic features of Russia that encouraged it to seek economic and political control beyond its boundaries. (An example has been provided.) Scarcity of warm-water ports

Geography and History For more on Russia's foreign policy in regard to controlling warm-water ports, see Unit 2, Global History.

that warms the climates in Western Europe. Therefore, it has short summers and long, cold winters.

Eastern Europe

The climate of Eastern Europe is somewhat cooler than that of Western Europe. However, the area enjoys four seasons and adequate rainfall. Nations on the Balkan Peninsula generally have warmer climates.

NATURAL RESOURCES

Northern Eurasia

MINERAL RESOURCES Russia possesses large reserves of coal, oil, iron ore, natural gas, manganese, bauxite, gold, and lead.

AGRICULTURAL RESOURCES The rich, black soil of the steppes, particularly in Ukraine, provides valuable farmland, but the harsh climates in other areas allow farmers to till only about 10 percent of the region's land. The principal products are wheat, rye, corn, potatoes, oats, and sugar beets. Even so, many nations of Northern Eurasia still must import large amounts of grain to feed their populations.

Eastern Europe

MINERAL RESOURCES The nations of Eastern Europe have deposits of coal, iron ore, lead, bauxite, zinc, copper, and natural gas.

AGRICULTURAL RESOURCES The principal crops in Eastern Europe are potatoes, grains, sugar beets, tobacco, and corn.

MAJOR GEOGRAPHIC THEMES

1. Russia spans two continents and has been influenced by ideas from regions both to the west and to the east.
2. Although the lack of natural barriers on the steppes has opened Russia to foreign invasions, the nation's large size and harsh climates have prevented easy conquest and made it difficult to govern.
3. The desire for warm-water ports has influenced Russia's foreign policy for centuries and led the Soviets to control satellite nations in Eastern Europe.
4. The large size of Northern Eurasia and its topography, such as the tundra, taiga, and deserts, have led to much cultural diversity within the region.
5. The location and geographic features of Eastern Europe have encouraged cultural diversity among its nations and made them subject to invasions and conquest throughout their histories.

Regents Questions for Practice

Review the Test-Taking Strategies section of this book. Then answer the following questions, drawn from actual Regents examinations. Circle the *number* of the word or expression that best completes the statement or answers the question. Write your answers to essay questions on a separate piece of paper. Hints on good ways to approach these questions are provided in the margins.

MAKING CONNECTIONS

1. Which is the *best* example of the fact that culture is partially influenced by the geography of an area?
1 Moslems are required to pray five times daily.
2 Jews are prohibited from eating pork.
3 Several political parties are found in India today.
4 Agriculture is a common occupation in the Nile River Valley.

Test Hint This question asks you to consider a cause (the geography of an area) and to determine its most likely effect on a particular culture. Of the choices given, eliminate any that are not related directly to geography.

2. The geography of a region will have the *most* direct influence on its people's
1 means of support.
2 form of worship.
3 system of education.
4 system of government.

Test Hint This question, too, asks you to consider a cause and its effect, but in a more general way.

3. The geographic isolation of a people frequently reinforces
1 a traditional way of life.
2 the development of scientific investigation.
3 the need for higher education.
4 a process of cultural diffusion.

4. The river valleys of the Tigris-Euphrates, the Nile, and the Indus were centers of civilization because they
1 had rich deposits of iron ore and coal.
2 were isolated from other cultural influences.
3 were easy to defend from invasion.
4 provided a means of transportation and irrigation.

Test Hint Before looking at the possible answers, always note the key words in the question—in this case, "river valleys."

5. The geographic features of the African continent are partly responsible for the
1 use of French or English as the official language of many African nations.
2 diversity of cultures found in Africa.
3 decline of the slave trade in the nineteenth century.
4 recent advances in technology in African nations.

6. Which statement best describes the effects of the geography of Africa?
1 Geography has encouraged physical mobility throughout Africa.
2 The geography of Africa has hindered economic development.

3 The geography of Africa has stimulated political and cultural unity.
4 The geography of Africa has resulted in most African countries having similar economic and social systems.

Building Skills: Reading a Cartoon

Base your answer to question 7 on the cartoon below and on your knowledge of social studies.

Now, remove that and fix this one.

7. The cartoon illustrates India's problems with
1 an inadequate transportation system.
2 inefficient government agencies.
3 conflict between religious groups.
4 the monsoon cycle.

8. Most of the Egyptian population is clustered in the Nile River Valley mainly because
1 the river is one of great military importance.
2 heavy industry is located along the river.
3 it is the most scenic area in the country.
4 the river is the major source of water for agriculture.

9. Which statement *best* describes the geography of Africa?
1 Most of the continent is made up of tropical rain forests.
2 Deserts and savannas cover almost half of the continent.
3 Most major rivers are navigable for their entire length.
4 The irregular coastline provides many natural harbors.

10. Which is a major effect of geography on Southeast Asia?
1 Monsoons help determine the types of agricultural products grown.
2 The wealth of natural resources led to early industrialization.
3 Climatic conditions have led to chronic food shortages.
4 Geography has created a sense of unity among all the peoples.

11. In Southeast Asia, the continued importance of the monsoon cycle indicates that this region is
1 becoming a major exporter of oil.
2 developing heavy industry.
3 dependent on traditional farming methods.
4 opposed to the use of nuclear power.

12. Which statement *best* explains why most of the population of the People's Republic of China live in the eastern third of the nation?
1 The best agricultural land is in the east.
2 The largest forests are in the east.
3 The best fishing areas are on the eastern coast.
4 The largest oil deposits are in the east.

13. Which is the main reason for the heavy population concentration in the eastern regions of the People's Republic of China?
1 China's capital is located in the east.
2 Most of China's fertile farmland is located in the east.
3 Most of China's oil resources are located in the Yangtze River Valley.
4 Overland trade with China's neighbors declined.

14. Which geographic feature has been *most* responsible for the population distribution in the Middle East?
1 abundance of oil deposits
2 location of water
3 presence of high plateaus
4 availability of natural harbors

15. Which generalization about the geography of Latin America is accurate?
1 Geographic features prevented foreign imperialism.
2 Harsh climatic conditions have prevented the development of large-scale agriculture.
3 The lack of geographic barriers facilitated the development of transportation and communication systems.
4 Great variations in latitude and land forms resulted in a diversity of climates.

16. The history of Russia was influenced by its lack of
1 warm-water ports.
2 mineral deposits.
3 different climates.
4 navigable river systems.

Essay Questions

1. Many problems of regions and nations of the world are related to geography.

Geographic Characteristics

Climate	Lack of natural barriers
Location	Scarcity of water
Mountains	Scarcity of mineral resources

Select three geographic characteristics from the list above and for each characteristic:

- Discuss how that characteristic has created a problem for a specific region or nation selected from Africa, Asia, Europe, the Middle East, or Latin America.
(You must use a different region or nation for each characteristic discussed.)
- Explain an action the region or nation has taken to adapt to or modify the effect of the geographic characteristic.

2. Geography often influences the course of human history.

Nations

South Africa	Soviet Union
Japan	Brazil
Poland	Israel

Select three of the nations listed. Discuss how geographic features of each nation chosen have influenced its political, economic, or historical development.

UNIT 2 Global History

MAKING CONNECTIONS

As you review each unit, you will find additional information in this column: major ideas, connecting themes, and questions to reinforce your learning. These items are closely tied to the Regents examination. Read this material carefully, and jot down any other facts that you would like to remember in the column's blank spaces. Using this column will **add to your success on the Regents exam.**

Section 1 Africa

Section 2 India

Section 3 Southeast Asia

Section 4 China

Section 5 Japan

Section 6 Latin America

Section 7 The Middle East

Section 8 Western Europe

Section 9 Northern Eurasia and Eastern Europe

Each section of the Global History Unit contains comprehensive coverage of the events that shaped the formation of human culture in each region. The unit as a whole traces important concepts in history such as **cultural diffusion** (the exchange of ideas among groups of people), growing global **interdependence**, the effect of **technology** (particularly the Neolithic and Industrial Revolutions), and shifting patterns of **power**. Key concepts and major ideas in the side column indicate other important concepts to help you review key themes in global history.

SECTION 1 Historic Setting: Africa

Time Frame

3000 B.C.–A.D. 1600	Rise of African Kingdoms and Empires
1440s	Arrival of Europeans on West African Coast
1500–1800	Peak of African Slave Trade
1870–1945	European Domination of Africa
1950s–1990	African Independence

OVERVIEW

Diversity is one of the key themes in African history. The continent's immense size and varied landforms have contributed to the development of diverse traditions and cultures. Scholars have identified between 800 and 1,000 distinct linguistic groups in sub-Saharan Africa. There are more than 2,000 distinct cultural groups.

Cultural diversity has worked against unity in Africa. In recent times, **tribalism** has often competed with **nationalism**—that is, loyalty to one's cultural or ethnic group has often been stronger than loyalty to one's nation. In addition, international disputes over territory often occur in Africa because political boundaries have divided cultural groups.

EARLY AFRICAN HISTORY

Ancient Africa

Some of the oldest objects made by humans have been found in the Great Rift Valley. Rock paintings have also been found in the west central Sahara and date from 6000 to 600 B.C. They were painted by early hunters who lived in the area of the Sahara at a time when it was less arid.

African Kingdoms and Empires

Several African kingdoms and empires flourished between 3000 B.C. and A.D. 1600.

KINGDOM OF GHANA The kingdom of Ghana developed a profitable trade in gold and salt and flourished between A.D. 400 and 1200.

MAKING CONNECTIONS

History and Geography Natural barriers hindered but did not prevent contacts and information exchanges with other continents or within the African continent. North Africa especially had early contacts with the Mesopotamians, Greeks, and Romans.

History and Politics An example of tribalism that resulted in civil war occurred in the late 1960s in Nigeria when the Ibo ethnic group attempted to secede and establish the Republic of Biafra.

History and Culture Historians rely on a variety of tools including archaeology, oral tradition (such as myths and legends), radiocarbon dating, and anthropology to learn about the cultures of the past.

MAKING CONNECTIONS

History and Society Arabs from North Africa spread Islamic religion and culture into sub-Saharan Africa in the eleventh century. For more on the spread of Islam, see Historic Setting: Middle East.

EMPIRE OF MALI After its collapse, Ghana was absorbed by Mali, which developed between 1200 and 1450 into an empire. In 1324 Mali's Muslim ruler, Mansa Musa, achieved international fame for his lavish display of wealth when he made a pilgrimage to the holy shrine at Mecca.

EMPIRE OF SONGHAI After civil wars weakened Mali, it was replaced by the even larger and more powerful empire of Songhai, which lasted until it was conquered by Morocco in 1590. A university at the capital of Timbuktu became a great center of Islamic learning. Like its predecessors, Songhai derived its wealth by controlling sub-Saharan trade routes and by trading in gold and salt with North Africa, Europe, and the Middle East.

Regents Tip List several examples of how trade contributed to cultural diffusion in early African history. (An example has been listed.)
Helped spread Islam from Middle East

ZIMBABWE In southern Africa, a wealthy trading empire developed at Zimbabwe following the discovery of gold around A.D. 1000. At the impressive ruins of Zimbabwe, archaeologists have found Chinese and Indian goods, testifying to distant trading contacts. These archaeological remains are indicative of the architectural skills of its builders.

KUSH AND AXUM The kingdom of Kush developed along the Nile at the same time as ancient Egypt. After Kush conquered Egypt in 750 B.C., it briefly controlled an empire stretching from the Mediterranean to present-day Ethiopia. After the decline of Kush around A.D. 200, power shifted to nearby Axum, which converted to Christianity in A.D. 324. The Ethiopians trace their Christian heritage to Axum.

THE DYNAMICS OF CHANGE

The Slave Trade

History and Society Blacks and Arabs as well as Europeans took part in the Atlantic slave trade for a variety of reasons. It is estimated that 50 million Africans died as a result of the trade, especially through disease aboard slave ships.

CAUSES Slavery existed in Africa before the arrival of the Europeans. But it grew to enormous proportions after the European discovery of the Americas. Plantations built in the Americas required many laborers. European attempts to enslave the Native American population were commercially unsuccessful so plantation owners turned to African slaves as a source of labor. Some scholars estimate that 15 million Africans may have been brought to the Americas against their will.

EFFECTS The slave trade encouraged **cultural diffusion**, or the exchange of ideas and goods among cultures, on four continents—Africa, Europe, North America, and South America. However, the slave trade had a devastating impact on Africa. Slave traders promoted local wars, which undermined traditional African political structures and deprived African societies of the talents of many of their people. Slave-trading nations justified this brutal trade by appealing to **racism**, or the false belief that one race is superior to another. Even after the slave trade ended in the mid-1800s, Africans struggled against racism's bitter legacy.

European Imperialism

After 1870, European nations entered into an age of imperialism. Under **imperialism**, one nation seeks to dominate another. Europeans were aided in their conquests by the technological breakthroughs of the Industrial Revolution. Guns allowed Europeans to conquer Africa within a 20-year period (1870–1890). Europeans chose to divide Africa for many reasons:

Reasons for European Imperialism

- Slavery's legacy of racism led Europeans to believe in the superiority of European civilization. They felt it was the "White Man's Burden," or duty of Europeans, to expose Africans to Christianity and Western culture. They used the false doctrine of racial inequality to justify the conquest of Africa.
- The Industrial Revolution led European nations to seek raw materials and markets for manufactured goods through **colonialism**, or possession of overseas territories. Under colonialism, colonies existed solely for the benefit of the home country.
- The rise of **nationalism**, or feelings of pride in one's country, sparked a desire for an empire. Europeans equated colonies with national power and prestige.
- International rivalries caused Europeans to expand their navies and seek fueling stations on bases around the world.

Great Britain and France established the largest African empires. But Spain, Portugal, Belgium, Italy, and Germany took land, too.

Effects of European Rule on Africa

Negative

- Downgraded traditional African culture and weakened family ties.
- Led to forced labor and abuses of human rights.
- Created artificial colonial boundaries that cut across historical, ethnic, and cultural boundaries.

Positive

- Improved medical care, sanitation, and nutrition.
- Expanded transportation and communication.
- Increased agricultural production with new seeds and fertilizers.
- Created new educational and career opportunities.

MAKING CONNECTIONS

Key Concepts: Technology European technology enabled Europeans to conquer Africa more swiftly, less expensively, and with less risk to their own health than would have been possible before the Industrial Revolution.

History and Politics The colonial powers contributed to African political unity by drawing together diverse ethnic and political units. However, the colonies' artificial boundaries often added to political instability within and among the independent African nations.

The Scramble for Africa, 1880 – 1914

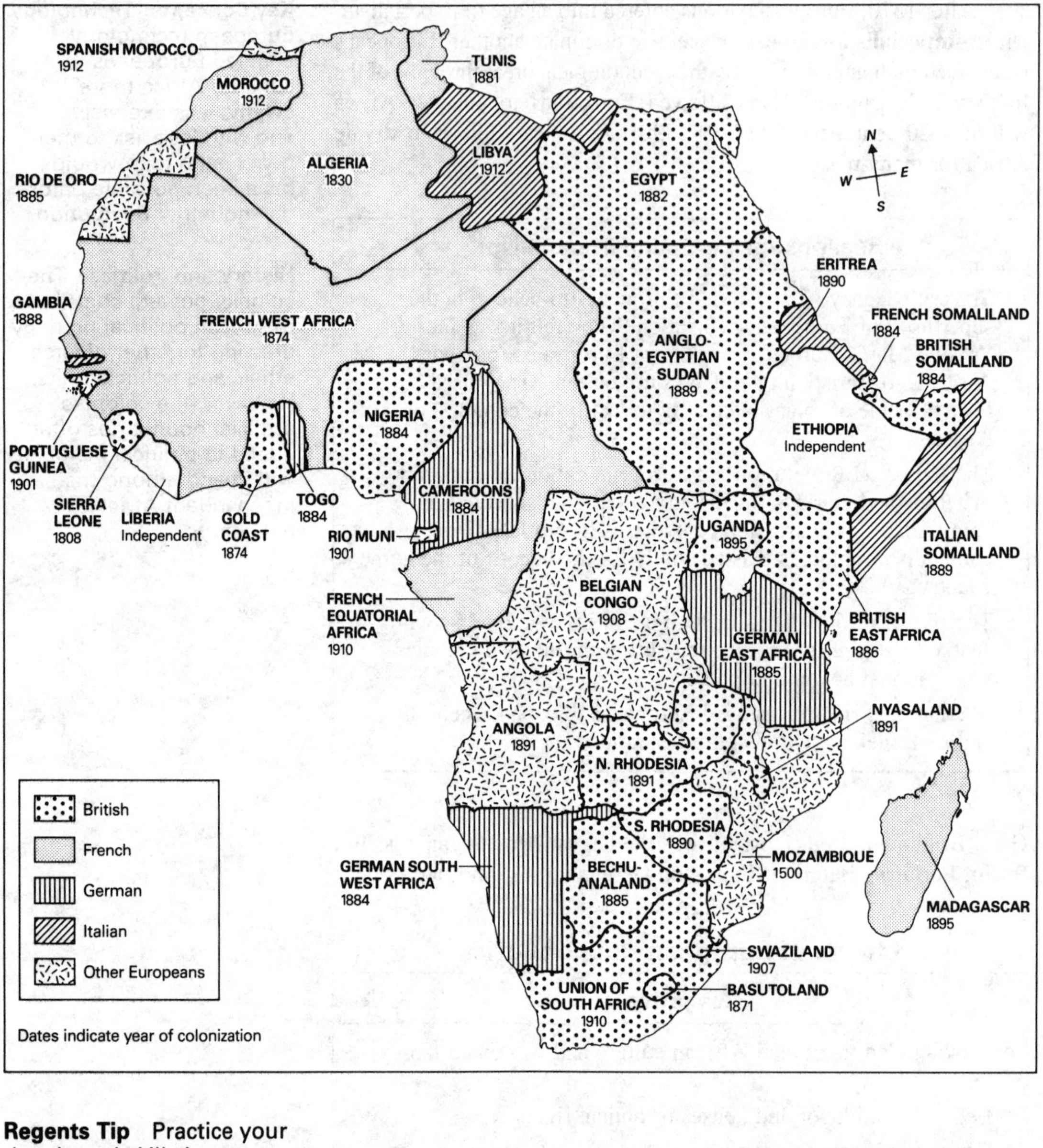

Regents Tip Practice your data-based skills by answering the following questions about the map: Which two African nations remained independent after 1880? Which two European nations were the major colonial powers ruling Africa?

EMERGENCE OF MODERN AFRICA

In the mid-1900s, colony after colony demanded **self-determination**, or the right to decide its own future. Several factors combined to produce this wave of African nationalism.

World War II

During World War II (1939–1945), many Africans fought to defeat the Nazis and Fascists. The war weakened racist arguments and advanced the idea of freedom in Africa. The United Nations Charter, adopted in 1945, set forth the principle of self-determination and accelerated African desires for independence.

Pan-Africanism

A movement for **Pan-Africanism**, or a united or allied Africa, had existed since the early 1900s. In 1963, the Organization of African Unity was formed specifically to promote this goal and to end colonialism in Africa. Today, it serves as a forum for promoting cooperation among its member nations.

Within the Pan-African movement, nationalist figures who promoted independence in the 1950s and 1960s, were once again active. Among these people were Jomo Kenyatta of Kenya, Kwame Nkrumah of Ghana, and Felix Houpouet-Boigney of Côte d'Ivoire.

CONTEMPORARY AFRICA

With the independence of Namibia in 1990, colonialism in Africa ended. Since independence, most African nations have tried to follow a policy of **nonalignment**, or noninvolvement with either the Communist bloc of nations or the Western bloc of nations. However, persistent economic crises have repeatedly forced African nations to accept aid from both East and West. Instability within Africa has also led some African nations to keep close economic and diplomatic ties with former colonial rulers.

Causes for African Instability
• Tribalism in several nations has undermined national unity.
• Authoritarian single-party rule has often prevented the development of democratic states.
• Military rule imposed through **coups d'état**, or forcible military takeovers, has often resulted in violent oppression.
• Large international debts and drought-induced famines have prevented economic development in several African nations.

MAKING CONNECTIONS

History and Politics Most African countries have depended heavily on the United Nations as a forum for discussing problems of colonialism and apartheid.

History and Politics Between the 1950s and 1990, the Cold War between the United States and the Soviet Union played a large part in shaping the foreign policies of the superpowers toward African nations.

History and Politics An instance of a military takeover that resulted in violent oppression occurred in Uganda in 1971, when General Idi Amin overthrew the government.

MAKING CONNECTIONS

History and Society
"Boers" is a Dutch word meaning "farmers." Present-day conflicts over ownership and control of the land in South Africa date back to these earliest European settlers. Along with English, the Boer dialect of Dutch, called Afrikaans, is the country's official language. However, native Bantu languages are more widely spoken.

History and Politics None of the supposedly independent homelands created by South Africa since the 1970s has received international recognition.

Regents Tip List ways in which apartheid contributed to instability in South Africa. (An example has been listed.)
It denied political rights to the majority of the people.

South Africa and Apartheid

DUTCH AND BRITISH SETTLERS South Africa is one of the few nations on the continent with a substantial population that is of European ancestry—approximately 5 million. In the 1600s, Dutch settlers called **Boers** arrived, followed by the British, who eventually gained control of the area. After the British abolished slavery in 1833, the Boers moved farther north. However, the British laid claim to this area, too, after gold and diamonds were discovered there. The resulting disputes led to the Boer War (1899–1902), which the British won. In 1910 they united all the colonies in the area under one state—the Union of South Africa.

"WHITES ONLY" In 1948 the **Afrikaners**, the Dutch-speaking descendants of the Boers, gained control of government. They formalized their racist policies in a program of **apartheid**, which literally means "apartness." Blacks, who make up about 68 percent of the present population, were denied citizenship in South Africa as well as access to many public facilities, such as libraries. Theoretically, separate, independent "homelands" were set aside for them. In reality, most of the nation's territory was reserved for the white minority—less than a fifth of the population. Coloreds (people of mixed race) and Asians were also denied many basic rights. South Africa's racial policies left it isolated from the rest of the world.

THE AFRICAN NATIONAL CONGRESS Inside South Africa, opponents to apartheid formed the African National Congress (A N C), which until recently had been outlawed. In 1990 the government of South Africa released the A N C leader, Nelson Mandela, after imprisoning him for 28 years. Increased pressure by black nationalists and the international community led to negotiations between Mandela and South African president F.W. DeKlerk to end apartheid. In April 1994 the first multi-racial election resulted in Nelson Mandela becoming president of South Africa.

MAJOR HISTORICAL THEMES

1. Africa has a history of ethnic and linguistic diversity.
2. Early African kingdoms developed advanced civilizations.
3. The slave trade disrupted African political and social structures and left a legacy of racism.
4. European imperialists divided most of Africa and formed political units with little regard to their ethnic makeup.
5. Africans won independence after the 1950s, but have faced continuing economic and political instability.
6. South Africa's internal racist policy of apartheid became a matter of international concern.

SECTION 2 Historic Setting: India

Time Frame

MAKING CONNECTIONS

3000 B.C.–1500 B.C.	Harappan Civilization
320 B.C.–535 A.D.	Maurya and Gupta Empires
1526–1857	Mogul Empire
1756–1947	British Rule in India
1947–present	Independence

OVERVIEW

A key theme in Indian history has been cultural diffusion. This pattern of civilization has resulted from an interplay between native Indian civilizations and the foreign cultures brought into India through a succession of invasions. This complicated mix of cultures—native and foreign—has created diversity and tensions within Indian society.

Key Concepts: Culture
Religious and cultural differences hindered national unity in India.

EARLY INDIAN HISTORY

Human civilization emerged in India along the rich farmlands of a **river valley**, a pattern repeated elsewhere in the world.

Indus Valley Civilization

Between 3000 and 1500 B.C., the **Harappan** civilization developed along the Indus River. Harappans built dams and levees to irrigate large crops for trade. Food surpluses allowed the Harappans to support an **urban**, or city-based, society. Archaeological digs show evidence of a well-organized central government.

Foreign Invasion and Conquest

India's wealth attracted repeated foreign invasion.

ARYANS Between 1500 and 1200 B.C., the Aryans swept into India out of Central Asia. Aryan and Harappan cultures blended to provide the basis for later Indian cultures. Two key developments appeared: (1) an early form of the **Hindu** religion and (2) a **caste system**, or society based on well-organized, hereditary social classes.

History and Society
Though the Republic of India prohibits discrimination based on caste, social inequality still exists within Indian society.

MUSLIMS In the eighth century, a succession of Islamic invaders brought the Muslim religion to India. By the 1500s, another Muslim group, the Mongols, founded the great **Mogul Empire**. From their

MAKING CONNECTIONS

Regents Tip Practice your data-based skills by answering the following questions about the map: Which river flows through a delta into the Bay of Bengal?

The Khyber Pass allows passage through which geographical barrier? Circle the correct choice.
a Himalaya Mountains
b Vindhya Mountains
c Hindu Kush Mountains
d Eastern Ghats

Geography of Ancient India

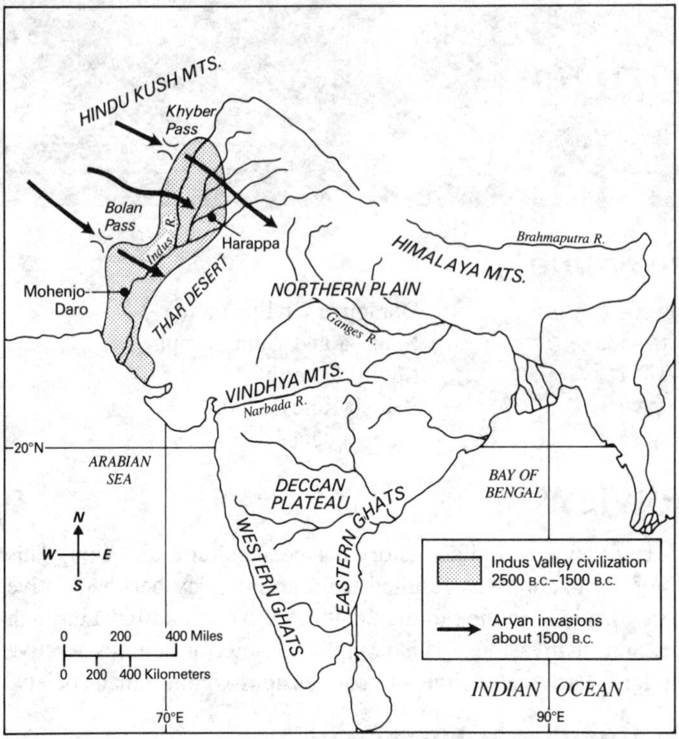

capital of Delhi, Mogul rulers led the country for over 300 years and stimulated a new cultural flowering. Starting in the 1700s, British imperial expansion gradually eroded Mogul control.

Classical Indian Empires

Between foreign invasions, two great native Indian empires arose.

Key Concepts: Culture Buddhism spread to Southeast Asia, Tibet, China, Korea, and Japan, where it was adapted by the various native cultures.

MAURYA EMPIRE (321–185 B.C.) The Maurya **dynasty**, or hereditary ruling family, built a well-run empire that included much of the subcontinent. **Ashoka the Great**, the best-known Maurya ruler, converted to Buddhism and sent missionaries to spread Buddhist teachings elsewhere in Asia.

GUPTA EMPIRE (A.D. 320–535) Under the Gupta dynasty, Hinduism dominated Indian life. Because of great progress in the arts and sciences, the Gupta era became known as the Golden Age of Hindu culture. The accomplishments of the Guptas included creating a numeral system with the concept of zero, making discoveries in astronomy, and using surgery. A wave of invasions by the Huns broke up the Gupta empire into small kingdoms. But the influence of Hinduism remained strong.

History and Society In India, religious beliefs and social organization are closely related.

BRITISH IMPERIALISM AND INDIAN NATIONALISM

In the 1600s, Great Britain entered into a period of commercial empire-building. The British government granted a charter to the British East India Company to build trading bases in India. By 1756, the British had used these bases to force rivals, especially the French, from the subcontinent.

British Colonial Rule

The British used a policy of "divide and conquer" to take over India. They undermined efforts by Indian princes to unify. Also, the British possessed better weapons and armed Indian soldiers known as **sepoys** to protect British holdings. In 1857, the sepoys revolted when the British violated their religious beliefs. The British suppressed the **Sepoy Mutiny** and took control of India from the East India Company in 1858. British governors ruled about two-thirds of India directly and closely supervised local Indian princes in the rest of the country. The colonial government improved health conditions, expanded transportation and communication systems, and widened educational opportunities. But the British generally treated Indian culture as inferior.

The Independence Movement

Two centuries of British rule unified India and created a sense of Indian identity. However, Indian leaders resented being banned from positions of top authority. They also were stung by Christian criticisms of the Hindu and Muslim religions. In 1885 urban intellectuals from India's middle class formed the **Indian National Congress**. Religious divisions between Hindus and Muslims led to the creation of the nationalist **Muslim League** in 1906.

When World War I erupted, many Indians served with the British. They hoped their loyalty would loosen British colonial bonds. When the British refused the Indians greater freedom, **Mohandas K. Gandhi** organized a mass political movement for independence. Gandhi called for broad-based reform, including improved status for women and "untouchables," the lowest social caste in India.

Gandhi's Methods

- **Passive Resistance**: A campaign of nonviolent noncooperation.
- **Civil Disobedience**: Refusal to obey unjust laws and a willingness to suffer punishment (including beatings and imprisonment) with patience and self-control.
- **Economic Boycott**: Refusal to buy British-made cloth (with a return to cottage, or domestic, industries).
- **Dandi Salt March**: Protest march against British tax on salt and ban on making salt.

MAKING CONNECTIONS

Key Concepts: Change The changes introduced by the British under imperialism were designed primarily to strengthen colonial rule.

History and Politics Dr. Martin Luther King, Jr., used methods practiced by Gandhi to combat racial segregation in the United States in the 1950s and 1960s.

MAKING CONNECTIONS

Regents Tip Explain how religious differences have contributed to political instability in India.

Freedom and Partition

World War II weakened British control of India. In 1947 British leaders agreed to Indian demands for independence. To avoid civil war between Hindus and Muslims, the British partitioned the subcontinent into the Hindu nation of India and the Muslim nation of Pakistan.

Independence set off a mass migration, or movement, of people. About twelve million refugees—Muslim minorities from India and Hindu minorities from Pakistan—left their homes to resettle in one of the two new nations. Thousands of people were killed in bloody rioting. Gandhi tried to restore peace, but a Hindu fanatic assassinated him in January 1948. **Jawaharlal Nehru**, India's first prime minister, steered India through its first difficult years of nationhood.

INDIA AFTER INDEPENDENCE

India's huge population and its economic and political power made it a leader among the **Third World**, or developing nations of the post war era. Like many African nations, India tried to follow a policy of nonalignment.

Democracy Amid Strife

History and Politics For more on India as a democratic republic, see Unit 5, Global Politics.

Despite great religious and economic turmoil, India has retained its democratic institutions. In 1966, Nehru's daughter, Indira Gandhi, became prime minister. Voters turned Gandhi out of office in 1977 for her suspension of civil liberties. She returned to power in 1981 and governed until her assassination in 1984 by Sikhs who sought the creation of a separate Sikh state. Today India functions as a democratic republic, similar to the United States. Power is divided between national and state governments. Since independence India has preserved its democratic institutions despite problems from religious conflicts and the suspension of civil liberties (1975–1977) by Indira Gandhi.

History and Politics Political and territorial disputes with both Pakistan and China encouraged India to develop nuclear weapons. The spread of nuclear weapons in a traditionally unstable region is a cause of global concern.

Economic Progress

When India achieved independence, it began to develop its industrial potential. India's technological progress was demonstrated in 1974 when Indian scientists exploded a nuclear device. The entry of a Third World nation into the "nuclear club" marked a major shift in global power.

History and Society Technological progress and industrial growth have had uneven effects on the standard of living of the Indian people. For more on food production and overpopulation in India see Unit 6, The World Today.

Agriculture, however, remains the mainstay of the Indian economy. In the early 1960s, use of new high-yield grains created a "green revolution." While India has doubled its food production since 1947, this gain has been matched by doubling of the population.

Pakistan and Bangladesh

After independence, Pakistan was governed by a succession of military regimes. Notable exceptions included the civilian governments of President **Zulfikar Bhutto** (1971–1977) and his daughter, **Benazir Bhutto** (1989–1990), the first woman to head a Muslim nation.

Boundary disputes between Pakistan and India have occasionally erupted into armed conflict. In 1971 with the military assistance of India, the area called East Pakistan became the independent nation of Bangladesh. Three years later, West Pakistan (known today as Pakistan) agreed to recognize Bangladesh. However, tensions over another disputed area—Kashmir—have remained high.

MAKING CONNECTIONS

History and Geography
See the map in Unit 1, The Geographic Setting, for the political boundaries of India and Pakistan.

MAJOR HISTORIC THEMES

1. India's earliest civilization emerged in the Indus River Valley.
2. India's history reflects an intermingling of native cultures with the cultures imported by foreign conquerors. This blending of cultures has produced great human diversity on the subcontinent.
3. British colonial rule helped create a sense of Indian identity.
4. After independence, cultural differences continued to trouble the partitioned subcontinent.

SECTION 3 Historic Setting: Southeast Asia

MAKING CONNECTIONS

Time Frame

800s–1500s	Early Southeast Asian Empires
1500s–1900s	European Imperialism
1945–present	Independence and Nationhood

OVERVIEW

Southeast Asia's location on major trade and migration routes has exposed it to a wide variety of foreign influences, first from China and India and later from European powers. In this century, the peoples of Southeast Asia rebelled against colonial rule and began to develop national identities of their own.

AN EARLY CROSSROADS

The region's location along a crossroads for trade and migration has resulted in many different ethnic groups, speaking more than 1,000 languages and dialects. The topography of Southeast Asia, with its dense rain forests, mountains, and archipelagoes, also contributed to the formation of a diverse cultural heritage.

Key Concepts: Change
In Malaysia, Chinese make up 32 percent of the population. In Singapore, which formerly was part of Malaysia, Chinese make up 77 percent of the population. Tensions between Chinese and Malaysians led to a major political change when Singapore seceded from Malaysia in 1965.

Chinese from the North

A pattern of foreign influence and domination in Southeast Asia started about 2,000 years ago. Despite a long history of expansionist policies from China on the north and the Khmer people to the west, Vietnam has vigorously sought to preserve its independence from foreign domination. The Chinese commercial presence in the region has been, on occasion, the cause of anti-Chinese resentment in this area.

Indians from the West

While the Chinese came to Southeast Asia mainly by overland routes, the Indians arrived by sea. In the first century A.D., Indian merchants established trading centers in the region. They introduced many aspects of Indian culture, including the Hindu and Buddhist religions. Two early Southeast Asian empires reflected this influence.

THE KHMER EMPIRE In what is now northwestern Cambodia, the **Khmer** established a great empire that flourished from around 800 to the 1430s. Ruins of a great temple at Angkor Wat give ample evidence of Hindu architectural influence.

THE SRIVIJAYA EMPIRE On the Indonesian island of Sumatra, the Buddhist dynasty of **Srivijaya** lasted from the 800s to the 1200s. It dominated other islands in the archipelago and became rich by taxing trading vessels that passed through the Malaccan Strait.

MAKING CONNECTIONS

History and Geography The Srivijaya Empire controlled the Malaccan Strait, which was important because it connected the Indian Ocean to the South China Sea and the countries of East Asia.

The Arrival of Islam

Arab traders brought Islam to Southeast Asia in the 1200s. A majority of people in Malaysia and Indonesia adopted Islam. Today Indonesia is the most populous Muslim nation in the world.

FOUR CENTURIES OF EUROPEAN COLONIALISM

The first Europeans to arrive in Southeast Asia were the Portuguese, drawn there in 1511 by the promise of wealth from the spice trade. Other European merchant ships soon followed. Eventually, all Southeast Asia came under European domination, with the sole exception of Siam (present-day Thailand), which was able to remain independent by acting as a **buffer state** separating the colonial territories of Britain and France.

Colonies in Southeast Asia

European Power	Colonies
Britain	Burma, Malaya, Singapore, Sarawak, Brunei, Northern Borneo, Southern New Guinea
France	Indochina (present-day Laos, Cambodia, Vietnam)
Germany	Northern New Guinea
Netherlands	East Indies (present-day Indonesia)
Portugal	Malacca, Timor
Spain	Philippine Islands

Profits of Empire

Spices lured Europeans to Southeast Asia, but the Industrial Revolution was a further incentive to establish and expand European colonial empires in this region. Colonies guaranteed a ready supply of natural resources and land to produce **cash crops**, or crops sold on the world market for money. Imperial powers set up plantations to grow sugar, coffee, tea, cotton, and rice. They also exploited existing reserves of hardwood trees, rubber plants, and deposits of tin and oil. The pattern of colonial activity was to import raw materials from the colonies, turn them into manufactured goods in factories at home, and then export them to the world as finished products. This system prevented development in the colonies.

Regents Tip List several reasons why Europeans sought colonies in Southeast Asia. (An example has been listed.)
Source of raw materials

Southeast Asia: Land Use and Resources

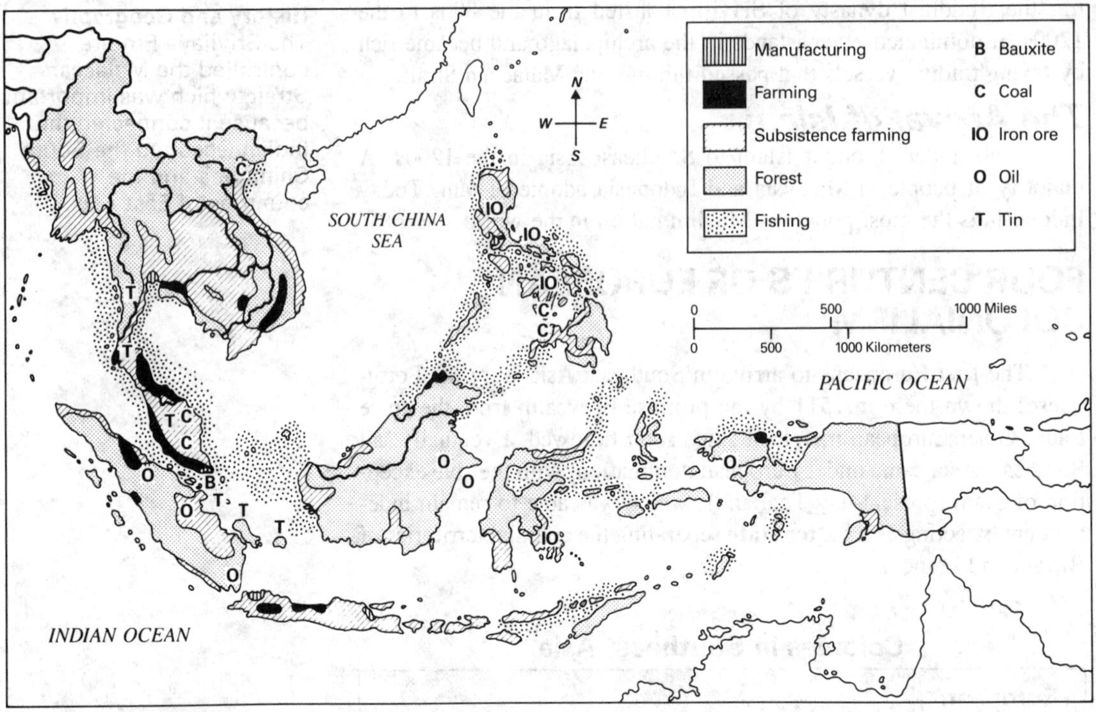

MAKING CONNECTIONS

Regents Tip Practice your data-based skills by answering the following question about the map: Which is most likely a true assumption based on the data shown on the map?

a Manufacturing dominates land use in Southeast Asia.
b Forest still cover much of the area of Southeast Asia.
c Fishing is of minor commercial importance in the region.
d Oil is not widely distributed in the region.

History and Economics For more on the reasons behind Japanese imperialism, see Historic Setting: Japan.

Growing Resentment

For the people of Southeast Asia, the colonial system brought hard work with little improvement in their standard of living. Forced labor and poor living conditions were common. The production of cash crops on huge plantations left farmers with little time or energy for growing enough food for themselves.

Many European powers fueled local dissatisfaction by encouraging the immigration of Indian and Chinese laborers to work on plantations and to build new transportation systems. Many of these immigrants came to the area to better their lot. Eventually, they settled in cities where they became merchants and bankers. The Southeast Asians often resented their success.

THE STRUGGLE FOR INDEPENDENCE

World War II (1939–1945) helped end colonialism. While war raged in Europe, Japan seized control of much of Southeast Asia and the European imperial powers were incapable of preserving their colonial empires in the face of a growing surge of local nationalism.

Peaceful Transitions

The United States, which had acquired possession of the Philippines from Spain in 1898, gave the islands independence in 1946 as it had promised. The Europeans wanted to resume control of their colonies, but nationalist leaders had emerged during the war. The British, weakened by the war, freed their colonies in a largely nonviolent transition of political power.

Armed Conflicts

INDONESIA A war lasting from 1946 to 1949 ended Dutch rule of Indonesia. The government of Indonesia faced the challenge of uniting about 300 ethnic groups that spoke over 250 languages and lived on thousands of islands.

INDOCHINA In French Indochina, the drive toward independence was spearheaded by the **Viet Minh**, a Communist-dominated movement under the leadership of **Ho Chi Minh**. After the Japanese occupation forces surrendered in 1945, Ho Chi Minh proclaimed independence for Indochina. However, France had no intention of giving up its old colony. The Viet Minh responded with guerrilla warfare. After eight years of struggle, a plan for withdrawal was arrived at the **Geneva Conference of 1954**. The plan created the independent countries of Cambodia, Laos, and Vietnam, which was divided into northern and southern sectors.

VIETNAM According to the Geneva plan, the division of Vietnam was to be temporary until general elections could be held to determine the nation's leadership. However, elections never took place. A Communist-backed government under Ho Chi Minh took over North Vietnam, while a non-Communist government supported by the United States took over South Vietnam.

In 1960 a Communist-directed **insurgency**, or rebellion, began in the south. The United States sent military forces to Vietnam as part of a larger plan to stop the worldwide spread of communism. Direct American involvement ended with the **Paris Peace Treaty of 1973**, which called for the withdrawal of foreign forces and an exchange of prisoners-of-war. In 1975 North Vietnamese forces overran South Vietnam and reunited the country.

SOUTHEAST ASIA SINCE INDEPENDENCE

Cambodia and Laos

After the reunification of Vietnam, Communist leaders in Cambodia and Laos also seized power. In Cambodia, which became known as Kampuchea, a totalitarian government forced hundreds of thousands of city-dwellers into the country where they often died in work camps.

Border clashes with Vietnam led to an invasion by the Vietnamese in 1978. This move was countered by a border incursion from China, which sided with Cambodia in the dispute. Vietnam withdrew its forces in 1989.

MAKING CONNECTIONS

History and Economics
The end of colonialism brought new economic challenges to the nations of Southeast Asia. For more on how these nations faced the challenges, see Unit 4, Global Economics.

Key Concepts: Power and Change
Internal struggles for power, such as those that occurred in Vietnam and Cambodia, sometimes lead to radical societal changes and political turmoil.

Key Concepts: Culture
The crime of genocide crosses cultures and eras. Under the repressive regime of the Khmer Rouge, the Cambodian government waged genocide on its own people. It is estimated that over one million Cambodians died in the 1970s as a result of the Khmer Rouge's efforts to restructure Cambodian society.

MAKING CONNECTIONS

Regents Tip Practice your data-based skills by answering the following question about the map: North Vietnamese troops used the Ho Chi Minh Trail to invade South Vietnam. Which two nations became involved in the Vietnam War because the trail passed through their territories?

a Cambodia and Thailand
b Laos and China
c Thailand and China
d Laos and Cambodia

War in Southeast Asia

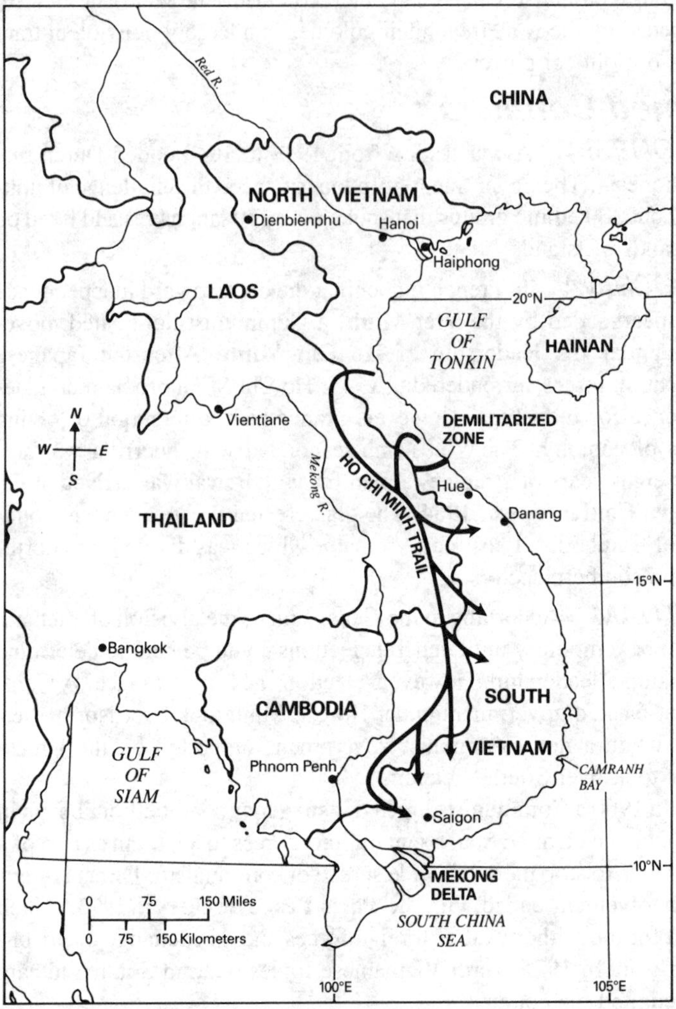

History and Politics For more on policies of the governments in this region, see Unit 5, Global Politics.

A Flood of Refugees

Years of warfare and political strife have disrupted the economies of Vietnam, Cambodia, and Laos and left many homeless. Hundreds of thousands of refugees have fled the communist dictatorships in these countries and strained the regional facilities set up to help them.

Turmoil in the Philippines

In 1986 rebels in the Philippines overthrew the dictatorship of Ferdinand Marcos and restored democracy under **Corazon Aquino**. Aquino, however, faced an ongoing Communist insurgency, attempted military coups, inflation, and a devastating earthquake in 1990.

Efforts at Stability

Because the new nations of Southeast Asia lack a long tradition of self-government, many of them have suffered political repression and economic hardship. Others, however, such as Singapore and Brunei, enjoy great prosperity. In order to promote social, economic, and cultural cooperation among themselves, non-Communist nations in the region formed the Association of Southeast Asian Nations (ASEAN) in 1967.

MAKING CONNECTIONS

Regents Tip List several factors that have contributed to instability in Southeast Asia. (An example has been listed.)
Internal struggles for power

MAJOR HISTORIC THEMES

1. Southeast Asia is a diverse cultural region with a long history of cultural interaction with China, India, and the Middle East.
2. Under European imperialism, Southeast Asia failed to develop diversified economies to sustain them after independence.
3. World War II loosened European colonial bonds on Southeast Asia, but without long-standing traditions of democratic rule many governments adopted communist dictatorships and military regimes.
4. Geopolitical factors, especially United States efforts to stop the spread of communism, have influenced the recent history of Southeast Asia.

SECTION 4 Historic Setting: China

MAKING CONNECTIONS

Time Frame

1500 B.C.–A.D. 1911	Rule by Imperial Dynasties
1839–1945	Period of European and Japanese Imperialism
1912–1949	Republic of China
1949–present	People's Republic of China

OVERVIEW

A key theme in Chinese history has been political change through the dynastic cycle. For thousands of years, the Chinese have seen the rise and fall of governments—periods of strong, authoritarian rule followed by periods of disunity and unrest. In recent times, this pattern has repeated itself with a half century of struggle among rival nationalist factions followed by centralized rule under the Chinese communists.

EARLY CHINESE HISTORY

Ancient Civilizations

As in other parts of the world, China's first civilizations developed in the region's fertile river valleys.

Imperial Dynasties

During China's nearly 4,000 years of history, it has experienced rule by a number of imperial dynasties. The Chinese came to view history as a series of dynastic cycles rather than as a movement forward in time. They saw dynastic cycles as a process that repeated itself in China's history. Although the Chinese understood that a dynasty's length might be influenced by the quality of its individual rulers, they anticipated that it would come full circle and be succeeded by a different dynasty.

Key Concepts: Political System
The ideas of the philosopher Confucius (551–479 B.C.) had a powerful influence on political structures that developed in China. Confucianism also shaped the educational and social systems.

China's Dynastic Cycles

Shang Dynasty	1500–1122 B.C.
Chou Dynasty	1122–256 B.C.
Period of Disunity	256–221 B.C.
Ch'in Dynasty	221–206 B.C.
Han Dynasty	206 B.C.–A.D. 220
Period of Disunity in Northern China/Six Dynasties in Southern China	220–589
Sui Dynasty	589–618
T'ang Dynasty	618–907
Period of Disunity	907–960
Sung Dynasty	960–1279
Yuan (Mongol) Dynasty	1279–1368
Ming Dynasty	1368–1644
Ch'ing (Manchu) Dynasty	1644–1911

The Mandate of Heaven

The Chinese explained the operation of the dynastic cycle through a belief in the **Mandate of Heaven**, or divine right of an emperor or empress to rule. So long as rulers kept political control, they were thought to hold the Mandate, or divine backing. However, if a ruler became corrupt or incompetent, or if subjects successfully rebelled, the Mandate was lost. Accordingly, anyone who overthrew a ruler could claim the Mandate of Heaven.

PERIODS OF DISUNITY Between the fall of one dynasty and the rise of a new one, a period of disunity sometimes occurred during which the Mandate of Heaven seemed to be withheld and no one family ruled the entire country. A period of disunity sometimes allowed new ideas to gain a foothold in China. Acceptance of Buddhism, for example, took place between the Han and Sui dynasties.

LENGTH OF DYNASTIES The rule of some dynasties was relatively brief, which suggests that they were "conquest dynasties," or dynasties that could conquer China but not effectively control it. Usually these dynasties were followed by dynasties with a more enduring period of political control, for example, the Sui and the T'ang dynasties.

FOREIGN DYNASTIES The Chinese also believed the Mandate of Heaven could be extended to foreign rulers. The Yuan dynasty originated in Mongolia and the Ch'ing dynasty in Manchuria. However, both the Yuan and Ch'ing accepted Chinese culture and governed traditionally.

MAKING CONNECTIONS

History and Politics The concept of the Mandate of Heaven was introduced by a Confucian philosopher named Mencius in the 300s B.C. By teaching that the Mandate could be withdrawn, Mencius acknowledged the right of the people to rebel against unjust rulers.

Key Concepts: Culture The Yuan dynasty created an empire in the 1200s that stretched across Asia to the Danube River in the west. Yuan rulers encouraged East-West trade and tolerated Christianity and the spread of Islam. Marco Polo established direct European trade with China during the Yuan dynasty. Cultures of both East and West were enriched by the interchange of ideas and innovations.

MAKING CONNECTIONS

Regents Tip Practice your data-based skills by answering the following question about the map: In whose sphere of influence was the port city of Shanghai?

a Japan c Russia
b Britain d France

Spheres of Influence in China to 1914

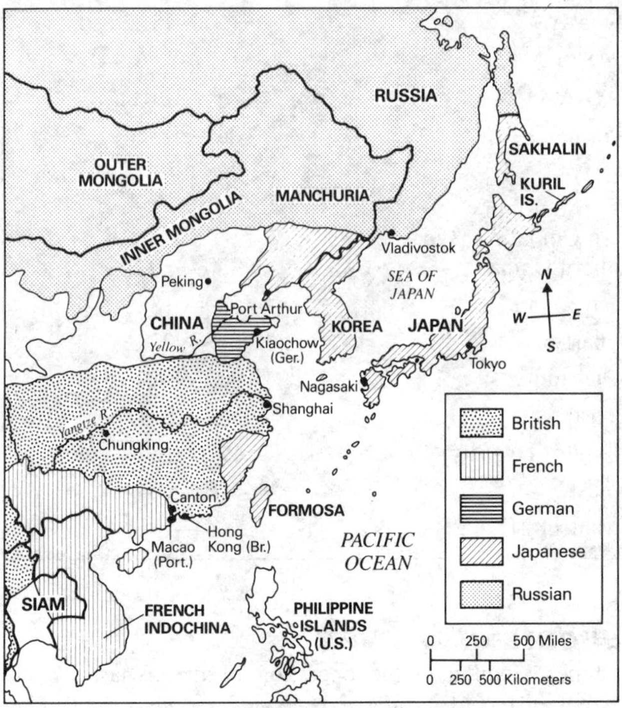

The Middle Kingdom

The traditional Chinese world view was **ethnocentric**. China was the center of the universe, known as **Zhung Guo** or the **Middle Kingdom**. The Chinese considered their culture superior to all others. Foreigners were ''barbarians'' who were expected to render a **tribute**—a payment or gift acknowledging submission to the ruling dynasty.

History and Economics For more background on imperialism, see Historic Setting: Western Europe.

THE CHALLENGE OF IMPERIALISM

In the 1800s Chinese civilization came in contact with European civilization, which held a conflicting world view—imperialism.

Key Concepts: Power and Technology The technology of the imperialist nations, especially in armaments, helped these nations gain power over China in the 1800s.

Foreign Intrusion

The economic, political, and military strength of European imperialism shattered China's ethnocentrism. The Chinese faced powers that did not accept Chinese culture as superior or even equal to their own. Imperialist powers challenged many traditional Chinese cultural values, including the idea of dynastic rule.

OPIUM WAR (1839–1842) AND ITS AFTERMATH

When British merchants introduced the opium trade into China, the Chinese government tried to stop it. British troops eventually took control of parts of the country, including Hong Kong and five ports. They demanded other concessions from China, too. The opium trade continued to flourish and had a devastating effect on the Chinese population.

SPHERES OF INFLUENCE Following Britain's example, other foreign powers, including France, Portugal, Russia, Germany, and Japan, acquired **spheres of influence**, or areas of economic control, in China.

The Boxer Rebellion

The 1900s opened with a large-scale Chinese revolt against foreign domination. A group known as the "Boxers" was originally opposed to the Ch'ing dynasty but was manipulated by government officials into becoming a primarily anti-western force. They attacked both the imperialists and Chinese who associated with them. A multinational army made up of troops supplied by Britain, France, Japan, and the United States ultimately crushed the rebellion. The victors forced China to pay war damages and grant even more concessions to foreigners.

MAKING CONNECTIONS

History and Politics The United States feared the imperial powers would exclude Americans from Chinese trade. In 1899 the United States government established an "Open Door Policy" that proposed equal trade in China for all nations.

THE REPUBLIC OF CHINA

Soon after the Boxer Rebellion, Chinese nationalists revolted against dynastic rule. The repeated failure of the Ch'ing Dynasty to protect China's **sovereignty**, or right to rule, had discredited it. On October 10, 1911, nationalist forces overthrew the last emperor and proclaimed the Republic of China.

Another Period of Disunity

The overthrow of the Ch'ing Dynasty was followed by a period of unrest and instability similar to the disunity that sometimes followed the collapse of traditional Chinese dynasties.

NATIONALISTS **Dr. Sun Yat-sen** formed a new political party, the **Kuomintang**, or Nationalist Party. He faced opposition from many forces: local Chinese warlords who supported dynastic rule, Japanese intent on imperialism, and a growing number of Chinese communists. When Sun died in 1925, **Chiang Kai-shek** took control of the Nationalists.

Regents Tip List reasons why Sun Yat-Sen's attempt to build a democratic republic failed. (An example has been listed.) The Chinese people had no tradition of democracy.

COMMUNISTS Chiang defeated Chinese warlords and united most of China. However, he faced a growing threat from the Communists. In 1934 Chiang succeeded in surrounding the Communists. The Communists broke out of the Nationalist encirclement and began the **Long March**, a 6,000-mile trek into the northwestern part of China. During the Long March, **Mao Zedong** emerged as leader of the Communist Party. Out of about 100,000 participants, fewer than 20,000 survived.

War and Its Aftermath

The outbreak of World War II temporarily halted civil strife, as both nationalists and communists battled a takeover of China by Japan. Following Japanese surrender, however, civil war resumed. Now

MAKING CONNECTIONS

better equipped than before and with a broader base of peasant support, the communists drove the nationalists off the mainland and onto the island of Taiwan. In 1949 Mao Zedong proclaimed the birth of the **People's Republic of China**. Chiang named his island-government Nationalist China.

History and Economics The Chinese under Mao adopted Marxism, hoping to achieve industrialization and share the benefits of economic development equally among the *proletariat* (industrial workers) and *peasantry* (farmers).

THE PEOPLE'S REPUBLIC OF CHINA

The communist regime reestablished a strong, centralized, authoritarian government. It offered a sense of unity and stability after years of unrest. But in many other ways, it built a totally new society. With support from the Soviet Union, Mao put communist political and economic principles into practice. Using these ideas, he reshaped traditional Chinese society.

The Great Leap Forward

During the 1950s and 1960s, the communists abolished private ownership of farms and created **communes**—huge cooperative farms where as many as 20,000 people might collectively work the land. Mao called this reorganization the Great Leap Forward. Because land could not be passed on from generation to generation, the new policy weakened the traditional Chinese family and undermined ancestor worship.

History and Society Mao Zedong's vision of the Chinese Revolution dominated developments in China from the founding of the People's Republic of China until Mao's death in 1976.

The Cultural Revolution

Mao tried to promote communism in other ways, too. He started schools on communes and in cities. Here students read from the **Thoughts of Chairman Mao**, the so-called Little Red Book. However, splits developed within the Communist Party. Some officials opposed Mao's later efforts to break with the Soviet Union. Others objected to his plans for agricultural and industrial reform. Mao feared that his revolution might be in danger, and so he launched the Cultural Revolution of 1966.

THE RED GUARDS To promote the Cultural Revolution, Mao shut down schools and universities all over China. He urged some eleven million communist-trained students to join the **Red Guards**. The Red Guards organized demonstrations in support of Mao. They upheld the ideal of rule by the peasants and workers through attacks on writers, intellectuals, and other "anti-party" figures. Thousands of professionals were imprisoned or sent to do manual work in the fields or factories. Mao ended the Cultural Revolution in 1969, but it disrupted Chinese life until his death in 1976.

History and Economics For more on how modernization has affected China's economy, see Unit 4, Global Economics.

Changes After Mao

A power struggle broke out when Mao died. Mao's widow, Jiang Qing, sought to renew the Cultural Revolution. But moderate leaders under **Deng Xiaoping** triumphed. Deng set aside some of Mao's more radical policies and promised to make China a modern nation by the year 2000. To achieve this goal, Deng opened China to foreign trade and greater contact with the West. He also introduced a program called the Four Modernizations. The program's goals included:

- Modernization and mechanization of agriculture
- Improvement of military forces
- Upgrading and expansion of industry
- Development of science and industry

RAPID CHANGE Deng's more open policies exposed the Chinese to Western culture and encouraged greater individual expression. In June 1989, government troops crushed a pro-democracy demonstration in Beijing's Tiananmen Square, causing thousands of deaths and injuries. The violence strained China's relations with the United States. In the 1990s, the United States and China continued to argue about human rights, as well as trade issues and the status of Taiwan. China's leaders, meanwhile, looked for ways to stay in power during a time of rapid social and economic change.

MAKING CONNECTIONS

History and Society
China's Confucian tradition was rejected in recent decades as unsuitable for modern times. Today, however, Chinese intellectuals are looking at Confucianism again to see how it might be reconciled with Chinese Marxism.

MAJOR HISTORIC THEMES

1. The traditional Chinese political system was based on dynastic cycles and the Mandate of Heaven.
2. China's ethnocentrism was challenged by foreign imperialism.
3. After a period of disunity, communists led by Mao Zedong established a strong central government that sought to build a pure communist state.
4. After Mao's death, Deng Xiaoping allowed greater contact with Western culture. However, he ensured continuation of communist rule by crushing democratic protests in Tiananmen Square.

SECTION 5 Historic Setting: Japan

MAKING CONNECTIONS

Time Frame

660 B.C.–A.D. 1185	Imperial Period
1185–1600	Feudal Period
1868–1912	Meiji Restoration
1945–1952	U.S. Occupation of Japan
1953–present	Parliamentary Democracy

OVERVIEW

Key Concepts: Identity The secure boundaries and remoteness of their island setting permitted the Japanese to develop a sense of identity very early in their history.

As an island nation located near China, Japan benefitted from cultural diffusion. By establishing an early pattern of selective borrowing, Japan acquired many Chinese cultural elements without being overwhelmed by them. In recent times, Japan has modernized by selectively borrowing from Western technology and culture.

EARLY HISTORY

Key Concepts: Culture Migrations lead to cultural diffusion because the people moving from one place to another carry their ideas and ways of life with them.

Archaeologists believe the first people to migrate to Japan may have come from the Asian mainland or islands in the Pacific. By 660 B.C., a single emperor, claiming descent from the sun goddess, emerged to unite the Japanese under his rule. For the next 1,500 years, the remoteness of the Japanese islands allowed the Japanese to develop a sense of identity. They borrowed many ideas from the mainland—religion, architectural styles, symbols for words (characters), and others. But they freely adapted these ideas to their own culture. The Japanese, for example, integrated the Chinese system of characters with their own phonetic writing system. They accepted many Buddhist and Confucian beliefs, but these ideas existed alongside the beliefs of **Shinto**, their own religion.

Rise of Feudalism (1185–1600)

History and Politics While Chinese history is divided by dynasties, Japanese history is divided, not by emperors, but by the family that actually held power at a given time. Each family used the emperor to back up its control.

The **imperial system**, or rule by an emperor, gradually weakened as noble families gained power in the 800s. The emperor's role became primarily religious and ceremonial. In the late 1100s, the imperial system gave way to **feudalism**—a social, political, and economic system based on personal loyalties, class distinctions, and the granting of land rights. Under feudalism, political power rested in the hands of military warlords.

THE SHOGUN The **shogun**, or military governor general, assumed the political power of the emperor and ruled with the support of a noble class of landowners.

DAIMYO Great landholders called **daimyo** swore allegiance to the shogun, but were very powerful lords in their own right.

SAMURAI Warriors called **samurai** swore allegiance to a daimyo or to the shogun, and, in return for their military support, were granted land and states. Their code of conduct, called **bushido**, stressed simplicity, courage, honor, and unquestioning obedience to one's lord. Warriors with no overlord to serve were called **ronin** and could be hired by other nobles.

PEASANTS AND ARTISANS Beneath the samurai class were peasants who worked the farms and artisans who made their weapons. In return for their services, they received the protection of the samurai.

MERCHANTS Merchants held low social status despite the fact that they might possess considerably more wealth than members of other social classes.

MODERNIZATION OF JAPAN

Although European traders and missionaries first arrived in Japan in the 1500s, the Japanese feared the foreigners might try to conquer them. In the early 1600s, shoguns banned almost all contact with the outside world. This self-imposed **isolation** lasted 250 years. As a result, Japan became cut off from Western technological and scientific advancement, including the Industrial Revolution.

The Opening of Japan

In 1853 the United States government sent **Commodore Matthew Perry** to Japan to seek protection for shipwrecked sailors and to institute trade negotiations. Fearing United States military action, the shogun opened Japan's doors to American trade in 1854. Soon after, Japan entered into trade agreements with other nations.

The Meiji Restoration (1868–1912)

The daimyo, angered by the shogun's agreements with foreigners, broke his power and brought back imperial rule under Emperor Meiji. In a process of reforms called the **Meiji Restoration** (Meiji is Japanese for "enlightened rule"), the Japanese ended feudalism and began to modernize by selectively borrowing from the West.

Modernization Programs

- Sent Japanese students abroad to learn Western methods and to bring Western technology back to Japan
- Instituted a broad-based program of public education

MAKING CONNECTIONS

Feudal Society in Japan

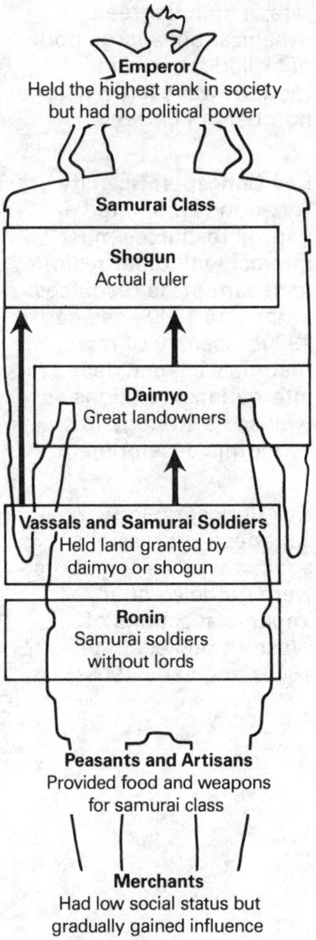
Emperor
Held the highest rank in society but had no political power
Samurai Class
Shogun
Actual ruler
Daimyo
Great landowners
Vassals and Samurai Soldiers
Held land granted by daimyo or shogun
Ronin
Samurai soldiers without lords
Peasants and Artisans
Provided food and weapons for samurai class
Merchants
Had low social status but gradually gained influence

Regents Tip Practice your data-based skills by answering the following question about the diagram:

To whom did samurai soldiers most directly owe their loyalty?

a the emperor and shogun
b the emperor
c the shogun and daimyo
d the daimyo and ronin

MAKING CONNECTIONS

History and Society At the time of the Meiji Restoration, Japan was already modernized in terms of a high literacy rate, a high degree of urbanization, a large pool of skilled labor, and modern ways to train large numbers of citizens.

Key Concepts: Scarcity A nation with limited natural resources must interact with other nations to secure these resources. In the late 1800s and early 1900s, scarcity of raw materials shaped Japan's international relations as well as its strategy for economic development.

Key Concepts: Power Japanese aggressions against weaker neighbors were modeled after imperialist actions of Western powers in the late 1800s and early 1900s.

- Built a modern army based on the **draft**, or enforced enlistment
- Constructed a fleet of steam-powered iron ships
- Adopted a written constitution in 1889 and implemented a parliamentary government with the emperor as its head

Due to these reforms, Japan avoided falling victim to the Western imperialists who divided China in the late 1800s. It, too, soon entered the race for empire.

JAPANESE IMPERIALISM

As a small country with limited resources, Japan felt its industrial success depended upon the acquisition of colonies for raw materials and markets. It won these colonies through a policy of war.

Sino-Japanese War (1894–95)

In a conflict with China, Japan emerged the winner and gained Formosa (present-day Taiwan), the Pescadores Islands, and part of Manchuria. In 1910, Japan had also annexed Korea.

Russo-Japanese War (1904–05)

After a brief war with Russia, Japan seized the southern half of Sakhalin Island and Russia's port and rail rights in Manchuria.

Second Sino-Japanese War (1937–1945)

In a later war against China, Japan invaded Manchuria and set up a puppet government. From there Japan went on to conquer China's coastal areas, major cities, and railroad lines.

World War I (1914–1919)

During World War I, Japan joined with the Allied Powers, who rewarded Japan by giving it former German possessions in the Pacific.

WORLD WAR II

Japan's territorial ambitions grew in the 1930s. It joined with aggressor nations, such as Germany and Italy, who sought to build worldwide empires. The three nations formed what was known as the **Axis Powers**. In 1931 Japan attacked Manchuria and in 1937 it began a full scale war against China in an effort to expand its control on the Asian mainland. In 1940 it seized French Indochina and eventually conquered a significant portion of Southeast Asia.

Pearl Harbor

The United States did not enter the war right away. But it felt that Japanese aggression in the Pacific threatened United States interests in the region. So the United States joined the Allies in cutting off Japan's oil supply. On December 7, 1941, Japan bombed the American naval base at Pearl Harbor, Hawaii. It hoped to knock United States forces out of the Pacific and negotiate a favorable peace treaty. Instead, the United States declared war against Japan.

War in the Pacific (1941–1945)

Japan had expected the Americans to cave in quickly, but the war dragged on for four years. United States troops drove the Japanese from the Pacific in a program of "island hopping." By 1945, the Japanese had retreated to their own shores.

The Atomic Bomb

After the Allies won the war in Europe, the United States turned its full attention to the war in the Pacific. A decision was made to use a powerful secret weapon, the **atomic bomb**, on the cities of **Hiroshima** and **Nagasaki**. The United States hoped to save the lives of thousands of American troops by ending the war quickly. On August 14, 1945, Japan surrendered unconditionally to the United States.

POSTWAR JAPAN

Japan's devastating defeat discredited the military and left the country in deep need of help in rebuilding.

United States Occupation (1945–1952)

United States armed forces under **General Douglas MacArthur** occupied Japan after the war. The Americans helped the Japanese write a new democratic constitution that went into effect in 1947. Under the constitution, Japan renounced its right to wage war and dismantled its military. **Emperor Hirohito** publicly gave up all claims to divinity. The Japanese legislature, called the **Diet**, assumed all lawmaking powers.

Economic Recovery

The United States and 42 other noncommunist nations signed a peace treaty with Japan. The United States and Japan also signed a **bilateral**, or two-nation, defense agreement. The United States speeded Japan's economic recovery through direct aid and orders for supplies during the Korean War (1950–1953). United States policies at this time laid the basis for future economic interdependence.

Today Japan is the world's third largest economic power and it plays an important role in international affairs. It is a leading producer of automobiles, electronic goods, and ships. As part of its economic expansion, it has bought a number of well-known businesses and a considerable amount of real estate in the United States—a cause for alarm in some quarters. A more legitimate concern, however, has focused on **trade imbalances**. Japan exports far more goods to the United States than it allows the United States to send into Japan.

MAKING CONNECTIONS

History and Technology The decision of the United States to use the atomic bomb has affected global politics ever since. See Unit 6, The World Today.

Key Concepts: Culture and Change The United States occupation introduced some American ideas and practices into Japanese culture. Reforms that produced lasting changes in postwar Japan were those that already had some basis in Japanese society.

History and Economics For more on Japan's role in the modern world economy, see Unit 4, Global Economics.

Regents Tip List several reasons why Japan was able to recover successfully after its defeat in World War II. (An example has been listed.)
The United States directly aided Japan's economic recovery.

MAKING CONNECTIONS

MAJOR HISTORIC THEMES

1. As an island nation close to the Asian mainland, Japan has been influenced by other cultures while maintaining a unique identity.
2. In a relatively short period of time, Japan was able to modernize and become a major world power.
3. Imperial expansion led to a war with the United States, in which Japan suffered a devastating defeat.
4. Postwar economic recovery has led to interdependence between the United States and Japan.

SECTION 6 Historic Setting: Latin America

Time Frame

50,000–10,000 B.C.	Migrations from Asia
1500 B.C.–A.D. 1530	Pre-Columbian Civilizations
1492–1546	European Exploration and Conquest
1520–1808	Era of European Colonialism
1808–1825	Latin American Independence Movements
1825–1910	Rule by Caudillos
1823–present	U.S. Involvement in Latin America

MAKING CONNECTIONS

OVERVIEW

For thousands of years, the native peoples of the Americas developed independently from the rest of the world. After 1492 European voyages of exploration and conquest created increasing interdependence between Europe and Latin America. European ethnocentric attitudes contributed to the exploitation of the peoples and resources of Latin America. The region's great geographic and cultural diversity made it difficult to organize unified opposition to colonial rule.

PRE-COLUMBIAN HISTORY

The term **pre-Columbian** refers to the period before the arrival of Christopher Columbus in the Americas in 1492. Three highly developed civilizations flourished in Latin America in pre-Columbian times.

Key Concepts: Political Systems
Although the rich pre-Columbian heritage has survived to this day in Latin America, it did not become an essential component of the political systems of the area.

The Maya (300–900)

The Maya developed a complex agricultural society centered in present-day southern Mexico and the northern part of Central America. The Maya practiced **polytheism**, or the worship of many gods. Their religious rituals revolved around agricultural seasons.

Mayan Accomplishments

- Systems of writing and mathematics, including use of zero
- A more accurate calendar than Europeans had at the time
- Astronomical observatories

MAKING CONNECTIONS

- Elaborate art, including stone sculptures, wall paintings, and huge works of architecture such as flat-topped pyramids
- Great cities that served as administrative and ceremonial centers and supported large populations

The Aztecs (1200–1521)

The Aztecs, a warrior group with a rigid class structure, settled in Mexico around A.D. 1200. Through the process of cultural diffusion, the Aztecs borrowed ideas from conquered peoples. For example, Aztec priests used knowledge of astronomy and mathematics acquired from other cultures to develop a calendar and a counting system. The Aztecs built a huge empire, forced conquered people to pay tribute, and used prisoners for human sacrifice to the Aztec gods.

Key Concepts: Scarcity
Among the Inca, a highly regimented state essentially eliminated scarcity of such essentials as food and housing.

The Inca (1200–1535)

The Inca ruled an extensive empire of several million people in the Andes Mountains of western South America. The emperor—thought to be a descendant of the sun god—strictly controlled the people and their activities through a network of officials and priests.

Incan Accomplishments

- An extensive road network
- Systems of measurement and record keeping
- Medical knowledge of surgery and diseases
- Elaborate building and engineering feats

Key Concepts: Culture
The Europeans' mistaken notion that they were the first to "discover" a "New World" in the Western Hemisphere is an example of Eurocentrism, the belief that European culture is superior to all others.

EUROPEAN EXPLORATION AND CONQUEST OF LATIN AMERICA

In 1492 Christopher Columbus, flying the flag of Spain, attempted to find a new commercial route to Asia by sailing west. What he found instead was a "New World," unknown to Europeans.

Key Concepts: Technology
Schools of navigation in Spain and Portugal, the development of ocean-worthy sailing ships called **carracks**, and the invention of the rifle in the late 1400s aided the European conquest of Latin America.

The Conquistadores

To explore and subdue the New World, Spain employed **conquistadores**, literally "conquerors," such as Vasco de Balboa, Hernán Cortés, and Francisco Pizarro. They sought adventure, personal wealth, and glory for their country. Added to these motives was Spain's desire to spread the Roman Catholic religion.

In 1521 the Aztec Empire fell to Cortés and his small band of soldiers. Pizarro conquered the Inca Empire in 1535. Guns, cannons, and horses—all unknown in the Americas—contributed to the conquistadores' easy victories. European diseases also did much to destroy these empires. The conquistadores enslaved survivors and shipped their wealth to Europe.

Dividing the Spoils

When European monarchs realized the extent and abundance of the Americas, they claimed **sovereignty**, or sole control, over various areas. They established settlements that grew into colonies. Spain dominated most of Latin America. But Portugal claimed a huge territory known as Brazil. England, France, and the Netherlands all established smaller colonies, especially on islands in the Caribbean.

MAKING CONNECTIONS

History and Politics
Portugal later consolidated its claim to Brazil in 1494 with the Treaty of Tordesillas, which divided the New World between Spain and Portugal.

COLONIAL RULE OF LATIN AMERICA

The Spanish ruled their Latin American colonies for almost 300 years. The ideas behind their system of rule were common in Europe at the time. Just as dissatisfaction with conditions in society led to the French Revolution in 1789, similar conditions led to independence movements in Latin America.

Key Concepts: Interdependence
The voyages and claims of the explorers led to an increasing interdependence between Europe and Latin America.

Absolutism

The government of Spain was an **absolute monarchy**. The absolute power of Spanish monarchs extended to their overseas empires. **Viceroys**, or colonial representatives of the king or queen, exercised great power over Spanish colonies. The majority of people lacked political rights and a voice in government.

Regents Tip Briefly define the following terms associated with Latin American history.

Conquistador:

Sovereignty:

Absolutism:

Viceroy:

Mercantilism:

Monopoly:

Encomienda System:

Mercantilism

Spain, like other European colonial powers, adopted a policy of **mercantilism**—that is, the colonies were expected to provide raw materials and markets for the home country. Moreover, Spain maintained a **monopoly**, or total control, over colonial trade. These practices guaranteed trading partners for Spain and ensured a steady flow of gold and silver into the Spanish treasury. Spain also benefitted from the discovery of large deposits of precious metals in some of its colonies.

Encomienda System

In addition to mining gold and silver, the Spanish began the large-scale cultivation of cash crops such as coffee, sugar, and tobacco. Land was concentrated in the hands of a few. The **encomienda system** gave certain Spanish settlers grants of land and control of the labor of specific groups of native peoples. On the Caribbean sugar plantations, a scarcity of local Indian labor led Europeans to import African slaves in large numbers. Eventually, the use of African slaves was extended to other colonies.

History and Society
Though concerned with the plight of Latin American Indians, the Roman Catholic Church nevertheless justified their enslavement.

Role of the Roman Catholic Church

Spain became a strong supporter of the **Counter-Reformation**, the movement to stop the spread of Protestantism. It sent missionaries to Latin America to convert the Indians. Roman Catholic priests

MAKING CONNECTIONS

established schools, taught agriculture, and worked to end abuses against the Indians. The Catholic Church grew rich in Latin America through gifts, grants of land, and church taxes. It gradually became more conservative and supported the ruling elite, or upper class.

Rigid Class Structure

Key Concepts: Power
The rigid class structure of Latin American society permitted a small privileged class to control vast areas of land, and thus its political and economic power.

Latin American society was rigidly structured into four classes.

PENINSULARES These were a select group of Spanish officials sent to Latin America to govern the colonies. They held the most prestige.

CRIOLLOS This class was made up of people born in the colonies of Spanish parents. Spanish officials looked down on the criollos and barred them from the highest positions in government and the church. The criollos, many of whom were educated and wealthy, developed feelings of bitterness and became the leaders of revolutions.

MESTIZOS AND MULATTOES These were people of mixed Spanish, Indian, or African parentage. This class consisted of laborers and townspeople. They had few political rights, and as their numbers grew so did their resentment of unfair treatment and low social status.

NATIVE AMERICANS AND AFRICAN SLAVES This class formed the bottom of the social structure in Latin America. They worked on the estates or in the mines and had little or no freedom.

LATIN AMERICAN MOVEMENTS FOR INDEPENDENCE

Key Concepts: Interdependence
The spread of revolutionary ideas from one area to another is an example of interdependence.

Independence movements formed in Latin America during the late 1700s and early 1800s for a variety of reasons.

Reasons for Independence Movements

- Unjust conditions stemming from colonial rule
- Spread of the democratic ideals of the European Enlightenment
- Successes of the American and French Revolutions
- Wars fought against French emperor Napoleon Bonaparte, which diverted Spanish and Portuguese attention from Latin America

Leaders of Latin American Independence

TOUSSAINT L'OUVERTURE In 1791 slaves in the French colony of Haiti, on the western half of the Caribbean island of Hispaniola, revolted under the leadership of **Toussaint L'Ouverture**. The struggle lasted many years, but in 1804 Haiti became the first independent country in Latin America.

SIMÓN BOLÍVAR Perhaps the greatest nationalist leader of this period was **Simón Bolívar**, known as "the Liberator." An educated and wealthy criollo, he fought for an independent and unified Latin America. In 1819 Bolívar organized an army and led a successful revolt against the Spanish. He was later named president of the republic of Gran Colombia (present-day Venezuela, Colombia, Ecuador, and Panama).

JOSÉ DE SAN MARTÍN AND BERNARDO O'HIGGINS Bolívar's counterpart in the south was **José de San Martín**, a professional soldier. San Martín's rebel army won independence for his native Argentina in 1816. He then joined forces with Chilean general **Bernardo O'Higgins**. Together they crossed the Andes and drove the Spanish from Chile, which declared independence in 1818. In the 1820s San Martín freed parts of Peru and Argentina.

MIGUEL HIDALGO AND JOSÉ MORELOS Mexico achieved its independence in the early 1800s with the help of two Catholic priests—Miguel Hidalgo and José Morelos. Although criollos, they led Indians and mestizos in revolution. The two leaders promised liberal reforms, including the abolition of slavery and land for the peasants. The Spanish executed the priests, but the revolution continued. In 1821, Mexico declared its independence.

Independence for Brazil and the Caribbean

Unlike Spanish colonies, Brazil experienced a peaceful transition to freedom when Portugal granted it independence in 1822. In the Caribbean, independence came more slowly, if at all. France, the Netherlands, and Great Britain retain possessions in the West Indies today. (See the map in Unit 1, The Geographic Setting, for independence dates in Latin America.)

LATIN AMERICA AFTER INDEPENDENCE

Post-Independence Instability

A variety of obstacles made it hard for Latin American nations to realize the revolutionary ideals for which they had fought.

REGIONAL DIFFERENCES Although Bolívar had encouraged the creation of a unified Latin America, geographic barriers, border disputes, and regional rivalries for power made this impossible.

CAUDILLOS The long tradition of absolute rule in Latin America left the people—most of whom were illiterate—ill-prepared to create representative democracies. **Caudillos**, leaders backed by the military, soon emerged in many Latin American nations. These military dictators used repressive law-and-order tactics that often favored the upper class.

MAKING CONNECTIONS

History and Politics
Throughout the colonial period, Portugal exerted less political control over Brazil than Spain did over its colonies. Whereas Spain was reluctant to recognize the independence of its former colonies, Portugal did not resist (the son of the Portuguese king proclaimed Brazil an independent kingdom). Brazil was not declared a republic until 1889.

Key Concepts: Political System
The military has played—and continues to play—an important role in the political system of most Latin American countries.

South America: 1790

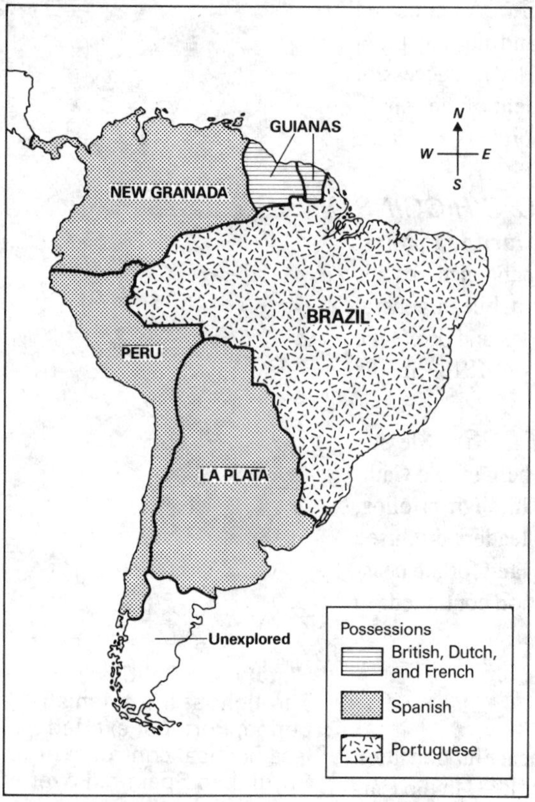

South America: 1828

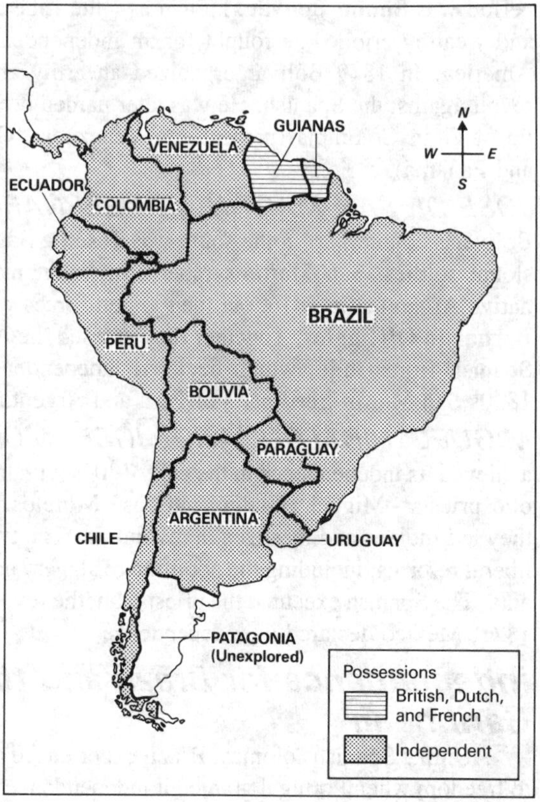

MAKING CONNECTIONS

Regents Tip Practice your data-based skills by answering the following questions about the maps: What political event is illustrated by comparing the two maps?

a the emergence of independent nations in South America
b Spanish exploration of the New World
c the rise of colonialism in South America
d United States involvement in Latin America

ECONOMIC AND SOCIAL INEQUALITY Overthrow of colonial rule ended mercantilism, but land and wealth still remained in the hands of a few criollos. The gap between rich and poor grew even wider. Mestizos and mulattos continued to be denied equal status. Although slavery was abolished, Indians and blacks had few rights.

CONSERVATISM OF THE CHURCH The Catholic Church continued to be a powerful force in Latin American society. The conservative nature of church leaders caused them to oppose liberal changes that might have benefitted the majority. Only in recent years has the church become more involved in promoting human rights and reform in Latin America.

The Monroe Doctrine

To prevent European powers from intervening in unstable Latin American nations, the United States issued the **Monroe Doctrine** in 1823. The doctrine declared the Western Hemisphere closed to further European colonization. Great Britain saw a link between Latin American independence and new markets, so it supported the United States.

ECONOMIC IMPERIALISM IN LATIN AMERICA

Latin American nations won political independence, but they soon fell subject to **economic imperialism**, or foreign economic control.

Foreign Investment

In the late 1800s, Americans and Europeans invested billions of dollars in underdeveloped areas of Latin America. Foreign investment helped countries such as Argentina and Brazil develop prosperous economies. This encouraged large-scale immigration from Europe as well as more investment, often in the form of loans.

Foreign Intervention

Economic investment and foreign intervention went hand-in-hand in Latin America. Investor nations sent warships to collect over-due loan payments or demanded economic concessions instead. Political instability and frequent changes in Latin American governments were viewed as threats to the foreign-owned businesses and investments. The United States and many European nations therefore supported caudillos who could provide law and order.

The Spanish-American War

In 1898 the United States became engaged in a conflict with Spain that centered on the rebellious Spanish colony of Cuba. The war resulted from United States' support of Cuban nationalism. The United States wanted a government in Cuba favorable to United States investors. Defeat of Spain expanded United States influence in the Caribbean. Cuba became an independent nation, but the United States imposed the Platt Amendment on Cuba's constitution. The amendment gave the United States the right to intervene in Cuban affairs to protect American lives and property and the right to set up two naval bases in Cuba. As a result of the war, the United States won control of Puerto Rico, Guam, and the Philippines.

The Panama Canal

The position of the United States as a world power led to increased United States interest in building a canal across Central America. A canal would allow United States ships easy access to both coasts, as well as overseas markets and possessions. The United States won the right to build such a canal by backing a revolution in Panama, which sought independence from Colombia. Panama lay on an **isthmus**, or narrow strip of land between the Americas. Work began on the Panama Canal in 1904 and ended in 1914. In 1978 Panamanians negotiated a treaty with the United States to regain control of the canal zone in 2000.

MAKING CONNECTIONS

Key Concepts: Change
Latin America has experienced a profound demographic change as a result of immigration, population growth, and widespread urbanization.

History and Economics
Latin America has a pattern of economic dependence, first upon the colonial powers, then upon other European countries, and then upon the United States.

History and Politics
Though Cuba and the Philippines are now entirely independent politically of the United States, Puerto Rico remains associated with the United States through its status as a commonwealth. Though not a state, Puerto Rico enjoys many of the benefits of statehood, such as United States citizenship for its people.

MAKING CONNECTIONS

Regents Tip Practice your data-based skills by answering the following question about the cartoon which depicts President Theodore Roosevelt: The cartoon is a political commentary on

a the building of the Panama Canal
b the Spanish-American War
c the Roosevelt Corollary
d Cuban independence

Key Concepts: Interdependence
Although politically independent and suspicious of United States intentions, most Latin American countries have been, and continue to be, heavily influenced by the United States.

The Roosevelt Corollary

In 1904 President Theodore Roosevelt announced the **Roosevelt Corollary** to the Monroe Doctrine to keep European warships out of Latin America. Roosevelt declared that the United States would exercise "international police power" in Latin American countries to protect foreign investments and to ensure repayment of loans. The corollary was used several times to justify American actions in Latin America.

LATIN AMERICA IN THE TWENTIETH CENTURY

Continuing Instability

Economic imperialism, especially on the part of the United States, promoted bitterness against foreign intruders and against Latin American leaders who allowed the exploitation. Because the United States had become the leading investor in Latin America after World War I (1914–1918), the Great Depression of 1929 devastated Latin American economies. Economic hardship combined with problems of autocratic rule, political corruption, and social inequality stimulated reform movements and revolutions in the region.

Mexico

Mexico was the first Latin American country to undergo a revolution in the 1900s. Demands for land reform and an end to foreign economic domination drove dictator Porfirio Díaz from power in 1911. However, revolutionaries split into several factions, causing six years of civil war. In 1917 Mexico adopted a new constitution. It provided for democratic reforms as well as curbs on the power and wealth of the Catholic Church and a redistribution of land. These changes were put into effect in the 1920s and 1930s.

MAKING CONNECTIONS

Regents Tip List several factors that have contributed to instability in much of Latin America. (An example has been listed.)
Economic dependence on foreign powers

Argentina

In the 1930s and 1940s, **totalitarian regimes**, or governments with complete control over the lives of the people, took shape in Europe and Japan. Several nations in Latin America followed their example. As the devastating economic effects of the Great Depression of 1929 hit, Latin American countries looked to strong leaders to help them. In Argentina, for example, **Juan D. Perón** came to power in 1946. Known as a "populist caudillo," he initiated policies that favored the middle class and workers. In general, however, his programs had a negative impact on the economy, especially on agriculture. Like most Latin American dictators, Perón's power rested on the military. In 1955 he lost military support and fled from the country. Perón returned to power for a short while in the 1970s.

Cuba

In 1952 **Fulgencio Batista**, an army sergeant, seized power in Cuba. He did little to improve conditions of unemployment and near starvation in rural areas. In 1956 a revolution erupted in Cuba.

CAUSES OF THE CUBAN REVOLUTION

Political Causes

- Institution of a repressive **police state**, or dictatorship, backed by a military and secret police
- Corruption and bribery among government officials

Economic Causes

- Control of Cuba's sugar plantations by an elite upper class
- Unequal distribution of wealth within Cuban society
- Concessions and special favors to foreign investors and high Cuban unemployment despite prosperity

Social Causes

- Lack of adequate housing, education, and medical care for the majority of Cubans
- Discrimination against blacks and the poor

MAKING CONNECTIONS

Regents Tip List factors in Latin American history that may have compelled Fidel Castro to model his government after the Soviet Union rather than the United States. (An example has been listed.)
Long tradition of dictatorships in Latin America

Moved by injustices, a young lawyer named **Fidel Castro** organized a guerrilla army that launched a three-year fight against Batista's forces. Castro's revolution gained popular support by promising political, economic, and social reforms. In 1959 he forced Batista from power and took control of the government.

After attempts to establish a relationship with the United States failed, Castro turned to the Soviet Union for support and used it as a model for Cuba's government and society.

EFFECTS OF THE CUBAN REVOLUTION

Political Changes

- Institution of a totalitarian regime, controlling all aspects of Cuban life
- Denial of basic political rights such as freedom of the press, assembly, and speech
- Violation of human rights and suppression of political opposition

Economic Changes

- Reorganization of private estates into **collective farms**, or farms jointly operated under government supervision
- **Nationalization**, or government control, of business and industry
- Seizure of foreign property with little or no compensation

Social Changes

- Prohibition of discrimination based on race, sex, or class
- Expansion of public education and an end to widespread illiteracy
- Improvements in housing and medical care

History and Politics For more on the course of communism, see Unit 5, Global Politics, and Unit 6, The World Today.

Castro's policies led many Cubans from the upper and middle classes to flee their homeland. Many of them came to the United States. In April 1961, the United States secretly sponsored an assault by Cuban exiles against Castro. When the **Bay of Pigs invasion** failed, tensions between the two nations increased. The United States still maintains a trade **embargo**, or ban, against Cuba, which has hurt the Cuban economy. Since the breakup of the Soviet Union in 1991, Cuba has maintained trade agreements with some of the former republics but can no longer rely heavily on financial support. Castro, however, has continued to follow a hard-line communist policy.

Nicaragua

THE SOMOZA DICTATORSHIP Castro's government has supported communist movements in other countries. In the 1970s, Castro backed Marxist guerrillas in Nicaragua known as the **Sandinistas**. The Sandinistas led a popular revolt against the dictatorship of **Anastasio Somoza**, whose family had ruled Nicaragua since 1936.

The United States supported the Somoza regime because of its anti-communist stand. The Somozas, however, used the military to rule and gained enormous personal wealth through political corruption and deal-making.

THE SANDINISTA EXPERIMENT In 1979 the Sandinistas overthrew Somoza and set up a Marxist regime under the leadership of **Daniel Ortega**. To solidify their position, the Sandinistas restricted some opposition activities and denied basic civil rights. Nonetheless, the Sandinistas undertook social and land reforms and improved education, housing, and medical care.

UNITED STATES AND CONTRA OPPOSITION Throughout the 1980s, the Sandinista government faced an armed counter-revolutionary group known as the **Contras**, financed mainly by the United States. In addition, the United States put a trade embargo on Nicaragua to pressure it into making reforms. In 1987 a group of neutral Latin American countries, known as the **Contadora Nations**, met to seek a solution to the crisis. **Oscar Arias Sanchez**, president of Costa Rica, proposed a peace plan that called for negotiations and an end to outside aid to guerrillas. In 1988 the United States Congress cut off aid, and an uneasy truce was declared.

DEMOCRATIC ELECTIONS In elections held in February 1990, **Violeta Chamorro** won an upset victory over Daniel Ortega. High inflation and unemployment led the people to withdraw support from the Sandinistas. Nevertheless, the Sandinistas remain an influential force in the country, especially in the military. Chamorro began her attempt at democratic government amid severe economic problems and strained political relations with communist factions.

MAKING CONNECTIONS

History and Politics
United States troops have directly intervened in Nicaraguan affairs several times in the twentieth century. For example, U.S. Marines occupied the country from 1926 to 1933. Such involvement has contributed to Nicaraguan resentment of United States policy.

UNITED STATES RELATIONS WITH LATIN AMERICA

Latin American resentment toward the United States began with economic imperialism and continues to this day, despite attempts by the United States to change its image.

Efforts at Cooperation

GOOD NEIGHBOR POLICY (1933) The United States canceled the Platt Amendment, which limited Cuba's sovereignty. The United States also entered into several trade agreements in Latin America and promised to consult with Latin American nations before enforcing the Monroe Doctrine through intervention.

ORGANIZATION OF AMERICAN STATES (1948) The OAS, as the organization is known, was formed to promote international cooperation and to provide a peaceful forum for settling regional disputes. Currently the OAS includes 35 member nations from the Americas, including the United States.

History and Politics
Although Cuba has been excluded from the OAS since 1962, it has maintained links with several Latin American countries.

MAKING CONNECTIONS

ALLIANCE FOR PROGRESS (1961) The United States instituted the Alliance for Progress to improve political, economic, and social conditions in Latin America, but abandoned it in 1974 because it was ineffective.

TREATY WITH PANAMA (1978) Under the treaty, the United States has agreed to turn over control of the canal to Panama by 2000.

United States Intervention in Latin America

Despite efforts to improve relations with Latin America, the United States has generally acted to promote its national interests.

CUBAN MISSILE CRISIS (1962) The United States "quarantined" Cuba, or imposed a blockade, to stop the Soviet Union from placing nuclear weapons on the island.

OVERTHROW OF ALLENDE (1973) The United States Central Intelligence Agency (CIA) helped overthrow the freely elected Marxist government of Salvador Allende in Chile. A dictatorship was subsequently established.

History and Politics The revolution in Grenada is an example of Fidel Castro's policy of exporting the Cuban Revolution to other nations in Latin America.

INVASION OF GRENADA (1983) United States troops invaded this Caribbean island after a revolution there raised fears that the island would become a base for exporting communist revolution in the region.

SUPPORT FOR EL SALVADOR (1980s) United States military and economic aid helped the government resist rebel forces in the region.

INVASION OF PANAMA (1989) United States troops overthrew the corrupt dictatorship of **Manuel Noriega**. Noriega was arrested and brought to the United States to stand trial for drug smuggling.

MAJOR HISTORIC THEMES

1. Advanced societies existed in Latin America prior to the arrival of Europeans.
2. Colonial exploitation led to nationalist movements for independence.
3. Problems such as geographic barriers prevented Latin America from becoming unified.
4. Colonial traditions of autocratic rule and foreign domination continued to influence Latin American society after independence.
5. The role of the United States in Latin America has alternated between intervention and cooperation.

SECTION 7 Historic Setting: The Middle East

MAKING CONNECTIONS

Time Frame

10,000–3500 B.C.	Neolithic Revolution
3500–612 B.C.	Early Mesopotamian and Egyptian Civilizations
1230–586 B.C.	Hebrew Conquest of Canaan; Kingdom of Israel
334 B.C.–A.D. 395	Greek and Roman Domination
395–1453	Byzantine Empire
750–1058	Golden Age of Islam
1453–1918	Ottoman Empire
1830–present	European Involvement and Arab Nationalism

OVERVIEW

Out of the Middle East came many of the world's great civilizations and three great religions. Two of them, Judaism and Christianity, spread to other parts of the world, leaving Islam as the region's unifying cultural element. Today, much of that unity has been destroyed by bitter conflicts among the newly formed nations.

EARLY RIVER VALLEY CIVILIZATIONS

The Neolithic Revolution (10,000–3500 B.C.)

Sometimes called the single most important innovation in human history, the **Neolithic Revolution** was a technological development that radically changed the nature of society. Between 10,000 B.C. and 3500 B.C., people in the Middle East began to develop farming techniques and to use stone tools. These developments led to the building of the first cities and to the rise of political systems. Trade also developed between these **city-states**. Toward the end of this period, people discovered how to make tools and weapons out of metal.

Key Concepts: Culture
The development of writing systems in the Middle East meant that information pertaining to trade, government, and ideas could be recorded and transferred to other regions and areas. This resulted in cultural diffusion.

Mesopotamian Civilizations (3500–612 B.C.)

Mesopotamia, the land between the Tigris and Euphrates rivers (see the map in Unit 1, The Geographic Setting), was the site of a succession of early civilizations, including Sumer, Babylonia, and

MAKING CONNECTIONS

Key Concepts: Technology The invention of writing made more advanced civilizations and more complex technology possible.

Assyria. During this time, writing was invented. Organized religions evolved, as did governments based on kingship and written codes of law. Technology and the arts flourished, too.

Ancient Egypt (3500–1090 B.C.)

A civilization also emerged along the Nile River. The Egyptians developed a government and religion centered on a **pharaoh**, or god-king, believed to be immortal and capable of ruling after death. This concept of an afterlife resulted in funeral practices to preserve the pharaoh's body and in the building of elaborate tombs, such as the **pyramids**.

THE HEBREWS

Key Concepts: Change The Hebrew's rejection of polytheism and insistence on monotheism marked a significant change in the development of Middle Eastern cultures and has had global effects.

Early Middle Eastern civilizations practiced religions based on **polytheism**, or belief in many gods. However, the region was also the birthplace of three great religions distinguished by **monotheism**, or belief in one God. The earliest of these, **Judaism**, was the religion of the **Hebrews**.

Development of Judaism and the Kingdom of Israel

The Hebrews originated in Sumer. Around 2000 B.C., they moved west and settled in Palestine on the Jordan River, the land they called Canaan (present-day Israel). Around 1800 B.C., drought forced some of the Hebrews into Egypt. There the pharaohs enslaved them. Around 1230 B.C., a leader named **Moses** led the Hebrews out of Egypt and back to Canaan. After conquering the Philistines and others, the Hebrew tribes united under a single government, forming the **Kingdom of Israel**. This kingdom achieved its greatest prosperity under **King David** and his son **Solomon**, who built a temple in Jerusalem in the 900s B.C. to glorify the God of the Hebrew people, "Yahweh" ("Jehovah" in modern English).

Departure from the Homeland

Israel's strategic location between Egypt and Mesopotamia made it the target of invasions by Assyrians, Babylonians, Greeks, and Romans. In 586 B.C., the Babylonians conquered Jerusalem and destroyed Solomon's temple. The **Jews**, as the Hebrews came to be known, were sent into exile. Though their kingdom was destroyed, the Jews held fast to their religion. Eventually, they returned to their homeland, but in A.D. 70 the Romans destroyed Jerusalem and a second temple that the Jews had built.

Key Concepts: Identity The formation of Jewish identity was influenced by the religious beliefs of the Hebrews and their treatment after exile from Jerusalem.

The **Babylonian exile** and repeated conquests scattered the Jews to other parts of the world in what is called the **diaspora**, or dispersing. Many Jews settled in Europe where they often became the victims of **anti-Semitism**—discrimination against and persecution of Jews. As a result, some Jews dreamed of a return to their historic homeland. This desire led to the **Zionist movement** of the late 1800s and creation of the modern state of Israel.

THE ROMAN EMPIRE AND THE SPREAD OF CHRISTIANITY

All of the Middle East adjacent to the Mediterranean Sea came under Roman control by A.D. 120. Around this time, missionaries began to spread **Christianity** throughout the Roman Empire, which had developed from Judaism about 75 years earlier. The promise of salvation for all peoples made the Christian concept of one God attractive to non-Jews. At first, Roman emperors persecuted Christians. But by the end of the fourth century, Christianity had become the empire's official religion.

THE BYZANTINE EMPIRE

In 286 and 395 the Roman Empire split into western and eastern halves. After the fall of the western half in 476, the Eastern Roman Empire, which included those areas of the Middle East from **Asia Minor** to Egypt, became known as the **Byzantine Empire**. The Byzantines inherited the Christian religion as well as Roman laws and the Roman system of government. Until the fall of the capital at Constantinople (present-day Istanbul in Turkey) in 1453, the Byzantine Empire exerted a great influence over much of the Middle East, Eastern Europe, and Russia.

THE RISE OF ISLAM

Islam, the third great monotheistic religion to come from the Middle East, was influenced by both Judaism and Christianity. Although it, too, spread far beyond its place of origin, it remained strongest in the Middle East. Islam provided cultural unity for the region. Today the vast majority of people who live there are **Muslim** (followers of Islam).

Origins of Islam

The founder of Islam, **Muhammad** (around 570–632), was born in **Mecca** in present-day Saudi Arabia. Mecca in Muhammad's time was a holy city for Arabs, as it is today. But then the people worshiped hundreds of gods. Muhammad began to preach a new faith in one God, called **Allah**. Facing persecution, Muhammad and his followers fled in 622 to nearby Medina, where the new faith grew. The Islamic calendar dates from the year of Muhammad's flight, which is called **hijra**. In 630 Muhammad returned to Mecca, captured the city, and proclaimed Allah to be the one God.

The Spread of Islam

Soon after Muhammad's death, his teachings were recorded in the **Koran**, the holy book of Islam. Within a little more than a hundred years, Muslim armies spread Islam west across North Africa and into Spain, east as far as India, and north into Asia Minor.

MAKING CONNECTIONS

Key Concepts: Change
Christianity brought about great changes in Greco-Roman civilization. The Judeo-Christian ethic shaped Western values, ideals, and culture.

Key Concepts: Culture and Political System
The Byzantine Empire dominated the Mediterranean world for 11 centuries with its unique blend of Greek and eastern Mediterranean culture. At a time when Europe was fragmented into small feudal units, the Byzantines developed the Orthodox Christian religion and continued the Roman political and legal system.

Key Concepts: Identity
As a way of life, Islam has preserved the cultural identity of the Middle East. Over the centuries, it has changed very little in terms of its religious beliefs, values, and ethics.

History and Society As Islam spread, so did Arabic—the language of the Koran. As a result, many diverse peoples became unified under a common religion and language.

THE MUSLIM GOLDEN AGE After 750, Islamic culture enjoyed a golden age under political and religious leaders—known as **caliphs**—who ruled from Baghdad (the capital of present-day Iraq). Baghdad prospered under the Abbasids.

INVADERS FROM CENTRAL ASIA AND EUROPE In the eleventh century, the **Seljuk Turks**, converts to Islam, invaded Baghdad and overthrew the caliphs. They then conquered Asia Minor and most of the Byzantine Empire. Another threat to Muslims and to the Byzantines came from Christian **crusaders** from Europe. They sacked Constantinople and other cities on their way to the Holy Land, which they hoped to seize from the Seljuk Turks. For a time in the 1100s, they controlled Jerusalem and other Mediterranean cities.

THE OTTOMAN EMPIRE In the 1300s, the **Ottoman Turks** invaded Asia Minor and were converted to Islam. Constantinople fell to them in 1453. By 1566, Ottoman rulers called **sultans** controlled an empire that included most of the Middle East and part of Europe.

By the 1800s, the vitality of the Ottoman Empire had declined as ethnic groups within the empire fought for independence or self-rule. One group, the **Armenians**, who are Christian, was continually persecuted by the Ottomans. During World War I, more than a million Armenians were massacred in an attempt at **genocide**—systematic destruction of an entire group of people.

Because of their involvement on the losing side in World War I, the Turks lost all their territory except present-day Turkey. In 1922 **Mustafa Kemal Ataturk** overthrew the sultan and in 1923 he created the Republic of Turkey. As president, Ataturk instituted major reforms to transform Turkey into a modern, European-style nation.

EUROPEAN IMPERIALISM AND ARAB NATIONALISM

As the Ottoman Empire declined in the 1800s, the industrialized nations of Europe tried to take greater economic control of the area. European imperialism formed the basis of much of the resentment and conflict in the Arab world today.

The Suez Canal

Completed by the French in 1869, the Suez Canal links the Mediterranean Sea to the Red Sea and the Indian Ocean beyond. The canal especially benefitted Great Britain by giving it better access to its most important colony, India. To control this strategic waterway, Britain sent an army to Egypt in 1882 and made it a protectorate. Egypt did not regain control of the canal until 1956.

Spheres of Influence

After World War I, Britain and France divided the former Ottoman territories in the Middle East. Britain assumed control of Iraq and Palestine, while France controlled Syria and Lebanon. Resentment

MAKING CONNECTIONS

History and Culture
Between the ninth and fourteenth centuries, the Islamic world preserved the knowledge of Greece and Rome. Arab scholars also broadened classical scientific and mathematical knowledge and laid the foundations for modern science and mathematics.

Key Concepts: Culture
One significant effect of the Crusades was the diffusion of Middle Eastern ideas and culture into western Europe.

Key Concepts: Power
After the 1600s, Ottoman power declined and the empire became a pawn in the balance-of-power struggle among European nations.

History and Politics
European involvement in the Middle East increased after France took control of Algeria in 1830. Besides France and Britain, Italy established a presence in the Middle East by taking over Libya in 1912.

History and Politics Egypt closed the Suez Canal to all traffic after the 1967 Arab-Israeli War. It remained closed until 1975.

grew when the Europeans failed to keep their wartime promise to support Arab national interests and to create a Jewish homeland.

Nationalist Movements

In the twentieth century, Arab **nationalism** led to the creation of independent Arab states. Another development has been the emergence of Islamic **fundamentalism**, a movement based on strict following of Muslim religious traditions. These forces have often been hostile to Western influence in the region. For example, in 1979 Islamic fundamentalists in Iran overthrew the pro-Western **shah**, or ruler, and held 59 Americans hostage for 444 days.

ISRAEL AND THE PALESTINIANS A United Nations plan for the partition of Palestine into an Arab state and a Jewish state was rejected by the Arabs but accepted by the Jews. When Israel announced its independence in 1948, it was immediately attacked by neighboring Arab states. Israel defeated the Arabs and took control of Arab territory. Many Palestinians became refugees. Other clashes with Arab states came in 1956, 1967, 1973, and 1982.

In the 1967 war, Israel occupied the **West Bank** of the Jordan River as well as other Arab territories where many Palestinians lived. Though Egypt signed a peace treaty with Israel in 1979, other Arab nations continued to oppose Israel's existence. In 1988 the Palestinians in the Israeli-occupied territories began a revolt called the **intifada**. In May 1994 the Palestine Liberation Organization and the state of Israel agreed to Palestinian self-rule in the Gaza Strip and Jericho on the West Bank.

OTHER CONFLICTS Arab nations formed the **Arab League** in 1945 to coordinate the region's political and economic policies. Yet Cold War rivalries, land disputes, and local power struggles led to frequent clashes, such as the **Iran-Iraq War** (1980–1988) and the Iraqi invasion of **Kuwait** in 1990. Since the 1970s, a bloody civil war in **Lebanon** between Christians and Muslims has been complicated by Israeli and Syrian intervention. In 1991 a United States led coalition under a United Nations mandate defeated Iraqi forces and forced their withdrawal from Kuwait.

MAJOR HISTORIC THEMES

1. Early technological advances resulted in several major river valley civilizations in the ancient Middle East.
2. Successive invasions and empire-building by various groups resulted in rich cultural diversity in the region.
3. Cultural diffusion spread Middle Eastern religions, technology, and ideas far beyond the region.
4. European imperialism helped create anti-Western hostility felt by many Arabs today.
5. Conflicts in the Middle East today threaten global stability.

MAKING CONNECTIONS

History and Politics Israeli security and Palestinian nationalism are central issues in the Arab-Israeli conflict.

Regents Tip Practice your data-based skills by answering the following question about the map: In 1948 Jerusalem lay on the border of which two nations?

a Israel and Syria
b Transjordan and Israel
c Egypt and Israel
d Lebanon and Syria

Israel: 1948

SECTION 8 Historic Setting: Western Europe

MAKING CONNECTIONS

Time Frame

Pre-history–3500 B.C.	Emergence of Civilization
2000 B.C.–A.D. 476	Ancient Greece and Rome
500–1500	Middle Ages and the Rise of Nations
1350–1650	Renaissance and Reformation
1450–1750	Exploration and Colonization
1500–1789	Establishment of Absolute Monarchies
1500–1800	Scientific Revolution and Enlightenment
1789–1848	Age of Revolutions
1750–1914	Industrial Revolution
1830–1914	Age of New Imperialism
1914–1919	World War I/Treaty of Versailles
1922–1939	Rise of Totalitarianism
1939–1945	World War II
1945–present	Cold War and Recovery

OVERVIEW

Key Concepts: Identity
Cultural diffusion and economic interdependence have produced a unique European identity that sets the region apart from other regions in the world.

Although western Europe has a diversity of landscapes and cultures, the independent nations of the region share a common heritage rooted in the ancient civilizations of Greece and Rome. Key themes in western European history include cultural diffusion and economic interdependence.

EMERGENCE OF CIVILIZATION

Key Concepts: Political System and Environment
Some Greek city-states developed a democratic political system that created an environment conducive to individual expression and creativity.

Between 10,000 B.C. and 3500 B.C., the nomadic people of western Europe developed methods of farming that allowed them to settle down and eventually to produce and develop new skills. People used this new technology to build complex societies called civilizations. The characteristics of early civilizations included complex governments and religions, a division of labor, cities, social classes, and methods of keeping records.

RISE OF CLASSICAL CIVILIZATIONS

The ancient civilizations of Greece and Rome emerged thousands of years ago. Yet they established a standard of excellence by which later societies measured their cultures. Through the process of cultural diffusion, the Greeks and the Romans influenced people from the Atlantic Ocean in the west to the Fertile Crescent and India in the east.

Ancient Greece

Greece is a nation composed of islands and peninsulas located in the Mediterranean Sea. Geography and location led the early Greek people to trade with other groups, such as the Minoans on the island of Crete, and to borrow beneficial ideas. Cultural diffusion, therefore, helped the Greeks to develop a highly advanced culture.

Greece's mountainous terrain made it difficult for the people to unite. Cut off from each other, isolated communities developed into independent political units called **city-states**. Each city-state, or polis, was different, having its own form of government, laws, and army. The two most important city-states were Athens and Sparta.

SPARTA Spartan society revolved around physical training and the military. It may be described as **monolithic**, since there was only one acceptable way of thinking and behaving. Sparta was a **totalitarian state** in that the government controlled every part of the lives of its people, limiting their freedom and demanding complete loyalty and obedience.

ATHENS Athens was a **pluralistic society**, which encouraged free expression, new ideas, and change. A well-rounded education was emphasized, the goal of which was a "sound mind and sound body." The ideal Athenian citizen was educated, loyal, and willing to be involved in the running of the city-state. Athens had a **direct democracy**. All citizens (native-born, free males over eighteen) had the right to take part in lawmaking in the Assembly.

THE GOLDEN AGE OF GREECE The Greeks, led by Athens, entered a golden age following the defeat of the Persians. This period is also referred to as the Age of Pericles (461–429 B.C.) since, as leader of Athens, Pericles encouraged the growth of democracy as well as cultural and scientific achievement. Pericles ordered the building of the Parthenon, a temple to the goddess Athena. The Parthenon is an example of Greek architectural excellence.

As the influence of Athens grew, so did resentment among other city-states, especially Sparta. This resentment led to conflicts among the city-states known as the Peloponnesian Wars (431–404 B.C.). These civil wars weakened Greece and allowed it to be easily conquered by the Macedonians, led first by Philip II and then by his son Alexander.

ALEXANDER THE GREAT (356–323 B.C.) Alexander the Great extended his territory from Greece, creating a vast empire that stretched all the way to India. He appreciated Greek culture and helped to spread it throughout the Mediterranean area and beyond. His rule marked a unique blending of Greek and Middle Eastern cultures known as the Hellenistic Period. The achievements of this age became part of the Greek heritage to Western civilization.

MAKING CONNECTIONS

History and Geography Unlike other early civilizations (for example, India and China), Greece did not develop in a river valley.

Regents Tip Compare Sparta with twentieth-century totalitarian states (for example, Nazi Germany and the Soviet Union).

Regents Tip Compare Athenian democracy with democracy in the United States. In what ways was Athens undemocratic?

Regents Tip List some significant ways that Athenian society differed from Spartan society. (An example has been listed.) Pluralistic rather than monolithic society

MAKING CONNECTIONS

Key Concepts: Culture
Examples of the lasting impact of Greek culture on Western civilization include today's Olympic games, the study of geometry, and a belief in democracy.

Key Concepts: Change
The treatment of Socrates shows that acceptance of new ideas was limited.

Key Concepts: Culture
Greek architecture reflected the value that Greek culture placed on order and balance.

Greek Column Styles

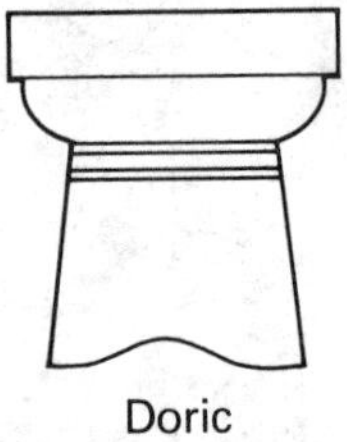

Doric

Ionic

Corinthian

Greek Contributions to Civilization

Theater

Produced tragedies and comedies, performing them in outdoor amphitheaters. One of the most famous Greek playwrights was **Sophocles**, author of *Oedipus Rex*.

Poetry

Celebrated Greek history, legends, and heroes. **Homer** wrote the *Iliad* and the *Odyssey*, which tell the stories of the Trojan War and serve as a source of information about early Greece.

Philosophy

A philosophy is an attitude or belief that affects how a person lives. A philosopher is a person who looks for wisdom. The three great Greek philosophers were:

- **Socrates** Formulated the Socratic method by which a person arrives at the truth through questions and answers. Socrates' advice to his students was ''Know thyself.'' He was eventually accused of corrupting the youth of Athens and was put to death for his controversial methods.
- **Plato** Student of Socrates. Plato is most famous as the author of the *Republic*, in which he attacked democracy and suggested that philosophers govern the state.
- **Aristotle** Student of Plato. Aristotle's philosophical and scientific works influenced thinking in Europe for almost 2,000 years.

Architecture

Constructed many well-proportioned marble buildings and developed three styles of columns (Doric, Ionic, and Corinthian)

Sculpture

Emphasized beauty and perfection. The Greeks idealized the human body, often using the gods as their subjects.

Mathematics

Made tremendous contributions in the field of geometry:

- **Pythagoras** developed the theorem pertaining to right triangles.
- **Euclid** created a branch of geometry based on deductive reasoning.

Science

Major advancements were made in a number of areas:

- **Archimedes**, a physicist, discovered the uses of the lever and the pulley.
- **Hippocrates** is called the ''Father of Medicine.'' Doctors today still adhere to the ethical standards of the Hippocratic Oath.

Ancient Rome

EARLY ROME Unlike the geography of Greece, which divided its people, the geography of the Italian peninsula allowed the people to unite under one government centered in Rome. A monarchy existed in Rome from 753–509 B.C., when the kings were overthrown and a democracy was established.

THE ROMAN REPUBLIC Since the population of Rome was much larger than that of any of the Greek city-states, the citizens were not able to take part directly in the running of the government. An **indirect democracy** was therefore established in which the people chose representatives to run the state for them. The Roman **Republic** was a government headed by elected leaders. Real power was held by the Senate, which represented the upper class, and two consuls, who served as heads of state. The rights of all Roman citizens were protected by the code of laws known as the **Twelve Tables of Law**. Over a two-hundred-year period, democracy was expanded, as the lower class achieved more power and greater political equality.

MAKING CONNECTIONS

Key Concepts: Culture
The word *democracy* is from the Greek and means rule by the people.

Key Concepts: Human Rights
Initially, Roman law offered limited human rights to its citizens.

Empire of Alexander the Great

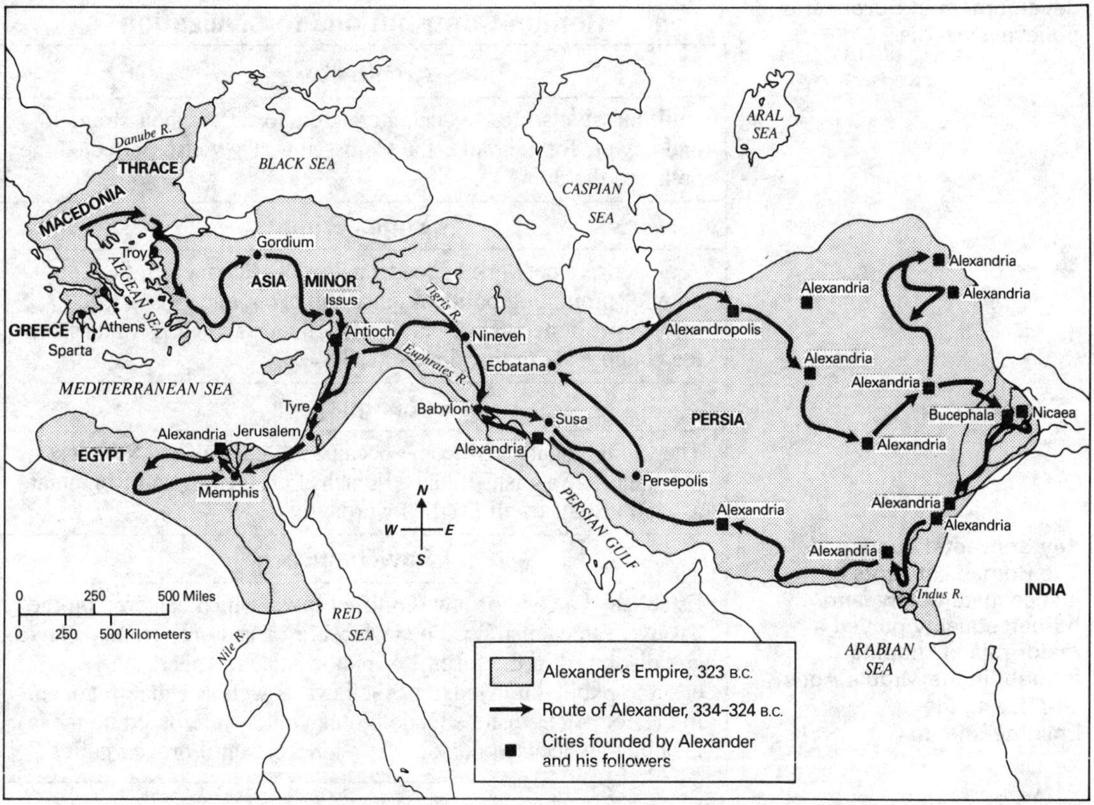

MAKING CONNECTIONS

FROM REPUBLIC TO EMPIRE Through a series of wars, Rome expanded its territory and became the dominant power in the Mediterranean area. The Romans selectively borrowed from the people they conquered, especially from the Greeks, and through this process of cultural diffusion improved their society. The benefits of Roman conquests were offset, however, by problems within Rome itself. As Rome grew, so did the gap between the rich and poor. Conflict between these groups led to the decline of the republic and set the stage for the rise of a strong leader, who first appeared in the form of a dictator—Julius Caesar—and then as an emperor—Augustus.

Key Concepts: Political System
People support strong rulers during times of crisis.

The Roman Empire (27 B.C.–A.D. 476) was an **autocracy** in which power was held by one man—the emperor. Augustus established a strong central government and a civil service through which he ruled his huge empire. Although he was an absolute ruler, he believed in governing for the good of the people and brought about reforms such as fairer tax collection.

THE PAX ROMANA Augustus established a period of great peace during which Rome flourished. The Pax Romana led to the start of Rome's golden age, the peak of Rome's civilization. The Romans depended largely on the Greeks for their style of art, literature, and drama, but they also made lasting contributions of their own.

Key Concepts: Political System
The Roman political system, unlike the Greek, was able to govern a large Mediterranean empire that strongly influenced the development of European political systems.

Roman Contributions to Civilization

Architecture
Built massive structures using concrete to reflect their strength and power, for example, the Colosseum. They also perfected the arch and the dome.
Engineering
An extensive network of roads and bridges connected the empire, promoting political unity and economic **interdependence**. They also built aqueducts to carry water from the countryside to the cities.
Language
The Latin language of Rome became the basis of the Romance languages—Spanish, Italian, French, Portuguese, and Romanian, as well as half of all English words.
Law/Justice
Established a code of law (**codified law**), which centered on the Twelve Tables of Law. The laws were carved onto stone tablets and displayed in the forum, or public square. This display ensured public knowledge of the laws as well as equal treatment in the courts. Decisions made by the courts were based on the idea that an accused person was "innocent until proven guilty."

Key Concepts: Justice
The Roman concepts of justice, natural law, and human equality played a major role in shaping thought in the Middle Ages and during the Enlightenment.

GROWTH OF CHRISTIANITY During the time of the Roman Empire, Jesus began to spread ideas that formed the basis of a new religion. Christianity was rooted in Hebrew religious traditions, such as the Ten Commandments, and was based on the idea of love of God and neighbor. The preaching of brotherhood and equality attracted the support of the poor and slaves, while the refusal to worship the emperor angered the Roman authorities. Although Christians faced persecution because of their beliefs, their numbers increased. Eventually, Emperor Constantine himself converted to Christianity and it became the official religion of Rome in A.D. 395. The Christian Church became one of the most important institutions in western Europe.

FALL OF ROME By the fourth century A.D. the government, economy, and character of the Romans had become weak. In A.D. 395 the Roman Empire was divided into two parts. The Eastern Roman Empire, also called the Byzantine Empire, centered around the capital of Constantinople and was able to regain its strength and productivity. The Western Roman Empire, ruled from Rome, continued to decline.

Causes of the Fall of Rome

Political
Government was weak and corrupt. There was also no orderly way to choose the next emperor; assassinations were common and the role of emperor often fell to the strongest general.
Economic
Heavy taxation, high unemployment, and a decline in trade and manufacturing contributed to economic decline.
Social
People developed a selfish attitude and put their needs above those of the empire. Lack of patriotism forced the government to rely on a mercenary army of non-Romans who sought only the spoils of war.

In such a weakened condition, Rome was opened to invasion. Germanic tribes, fleeing from the Huns of Asia, invaded and captured Roman territory. Rome itself fell to the Ostrogoths in A.D. 476, signaling the collapse of the empire.

THE MIDDLE AGES (A.D. 500–1500)

The time between the end of the Roman Empire and the start of modern European history is called the Middle Ages. The word **medieval** describes this period of transition when the people of Western Europe attempted to rebuild what had been lost as a result of Rome's collapse.

MAKING CONNECTIONS

Regents Tip Compare Christianity with Judaism and Islam. (An example has been provided.)
All three religions are monotheistic

Key Concepts: Interdependence
At its height, Rome actively participated in a globally interdependent economic system, which ultimately contributed to its decline as unfavorable balances of trade increased.

Regents Tip List some effects of the fall of the Western Roman Empire. (An example has been listed.)
Blending of Roman and Germanic cultures

MAKING CONNECTIONS

Early Middle Ages (A.D. 500–1000)

The first five hundred years of the Middle Ages are referred to as the Dark Ages since Europe was plagued by numerous problems.

LACK OF A STRONG CENTRAL GOVERNMENT The collapse of Rome threw Europe into chaos. Since there was no strong government to keep order, warfare was almost constant.

DECLINE IN TRADE Roman roads deteriorated and merchants became afraid to travel. The use of money nearly ceased and people had to resort to barter. As trade declined, so did the number of towns and cities.

DECLINE IN FORMAL LEARNING Constant warfare led to the destruction of many libraries, schools, and museums. Education and culture were neglected as people began to concentrate only on survival.

History and Society
During the Middle Ages, the Christian Church in western Europe, which maintained a centralized organization based in Rome, became the center of literacy in the region and a link with the Roman culture of the past.

The knowledge and culture of the ancient civilizations was not lost to future generations, however. The Christian Church helped to preserve Western civilization and kept learning alive through its educational system. The Byzantine Empire maintained schools, libraries, and museums, thus preserving the classical learning of the Greeks and the Romans. Constantinople became a center of trade and culture. Justinian's Code, a summary of Roman law, served as the basis for later legal systems by recording ideas such as equality before the law and guarantee of legal rights.

CHARLEMAGNE (A.D. 771–814) King of the Germanic tribe known as the Franks, Charlemagne established a great empire in Europe. He converted to Christianity and, through his conquests, not only united many tribes in Europe, but also spread his religion. He encouraged trade and, recognizing the importance of education, established schools. The pope, leader of the Christian Church, crowned Charlemagne "Emperor of the Romans" in A.D. 800. Charlemagne ruled effectively, but following his death in A.D. 814, his empire fell apart, leaving western Europe open to attack. Invasions by the Vikings from the north, the Magyars from the east, and the Muslims from the south created a climate of fear in Europe. The feudal system developed as a means of restoring order and insuring protection against the new invaders.

Key Concepts: Interdependence
The traditional society of feudal Europe was one in which each class understood its place and obligations within an interdependent system.

Feudalism

Feudalism grew out of Germanic customs. It provided western Europe with a form of government, an economic system, and a rigid but interdependent class structure. Through feudalism, the needs of each class were satisfied.

POLITICAL SYSTEM Feudalism was a system of local government based on the control of land. Kings granted land (a **fief**) to their nobles (called **lords** or **vassals**) in return for their pledge of loyalty and military support. Lords gradually became more powerful than kings as they increased the size of their landholdings. The feudal system lacked a strong central authority. Lords ruled over their own lands, made their own laws, and controlled their own armies made up of knights.

ECONOMIC SYSTEM Under feudalism, an economic system developed known as **manorialism**—a system in which land, rather than trade and commerce, was the major source of wealth. The manor, or estate of the lord, became the basic economic unit of society, replacing the disappearing towns and cities. Peasants were not permitted to own land, but could live under the security and protection of the lord on his manor. The peasants worked the land and provided food and services for the upper classes. The manor was almost entirely self-sufficient, producing the necessities of life with little need to trade.

SOCIAL SYSTEM Feudalism divided society into classes of greater lords, lesser lords, knights, peasants (or serfs), and townspeople. Class was determined at birth and there was little **social mobility**. Kings, lords, and knights were the noble elite, not only because they controlled land, wealth, and power, but also because they were bound by oaths of loyalty and a code of behavior known as **chivalry**. The majority of the people were peasants and most were bound to the land as **serfs**. Their only hope of relief from poverty and hardship came from their religious beliefs, the Christian promise of heaven as a reward for a good life.

MAKING CONNECTIONS

The Structure of Feudal Society

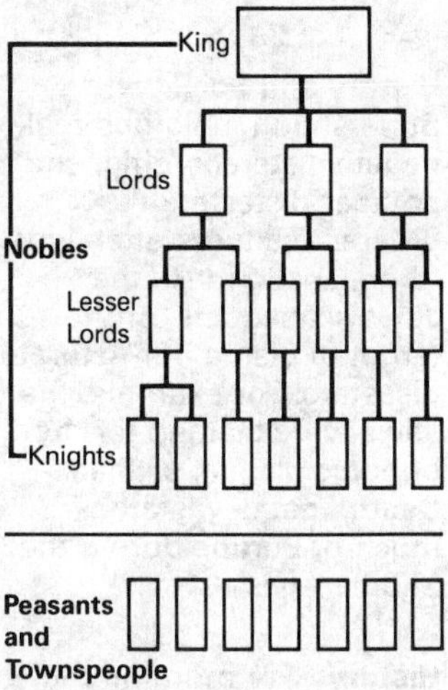

The Medieval Church

In A.D. 1054 when the Christian Church in Europe split into two churches, the Eastern or Orthodox Church became the church of the Byzantine Empire and Russia. The Roman Catholic Church became the dominant religious institution in western Europe. It helped to provide order and stability during feudal times. Since most of the people in western Europe belonged to the Catholic faith, the Church also served as a unifying force. The medieval Church fulfilled many functions.

RELIGIOUS FUNCTION The Church provided a place of refuge and hope. It taught that faith and good works ensured happiness in heaven. The Church threatened those who violated its laws with **excommunication**. An excommunicated person was barred from Church services and the rites believed to help secure salvation from punishment after death for past sins.

POLITICAL FUNCTION The educated Church leadership took on many of the responsibilities of a government during the Middle Ages. They kept records of births, marriages, and deaths and made religious laws. The Church claimed supremacy over civil authority, which led to many conflicts between feudal kings and popes.

ECONOMIC FUNCTION The Church became an important landowner in Western Europe. It also acquired considerable wealth through the collection of the **tithe**—a 10 percent tax on a person's income. Christians were not permitted to become bankers since the Church forbid usury, the charging of interest on loans.

Regents Tip List some ways in which the Roman Catholic Church helped unify western Europe during the Middle Ages. (An example has been listed.)
Had a centralized administration that spanned Europe

MAKING CONNECTIONS

SOCIAL FUNCTION The Church became responsible for maintaining education. Schools were set up in churches and monasteries. The Church also encouraged the first universities in western Europe. The cultural influence of the Church extended to music, sculpture, painting, and architecture. This influence is best reflected in Gothic cathedrals, whose statues and stained glass tell the stories of the Bible.

History and Society
Superstition, religious zeal, negative stereotyping, and popular distaste for different cultures often led Christians to make the Jews scapegoats, or the target of blame, for natural disasters. For example, the Jews were blamed for the bubonic plague, or Black Death, that devastated much of Europe during the Middle Ages.

History For more on the Crusades, see the section on the Middle East in this unit.

Late Middle Ages (1000–1500)

During the late Middle Ages, the Roman Catholic Church taught that "only those who believe (in the teachings of the Catholic Church) will be saved." Non-believers were often victims of discrimination. **Anti-Semitism**, or prejudice against Jews, was prevalent. Jews were forced to live apart from Christians in special sections of towns called **ghettos**.

Muslims were also considered to be enemies of the Church. In 1095, Pope Urban II called for a **crusade**, or holy war, against the Seljuk Turks. The Turks, followers of Islam, had captured Palestine, the birthplace of Jesus, and were threatening the Christians of the Byzantine Empire. There were seven Crusades over a period of 200 years and, though they failed to free the Holy Land permanently, they contributed to dramatic changes in Western Europe.

CULTURAL DIFFUSION Contact with the advanced civilizations of the Muslim world and the Byzantine Empire resulted in the exchange of ideas and a renewed interest in learning. People became curious about the world around them.

Key Concepts: Scarcity
The scarcity of Asian goods in Europe, particularly after the decline of the Byzantine Empire, led Europeans to expand outward in search of new trade routes.

REVIVAL OF TRADE European demand for goods from the East (silks, spices, perfumes), introduced by the returning Crusaders, helped to stimulate trade and the growth of cities. These cities began to replace the manors as the economic centers of society. The Italian cities became especially wealthy due to their location along the Mediterranean Sea—the main trade route to the East.

DECLINE OF FEUDALISM The revival of trade brought about the decline of feudalism as a political, economic, and social system. Coined money came back into use and a new middle class of merchants and craftsmen developed. These groups formed organizations called **guilds**, which regulated trade or crafts in a town. Members of guilds became wealthy and influential citizens. Serfs, who were once bound to the land, ran away to towns or bought their freedom and became tenant farmers.

Key Concepts: Power
Increased trade created the preconditions for the Renaissance—greater affluence and the rising power of the middle, or merchant, class.

The shift from land to money as the source of wealth contributed to a decline in the power of lords and an increase in the power of kings. The middle class needed the protection of a strong ruler and therefore supported the king over a lord. The wealth of the middle class allowed the king to hire an army so that he was no longer dependent on the loyalty of his lords. The feudal system eventually gave way to **nation-states** led by strong kings.

THE RENAISSANCE (1350–1650)

The changes that came in the late Middle Ages helped to pave the way for the Renaissance, a "rebirth" of culture and learning in western Europe. This period was marked by (1) a rediscovery of the classical civilizations of Greece and Rome; (2) renewed interest in secular, or worldly, matters; (3) increased emphasis upon the uniqueness and worth of the individual.

Beginnings in Italy

The Renaissance began in Italy during the fourteenth century. Italy had a rich heritage based on the traditions of Greece and Rome. Artists and writers used this history as a source of inspiration. Italian city-states such as Florence and Milan grew rich from the trade between Europe and the Middle East. Members of the middle class and nobility, such as Lorenzo de' Medici, used their wealth to become patrons of the arts. Officials of the Catholic Church also employed artists to decorate cathedrals and monasteries. Eventually, the Renaissance spread throughout Western Europe.

Humanism

The spirit of the Renaissance was represented by the philosophy known as **humanism**, which focused on man and his world. Unlike medieval scholars, who concerned themselves primarily with questions of religion and the afterlife, humanists concentrated on everyday human problems and relationships. The secular nature of humanism, as well as its questioning attitude, often brought it into conflict with the traditional teachings of the Catholic Church and of medieval thinking.

Accomplishments of the Renaissance

LITERATURE Although early humanists wrote in classical Latin, others began writing in the vernacular, or language of the people. This change, along with the invention of the printing press in the 1400s, encouraged learning and spread the ideas of humanism. Important and influential Renaissance authors include:

- **Niccolò Machiavelli** (1469–1527) of Florence wrote a handbook for rulers called *The Prince*. He promoted the idea of "power politics," arguing that "the end justifies the means" in gaining and keeping power. His realistic and sometimes ruthless approach to politics became a model for future leaders.
- **William Shakespeare** (1564–1616), an English playwright and poet, is considered to be one of the greatest writers of all time. In plays such as *Romeo and Juliet*, he explored the depths of human emotions and relationships.

MAKING CONNECTIONS

Key Concepts: Culture The travels of such European traders and missionaries as Marco Polo and John de Plano Carpini within the Mongol Empire vastly increased European knowledge of China, India, and the East Indies and helped prepare Europeans for overseas expansion.

History and Society The humanistic spirit of the Renaissance emphasized individual uniqueness and worth.

History and Society Although the printing press helped spread humanism by making books widely available, it also promoted the spread of traditional religious learning. Gutenberg's first printed book was the Bible, which remains the most widely published book in the world.

MAKING CONNECTIONS

ART In both sculpture and painting, Renaissance artists employed the Greco-Roman style and humanist themes. When dealing with religious subjects, a realistic approach was used rather than the two-dimensional style of the Middle Ages. Outstanding Renaissance artists include:

- **Leonardo da Vinci** (1452–1519) is considered to be a true "Renaissance person," an individual with an interest and talents in many areas. Today he is recognized as a genius who made contributions as an inventor, scientist, sculptor, architect, and painter. Best known among his artistic works are *The Last Supper* and the *Mona Lisa*.
- **Michelangelo** (1475–1564) also left behind an extraordinary legacy. His sculptures include *David* and the *Pietà*. He designed the dome of St. Peter's Basilica in Rome and painted biblical scenes on the ceiling of the Sistine Chapel.

Regents Tip List some historical causes of the Renaissance in Europe. (An example has been listed.) Cultural contacts with the Middle East after the Crusades

SCIENCE The curiosity encouraged by humanist philosophy led to scientific progress. During the thirteenth century, a monk named Roger Bacon encouraged the use of reason to solve problems. He developed a scientific method based on observation and experimentation. Renaissance scientists adopted these ideas and made discoveries that challenged existing theories. Since Renaissance science changed the way people looked at the world, it is sometimes considered the start of a **Scientific Revolution**. Leading Renaissance scientists include:

- **Nicolaus Copernicus** (1473–1543) developed the heliocentric theory. Using mathematical formulas, he determined that the sun, not the earth, was the center of the universe.
- **Galileo Galilei** (1564–1642) improved the telescope and thereby produced evidence to support the claims of Copernicus. Church leaders, who had taught for centuries that the sun revolved around the earth, were unwilling to allow what they perceived as a challenge to their authority. Galileo was tried as a **heretic**, a Christian who disagrees with official Church doctrine, and forced to admit his "error." Despite such opposition from the Church, scientific progress continued.

THE PROTESTANT REFORMATION (1517–1650)

The Protestant Reformation was a challenge to the Roman Catholic Church. Many people objected to certain teachings and practices of the Church and attempted to reform, or change, them. In 1517, a German monk named **Martin Luther** posted a list of complaints against the Church called the **Ninety-Five Theses**, or questions for debate. Luther condemned the Church's practice of selling **indulgences**, pardons for sins, claiming that religious faith alone guaranteed salvation. He believed that the Bible was the supreme religious authority on earth. He translated the New Testament into German and encouraged people to read and interpret it for themselves. In rejecting the power of the pope and his priests, Luther made the final break with the Church. The pope declared Luther a heretic and excommunicated him.

Through the use of the printing press, Luther's ideas spread and he gained many followers. Gradually, a new worship service and a religion that followed Luther's ideas developed. Lutheranism, the name given to the religion, spread from the German states to the Scandinavian countries and to some parts of central Europe.

MAKING CONNECTIONS

History and Society The Reformation ended western Europe's religious unity.

Underlying Causes of the Reformation

- *The Renaissance*, based on the philosophy of humanism, led people to question the authority of the Church and to place greater faith in human reason.
- *The rise of nation states* led some monarchs to resent the power of the pope in their countries. A growing sense of **nationalism** prompted people to feel more loyal to their king than to the pope.
- *Economic restrictions* such as the ban on usury, or lending money at interest, created opposition among members of the new middle class. People also resented the tithe, the 10 percent tax on income.
- *Worldliness and corruption within the Church* caused a crisis of faith among believers.

Key Concepts: Power During the Reformation a European social order based on the power and authority of the Church was challenged by nation-states and individuals.

Results of the Reformation

FORMATION OF NEW CHRISTIAN RELIGIONS Others followed the example of Luther and established their own religions. Religions that denied the universal authority of the pope and rested on the Bible as the source of truth were called **Protestant**.

- **John Calvin** established a religion based on the ideas of **predestination** and the **theory of the elect**. Predestination meant that whatever happened to a person after death was determined beforehand by God, and nothing could be done to change it. The elect, or those who would be saved from punishment for sins, would be known by their

MAKING CONNECTIONS

moral lives and by the success they achieved through hard work. Calvin's ideas became popular, especially among the middle class who saw success in business as a sign of salvation.

- **Henry VIII of England** was not a true religious reformer, yet he broke from the Catholic Church and the pope. After divorcing his wife to marry a woman he hoped would bear him a male heir, Henry VIII was excommunicated. Supported by his people, he convinced Parliament to pass the **Act of Supremacy** in 1534. This act created a **national religion**, the Anglican Church of England, with the English monarch as its head. Though the Anglican Church preserved many traditional Catholic beliefs and practices, it had differences.

Key Concepts: Culture Latin remained the language of the Christian Church in western Europe long after it disappeared as the language of the common people. It is still used by the Roman Catholic Church for official pronouncements.

GREATER POWER FOR CIVIL AUTHORITIES The Protestant Reformation enabled monarchs and civil governments to increase their power at the expense of the Catholic Church. The Church, though remaining an important institution, would never again enjoy the position it had during the Middle Ages. This was partly due to the fact that religious unity in Europe had ended, and the Church had lost many followers.

RELIGIOUS WARS Religious differences led to a century of warfare. For example, in 1588 Protestant England engaged in a naval war with Catholic Spain. Although the difference in religion was a major cause of the conflict, competition for trade and rivalry for power also were factors. An attempted invasion of England resulted in the defeat and near destruction of the **Spanish Armada**. Through victory over Spain, Queen Elizabeth I preserved Protestantism in England and helped her country to become a major world power. Other conflicts, such as the civil wars in Germany and France and the Thirty Year's War (1618–1648), began as religious conflicts but had political overtones. Through these wars, rulers attempted to increase and consolidate their own power and that of their countries.

Regents Tip Briefly describe the effect the Reformation had on political and social stability in western Europe.

The Counter Reformation

In order to stop the spread of Protestant religions, the Catholic Church attempted a Counter Reformation. For example, in 1545 the pope convened the **Council of Trent**. Over a number of years, Church officials confirmed certain teachings, such as the supremacy of the pope, that had been attacked. They also instituted reforms such as ending the sale of indulgences. The Index, a list of books Catholics were forbidden to read, was created by the council to prevent the spread of heresy, or anti-Church statements. Despite these moves, the Counter Reformation was unable to restore the former membership, power, and prestige of the Church.

AGE OF EXPLORATION AND COLONIZATION (1450–1750)

Two forces encouraged Europeans to undertake voyages of exploration in the fifteenth century: (1) a desire to find a new route to the riches of Asia and (2) a curiosity about the world inspired by the Crusades, the Renaissance, and the tales of travelers such as **Marco Polo**. Exploration was made possible by technological advances, such as the **compass** and the **astrolabe**, which made ocean navigation more exact. Other developments, including the use of **gunpowder**, made Europeans more confident to venture outside established borders and trade routes.

The Search for an All-Water Route

European desire for goods from the East grew as a result of the Crusades. But long and difficult trade routes made goods expensive and demand for goods hard to satisfy. The fall of Constantinople to the Muslims in 1453 added even more danger for merchants. These factors pushed countries into searching for a less expensive and safer all-water route to Asia.

Italian cities, which had a monopoly on the existing Mediterranean trade, had little interest in investing in risky sea explorations. The new nation states of western Europe had more desire to find a new trade route. Portugal and Spain, located on the Iberian Peninsula, led the way in exploration.

PORTUGAL **Prince Henry the Navigator** set up a school for sailors, got financing for expeditions, and sent explorers down the coast of Africa. In 1488, **Bartholomeu Dias** reached the southern tip of Africa, later called the Cape of Good Hope. In 1498, **Vasco da Gama** rounded the cape and reached India. The all-water route, though long, was easier, safer, and far more profitable than the overland routes.

SPAIN Queen Isabella, motivated by goals of power, wealth, and the spread of Christianity, sponsored the voyage of **Christopher Columbus**. He hoped to find a route to the East by sailing west. In 1492, he discovered what became known as the "New World," inhabited by people he mistakenly called "Indians." In 1519, Spain backed **Ferdinand Magellan**, whose crew completed the first **circumnavigation** of the earth.

Establishment of Colonial Empires

The discovery of new lands encouraged the European nations to set up **colonies**, foreign territories controlled by, and often exploited by, a stronger nation. Spain, Portugal, England, France, and Holland were the leading colonial powers during the seventeenth and eighteenth centuries. The building of empires had several important effects.

MAKING CONNECTIONS

Key Concepts: Change The Age of Exploration marks the end of an era of European regional isolation and the beginning of European global domination in much of Latin America, Africa, Southeast Asia, and China that lasted into the twentieth century.

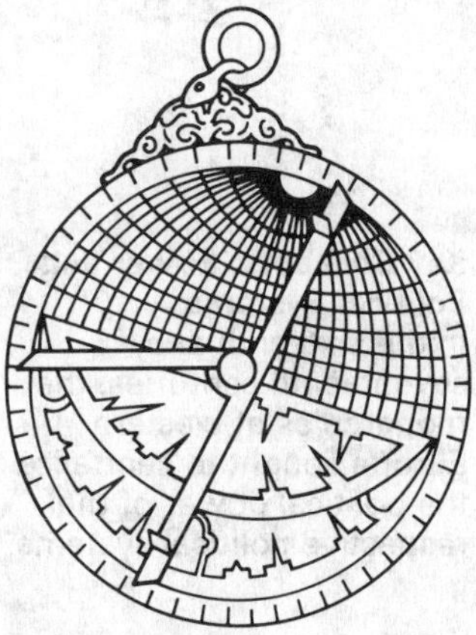

This instrument, the astrolabe, was used to calculate the exact latitude of one's ship.

History For more on Christopher Columbus and the exploration of the Western Hemisphere, see the section on Latin America in this unit.

History and Economics Raw materials obtained from colonies spurred the economic development of western Europe.

MAKING CONNECTIONS

- Overseas expansion led to increased power and wealth for European nations, but competition for colonies eventually led to war among them.
- Christianity and the culture of western Europe were spread throughout the world.
- The ethnocentric attitude of the Europeans resulted in the mistreatment of native peoples. Europeans regarded the cultures of the New World as inferior and attempted to change or destroy their civilizations. The Mayas, the Aztecs, and the Incas were almost totally wiped out by the Europeans.

History For more on the African slave trade, see the section on Africa in this unit.

- The trans-Atlantic slave trade brought millions of Africans to the Americas against their will. This violation of human rights had a harmful effect on the development of African civilizations. It also created a legacy of bitterness among Africans and the descendants of slaves.

THE AGE OF ABSOLUTISM (1500–1789)

Key Concepts: Power and Political Systems
In the sixteenth and seventeenth centuries, the monarchies of western Europe sought to centralize the political power of their respective political systems.

The Age of Absolutism was a period of European history in which almost all nations were ruled by monarchs who had total power. The governments of these nations were **autocracies**, and their leaders were called **absolute monarchs**.

Theory of Divine Right

Many monarchs justified their use of power with an idea known as the **divine right** of kings. James I of England (1603–1625) explained this idea by saying: "The king is from God and the law is from the king." In other words, the king was the agent of God on earth and laws made by the king had to be obeyed. This theory was similar to the Chinese Mandate of Heaven. However, the Chinese emperor lost the mandate if he ruled unjustly, and the people had the right to overthrow him. According to the theory of divine right, the people had no rights. The king, who was above the law, could rule in any way he wished.

History For more about the Mandate of Heaven, see the section on China in this unit.

Case Study: Louis XIV of France

Louis XIV believed he had a divine right to rule and pursued policies that concentrated power in the monarchy. He was an able and ambitious ruler who is said to have proclaimed "L'etat, c'est moi" ("I am the state"), thus commanding the complete loyalty and obedience of the people. During a time when many French people did not have shelter or enough to eat, he built the lavish **Palace of Versailles** outside of Paris. He hosted huge banquets and encouraged his nobles to stay at Versailles so as to keep an eye on them.

The luxury and brilliance of his court, as well as his symbol, the sun, earned him the name "Sun King." As the name implies, he believed the destiny of France revolved around him the way the earth revolves around the sun. Under Louis XIV's direction, France became a center of culture and an important trading power. The gains made during this period were offset, however, by the extravagance of his court and the numerous, costly wars he waged. When he died in 1715, he left a legacy of absolute rule, social unrest, and economic debt that would lead to revolution.

MAKING CONNECTIONS

THE GROWTH OF DEMOCRACY IN ENGLAND

Regents Tip Briefly explain how the political system in England encouraged the gradual growth of democracy.

While most of Europe was experiencing absolutism, England was undergoing an evolutionary change to democracy. Rule by the people came gradually, in a series of steps, until a **limited constitutional monarchy** was established.

Magna Carta (1215)

Signed by King John, the Magna Carta became the basis of English democracy. It limited the power of the king by law, forcing him to consult the legislature, or Parliament, in order to raise taxes.

Puritan Revolution (1642–1649)

During the 1600s, the **Stuart** rulers—James I and Charles I—attempted to rule as absolute monarchs. They disregarded the law and Parliament. In 1642, civil war broke out over the issue of absolutism and divine right. The Puritan forces in Parliament defeated the armies of Charles I, and the king was subsequently tried and executed. Between 1649 and 1660, the English experimented with a **republican** form of government, led by **Oliver Cromwell**. Following the death of Cromwell, the people decided to restore a limited monarchy to England.

Glorious Revolution (1688–1689)

James II was an unpopular ruler. He was a Catholic and believed in the divine right of kings. In a bloodless revolution, the people drove him from power. He was replaced by William and Mary, his daughter and son-in-law, who agreed to share their power with the people. The Glorious Revolution ensured that future monarchs would be Anglican and their powers would be limited.

English Bill of Rights (1689)

The English Bill of Rights placed further limits on the power of the king to tax and make laws. It also listed basic civil liberties of the people, including the right to a fair and speedy trial by jury. It became the model for the United States, which adopted a similar measure in 1791.

Key Concepts: Power The traditions of sharing political power and natural law, which date back to the Greek and Roman periods, were expressed in such documents as the Magna Carta and the English Bill of Rights, which limited royal absolutism.

The evolutionary changes that established democracy in England continued beyond 1689. In the centuries that followed, England became more democratic while the monarchy became less powerful, eventually being reduced to a figurehead.

MAKING CONNECTIONS

THE COMMERCIAL REVOLUTION

Overseas expansion, resulting from the voyages of exploration, helped to bring about a Commercial Revolution in Europe.

History and Economics By investing in overseas colonies, many capitalists helped expand Europe's global domination.

DEVELOPMENT OF CAPITALISM Increased trade and a greater supply of gold and silver taken from the New World led to the expansion of economic activities such as banking and investment. These activities were part of an economic system known as **capitalism**, which was based on the idea of private ownership of property. One result of the development of capitalism was the emergence of a middle class of merchants, businessmen, and bankers who eventually became a powerful force for change in Europe.

Key Concepts: Power Mercantilist policies strengthened the power of Europe's absolute monarchs.

MERCANTILISM During the 1600s, governments began to exert more control over economic affairs. The new economic policy of **mercantilism** was adopted by most European nations, which served to strengthen the absolute monarchies. Mercantilism stated that a country's power was measured by its wealth in gold and silver. It encouraged strict government control of the economy in order to create a **favorable balance of trade**, that is, to export more than import. Under this system, the government would promote domestic industry, place tariffs on imports, and obtain colonies to be used as sources of raw materials and markets. Competition for trade and colonies often led to wars such as the **French and Indian War** (1754–1763), in which France lost most of its North American possessions.

Key Concepts: Culture and Change Western Europe, unlike the cultures of the East, had all the preconditions necessary to achieve the transition from an agrarian economy to a capitalist one, including the existence of a class of merchants and bankers powerful enough to initiate change.

Effects of Mercantilism

- Strict mercantilist policies fostered resentment in the colonies. Such resentment was one of the chief causes of the American Revolution against England in 1775.
- The European middle class became dissatisfied with mercantilist policies. In France, for example, the **bourgeoisie** felt they could make more money with fewer restrictions. Since they lacked the political power to change government policy, the middle class grew increasingly discontented and anxious for an end to absolute rule.

History and Society The findings of the Scientific Revolution represent a secularization of scientific inquiry and a revolt against traditional authority. In addition, it represented a new approach to problem solving that set the West apart from other regions of the world.

THE ENLIGHTENMENT/AGE OF REASON (1500–1800)

The **Enlightenment** was an eighteenth century movement among writers and intellectuals that was inspired by the Scientific Revolution. The writers of the Enlightenment applied the scientific method of observation and investigation to problems they found in society. They challenged traditional authority and encouraged the improvement of society through the use of reason. Since the Enlightenment advocated changes in the existing system, it was supported by the bourgeoisie and opposed by the nobility and clergy.

Ideas Proposed by Enlightenment Thinkers

- **Democracy**, or rule by the people, as an alternative to absolutism, which denied people their basic natural rights
- **Laissez-faire capitalism**, an economic system in which the government has little control, as an alternative to mercantilism, which restricted free enterprise. **Laissez faire** is French for "Let people do as they choose."

Leaders of the Enlightenment

John Locke, author of *Two Treatises on Government* (1690), was actually a forerunner of the Enlightenment. Writing in defense of England's Glorious Revolution, Locke declared that all people have **natural rights** to life, liberty, and property. He further claimed that people had a contract with the king to protect those rights. Locke argued that the king got his power to rule from the people, who were entitled to rebel if he failed to rule in their interest. This concept of "government by the consent of the governed," was used to justify the American and French Revolutions.

The **philosophes** were a mostly French group of thinkers at the heart of the Enlightenment. They included the following writers:

- **Voltaire**, leader of the philosophes and author of *Letters on the English*, favored the idea of a limited monarchy. He fought against discrimination and intolerance, particularly on the part of the Catholic Church. His outlook can be summed up in the phrase "I may disapprove of what you say, but I will defend to the death your right to say it."
- **Jean Jacques Rousseau**, author of *The Social Contract*, believed in the equality of all people. He favored government based on the "general will," or the desires of the majority. Rousseau condemned political and social restrictions by stating, "Man is born free, and everywhere is in chains."
- **Baron de Montesquieu** In *The Spirit of Laws*, Montesquieu encouraged the separation of governmental power into three branches—judicial, legislative, and executive—in order to prevent dictatorship. This idea became part of the Constitution of the United States.

MAKING CONNECTIONS

History and Economics
For more about laissez-faire capitalism, see Unit 4, Global Economics.

Key Concepts: Power
Europe's middle class rejected the medieval class structure, which denied them political power. They insisted upon their right to participate in a government controlled by an elected representative legislature.

Regents Tip List the key idea associated with each of the following Enlightenment thinkers. (An example has been listed.)

Isaac Newton: law of gravity
John Locke:

Voltaire:

Jean Jacques Rousseau:

Baron de Montesquieu:

Population and Land Ownership in France, 1789

Percentage of Population by Estate

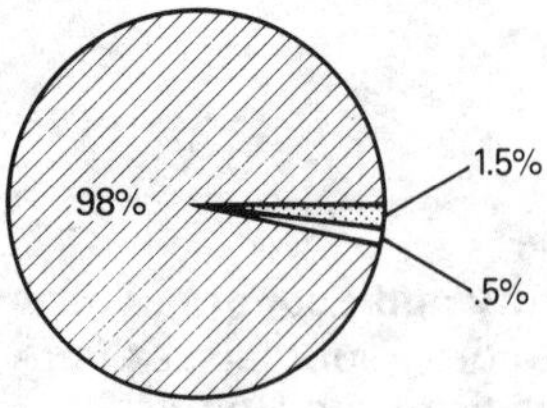

Percentage of Land Owned by Estate

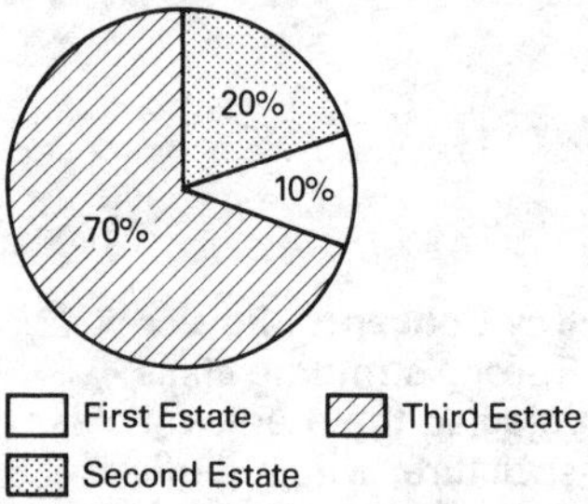

Approximate figures

The Enlightenment resulted in greater religious tolerance and some social reform. More dramatically, it inspired revolutions in America (1775), France (1789), and Latin America (nineteenth century).

THE FRENCH REVOLUTION (1789–1799)

By 1789, France was bankrupt. The national debt that resulted from the wars of Louis XIV had grown larger under his successors, creating a severe economic crisis. The inability of Louis XVI to deal effectively with this crisis, provided the spark that ignited revolution. The violence that erupted in 1789 was, however, centuries in the making.

Underlying Causes of the French Revolution

Political

- **Absolutism** The kings of France ruled with total power and denied the people their rights. Opposition was not tolerated. Enemies of the king were jailed without trial.
- **The Enlightenment** Writers pointed out the abuses of the Old Regime—the economic, social, and political system that supported absolutism. They called for a change to democracy.
- **Successful revolutions** The example of England's Glorious Revolution and the American Revolution inspired the French to challenge the existing authorities.

Social

- **Rigid social classes**, or **estates**, created inequality and limited social mobility. The First and Second Estates, made up of the Roman Catholic clergy and the French nobility, accounted for only two percent of the population. However, they received rights and privileges denied to the majority in the Third Estate, who were the middle class, peasants, and city workers.
- **Rise of the bourgeoisie**, a wealthy and educated middle class. They resented their lack of status and, inspired by the Enlightenment, became leaders of the revolution.

Economic

- **Unfair taxes** fell heaviest on the Third Estate, causing discontent among peasants, city workers, and the bourgeoisie.
- **Restrictive mercantilist laws** caused the bourgeoisie to lose profits.

Key Concepts: Change
The American and French revolutions represented a basic change in the western relationship between government and the governed. With these two revolutions, the West moved toward a more democratic system in which the equality and human rights of citizens were recognized and the power of government was based not upon divine right but upon the consent of the governed.

Stages of the French Revolution

The stages of the French Revolution represent the changes in leadership and the shifting of power during this period.

STAGE ONE (1789) The financial crisis forced Louis XVI to call a meeting of the French Parliament. Known as the **Estates General**, it had not met in over 150 years. Representatives of the Third Estate used this opportunity to demand the creation of a more democratic National Assembly. The king rejected their demands and ordered them to disband. Locked out of their meeting hall, the new National Assembly met on a tennis court. In what became known as the **Tennis Court Oath**, they vowed to stay together until they had a new constitution. Upon hearing rumors that the king intended to send troops to break up the National Assembly, mobs stormed and captured the **Bastille**, a former jail for political prisoners. Its capture symbolized the end of the Old Regime and signaled the start of the revolution.

STAGE TWO (1789–1791) The **National Assembly** was a provisional, or temporary, government that instituted a series of reforms.

- Adopted the *Declaration of the Rights of Man*, a document based on the ideas found in the English Bill of Rights and the American Declaration of Independence. It stated that "men are born free and remain free and equal in rights."
- Ended all special privileges of the clergy and nobility
- Wrote the Constitution of 1791, which established a limited monarchy

STAGE THREE (1791–1792) The **limited monarchy** was a government in which the king shared his power with a Legislative Assembly dominated by the bourgeoisie. Since the government faced opposition within France and pressure from outside France, this period was unstable.

Radicals, called **Jacobins**, favored more extreme change. They wanted to abolish the monarchy entirely and establish a **republic** dominated by the working classes. They were led by **Georges Danton**, **Jean Marat**, and **Maximilien Robespierre**.

Neighboring countries invaded France in 1792 in order to stop the spread of the revolution. This action intensified French nationalism and many people rallied in defense of the revolution and its goals of "liberty, equality, fraternity." The Limited Monarchy came to an end when Louis XVI, accused of treason, was arrested and executed as the birth of the republic was announced.

STAGE FOUR (1792–1795) During this period, the radical Jacobins seized power and established the Committee of Public Safety. The Jacobins used all means possible to safeguard the revolution. They instituted the first draft in European history. The execution of the king had brought on more invasions, and an army was needed to meet the threat. Nationalist spirit ensured its success.

The Committee of Public Safety began a **Reign of Terror** in which those suspected of opposing the revolution were executed.

MAKING CONNECTIONS

Key Concepts: Citizenship Throughout the world, the American and French revolutions have served as models for political action by those seeking to participate in the full rights and privileges of democratic citizenship.

Regents Tip Summarize the stages of the French Revolution.

Stage One:

Stage Two:

Stage Three:

Stage Four:

Stage Five:

MAKING CONNECTIONS

Marie Antoinette, wife of Louis XVI, was among the thousands that died on the **guillotine** during one year, 1793. The terror that was designed to protect the revolution eventually caused the downfall of its radical leadership. Constant and excessive violence led the people to turn on the Jacobins.

STAGE FIVE (1795–1799) Following the Reign of Terror, moderates regained power. More cautious and less extreme than the radicals, they set up the **Directory**. Inefficient and weak, it was overthrown in a **coup d'état** by the brilliant and ambitious revolutionary general, **Napoleon Bonaparte**. Napoleon, though claiming to be a "true son of the Revolution," established a military dictatorship in France. His rule restored stability and ended the revolution.

THE REIGN OF NAPOLEON (1799–1815)

The Revolution had thrown France into chaos and disunity. The people therefore supported the absolute rule of Napoleon, believing that a strong ruler would return the country to normalcy. Napoleon took a number of steps to rebuild France:

Europe at the Height of Napoleon's Power, 1812

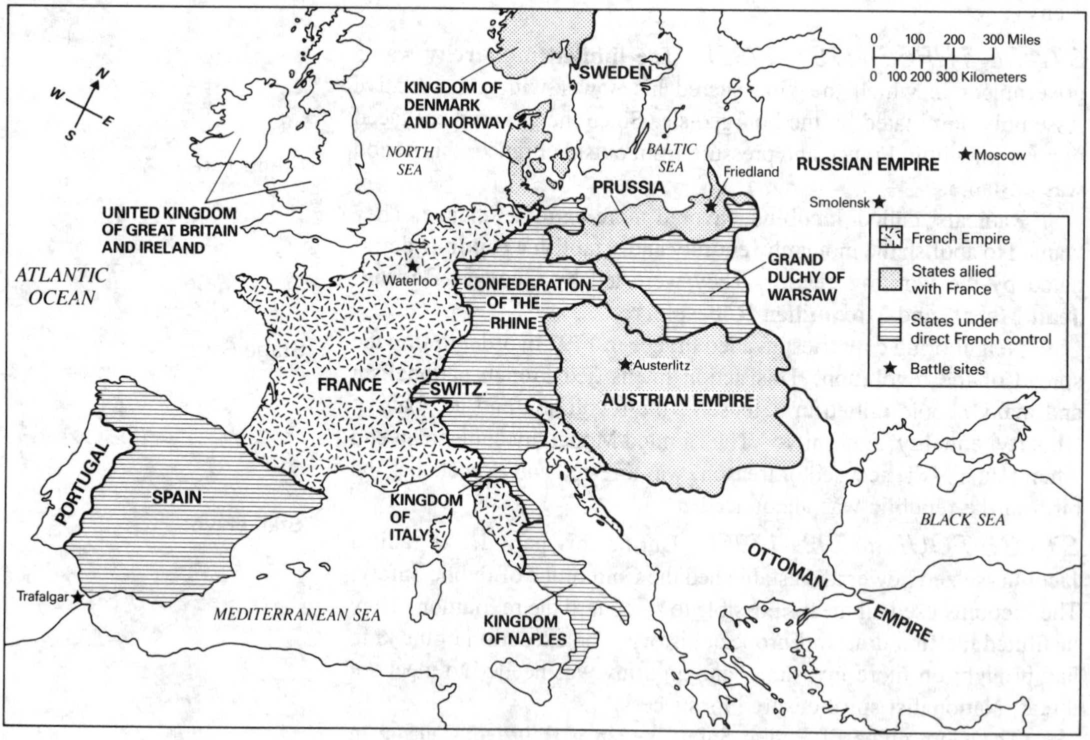

MAKING CONNECTIONS

- Set up an efficient, **centralized government** under his control. Although he restricted personal freedoms, he promoted such revolutionary goals as equality.
- Established the **Napoleonic Code**, a code of law that preserved revolutionary changes in the legal system. It guaranteed equal treatment before the law, trial by jury, and religious freedom.
- Strengthened the French economy through new tax laws and the creation of the Bank of France.
- Set up a system of public schools to encourage nationalism.

In addition to strengthening France from within, Napoleon created a great empire. By 1808, he dominated most of the European continent. The military might of France upset the **balance of power** in Europe. Other countries tried unsuccessfully to destroy Napoleon. In 1812, however, the disastrous invasion of Russia weakened Napoleon to the point where a strong alliance, led by England, was able to defeat him. He was exiled to St. Helena in 1815, where he died in 1821.

Effects of the French Revolution

- Ended absolutism in France. After the downfall of Napoleon, a limited monarchy was installed.
- Many of the reforms of Napoleon became permanent, such as the guarantee of social equality.
- Revolutionary ideas spread and inspired future struggles for "liberty, equality, fraternity."

History For information about the effect that the French and American revolutions had in Central and South America, see the section on Latin America in this unit.

CONGRESS OF VIENNA (1814–1815)

The **Congress of Vienna** was a meeting held by the leaders of Europe after the defeat of Napoleon. The goals of this group, led by Prince **Klemens von Metternich** of Austria, were **reactionary**. They wanted to return Europe to pre-revolutionary conditions. The armies of Napoleon had spread the ideas of liberty, equality, and fraternity, however, and people throughout Europe wanted to move forward, not backward. This conflict of interests resulted in revolutions by various groups (for example, Germans, Italians, Poles, and Greeks) from 1815 to 1848. Although most of these revolutions failed, the ideas of liberalism and nationalism that had inspired them did not die.

Key Concepts: Change Beginning in modern Europe but rapidly moving outward to other regions, nationalism and armed revolution have proved to be dynamic agents of change whose influence has helped to shape the destinies of people throughout the world.

GROWTH OF NATIONALISM

Nationalism, or strong devotion to one's country, is a feeling that develops within a group of people who share such things as common language, history, traditions, and goals for their country. Nationalism supports the idea of **self-determination**, which means that

MAKING CONNECTIONS

people of similar backgrounds have the right to join together in their own country and choose their own form of government, without outside interference. The growth of nationalism in the nineteenth century led to independence and unification movements throughout Europe.

Unification of Italy

Key Concepts: Political Systems
In Italy as in some other sections of Europe, nationalism was directed toward the overthrowing of foreign domination. In addition, it sought the installation of a unified, independent political system.

Italy in the early nineteenth century was a divided country, and much of it was dominated by Austria, its northern neighbor. Italian nationalism, rooted in the Roman Empire, had been reawakened by the armies of Napoleon. The goals of Italian nationalism, or "risorgimento," were unification and democracy.

The following leaders guided Italian nationalism:

- **Giuseppe Mazzini**, the "soul" of Italian unification, inspired nationalism through writings and speeches. He formed "Young Italy" in 1831, an organization dedicated to the removal of Austrian control and the establishment of an Italian **republic**.
- **Count Camillo Cavour**, the "brains" of Italian unification, orchestrated the plan that would unify Italy. In 1852, he became prime minister of Sardinia-Piedmont, a **limited monarchy** under King Victor Emanuel II. Sardinia-Piedmont represented democracy and became the center of the unification movement. As prime minister, Cavour formed an alliance with France in 1859 and then with Prussia in 1866, which allowed him to drive the Austrians out of northern Italy. This action inspired other Italians to rebel against their Austrian-dominated governments, and eventually to vote by **plebiscite** to join Sardinia-Piedmont.
- **Giuseppe Garibaldi**, the "sword" of Italian unification, organized an army called the "Red Shirts," which carried out a successful rebellion in the Kingdom of the Two Sicilies in 1860. In the spirit of nationalism, Garibaldi encouraged the people of Sicily to unite with Sardinia-Piedmont. He later joined with Cavour to take control of most of the Papal States, the Church-owned land in central Italy.

The formation of the Kingdom of Italy was announced in 1861, and King Victor Emmanuel II became its limited monarch. In 1870, French troops that had been guarding the pope in Rome were withdrawn to serve in the Franco-Prussian War. Italian troops took over the city and proclaimed it their capital. Although unification was complete, feelings of nationalism continued to grow. The desire on the part of many Italians for more territory and world power led to future conflicts.

History and Society
Before unification, Germany consisted of dozens of small principalities and kingdoms, linked mainly by a common language.

Unification of Germany

As in Italy, feelings of nationalism, aroused during the Napoleonic Wars, encouraged a movement to unite the German states. In

1848, **liberals** attempted to achieve unity and democracy. This attempt failed, and **conservatives** took control of the drive for unification. As a result, Germany was united under a strong, **autocratic** ruler.

OTTO VON BISMARCK The man who organized and carried out the plan for German unification was Otto von Bismarck, prime minister of Prussia, the strongest German state. Bismarck's approach to unification was a policy of "blood and iron," through which he created and used a powerful Prussian army to remove all obstacles to unity.

After the **Seven Weeks War** (1866), Austrian domination of the German states ended, and the northern states combined into a **confederation**. In order to provide a reason for the four southern states to join the north, Bismarck provoked France into declaring war on Prussia. During the **Franco-Prussian War** (1870–1871), the four southern states, compelled by feelings of nationalism, came to Prussia's aid, and eventually agreed to permanent unification. The Franco-Prussian War resulted in a humiliating defeat for France, for which the French people desired "revanche," or revenge.

THE GERMAN EMPIRE In 1871, the second German Empire, or Reich, was formed (the first had been the Holy Roman Empire). The government of Germany was **authoritarian**; power rested with Kaiser Wilhelm I and his chief minister, Bismarck. Under the direction of Bismarck, the "Iron Chancellor," Germany pursued policies of nationalism, militarism, industrialization, and social reform. A clever diplomat, Bismarck was able to prevent France from forming alliances. Isolated, France was unable to pose a threat to Germany, which continued to grow in strength, power, and confidence in alliance with Austria and Italy.

In 1888, a new Kaiser, Wilhelm II, came to the throne. Young and unwilling to share his power, he forced Bismarck to resign. Lacking Bismarck's skill, Wilhelm's policies gave France the opportunity to form alliances with Russia (1894) and England (1904). With the existence of two opposing alliances in Europe, the stage was set for the outbreak of World War I.

MAKING CONNECTIONS

History and Politics
Bismarck's policies became the foundation for the totalitarian Nazi regime that came to power in Germany after World War I.

THE INDUSTRIAL REVOLUTION (1750–1914)

The Industrial Revolution was one of the most significant events in history. During this period, the creation of new inventions, the development of the factory system, and the expansion of business took place. Industrialization changed the way goods were made, but it also resulted in profound economic, social, and political changes that affected the lives of people around the world.

The Industrial Revolution began in England in the mid-eighteenth century. England had certain advantages that helped to bring about industrialization.

MAKING CONNECTIONS

Regents Tip Briefly describe the major changes that resulted from each of the following revolutions.

Commercial Revolution:

The Intellectual Revolution known as the Enlightenment:

French Revolution:

Industrial Revolution:

NATURAL RESOURCES England had an abundance of coal and iron ore, two of the basic ingredients for industrialization.

FAVORABLE GEOGRAPHIC CONDITIONS As an island with an irregular coastline, England had many natural harbors. Navigable rivers served both as transportation routes and sources of power for factories.

COLONIAL EMPIRE England's colonies provided raw materials (such as cotton for textile factories) and markets for finished products (such as fabric and clothing).

CAPITAL Wealthy merchants had money to invest in new businesses and expanding industries.

LABOR SUPPLY In the late seventeenth century, Parliament passed the **Enclosure Acts**, which fenced off the "common lands" and deprived small farmers of land. Many of these unemployed farmers went to the cities to work in the factories.

The contributions of various inventors laid the groundwork for economic growth and the expansion of the Industrial Revolution.

Key Inventions of the Industrial Revolution

Inventors	Invention
James Watt (England)	**Steam Engine** (1775) The first successful use of steam as a source of power meant that factories no longer had to be built along rivers.
Robert Fulton (United States)	**Steamboat** (1807) The *Clermont* was the first commercially successful steamboat. Soon steam-powered boats and ships carried materials and goods on both rivers and oceans.
George Stephenson (England)	**Steam Locomotive** (1814)/**Locomotive Train** (1829) Trains provided a faster and easier means of moving goods across land.
Michael Faraday (England)	**Dynamo** (1831) The electrical generator provided a new source of power. The use of electricity affected not only manufacturing, but everyday life as well.
Henry Bessemer (England)	**Process for Making Steel** (1856) Steel became the most important metal used in industrialization.

Effects of the Industrial Revolution

As the Industrial Revolution spread across Europe and the United States, it brought about dramatic results.

Spread of Industry About 1870

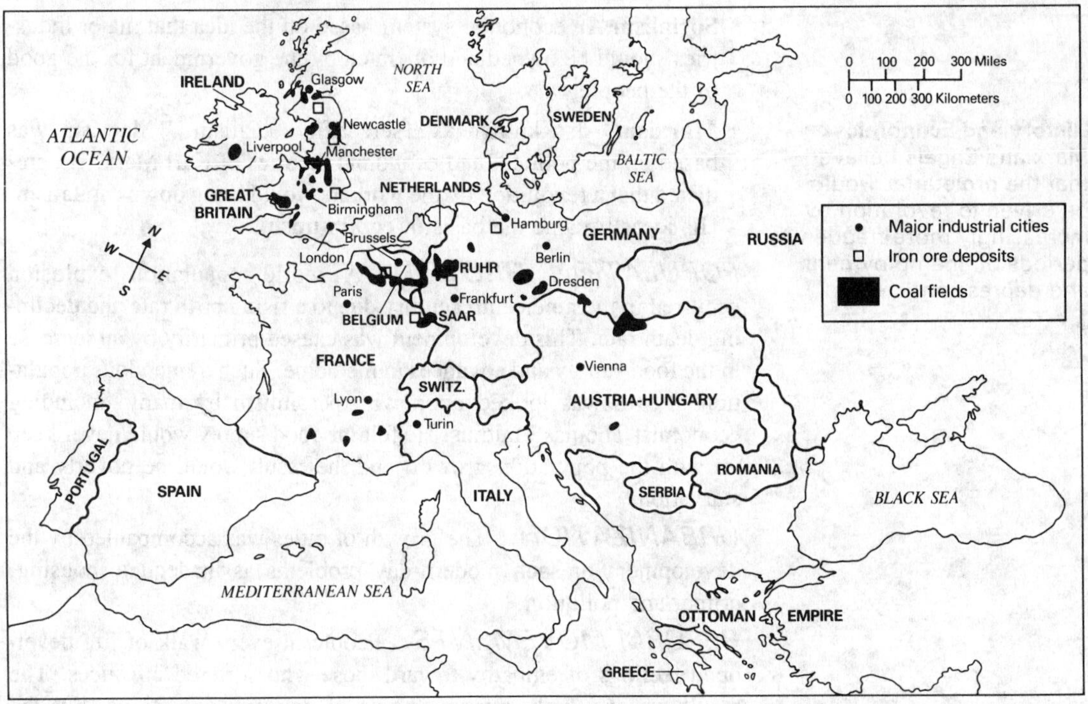

RISE OF THE FACTORY SYSTEM The method of manufacturing goods changed from the domestic system, in which work was done at home, to the factory system.

HIGHER STANDARD OF LIVING Due to the use of new methods such as mass production, division of labor, and the assembly line, prices came down and a greater amount and variety of goods became available to more people.

GROWTH OF CAPITALISM Capitalism expanded as governments adopted the idea of laissez faire and gave up much of their control over economic affairs.

CHANGES IN WORKING CONDITIONS In the early days of the Industrial Revolution, workers, including children, were subjected to unfair treatment—long hours, low pay, and poor working conditions. This situation gradually improved due to (1) the rise of labor unions to bargain with employers and (2) more government involvement in regulating working conditions. For example, the Sadler Commission was formed by the British Parliament in 1832 to investigate conditions in the factories. Various pieces of legislation were passed to end unfair practices. For example, the Factory Act of 1833 put limits on child labor in textile factories.

CHALLENGES TO CAPITALISM Different groups viewed capitalism as being unjust to the majority of people and developed alternatives.

MAKING CONNECTIONS

History and Society Many European novelists of the nineteenth century addressed the poor living and working conditions of those who labored under the factory system. Examples include Emile Zola's *Germinal* and Charles Dickens' *Oliver Twist* and *Hard Times.* Such works helped encourage reform.

MAKING CONNECTIONS

History and Economics
Marx and Engels believed that the proletariat would be driven to revolution by increasingly more frequent periods of unemployment and depression.

Key Concepts: Change, Power, and Political Systems
Changes in the European power structure brought about by the Industrial Revolution were reflected in the expansion of suffrage in European political systems throughout the late nineteenth and early twentieth centuries.

Alternatives to Capitalism

- **Socialism** An economic system based on the idea that major industries should be owned and operated by the government for the good of the people.
- **Marxism** Also known as "scientific socialism," Marxism was based on the political and economic theories of Karl Marx. He predicted that a revolution by the workers would bring down capitalism. His ideas became the basis of **communism**.

POPULATION GROWTH A world population explosion occurred in the nineteenth century due to a rising birth rate and declining death rate. This development was caused primarily by an increase in the food supply and advances in medicine. Such tremendous population growth was looked upon with pessimism by many, including economist Thomas Malthus. He felt the food supply would never keep up with the population growth, and the result would be poverty and starvation.

URBANIZATION The growth of cities was accompanied by the development of such modern-day problems as inadequate housing, crime, and pollution.

REFORM MOVEMENTS People in every walk of life developed feelings of empathy toward those who suffered injustices. The result was not only improvements in working conditions, but the growth of **humanitarianism**. Concern for the welfare of all people led to the abolition of slavery, public education, and improved treatment of the mentally ill.

EXTENSION OF DEMOCRACY The traditional social structure changed as a result of the growth of the middle and working classes. Concentration of these classes in the cities increased their power and furthered the development of democracy. In England, for example, the Reform Bill of 1832 extended suffrage, or the right to vote, to a large number of the middle class, thereby increasing their influence in government. By 1918, the right to vote had been extended to all adult males and, as a result of a feminist movement, all women were granted suffrage by 1928.

IMPERIALISM Industrializing countries attempted to gain colonies that would provide them with raw materials and markets. Competition for trade and colonies led to rivalry and war among the major powers.

AGE OF IMPERIALISM (1830–1914)

Imperialism is the domination by one country of the political, economic, or cultural life of another country or region in order to increase its own wealth and power. Imperialism during the period following the Age of Exploration (fifteenth–seventeenth centuries), when European countries acquired colonies to support mercantilism, can be called "old imperialism." In the nineteenth century, a new era of imperialism began, this time spurred on by the Industrial Revolution.

MAKING CONNECTIONS

Regents Tip Briefly describe each of the following historical movements and explain its effect on society.

Feudalism:

Nationalism:

Mercantilism:

Capitalism:

Imperialism:

Causes of Modern Imperialism

Political Causes

- Feelings of **nationalism** intensified throughout Europe during the nineteenth century. Nationalism in the extreme promotes the idea of national superiority. Industrialized countries therefore felt they had the right to take control of weaker areas.
- Countries attempted to increase their **power** through the control of more land and people.
- Imperialist activity involved shows of strength. Through such displays, countries gained the **respect** of other nations. The United States and Japan, for example, were imperialist in part because they wanted to be taken seriously as world powers.
- As the foreign affairs and trade practices of nations became global, countries tried to obtain **strategic military bases** from which to protect their interests.

Economic Causes

As a result of the Industrial Revolution, countries needed colonies for:

- **Raw materials** to feed the ever-increasing number of factories.
- **Markets** for finished products, since domestic markets could not consume all that was being produced.
- Places to **invest** surplus capital, based on the idea that an investment in an underdeveloped area would yield a greater profit.
- Places to send **surplus population**, which would alleviate domestic problems such as overcrowded cities and unemployment.

Social Causes

Many people believed in the words of the British poet **Rudyard Kipling**, who said it was the "white man's burden" to:

- Educate the people of the underdeveloped world.
- Spread the customs of what they perceived was a superior Western culture.
- Convert people to Christianity, since it was believed that the souls of nonbelievers would not be saved.

MAKING CONNECTIONS

Although many people were sincere in thinking that these goals would benefit the non-Western world, they revealed the **ethnocentric** attitude of the imperialist nations.

History For more on the effects of modern imperialism in Africa, India, Southeast Asia, and China, see the sections on these regions in this unit.

Effects of Modern Imperialism

The new era of imperialism brought about important and far-reaching effects. Through the creation of global empires, the imperial powers helped spread the Industrial Revolution and the capitalist system around the world. Christianity, western European languages, and organized systems of government were introduced in the colonies. Imperialism benefited underdeveloped regions through improved transportation, education, and medical care.

Imperialism also had its negative side. It undermined native cultures and exploited people and resources in undeveloped lands. Eventually, **colonial nationalist movements** developed to end imperial control. One such movement was the Boxer Rebellion in China. The most dangerous aspect of imperialism was competition among the colonial powers themselves. These rivalries held the potential for conflict and war.

WORLD WAR I (1914–1918)

In 1871, the balance of power changed in Europe. France had been defeated in the Franco-Prussian War and Italy and Germany had joined the competition among nations in Western Europe. The new era of imperialism intensified the competition until global conflict finally erupted in 1914.

Causes of World War I

The underlying causes of World War I revolved primarily around the European rivalries.

MILITARISM The buildup of strong armies caused fear and suspicion in Europe. Nations generally believed that war was a legitimate way to handle a crisis if diplomacy failed. There was no worldwide forum to help countries settle disputes.

Key Concepts: Power The economic rivalry between Great Britain and Germany poisoned relations between the two powers and ultimately led to war.

NAVALISM England's status as the number one naval power was being challenged by Germany. This contest, in addition to economic competition, led to a hostile relationship between the two countries.

NATIONALISM Nationalistic feelings contributed to the outbreak of war in a number of ways.

- Devotion to country led people to support the policies of their governments, even if that meant war.
- France, whose national pride had been hurt as a result of the Franco-Prussian War, wanted revenge against Germany, which had taken the French provinces of Alsace-Lorraine.

- Ethnic minorities, such as the **Slavic** people of eastern Europe, wanted unity and independence. Austria-Hungary attempted to stop the spread of these nationalistic ideas since they threatened the existence of the empire.

IMPERIALISM Competition for trade and colonies resulted in tense relationships between nations. In Europe, major powers, especially Russia and Austria-Hungary, became rivals for the **Balkans**, a region of southeastern Europe. Intense foreign interest in the area, combined with the desire of the Slavic people for their own unified and independent country, transformed the Balkans into the "powderkeg of Europe."

SYSTEM OF ALLIANCES In an effort to maintain a balance of power in Europe, the major powers created opposing alliances. By 1907, Europe was divided into the **Triple Entente** (Great Britain, France, Russia) and the **Triple Alliance** (Germany, Austria-Hungary, Italy). The existence of these alliances, whose terms were kept secret, turned a regional conflict into a world war.

Immediate Cause of the War

The spark that set off the "powderkeg" was the assassination of **Austrian Archduke Franz Ferdinand** in June of 1914. The assassin was a member of the **Black Hand**, a Serbian nationalist group. Serbia was a leader in the pan-Slavic movement to unite all Slavic people into their own country.

Germany gave Austria-Hungary a "blank check" in whatever action it wanted to take in revenge for the assassination. Backed by its ally, Austria-Hungary decided on war, seeing it as an easy way to get Balkan territory. Russia, the "big brother of the Slavs," was pledged to support Serbia. The crisis became an international conflict when war was declared and the system of alliances went into effect. The members of the Triple Entente led the **Allies**, a group that grew to over 20 nations. Germany and Austria-Hungary became part of the **Central Powers**. Italy declined to enter the war in 1914 since it viewed Germany as the aggressor. In 1915, however, Italy joined the Allies with the hope of gaining Austrian land.

The Course of the War

World War I was the first modern war. Countries made use of the advances in military technology that resulted from the Industrial Revolution. Weapons such as machine guns, grenades, poison gas, and flame throwers killed millions and changed the nature of war forever.

TRENCH WARFARE Although World War I was a global conflict, involving countries and colonies all over the world, the main theaters of combat were in eastern Europe and along a western front in France and Belgium. The failure of Germany to win a complete and

MAKING CONNECTIONS

Key Concepts: Diversity and Political Systems
The ferment of nationalism among the diverse ethnic groups of eastern Europe weakened the political system of Austria-Hungary and became a major factor leading to war.

Key Concepts: Power
The attempt to maintain a balance of power by means of opposing alliance systems escalated limited regional crises into major international incidents.

MAKING CONNECTIONS

History For more on the Russian Revolution, see the next section in this unit.

History and Politics The Germans' policy of using their submarines to sink the ships of neutral nations suspected of carrying supplies for the Allies contributed to the entry of the United States into the war. U.S. intervention had a profound effect on the isolationist tradition in the United States and set the stage for future interventionism in European affairs.

Regents Tip List several causes and results of World War I. (Examples have been listed.)

Causes: Economic rivalry between Britain and Germany

Results: Breakup of German and Austro-Hungarian empires

decisive victory produced a stalemate in the West. The method of fighting became known as trench warfare, since opposing armies dug in on either side of a "no man's land" over which they fought.

RUSSIAN WITHDRAWAL On the eastern front, Russia experienced heavy losses and by 1917 inadequately supplied soldiers began deserting in large numbers. This situation helped lead to the Russian Revolution, and the new Communist leadership subsequently pulled Russia out of the war. Russian withdrawal allowed Germany to concentrate only on the western front, but American participation in the war on the side of the Allies presented a new problem for Germany.

UNITED STATES ENTRY The United States declared war on Germany in April of 1917. Although it had tried to remain neutral, the United States was pushed into the war by Germany's use of **unrestricted submarine warfare**. President Woodrow Wilson felt that freedom of the seas and the rights of neutrals were issues worth fighting over. He also feared that a victory by the autocratic Germany would pose a threat to democracy. America's entrance into the war allowed the Allies to take the offensive until Germany agreed to an armistice. The fighting ended on November 11, 1918.

The Treaty of Versailles (1919)

The victorious Allies gathered at Versailles in France to work out the terms of peace. At the conference, the major decisions were made by the "Big Four"—the leaders of Great Britain, France, Italy, and the United States. Of the four Allied leaders, President Wilson of the United States was alone in not wanting to punish Germany or gain territory.

THE FOURTEEN POINTS Wilson presented his idealistic plans for peace called the Fourteen Points. His ideas included arms reduction, guaranteed freedom of the seas, and the right of self-determination for all nationalities. An essential part of his proposal was the formation of a League of Nations to help settle disputes and prevent future wars. Wilson was looked upon as a dreamer, and many of his ideas were ignored in the creation of the actual treaty.

TERMS OF THE TREATY OF VERSAILLES The provisions of the treaty applied to Germany alone:

- **Loss of Territory** Germany lost land, some of which was used to help create the new country of Poland.
- **Loss of colonies** German colonies were taken by the League of Nations and became "mandates" of the Allies, to be prepared for independence.
- **Disarmament** Germany's army and navy were drastically reduced. In addition, no troops were allowed in the Rhineland, an

Europe After World War I

MAKING CONNECTIONS

industrial area along the French border. War industries were shut down.

- **War Guilt Clause** Germany was forced to accept full responsibility for the war and to pay for the damages. Having to accept blame and pay reparations hurt national pride and caused much bitterness among the Germans.
- **League of Nations** The Treaty approved the formation of an international peacekeeping organization. Ironically, the United States Senate thought that participation in the League would involve the United States in future European conflicts, and therefore it signed a separate treaty with Germany. The United States never became a member of the League, and this lack of support contributed to the organization's weakness in enforcing the terms of the treaty.

MAKING CONNECTIONS

Other Treaties

As a result of treaties with other members of the Central Powers, Austria-Hungary was divided, and both countries had to limit their armies and pay reparations. Any future union between Austria and Germany ("anschluss") was forbidden. In an effort to carry out the ideal of **self-determination** (all people have the right to their own country and to choose their own government), new nations were created from territory taken from the Central Powers and Russia.

THE RISE OF NAZI TOTALITARIANISM

Germany's defeat in World War I led to the collapse of the Kaiser's government. In 1918, the **Weimar Republic** was established, despite the fact that Germany had had little experience with democracy. The new leadership was at first unpopular with the people. It appeared weak for having accepted the humiliating Treaty of Versailles and it seemed unable to deal with Germany's serious post-war economic problems. By the mid-1920s, Germany, with the help of loans from the United States, had begun to make a slow recovery and become politically stable. In 1929, however, the economy of the United States plunged into depression, taking Germany and the rest of the world with it. The **Great Depression** brought about the end of the Weimar Republic and paved the way for the rise of **Adolf Hitler** and the fascist **Nazi Party**.

History and Economics
For more on the Great Depression, see Unit 4, Global Economics.

Fascism is a political philosophy that is **totalitarian**, meaning that the government completely controls every part of the lives of its people. This ideology was created by **Benito Mussolini**, who established a fascist state in Italy in 1922. Mussolini was Adolf Hitler's model and **Nazism** was the German form of fascism.

Key Concepts: Citizenship and Human Rights
In totalitarian states, such as Nazi Germany, citizenship is measured by service to the state, and the expression of human rights is suppressed. What other societies adopted totalitarianism?

Nazi Party Platform

Hitler's Nazi Party platform was very appealing to the German people in the early 1930s for the following reasons:

- The Nazis promised to restore law and order to an unsettled Germany.
- The Nazis promised to improve the economy by breaking the terms of the Treaty of Versailles. Unemployment would be alleviated by increasing the size of the army and reopening the war materials factories.
- The pro-capitalist philosophy of the Nazis appealed to the middle-class businessmen who feared a Communist revolution in which they would lose their property.
- The Nazis blamed Germany's defeat in World War I and subsequent problems on "traitors," namely Communists and Jews, within German society. The use of the Jewish minority as a scapegoat represented the trend of **anti-Semitism** in European history.

History and Society
Racism and anti-Semitism were well established in European society, and the Nazis were able to use them to obtain and maintain political power.

- The Nazis promoted German **nationalism**. In his book, *Mein Kampf*, Hitler encouraged the unity of all Germans in Europe. He also outlined the theory of the "master race." According to Hitler, the Germans were a pure **Aryan** race and therefore superior to all others. He advocated German expansion, since in order to fulfill their potential, the German people needed "lebensraum," or living space. This was to be found in eastern Europe, whose people would become German slaves. Hitler used this racist philosophy to justify acts of aggression.

MAKING CONNECTIONS

Regents Tip A Regents essay might ask how an author's ideas affected his or her country or the world. What evidence do you see that Hitler tried to carry out the ideas he expressed in *Mein Kampf*?

The Third Reich (1933–1945)

As Führer, or leader, of Germany, Hitler created a **totalitarian** state based on the fascist philosophy. The Nazi Party was the only political party that was allowed to exist. The **Gestapo**, or secret police, was responsible for crushing any opposition to Hitler's rule. Nazi ideas were spread through **indoctrination**. Most German children attended public schools in which only Nazi ideas were taught. Children were also encouraged to join the "Hitler Youth." Support for Hitler's leadership and programs was gained through a **propaganda** campaign of speeches, giant rallies, and military parades. Through the use of **censorship**, the government controlled what the people saw, heard, and read. In addition, newspapers, radio, and movies promoted Nazism.

Campaign Against the Jews

Millions of people in Germany were denied their basic human rights, but the Jews especially were singled out for persecution. The **Nuremberg Laws of 1935** deprived Jews of their German citizenship and made discrimination against them legal. All Jews were required to wear a yellow Star of David to identify them. Treatment of the Jews grew increasingly worse until eventually they were sent to slave labor camps and then to death camps as Hitler implemented his "final solution"—a program of **genocide**, or planned destruction of a race.

THE ROAD TO WAR Hitler glorified war as a means of restoring German national pride. This tactic led to public support for a policy of expansion. In 1938, Germany took control of Austria. Although this seizure was a violation of the Treaty of Versailles, the former Allies did nothing. Later that year, Hitler threatened war if he was not given a region of Czechoslovakia known as the Sudetenland. The **Munich Pact**, signed by Great Britain, France, Italy, and Germany, authorized the transfer of territory on the condition that Hitler make no further demands. This policy of **appeasement**, promoted by British Prime Minister **Neville Chamberlain**, only encouraged more aggression. In 1939, Hitler took all of Czechoslovakia. In anticipation of a future conflict with Great Britain and France, Hitler took steps to secure Germany's eastern border. The **Nazi-Soviet Nonaggression Pact**, signed in August 1939, eliminated the possibility of a two-front war and allowed Hitler to invade Poland on September 1, 1939.

MAKING CONNECTIONS

History and Geography After the Communist Revolution, Russia became known as the Soviet Union.

Key Concepts: Change The political, economic, military, and colonial decline of Europe that began with World War I was greatly accelerated by World War II.

History For more on Japan's role in World War II, see the section on Japan in this unit.

Regents Tip The Regents exam often asks for examples of human rights violations. The Holocaust is a prime example. In addition to the Jews, the Nazis targeted several other groups for elimination, including Gypsies, the mentally ill, and homosexuals.

WORLD WAR II (1939–1945)

The invasion of Poland signaled the beginning of World War II as the **Allies** (Great Britain and France) finally took a stand against Germany. The war took on global proportions when Japan joined the **Axis Alliance** (Germany and Italy). Although the United States declared neutrality, it helped the Allies by all means short of war. In 1941, after the surprise Japanese attack on its **Pearl Harbor** naval base in Hawaii, the United States entered the war. In the same year, the Soviet Union joined the Allies when Hitler broke the Nonaggression Pact and invaded the Soviet Union.

Characteristics of World War II

A GLOBAL CONFLICT World War II was fought on land, sea, and air in Europe, Africa, Asia, and the Pacific. The Axis Powers were faced with armies from all over the world.

A TOTAL WAR The fighting in World War II was not confined to battlefields and soldiers. Civilian areas became targets of bombings, for example, in the Battle of Britain. Over 20 million innocent people were dead or wounded as a result of the war.

A MECHANIZED AND MOBILE WAR Countries made use of tanks, planes, aircraft carriers, and battleships. Hitler's "**blitzkrieg**," or lightening war tactics, brought easy victory against Poland and France. New technologies such as sonar and radar helped in defending against submarine and air attacks. Advances in technology and science also led to the development of offensive weapons capable of mass destruction. In July 1945, the United States secretly tested the first **atomic bomb**. Although the Germans had surrendered in May, the war in the Pacific went on. President **Harry Truman**, in an effort to end the war and save American lives, decided to use the new weapon on Japan. In August 1945, the United States dropped atomic bombs on the Japanese cities of Hiroshima and Nagasaki, resulting in 150,000 casualties and enormous destruction. Japan surrendered on August 14, 1945, ending World War II.

Results of World War II

World War II claimed millions of lives and destroyed millions of dollars in property. Such devastation had a profound impact on the world and helped determine the course of post-war history.

THE HOLOCAUST The war drastically changed the population make-up of Europe, especially central Europe. Nazi concentration camps claimed a total of 12 million lives. Six million Jews were victims of the **Holocaust**, the result of Hitler's "final solution" of systematically exterminating all the Jews in Europe. The discovery of the Nazi death camps such as **Auschwitz**, equipped with gas chambers and crematoria, revealed the depths of Hitler's hatred and brutality.

The World at War: World War II

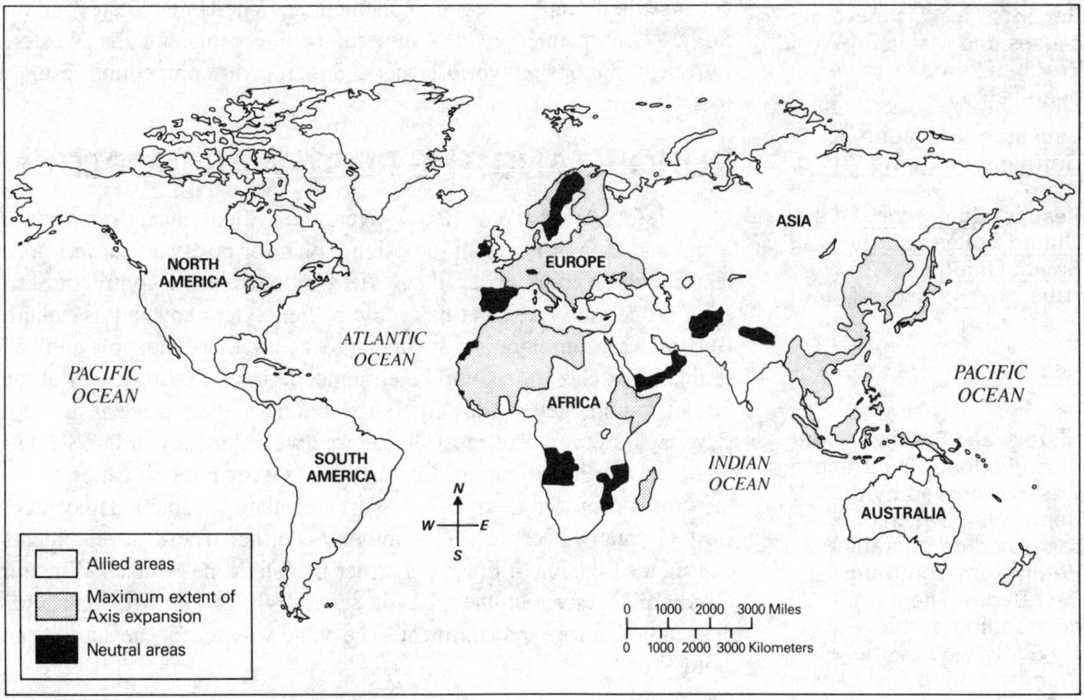

NUREMBERG TRIALS Nazi war criminals were brought to justice at the Nuremberg trials. Although Hitler had committed suicide, other Nazi leaders were tried for acts of aggression and such "crimes against humanity" as the torture and execution of prisoners and the attempted genocide of the Jewish population of Europe.

ESTABLISHMENT OF THE UNITED NATIONS The United Nations (UN) was formed as an international peacekeeping organization. The destruction of World War II, plus the development of atomic weapons encouraged world powers to work to avert future wars. Led by the Big Five—the United States, the Soviet Union, Great Britain, France, and China, the UN provides a forum for discussion and a means of settling disputes. Although it has not ended all war, it has been able to prevent World War III.

COLONIAL NATIONALISM Colonial people began to take advantage of the weakened condition of the imperial powers after World War II. They started or intensified movements for independence. Many new sovereign nations emerged between 1945 and 1965.

SHIFT IN GLOBAL POWER European domination of the world ended as a result of World War II. Despite being on the winning side, Great Britain and France lost great-power status. This was due

MAKING CONNECTIONS

History and Politics The United Nations was granted greater powers than the League of Nations. For more on these two organizations, see Unit 5, Global Politics.

MAKING CONNECTIONS

Regents Tip List several causes and results of World War II. (Examples have been listed.)

Causes: Humiliation of Germany following World War I
Results: Emergence of the United States and the Soviet Union as superpowers

History and Politics Until recently, the iron curtain was symbolized by the Berlin Wall, which separated democratic West Berlin from Communist East Berlin. The dismantling of the Wall in 1989 followed by the reunification of Germany in 1990 is viewed by many as a major step in ending the Cold War.

Regents Tip The Regents exam sometimes asks for an example of a foreign policy.
Containment is one example.
Name another.

Key Concepts: Power Because of the delicate balance within the European power structure after World War II, some European nations, such as Sweden, Finland, Austria, and Switzerland, have pursued a policy of neutrality.

not only to the destruction from which they had to recover, but also because their empires began to disintegrate. The United States and the Soviet Union emerged as "superpowers," replacing the Western European nations as world leaders. Superpower competition resulted in a 40-year "cold war."

EUROPE AND THE POST-WAR WORLD

Before World War II was over, the Allied leaders met first at Yalta and then at Potsdam to design a plan for post-war Europe. As a result of these conferences, the Soviet Union was given control of Eastern Europe until free elections could be held. Germany and its capital, Berlin, were temporarily divided into zones of occupation until all remnants of Nazi rule could be eliminated. **Josef Stalin**, leader of the Soviet Union, never allowed free elections to take place in Eastern Europe, however, and most of the area was transformed into "satellites" of the Soviet Union. Conflict over German reunification led to the creation of two Germanies. West Germany became a democracy, East Germany became a Communist satellite. These developments caused the division of Europe. Former British Prime Minister **Winston Churchill** described the line of separation as an "iron curtain" descending across the continent. The stage was set for the start of the Cold War.

Cold War Policies in Europe

Fought mainly with words in an atmosphere of tension, the Cold War began in the wake of World War II as former Allies became distrustful of each other. Differences in political and economic philosophies (democracy and capitalism vs. totalitarianism and communism) formed the basis of this war without fighting. In addition, the West feared that the Communists would seek to expand outside of Eastern Europe. The United States led the "free world" in trying to stop the spread of communism by adopting a policy of "containment."

TRUMAN DOCTRINE In 1947, President Truman announced an economic and military aid program designed to help people resist Communist aggression. Aimed chiefly at Greece and Turkey, it was successful in saving these countries from Communist threats.

MARSHALL PLAN Following World War II, Europe was a scene of devastation and destruction. Eastern Europe was already under Soviet control. The United States feared that poor economic conditions would make the rest of Europe vulnerable to Communist encroachment as well. The Marshall Plan, enacted in 1948, offered economic aid to all European countries as a means of lessening the appeal of communism.

EUROPEAN ECONOMIC COMMUNITY In an effort to improve their own economies, six Western European nations, led by

Europe After World War II

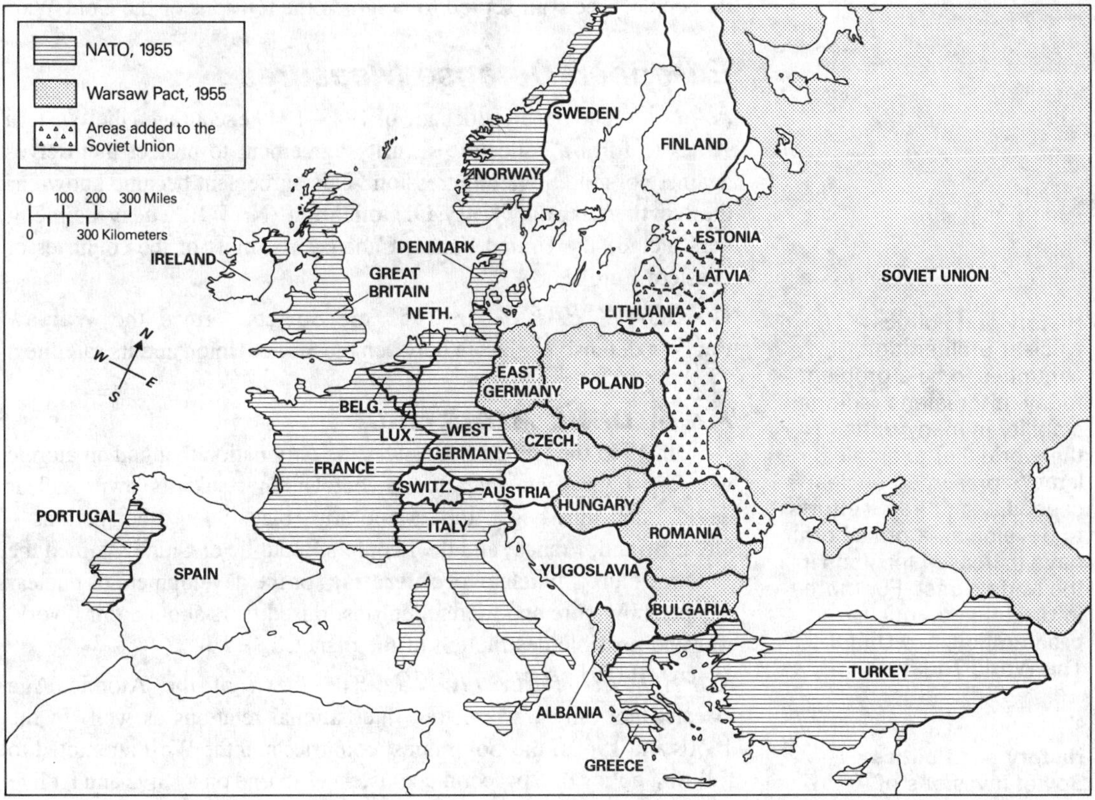

France, formed the European Economic Community (EEC) in 1957. Also known as the **Common Market**, the EEC encouraged free trade among members and uniform economic policies. Formation of this union helped economic stability return to the region and greatly reduced the threat of communism.

MAKING CONNECTIONS

History and Economics
For more on the EEC, see Unit 4, Global Economics.

Berlin: Focus of the Cold War

In 1948, and again in 1961, the city of Berlin, divided and occupied after World War II, became the focal point of the Cold War.

BERLIN AIRLIFT The city of Berlin lay in the Soviet zone of occupied Germany. In 1948, in an effort to drive the Western Allies out of Berlin, the Soviet Union cut off all land access routes to the city. Not wanting to lose control of the city to the Soviets, the Allies conducted a successful airlift, flying in tons of food and supplies for almost a year. Eventually the Soviets lifted the blockade, but Berlin remained divided and occupied by foreign powers.

BERLIN WALL West Berlin was a showplace of democracy and prosperity, and thousands of East Germans were using the city as a means of escaping communism. Embarrassed by this situation, the

MAKING CONNECTIONS

History and Politics Nuclear proliferation continues to be a problem today. It threatens regional stability in many parts of the world. For example, Israel's presumed nuclear capability and Iraq's efforts to develop an atomic bomb have increased tensions in the Middle East. For more information on nuclear proliferation, see Unit 6, The World Today.

History and Politics The Soviet invasions of Hungary in 1956 and of Czechoslovakia in 1968 to crush movements toward democracy within the Soviet bloc posed serious threats to peaceful coexistence.

History and Society Increasingly, the peoples of Eastern and Western Europe have rejected war as a means of resolving international conflict. For more information on the Soviet Union, see the section on Northern Eurasia and Eastern Europe in this unit and Unit 5, Global Economics.

East German government built a wall to prevent the loss of any more of its people. The wall served to heighten the tensions of the Cold War.

European Defense Measures

NATO The Berlin Blockade of 1948–1949 encouraged the Western Allies to form a collective security agreement to protect themselves against possible Soviet aggression. This agreement became known as the **North Atlantic Treaty Organization** (NATO). Today its members include the United States, Canada, and most of the countries of Western Europe.

WARSAW PACT In 1955 the Soviets formed the **Warsaw Pact**—a defensive alliance between the Soviet Union and its satellites.

An Atomic Arms Race

In 1945 the United States was the only nation that had an atomic weapon. Four years later the Soviet Union tested its own nuclear device, and thus began the atomic arms race. Soon other nations—Great Britain, France, and the People's Republic of China—joined the "atomic club." **Nuclear proliferation**, or the development of nuclear weapons by more and more countries, raised fears about a third world war and possible destruction of the planet.

IMPROVED RELATIONS The dawn of the Atomic Age affected not only warfare, but international relations as well. In the 1950s and 1960s, the Communist countries and the West attempted to follow a policy of "peaceful coexistence" based on a "live and let live attitude." This attempt at improving their relationship was often marred by incidents such as the Cuban Missile Crisis (1962). In the 1970s, the United States pursued **détente**, the easing of tensions in the Cold War, which resulted in some limited arms reduction agreements.

THE END OF THE COLD WAR In the late 1980s, Soviet policies of "glasnost" and reform, initiated by **Mikhail Gorbachev**, resulted in monumental changes. By the end of 1989, Eastern Europe was free from Soviet control and Communist domination; the Berlin Wall, symbol of the Cold War, had been torn down. In 1990, the Soviets agreed to the unification of Germany. The Soviet Union and the West cooperated in the United Nations actions against the aggression of Iraq. At an international meeting in Paris in November 1990, the Cold War was officially declared to be over. The Soviet Union itself ceased to exist in 1991. The former Soviet Republics now look to the West for support as they go through political and economic change.

The End of European World Domination

In the post-war period, the countries of Western Europe lost their positions of dominance in the world. Germany had been defeated and divided. Italy was completely devastated and in subsequent years experienced economic and political instability. Great Britain and France, though victors in the war, had to accept that they were not superpowers. In various places around the world, the Western Europeans were forced to face the reality of their changing role.

INDIA After World War II, Great Britain was forced to deal with growing nationalism in its colonies. In 1947, Great Britain lost India, the "jewel in the crown." Pressure to grant independence came as a result of a massive nonviolent civil disobedience movement led by Mohandas K. Gandhi.

SOUTHEAST ASIA The French-Indochina War (1945–1954) was an attempt by France to keep control of its empire in Southeast Asia. Many of the rebels were Communists as well as nationalists and so, as part of the policy of **containment**, the United States financed much of the French war. However, France's overwhelming defeat at the battle of Dien Bien Phu forced the French to accept the 1954 Geneva Agreement, which gave Indochina its independence and divided it into Laos, Cambodia, and North and South Vietnam.

MIDDLE EAST In 1956, Great Britain and France, along with Israel, invaded Egypt with the intention of blocking the nationalization of the Suez Canal. The **Suez Crisis** ended when the United Nations, prompted by the United States and the Soviet Union, condemned the action and ordered the invaders out. This defeat proved to be a major humiliation for the former global giants.

AFRICA In North Africa, the independence movement in **Algeria** turned into another bloody conflict for France. This struggle resulted in domestic turmoil and the creation of a new government headed by the World War II hero, **Charles de Gaulle**, who ended the war by granting Algeria its independence in 1962.

Great Britain withdrew from its African colonies in the late 1950s and 1960s. In Africa, the European minority often feared independence, and so nationalist movements sometimes became violent. In Kenya, for example, extremists known as the Mau Maus launched terrorist attacks against British settlers. Over 12,000 people were killed before independence was granted.

Two Modern Nationalists

Despite the loss of their empires, both France and Great Britain produced leaders who strengthened the position and prestige of their countries.

CHARLES DE GAULLE As president of France from 1959 to 1969, de Gaulle attempted to reassert French power and influence by following nationalist policies. Under his leadership, France developed its own atomic weapons instead of relying on the United States for

MAKING CONNECTIONS

Key Concepts: Power International organizations such as the Commonwealth of Nations and the United Nations can only be as powerful and effective as their member states wish them to be.

Regents Tip The Regents exam almost always asks about nationalist leaders and their policies. Also, a Regents essay may ask about nationalist groups, their goals, and their methods. For more on African nationalism, see the section on Africa in this unit.

MAKING CONNECTIONS

protection. Although France maintained its membership in NATO and continued to follow NATO policy, de Gaulle withdrew French troops from NATO forces in 1966. In order to preserve France's dominant role in the affairs of the continent, de Gaulle consistently vetoed Great Britain's entry into the Common Market (EEC). De Gaulle's policies set the tone for future leaders of France.

MARGARET THATCHER As British prime minister from 1979 to 1990, Margaret Thatcher followed conservative policies that lessened the role of the government in Great Britain's economy. Although greater prosperity was the result, social programs to help education and the poor were cut back. Some people criticized her domestic policies, but she was popular for the way she promoted Great Britain's role as a world power. In 1982, for example, she demonstrated that the British would protect what was left of the empire. When Argentine invaders attempted to take control of the Falkland Islands, a British possession off the coast of South America, a military force was sent to rescue the colony. She consistently proved that Great Britain was the strongest ally and a loyal supporter of the United States. The British supplied the second largest number of troops to the United Nations forces in support of Kuwait in 1990.

Western Europe Today

Although the countries of Western Europe individually declined as world powers following World War II, Western Europe as a bloc has become increasingly important in global affairs. Cooperation in the region on issues such as trade, defense, atomic energy, and the environment have provided Western Europe with a high degree of security and prosperity.

Regents Tip List some recent trends that have eased East-West tensions in Europe.
(An example has been listed.)
Soviet policy of glasnost

THE FUTURE OF EUROPE

The nations of Western Europe are undertaking steps to bring about greater political and economic unity. The plan builds upon the structure of the European Economic Community (EEC), which includes almost all the countries of Western Europe and has become a powerful economic force in the world. Steps toward the goal have already been taken. For example, the European Parliament deals with issues of concern to the whole region. Other plans are under discussion or in the process of being implemented in accordance with the Maastricht Treaty of 1991 such as the adoption of a common passport and a uniform currency for members of the European community.

One problem that has stood in the way of European unity has been feelings of **nationalism** and the pursuit of national interests by individual nations. Although several leaders are hesitant about greater integration, Margaret Thatcher of Great Britain was the most vocal in expressing her concerns. Her stand was seen as an obstacle to the creation of such a united Europe. In December 1990, she was forced to give up the leadership of the Conservative Party and resign as prime minister. The issue of nationalism remains to be dealt with despite the departure of Margaret Thatcher.

Several other factors are to be considered in analyzing plans for the future of Europe. The end of the Cold War has removed the Communist threat to Western Europe. In 1994, NATO members offered the Partnership for Peace plan to their former enemies. The plan calls for unprecedented cooperation on matters of peace and security in the region. Certain Eastern European countries may eventually be granted membership into NATO itself. Many former Soviet bloc countries also desire admission to the European Union. However, greater economic improvement is necessary before this would be possible.

MAKING CONNECTIONS

MAJOR HISTORICAL THEMES

1. The political and cultural achievements of Greece and Rome shaped Western civilization.
2. Feudalism was a political, economic, and social system.
3. As a result of the Crusades and exploration, cross-cultural contacts were made that brought about great change in Europe.
4. The Renaissance was a rebirth in education and the arts that started the modern era.
5. The Reformation challenged the power of the Catholic Church.
6. During the Age of Absolutism, power was concentrated in the hands of the monarch.
7. The ideas of Enlightenment writers such as Locke, Rousseau, and Montesquieu inspired revolutions.
8. The French Revolution and the Napoleonic Wars helped to spread the ideas of democracy and nationalism.
9. The combination of many positive factors made England the center of the Industrial Revolution.
10. Industrialization led to political, economic, and social changes.
11. The need for raw materials and markets led to imperialism.
12. World War I resulted from conflicting alliances, economic rivalries, nationalist feelings, and militarism.
13. World War II ended European world domination and led to the emergence of two superpowers—the United States and the Soviet Union.
14. The post-war struggle between democracy and communism resulted in a Cold War.
15. Since 1945, the countries of Europe and the world have become more interdependent.

SECTION 9 Historic Setting: Northern Eurasia and Eastern Europe

MAKING CONNECTIONS

Time Frame

800s–1240	First Russian State at Kiev
1240–1480	Mongol Control of Russia
1480–1598	Muscovite Rule
1613–1917	Romanov Dynasty
1917–1991	Communist Rule
1991 on	Democratic Rule

OVERVIEW

Russia began as a small city-state, but due to a policy of expansion, it developed into a vast empire. In order to control such a tremendous number of people, successive Russian leaders imposed absolute rule. There was little opportunity for the development of individual rights and responsibilities. In 1917, a revolution took place that transformed the Russian Empire into a Communist totalitarian state known as the Soviet Union. Little changed for the people, however, until the reforms of Mikhail Gorbachev in the last half of the 1980s.

EARLY RUSSIAN HISTORY

Key Concepts: Environment
Environmental and physical features have influenced the course of history of the peoples of Central Asia and eastern Europe.

Before the ninth century A.D. tribes of **Slavic** people from eastern Europe migrated into what is now the European part of the Soviet Union. They settled along the rivers and, since farming was difficult, they became traders. The site of the first Russian state was **Kiev**, a city that developed along the Dnieper River—a major trade route between the Baltic and Black Seas.

Byzantine Influences

From the ninth to the thirteenth centuries, Kiev carried on a profitable trade with the Byzantine Empire. The Byzantine Empire, or the Eastern Roman Empire, did not fall to invaders like the Western Roman Empire. Instead, its economy and culture continued to flourish. As a result of the contact between Kiev and the Byzantine Empire, cultural diffusion took place, which profoundly affected the development of Russian society.

AUTOCRACY The Byzantine belief in **autocracy**, or absolute rule, set an example for future Russian and Soviet leaders.

EASTERN ORTHODOX CHURCH Byzantine missionaries converted the Slavic people to Eastern Orthodox Christianity. The Russian Church was dominated by the government, as it was in the Byzantine Empire.

RELIGIOUS ART AND ARCHITECTURE Styles of early Russian art and architecture revolved around religion and reflected the Byzantine influence (for example, onion-shaped domes, spires, and small religious paintings called **icons**).

CYRILLIC ALPHABET Byzantine missionaries developed the Cyrillic alphabet as well as a written language for the Slavs.

MAKING CONNECTIONS

Key Concepts: Interdependence and Culture
Commercial interdependence, such as that between Kiev and Byzantium, often resulted in cultural diffusion.

Mongol Rule (1240–1480)

In the thirteenth century, the Mongols, or Tatars, from Central Asia invaded and took control of Russia. Their harsh, autocratic rule had lasting effects on Russia.

FEUDALISM Land became the most valued possession, and a class of nobles emerged who became privileged and powerful through their control of land. Peasants who worked the land gradually lost their freedom and became legally bound to the land as serfs.

Key Concepts: Political System
Absolutism and feudalism, two major themes in later Russian history, developed in Russia at the same time they developed in western Europe, China, and Japan.

ISOLATION Mongol rulers isolated Russia from western Europe. The Russians were not exposed to the cultural rebirth of the Renaissance, nor did they benefit from the commercial revolution that occurred in western Europe following the Crusades. The fall of the Byzantine capital of Constantinople to the Moslem Turks in 1453 helped to isolate Russia even further. As a result of this isolation, there was little change or advancement in Russia under Mongol rule.

DISTRUST OF FOREIGNERS The brutality of the Mongols caused the Russians to develop a mistrust of outsiders and a fear of foreign domination that persisted into modern times.

Muscovite Rule (1480–1598)

In the fourteenth century, the Mongols began to decline in power as the Russian princes of Muscovy grew in power. Muscovy was centered around the city of Moscow, which became an important commercial and religious center. The local princes copied the efficient and autocratic methods of the Mongols and used them to strengthen their own positions. By the end of the fifteenth century, the Mongols had been forced out of power and Moscow had become the heart of a new Russian state.

The creation of a unified Russian nation was accomplished by two leaders of Moscow:

- **Ivan III**, also known as Ivan the Great, extended Muscovy territory and united the lands under his rule. In 1547, he proclaimed himself **czar** (tsar), meaning emperor or Caesar. This title became official with the crowning of Ivan IV.

The Growth of Russia, 1300–1800

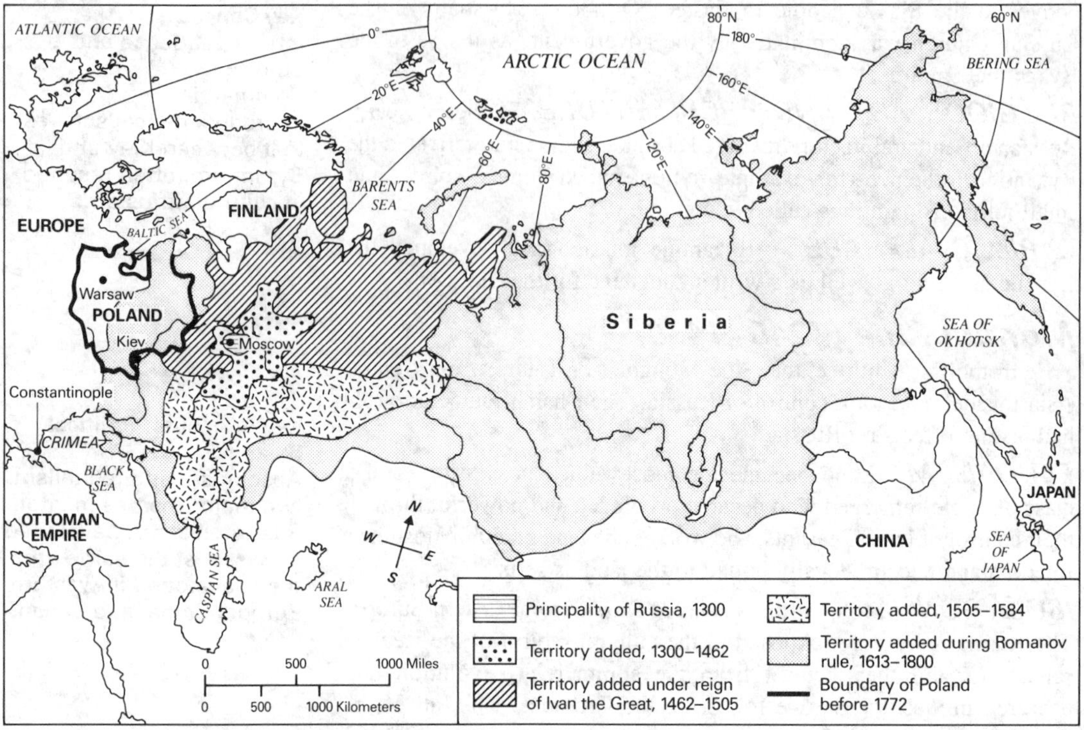

MAKING CONNECTIONS

- **Ivan IV**, also known as Ivan the Terrible, continued the policy of expansion and strengthened his own power at the expense of his nobles. He gained his name because of his use of a secret police and his harsh methods in dealing with those he felt were disloyal.

Ivan the Terrible was succeeded by several weak czars. As a result, Russia endured a 30-year period of political, economic, and social upheaval called the "Time of Troubles" (1584–1613). This period came to an end with the election of a new czar, who took firm hold of the country and resolved many of its troubles.

THE ROMANOV DYNASTY (1613–1917)

The election of Czar Michael Romanov in 1613 established a **dynasty** that would rule Russia for 300 years. The two most important Romanov leaders were Peter the Great and Catherine the Great. They not only expanded the empire, but were the first to turn Russia toward the cultural values of the West.

Regents Tip Regents essays often ask about leaders, their goals, and their methods.

Peter the Great (1682–1725)

Peter the Great was a true absolute monarch. He controlled the nobility and the Russian Orthodox clergy. He created an army that was loyal to him alone. Peter's goal was to transform Russia into a commercial and military power. He wished to expand Russian territory to gain the warm water port that Russia lacked. He realized, however, that his country would have to change if it was to compete with the modern nations of western Europe. Following a year's tour of major western European countries, Peter began a policy of **westernization**—a program to modernize Russia by establishing contact with the West and by adopting western ways. The process of westernization included a series of reforms.

MODERNIZATION OF THE ARMED FORCES Peter the Great modernized the Russian army and established a large and impressive navy. Using these forces, Peter was able to expand Russian territory to the south and to the north.

ESTABLISHMENT OF A NEW CAPITAL On newly acquired land, he built a seaport that he called his "window to the West." The city, St. Petersburg, was located on the Baltic Sea and served as the Russian capital until 1918. Today it is one of Russia's most important cities.

DEVELOPMENT OF COMMERCE He helped transform Russia into a commercial power by increasing manufacturing and trade.

ADOPTION OF WESTERN CUSTOMS Western customs such as smoking and shaving of beards were forced on the Russian nobles. However, these changes were superficial and did not really change the Russian character.

Peter the Great brought Russia into the modern world and made it a major power in Europe. But his improvements were costly. Under his rule the people had no rights and opposition to his policies was brutally put down. He used forced labor and raised taxes to make his ideas realities. Although the economy improved, the life of the Russian serf became even worse than it had been before.

Catherine the Great (1762–1796)

During the reign of Catherine the Great, Russia continued to expand. In a series of "partitions," Russia, Austria, and Prussia divided Polish territory among them. Poland, weakened by internal problems and lacking any protective geographic barriers, could do nothing to prevent the partitions and was ultimately erased from the map. Catherine also expanded Russian territory to the south so that by the end of her reign in 1796, Russia had become a vast empire.

Like Peter the Great, Catherine followed a policy of westernization. Although she was an absolute monarch, she attempted to rule as an "enlightened despot." She claimed that she based her policies on the liberal ideas of the European writers of the **Enlightenment**. She encouraged art, literature, and science. She gave lip service to the need for greater local self-government. Her reforms however, had little

MAKING CONNECTIONS

Key Concepts: Technology and Culture
Although anxious to adopt western technology and trade, many Russians rejected other aspects of western culture in favor of traditional Russian values.

Regents Tip Regents exams look for women who were leaders.

MAKING CONNECTIONS

effect on the majority of the people. She did not extend her liberal philosophy to peasants or serfs, whose protests for better conditions were ruthlessly crushed. She did not tolerate opposition and she continually raised taxes to pay for improvements and wars.

THE ROAD TO REVOLUTION

History and Politics Though Russia was isolated from western Europe, eastern European countries were oriented toward western Europe. Foreign invasions and internal dissension led to widespread regional instability in Hungary, Poland, and the Balkan states.

During the eighteenth century the countries of western Europe were profoundly changed by two major events—the French Revolution and the Industrial Revolution. The Russian czars desired the economic wealth that resulted from the Industrial Revolution, but they tried to keep the ideals of the French Revolution—"liberty, equality, fraternity"—from reaching their people. In contrast to the progress experienced by western Europe, Russia changed very little throughout the nineteenth century. The lack of progress and the existence of injustice combined to lay the groundwork for the major revolution that took place in 1917.

Economic Conditions

Russia began to modernize in the late nineteenth century in an effort to catch up with the industrialized nations of the world. For the most part, however, it remained a **traditional society** based on agriculture. The majority of peasants did not own their land, they used primitive methods, and most engaged in **subsistence farming**. These peasants were joined in their poverty and discontent by a new class in society, the industrial factory workers. Industrialization also led to the rise of the wealthy capitalists who wanted political as well as economic power. The **rigid class structure** prevented these business owners from gaining this power.

Social Conditions

Regents Tip Compare and contrast Russia during the Romanov dynasty to France under the Old Regime. (An example has been provided.)
Both Russia and France had absolute monarchs.

Traditional Russian society was unfair and resistant to change. The upper classes, composed of Russian Orthodox clergy and nobility, were granted special privileges and controlled most of Russia's wealth. The majority of people were commoners, and most were poor and uneducated. Social mobility was limited. Even the wealthy and educated middle class had no chance for advancement.

Political Conditions

The guiding principles of the Romanov dynasty were "nationality, orthodoxy, and autocracy."

NATIONALITY By the end of the nineteenth century, Russia was a vast empire, and it contained many **ethnic minorities**. The policy of the czars was to maintain tight control over these groups as well as to encourage feelings of unity and **nationality**. To accomplish this goal, the czars designed a policy of "Russification" to make all groups think, act, and believe as Russians. The attempt to destroy native cultures was strongly resisted by these groups.

Nationalities in Eastern Europe About 1870

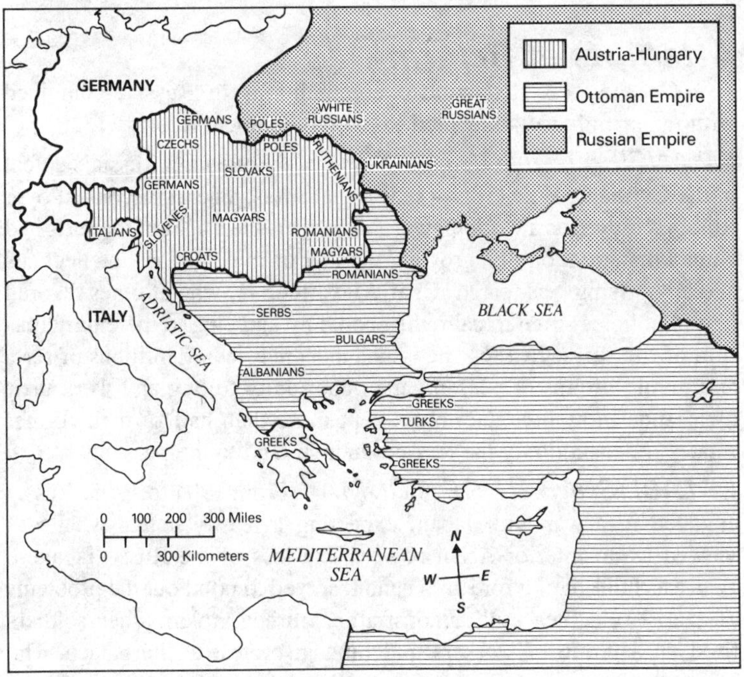

MAKING CONNECTIONS

ORTHODOXY Russia's many religious minorities were as threatening to unity and control as were its ethnic groups. The only fully acceptable belief was **Orthodoxy**, or the teachings of the Russian Orthodox Church. Suspicion and hatred of other religious groups was common. Throughout Russia and Eastern Europe, **anti-Semitism**, or prejudice against Jews, was a prevalent attitude. Jews were an ethnic as well as a religious minority, and therefore easy targets of persecution. When economic conditions were especially bad and the government feared an uprising of the people, Jews were used as scapegoats for the problems of the nation. The government played on the fears and anger of the people, channeling these feelings into violent attacks on the Jews. Such attacks, called **pogroms**, helped the people forget about their own troubles and allowed the government to avoid a confrontation with its subjects. Millions of Jews were forced to flee from Russia during the nineteenth century to escape the pogroms.

History and Society For more information on Russian Jews, see the section on Northern Eurasia and Eastern Europe in Unit 3, Global Society.

Regents Tip Compare the treatment of Jews in Russia with that in Nazi Germany. (An example has been provided.)
In both countries, Jews were used as scapegoats for problems.

AUTOCRACY While other countries were introducing elements of democracy into their societies, the czars attempted to maintain autocracy in Russia. Growing discontent among the people and the desire to change made control difficult. The majority of people, especially the educated middle class, began to feel that an end to absolutism would result in greater equality and improved living conditions. The czars often resorted to repressive measures, such as the use of secret

MAKING CONNECTIONS

police, to stop the spread of new ideas and prevent challenges to their authority.

Attempts at Reform

Growing dissatisfaction over conditions in Russia, combined with major military losses, led to two government reforms.

EMANCIPATION OF THE SERFS Following Russia's defeat in the **Crimean War** (1854–1856), there was general discontent over Russia's failure as a world power. Moreover, the plight of the serfs had gained the attention of a growing number of middle-class intellectuals and an uprising was feared. **Czar Alexander II**, who at times favored liberal policies, tried to calm the people by agreeing to the **emancipation of the serfs**. In 1861, he issued a decree freeing millions of serfs and giving groups of peasants the opportunity to buy and work their own land. In reality, the nobles kept more than half of their former estates, releasing only the less-productive land to the peasants.

ESTABLISHMENT OF A DUMA From 1904 to 1905, Russia engaged in a war with Japan, expecting to easily defeat what was viewed as an inferior Asian power. The loss of the Russo-Japanese War was humiliating for Russia and it served to point out the problems of czarist rule. Peaceful demonstrations turned violent when soldiers fired on a group of workers marching in protest to the palace. The massacre, known as "Bloody Sunday," touched off the **Revolution of 1905**. In an effort to calm the outrage of the people, **Czar Nicholas II** agreed to the establishment of a legislature, or Duma. Although the Czar promised basic civil rights and lawmaking powers to the Duma, he disregarded these promises once the revolution was put down. By refusing to deal honestly with the people, Nicholas II ensured the inevitability of the revolution that would destroy him and his dynasty.

Key Concepts: Human Rights and Justice The widespread denial of basic human rights in Russia led to demands for justice and reform.

THE REVOLUTION OF 1917

Between 1905 and 1917, there was a growing desire among the people to end absolute rule. The czar seemed unwilling or unable to deal effectively with the country's problems. The conditions for change were right, and all that was needed was a spark to ignite the people and create revolution. World War I provided that spark.

Key Concepts: Change Revolutions are more likely when many different groups in a country become discontented at the same time.

Russia in World War I (1914–1917)

World War I erupted in Europe in 1914. One of the basic causes was a conflict of interests. People throughout eastern Europe, guided by feelings of nationalism, wanted unity within their own independent nations. Countries such as Russia and Austria-Hungary, on the other hand, wished to maintain control over ethnic minorities living under their rule and possibly to extend their empires even further. When war broke out following the assassination of Austrian Archduke Franz Ferdinand by a Serbian nationalist, Russia joined Great Britain and France in the fight against Germany and Austria-Hungary. The czar himself took charge of Russia's military strategy.

History For more information on the outbreak of World War I, see the section on western Europe in this unit.

Russian troops met with many defeats. Soldiers lacked basic military supplies and became increasingly distrustful of their leaders. Although troops at the front remained loyal, by 1917 those serving behind the lines began to desert in great numbers.

The Outbreak of Revolution

While the czar was on the battlefront, directing the course of Russian action, he neglected the problems of the civilian population. Morale was low in the face of severe shortages of food, fuel, and housing. The people might have tolerated these shortages for the sake of **nationalism**, if the czar had been successful with his armies. However, he was not successful. Tensions and anger mounted.

In March 1917, the czar's troops refused to fire on a group of protesters, but instead joined them in sympathy. Widespread rioting resulted, bringing the country to near **anarchy**. Realizing he was no longer in control of his troops and was without the support of his people, Czar Nicholas II **abdicated**, or gave up his throne.

MAKING CONNECTIONS

Regents Tip List some of the causes of the Russian Revolution. (An example is listed.)
Denial of human rights for the peasants

The March Revolution

The March Revolution, which brought about the downfall of the czar, was a spontaneous reaction to an intolerable situation. It lacked strong leaders and a well-defined plan. Therefore, following the overthrow of the czar, a **provisional**, or temporary, government was set up. It was dominated mainly by members of the middle class who intended to write a **constitution** to establish a **democratic** government in Russia. This government brought only **moderate** changes. Major issues such as the peasants' desire for land were assigned further study. Such caution angered the people whose representatives—the **soviets**, or councils of workers and soldiers, and later intellectuals and peasants—demanded action that would bring about immediate results. The provisional government's already weak position was further hurt by its leaders' decision to honor Russia's commitment and continue participation in World War I.

The November Revolution

The new, open atmosphere in Russia following the events of March 1917 made it possible for revolutionaries living in exile to return home. Among these were **Nikolai Lenin** and **Leon Trotsky**, leaders of the **Bolsheviks**, radical socialists who followed the ideas of **Karl Marx**. Lenin immediately tried to gain the support of the people by promising to deliver everything they had been demanding. The Bolsheviks offered the people a program of "peace, land, and bread."

- **Peace** An end to Russia's role in World War I.
- **Land** The peasants could seize the lands of the nobles.
- **Bread** An end to the shortages in the cities and better conditions for the workers. The Bolsheviks promised the city workers a greater share in the wealth they worked to produce.

MAKING CONNECTIONS

Such promises of direct and extreme action were exactly what the majority of the people wanted to hear. Support for the Bolsheviks grew as the authority of the provisional government was undermined. In November 1917, the Bolsheviks led a second revolution. The provisional government was overthrown and a new government was installed with Lenin as premier and Trotsky as minister of war.

History and Politics
Revolutions can be inspired by ideology as well as by practical concerns. The ideology may have to be modified to govern a nation.

MARXIST–LENINIST PHILOSOPHY In order to bring about the November Revolution, Lenin adapted the theories of Karl Marx to the situation in Russia. Marx had predicted that a Communist revolution would first occur in an industrial society such as Great Britain. He believed that the exploited factory workers would be driven to overthrow the capitalist owners and would then take both economic and political control of the country. Russia in 1917 was industrializing, but was still primarily an agricultural nation. Lenin did not think it was necessary to wait until Russia was completely industrialized before bringing about the revolution that would result in a Marxist state. The ultimate goal, he believed, was the creation of a society based on political and economic equality. He was determined to use any means necessary to bring it about in Russia, in spite of its traditional economy.

DEVELOPMENT OF THE SOVIET STATE

The world's first modern Communist state became fully defined under the leadership of Nikolai Lenin and Joseph Stalin.

Russia Under Lenin (1917–1922)

Once in power, the Bolsheviks, or Communists as they became known, attempted to fulfill their revolutionary goals. As promised, Premier Lenin immediately took steps to establish terms of peace with Germany. The **Treaty of Brest-Litovsk** (1918) was very harsh in that Russia was forced to give up extensive territory. Lenin accepted the treaty, despite the objections of other Bolsheviks, since he felt peace at any price was imperative for the survival of Russia and the revolution.

History and Economics
For more on changes to the Russian economy, see Unit 4, Global Economics.

Economic problems that existed prior to 1917 were made worse by the devastation of war and revolution. In the midst of this economic disorder, Lenin attempted to transform capitalist Russia into a Communist state. Eventually, both industries and land were **nationalized**, or put under the ownership and control of the government. The majority of people were not familiar with Communist philosophy and did not understand Lenin's actions. He found it difficult therefore to gain the cooperation of the people. Some felt that the promises of "land" and "bread" were not being fulfilled, and opposition to Bolshevik rule began to grow.

CIVIL WAR (1918–1921) For three years after the Bolshevik takeover, civil war raged between the "Reds," who supported the revolutionary government and the "Whites," who represented many different groups with the same goal—the overthrow of the Bolsheviks. The White army was helped by Great Britain, France, Japan, and the United States, who wanted Russia to rejoin the Allies and who also feared the spread of communism to the rest of Europe.

The Bolsheviks appealed to the people's sense of **nationalism** in fighting the civil war and employed extreme measures to stop **counter-revolutionary** activities. They used a secret police to uncover opposition. Thousands suspected of being anti-Bolshevik and therefore anti-revolution were executed. In an effort to destroy a unifying force among the Whites, the Bolsheviks executed Czar Nicholas II and his entire family. Ultimately, the Whites were no match for the leadership and determination of the Reds, whose victory allowed the Communists to establish firm control over Russia.

MAKING CONNECTIONS

Regents Tip List the similarities between the period under Lenin and the Reign of Terror in France. (An example has been listed.)
Execution of suspected counter revolutionaries

NEW ECONOMIC POLICY (NEP) In order to rebuild his war-torn country and ease the transition to communism, Lenin altered his earlier economic program. The New Economic Policy allowed some private control of land and business and set Russia on the road to recovery.

FORMATION OF THE USSR (1922) The Communists organized the government into the **Union of Soviet Socialist Republics (USSR)**, or Soviet Union, which became the new name of the country. Initially, the union consisted of four republics; as more territory was acquired republics were added. By 1940 they numbered fifteen.

Key Concepts: Diversity Northern Eurasia is a region of great ethnic diversity. It is a "union" of many different nations and ethnic groups.

Soviet Union Under Stalin (1922–1953)

Lenin's death in 1924 led to a power struggle between **Trotsky**, Lenin's chosen successor, and **Joseph Stalin**, a ruthless and ambitious Communist Party leader whom Lenin feared. Through manipulation and political deal making, Stalin was able to force Trotsky out of office and out of the country. Stalin's rise to dictator marked Russia's return to stability under the authority of a strong ruler. Many of the policies he established endured long after his death.

Regents Tip Compare the Soviet Union under Stalin with Germany under Hitler. (An example has been provided.)
Both countries had totalitarian governments

TOTALITARIANISM As dictator with unlimited power, Stalin created a **totalitarian** police state more efficient and brutal than czarist Russia had ever been. A totalitarian government is one that has the power to completely control every part of the lives of its people. Stalin increased the size and power of the secret police who sought out and destroyed his opposition. He ruled through terror, trusting almost no one. **Purges**, which were moves to clean out the Communist Party of "disloyal" members, routinely occurred and even those closest to Stalin were not safe. Execution, imprisonment, or exile were common punishments for those found guilty by Stalin's courts. Eventually, the

MAKING CONNECTIONS

History, Economics, and Society Once revolutionary leaders have won a political revolution, they may begin economic and social revolutions. For more information, see Unit 3, Global Society, and Unit 4, Global Economics.

general population was affected by this ruthlessness and it has been estimated that millions of people died as a result of execution or slave labor during Stalin's regime. Only recently has the Soviet leadership fully acknowledged the atrocities committed by Stalin.

PLANNED ECONOMY Since the Communist, totalitarian philosophy of the Soviet Union was incompatible with that of the countries of Western Europe and the United States, Stalin realized that economic and military strength were necessary for the survival of the new system. In order to fully modernize the country, he initiated a series of Five-Year Plans. Under this planned economy, the government had complete control over production and distribution. Emphasis was placed on heavy industry, especially the manufacturing of war materials, while consumer goods were neglected. By putting the needs of the state first, Stalin succeeded in transforming Russia into a modern, industrial nation.

COLLECTIVIZATION Stalin forced the peasants to give up their small farms and join **collective farms** controlled by the government. Millions who opposed this policy were killed or sent to prison labor camps in Siberia or Soviet Central Asia. In the rich agricultural farmlands of the **Ukraine**, where opposition was particularly strong, all food supplies were seized by the government. In this way, peasants who stood in the way of Stalin's program starved to death.

THE SOVIET UNION IN WORLD WAR II (1941–1945)

On September 1, 1939, Hitler invaded Poland and World War II began. The outbreak of war gave Stalin the opportunity to carry out the historic Russian theme of expansion.

Agreement with Germany (1939)

The **Nazi-Soviet Nonaggression Pact** was an agreement in which the leaders of Germany and the Soviet Union promised not to attack each other's country. It also contained a secret provision for the division of Poland between them. In 1940, the **Baltic nations** of Estonia, Latvia, and Lithuania, were annexed to the Soviet Union as separate republics.

Joining the Allies

In 1941, Hitler broke his promise and staged a surprise attack on the Soviet Union. This move forced Stalin to join the Allies in the war against Germany. After a number of early defeats, the Soviets finally rallied, helped in part by the harsh Russian winter of 1942. Following the Battle of Stalingrad (1942–1943), the Soviet army went on the offensive, "freeing" Czechoslovakia, Poland, Hungary, and Romania from Nazi control. Germany surrendered in May 1945 with the fall of

Berlin. The war had been especially hard on the Soviet Union, and the people viewed Stalin as a father figure, who guided them to victory against the Nazis in the "Great Patriotic War."

MAKING CONNECTIONS

Control Over Eastern Europe

Guided by the principle of nationalism, Stalin took steps to ensure that his country would never again be vulnerable to foreign invasion. At the end of World War II, the Eastern European countries that had been liberated from the Nazis by the Soviet army came under Stalin's control. Although he had promised the Western Allies that these nations would have free elections, Stalin made sure that Communist regimes loyal to the Soviet government in Moscow were installed. These countries became known as **satellites** since they were not truly independent but rather revolved around the Soviet Union, following its directives. Since the Soviet Union lacked geographic barriers in the West, these satellites provided a buffer zone against any future attacks from Western Europe.

Key Concept: Power and Choice
World War II provided the Soviets with an opportunity to expand into Eastern Europe. The countries of Eastern Europe became Communist through Soviet military and diplomatic pressure rather than by democratic choice.

One country in Eastern Europe that eluded Stalin was **Yugoslavia**, which adopted the Communist philosophy but did not become a satellite. Under the leadership of **Marshal Tito**, the Communists in Yugoslavia had driven out the Nazis and taken control of the government without the help of Stalin. Although the Soviet leader attempted to force Yugoslavia into the satellite camp, Tito resisted and was able to follow a policy of **nonalignment**, or not formally taking sides with either the Communists or the West.

THE COLD WAR ERA (1948–1990)

History For more on the Cold War, see the section on Western Europe in this unit.

Before the end of World War II, Stalin had promised the Allies to help promote freedom, but after peace was declared he soon indicated he had other intentions. The Soviets blocked Western efforts to reunite Germany after a period of occupation. Instead, East Germany became a Communist satellite of the Soviet Union. When the Soviets attempted to force the Allies out of Berlin by blocking access routes, the Allies responded with a massive air lift. This was the first major incident of the Cold War—the struggle between the Communists and the West.

The Iron Curtain

Stalin was almost completely able to isolate the satellites from the free countries of the West. Winston Churchill, the World War II prime minister of England, compared this separation to an "iron curtain" descending across Europe; future historians cited it as the basis of the **Cold War**. Since Eastern Europe was cut off from the rest of the world, its political and economic systems became interdependent with those of the Soviet Union. Movements by countries such as Poland and East Germany to break from Soviet domination were not tolerated.

MAKING CONNECTIONS

The Khrushchev Regime (1953–1964)

Following the death of Stalin, a power struggle occurred as it had after the death of Lenin. **Nikita Khrushchev** eventually emerged as the undisputed leader of the Soviet Union. Although he stunned fellow Communists by denouncing the excesses of Stalin, Khrushchev nonetheless assumed dictatorial powers. Khrushchev encouraged a policy of "peaceful coexistence" with the West, but Cold War tensions were heightened by several incidents.

REVOLT IN HUNGARY In 1956, Hungary's attempt to revolt against Soviet control was crushed. Khrushchev made it clear that Eastern Europe would remain under Soviet domination.

CUBAN MISSILE CRISIS In 1962, the United States learned that the Soviets had installed missile bases in Cuba, from which it was possible to launch a nuclear attack. After President John F. Kennedy ordered a naval blockade of Cuba, Khrushchev removed the missile sites.

The Brezhnev Years (1964–1982)

Khrushchev's failure in the Cuban missile crisis, along with a poor Soviet economy and growing split between the Soviet Union and Communist China, helped lead to his removal from office in 1964. **Leonid Brezhnev** succeeded Khrushchev as leader of the USSR. Brezhnev was a hardline Communist who took a Stalinist approach in dealing with opposition in his own country as well as in the satellites.

Regents Tip **Dissident** is a key vocabulary word.

REPRESSION OF DISSIDENTS Brezhnev did not tolerate any form of dissent. Those who disagreed with government policies or the Communist system were subjected to punishment or exile. Extensive violations of human rights during Brezhnev's rule aroused much concern among Western nations.

PRAGUE SPRING In the spring of 1968, the government of Czechoslovakia attempted to improve political, economic, and social conditions in the country. Calling its reforms "socialism with a human face," the government began to allow the people greater rights and freedoms as well as economic contact with the West. Brezhnev sent in troops to occupy the country and put an end to the experimental reforms.

MARTIAL LAW IN POLAND Severe economic problems during the 1970s pushed Polish workers to demand change. In 1980, **Solidarity**, a ten-million-member labor union, was formed. Led by **Lech Walesa**, it demanded an end to the Communist monopoly of power and pushed for economic reforms that would improve the working and living conditions for the people. Pressured by the Soviets, the Polish government imposed martial law. Solidarity was outlawed and Walesa was jailed. These actions were condemned by the Catholic Church in Poland, a long-time opponent of the Communists, as well as by the pope and the leaders of the West. Lech Walesa was finally freed in 1983 and, for leading a fight for freedom by peaceful means such as strikes and demonstrations, he was awarded the Nobel Peace Prize. Suppression of protests continued, however, until 1988.

MAKING CONNECTIONS

Détente

The massive nuclear arsenals controlled by the Soviets and the Americans caused fear that a war between the countries could mean mutual destruction. This fear prompted the adoption of a policy of **détente** by both the United States and the Soviet Union during the 1970s. Détente, or a easing of tensions in the Cold War, included arms control talks and cultural exchanges. Improved relations between the Soviet Union and the U.S. were hurt, however, by such events as the Soviet invasion of Afghanistan in 1979.

History and Political Science For more on détente, see the section on Northern Eurasia and Eastern Europe in Unit 5, Global Politics.

NORTHERN EURASIA SINCE 1985

Mikhail Gorbachev assumed the role of leader of the Soviet Union in 1985. Compared to previous Soviet rulers, he was young and energetic as well as determined to change his country for the better. In his five years in power, Gorbachev pursued three major reform programs.

GLASNOST **Glasnost** was a policy of greater "openness" within Soviet society and in dealings with other countries. This policy allowed the people more freedom to criticize the government, and political dissidents had better treatment. Gorbachev also met with Western leaders to work out arms reductions and cultural exchanges.

History and Political Science For more on glasnost and democratization, see the section on Northern Eurasia and Eastern Europe in Unit 5, Global Politics.

DEMOCRATIZATION Under democratization the people of the Soviet Union were granted a more meaningful voice in the government. A freely elected government body was created and political parties other than the Communist Party were allowed to exist and function.

PERESTROIKA Gorbachev's plan for economic reform was called **perestroika**, which means "restructuring." It was a loosening of the government's grip on the Soviet economy.

A NEW ERA A group of hard-line Communist leaders tried to seize power in August 1991. The Soviet people, led by Russian Republic president Boris Yeltsin, resisted the takeover attempt, and it failed in less than a week. Gorbachev returned to power as Soviet president but resigned amid turmoil a few months later. As the Soviet Union was disbanded, Boris Yeltsin emerged as the leader of a new Russia. He experienced difficulty in ruling and found it necessary to dissolve the parliament in September 1993. As a result, there was an attempted coup d'etat but this too was unsuccessful.

THE ODD COUPLE

MAKING CONNECTIONS

HOPES AND FEARS Gorbachev's reforms helped lead to such events as the end of the Cold War, the collapse of communism in Eastern Europe, and the breakup of the Soviet Union in 1991. Under Boris Yeltsin, Russia began the transition to a free-market economy and a democratic government. But Yeltsin also sent Russian troops into the province of Chechnya, which was seeking independence. The war in Chechnya cost thousands of lives and damaged Yeltsin's support. Rising crime and corruption hurt Yeltsin as well.

MAJOR HISTORICAL THEMES

1. Both Russian and Soviet history were influenced by a policy of expansion.
2. The idea of autocracy came from the example of the Byzantine Empire and the Mongols. Autocracy has been useful in governing a large amount of territory and number of people.
3. The Revolution of 1917 was brought on by a number of factors that created an intolerable situation.
4. Lenin adapted the theories of Marx to fit the Russian situation in bringing about the Communist revolution.
5. Stalin used brutal tactics to establish a totalitarian state, which was maintained by his successors.
6. The history of eastern Europe has been marked by domination by foreign powers.
7. The reform policies of Mikhail Gorbachev led to dramatic changes in Northern Eurasia, Eastern Europe, and the world.

Regents Questions for Practice

Review the Test-Taking Strategies section of this book. Then answer the following questions. Circle the *number* of the word or expression that best completes the statement or answers the question. Write your answers to essay questions on a separate piece of paper.

1. During the 1950s and 1960s, the history of most African countries was characterized by
   1 colonization by imperialist nations
   2 the achievement of political independence
   3 a sharp decrease in the birth rate
   4 the development of economic self-sufficiency

2. The term "Pan-Africanism" can *best* be defined as a movement whose purpose is to
   1 promote African unity
   2 support cultural diversity
   3 encourage European investment in Africa
   4 advocate a return to colonial conditions

MAKING CONNECTIONS

Test Hint Questions 2 and 3 ask for "the best" of the answer choices. Others may be partially correct, so read all choices carefully to select the best answer.

3. Which generalization *best* explains the creation of the nations of India and Pakistan in 1947?
   1 Armed conflict is necessary for independence movements to succeed.
   2 Religious movements may have a strong influence on political events.
   3 Industrialization needs to reach a high level before a nation can become independent.
   4 Similar geographic and historical conditions may promote unity between nations.

4. The primary goal of the Palestine Liberation Organization (PLO) has been to
   1 establish a home state for Palestinian Arabs
   2 eliminate Communist influence in the Arab nations
   3 bring about a peaceful settlement of the conflicts between Egypt and Palestinian Arabs
   4 control the Organization of Petroleum Exporting Countries (OPEC)

5. The major factor that enabled western Europe to dominate large parts of Asia and Africa in the 19th and early 20th centuries was the
   1 technological and military superiority of European nations
   2 acceptance of Christianity by many Asians and Africans
   3 desire of Asians and Africans for European raw materials
   4 refusal of Asians and Africans to fight against European imperialism

Test Hint Be alert to dates and time periods in questions. In questions 5, 6, and 8, time periods are important.

6. Eighteenth-century Russia and 19th-century Japan were similar in that both countries
   1 began the process of modernization after a long period of isolation
   2 developed democratic governments after years under absolute monarchies
   3 refused to accept Western technological ideas
   4 adopted socialist economic systems after capitalism had failed

MAKING CONNECTIONS

7. Which was a direct result of the European slave trade in Africa?
   1 It promoted a feeling of racial superiority among Europeans.
   2 West African kingdoms prospered.
   3 Africans moved in large numbers to rural areas.
   4 African military forces ended the slave trade.

8. A major factor in the development of 20th-century nationalist movements throughout Africa was a common
   1 language throughout most of Africa
   2 goal to end European rule in Africa
   3 ethnic bond among the people of sub-Saharan Africa
   4 religion throughout most of Africa

---

9. Tribalism in modern African nations has frequently resulted in political
   1 disunity
   2 equality
   3 interdependence
   4 harmony

10. The boundaries of modern African nations do not usually follow tribal boundaries mainly because
   1 African nations are trying to decrease tribal influence
   2 most tribes are unwilling to cooperate with the new national governments
   3 tribes have lost their importance in the lives of modern Africans
   4 modern national boundaries tend to follow former colonial boundaries

11. Since independence, India's official foreign policy has been characterized by
   1 military alliance with the United States
   2 friendship with Pakistan
   3 hostility toward Third World nations
   4 nonalignment with the major powers

12. One factor that accounted for Chinese influence on traditional Japanese culture was the
   1 continuous warfare between the countries
   2 geographical location of the countries
   3 refusal of Western nations to trade with Japan
   4 annexation of Japan into the Chinese Empire

13. The Boxer Rebellion of the early 20th-century was an attempt to
   1 eliminate poverty among the Chinese peasants
   2 bring western-style democracy to China
   3 restore trade between China and European nations
   4 remove foreign influence from China

14. The spread of Islam throughout the African continent is an example of
   1 national security
   2 socialism
   3 cultural diffusion
   4 self-determination

15. Which was a major effect of European rule in Africa?
1 decreased dependence of African nations on imports
2 development of subsistence agriculture
3 improved transportation and communication systems
4 increased use of barter

16. Which was a characteristic of feudalism in both medieval Europe and Japan?
1 The middle class acquired more power than did any other class.
2 Political power was held by a strong centralized government.
3 The army encouraged strong nationalistic feeling among the people.
4 All the people knew their roles in a rigid class system.

17. European imperialism promoted the development of nationalism in Asian and African countries by
1 unintentionally uniting people to oppose foreign domination
2 promoting free trade associations among colonies
3 establishing Christianity as the common religion
4 discouraging patriotic feelings toward the mother country

Base your answer to question 18 on the cartoon below and on your knowledge of social studies.

Auth, The Philadelphia Inquirer

18. The situation illustrated in the cartoon was mainly caused by the
1 policies of the government of the Republic of South Africa towards blacks
2 abundance of oil resources in the Republic of South Africa
3 secession of the Republic of South Africa from the United Nations
4 refusal of the Republic of South Africa to trade with other African nations

Base your answers to question 19 and 20 on the cartoon below and on your knowledge of social studies.

Shanks in The Buffalo Evening News

19. The crisis illustrated in the cartoon involves the
1 internal problems in the Philippines
2 border conflicts between Honduras and Nicaragua
3 conflict between Israel and its Arab neighbors
4 flight of Afghan refugees into Pakistan

20. The main idea of the cartoon is that the crisis will
1 be confined to the Middle East
2 be controlled by Western democracies
3 totally destroy the Islamic religion
4 eventually affect the entire world

21. Which statement *best* explains why British India was partitioned in 1947?
1 The British feared a united India.
2 One region of India wanted to remain under British control.
3 Religious differences led to political division.
4 Communist forces refused to participate in a centralized Indian government.

22. Movements to achieve Arab unity have not been successful primarily because of the problems created by the
1 issue of human rights violations
2 strength of nationalistic interests
3 growth of internationalism
4 need for free trade

23. Which statement is *best* supported by a study of the history of the Middle East?
1 Differing religious beliefs have been a frequent source of conflict in the region.
2 Few cultural and political differences are found among the nations of the region.
3 The nations of the region have been instrumental in the development of democratic ideas.
4 The people of the region have generally adopted the ideas and values of Western culture.

24. Which was a major result of the struggle for Africa by European powers between the 1880s and World War I?
1 an increase in the slave trade
2 the strengthening of traditional village ties
3 an increase in tribal warfare
4 the creation of arbitrary colonial boundaries

25. The primary reason that the Japanese policy of near-isolation ended in 1853–1864 was that Japan
1 needed additional territory as an outlet for its surplus population
2 needed European markets for its manufactured goods
3 became involved in a war with China
4 was pressured by the United States naval power to open its ports

26. Feudalism in western Europe was similar to feudalism in Japan in that
1 power was based on class relationships
2 the national government controlled the nobility
3 social mobility was easily achieved
4 most of the people lived in cities

27. Which has occurred in Southeast Asia since the end of the Vietnam War in the early 1970s?
1 Military dictatorships have been replaced by democratic governments.
2 Communist economic practices have brought about substantial industrial growth.
3 A strong middle class has emerged as the dominant economic force.
4 Conflicts have developed among the Communist factions in the area.

28. Which statement is *most* consistent with the political views of Mahatma Gandhi?
1 Not until the last Englishman has left India will I put down my sword.
2 To protest injustice is to use one's time unproductively.
3 Independence is a goal that we may seek but never attain.
4 Opposition to evil is as much a duty as is cooperation with good.

29. The government of which nation accepts racism as a part of its legal system?
1 Japan
2 Ghana
3 United Kingdom
4 South Africa

30. Which observation about the impact of colonialism on African kingdoms is *most* valid?
1 European nations respected the heritage of the ancient African kingdoms.
2 Historians have proved that the positive effects of colonialism have outweighed the negative effects.
3 Colonialism introduced Africans to a variety of non-African cultures.
4 Without the colonization of Africa, the continent would have continued in a period of stagnation.

31. Which problem has proved historically to be the major stumbling block to settlement of the Arab-Israeli conflict in the Middle East?
1 claims by both sides to the same territory
2 interference by outside religious groups
3 failure of the United Nations to become involved
4 desire of both sides to control the oil resources in the area

32. The ancient Chinese and Egyptian civilizations were similar in that they
1 had little impact on later societies
2 had democratic forms of government
3 developed in river valleys
4 shared a universal language

33. Japan's current position as a world power is most directly based upon Japan's
1 economic strength
2 abundance of natural resources
3 diversity of cultures
4 military superiority

34. The Boxer Rebellion in China in 1900 and the Iranian Revolution in 1979 were similar in that both
1 blamed foreigners for the erosion of traditional cultures
2 were led by young radicals who wished to modernize their country
3 spared the rights and property of foreign diplomats
4 were successfully suppressed by foreign military intervention

35. Which was a major result of European imperialism in sub-Saharan Africa during the late 19th and early 20th centuries?
1 adoption of Islam as the dominant African religion
2 decline of traditional Africa cultures
3 strengthening of tribal organizations
4 beginning of slavery

36. The histories of England and Japan are *most* different with respect to the
1 existence of significant dependence upon foreign imports
2 pursuit of imperial policies that led to friction with the United States
3 length of time during which democratic political practices developed
4 acceptance of 20th-century technology

37. Which was a common feature of feudal societies in both Japan and Europe?
1 extensive contact with citizens of other countries
2 opportunity for social mobility
3 domination by a military class
4 strong central government

38. Which was the characteristic of Western European nations that *most* enabled them to establish colonies in Asia and Africa?
1 rigid social class structures
2 self-sufficiency in natural resources
3 frequent political revolutions
4 advanced technology

39. Which was common to both European and Japanese feudalism?
1 flourishing trade
2 development of industry
3 cultural diversity
4 decentralized government

Essay Questions

1. Traditional colonial empires no longer exist in the modern world. However the influence of imperialism continues today. Identify *three* Third World nations that have been affected by imperialism. For *each* one chosen:

- Show how current political, economic or cultural conditions reflect the influence of imperialism
- Show how that nation has tried to promote its own national identity

2. Nationalism is a major factor that helps to shape the foreign policy of a country. Choose *three* of the countries listed below. For *each* one chosen, describe a nationalistic goal of that country in the time period indicated. Show how that goal helped to shape a policy of that country toward one or more other nations.

Countries
United States in the 19th century
Prussia in the 19th century
Israel in the 20th century
Vietnam in the 20th century
Nigeria in the 20th century

3. A strong leader acts decisively not only to influence events within his or her nation but also to influence relations with other nations.

Leaders
Corazon Aquino
Indira Gandhi
Ayatollah Khomeini
Deng Xiaoping
Fidel Castro
Napoleon Bonaparte
Jomo Kenyatta

Select *three* leaders listed and for each leader

- Identify the nation in which the leader acted
- Discuss *one* domestic or *one* foreign policy of the leader
- Discuss a method used by the leader to put his or her policies into effect

4. Throughout history, great civilizations have existed in different parts of the world.

Civilizations
Ancient Mesopotamia
Ancient Africa
Golden Age of Athens
Golden Age of China
Ancient Latin American Empires
Golden Age of Muslim Culture

Select *three* of the civilizations listed and discuss *two* specific characteristics or achievements of each civilization.

5. Nations and regions often adopt ideas and practices from other parts of the world. The nations mentioned below have experienced cultural diffusion.

Japan from China
Mexico from Spain
Europe from Africa
Russia from the Byzantine Empire
Southeast Asia from India

Select *three* of the examples listed and for each example:

- Describe one idea or practice that was acquired by the first nation or region from the second
- Discuss the effect of the idea or practice on the nation that adopted it

6. Many leaders have changed their nation's history by the political, economic, or social policies.

Leaders
Otto von Bismarck
Ho Chi Minh
Mohandas Gandhi
Jomo Kenyatta
Margaret Thatcher
Mikhail Gorbachev

a Select *three* of the leaders from the list. For *each* leader chosen, describe a specific political, economic, or social policy of that leader that brought about change in his or her nation.

b For *one* of the leaders discussed in answer *a*, explain how that leader's policy has had either a positive or negative effect on his or her nation.

7. Revolutions can be political, social and/or economic. They produce long-term effects on regions and countries.

Regions/Countries

Africa	Japan
China	Latin America
Iran	Western Europe

Select *three* regions or countries listed. For *each* one selected:

- Identify a specific revolution that occurred in the region or country
- Describe *one* major cause of the revolution
- Explain *one* long-term effect of the revolution on that region or country

8. Since World War II, the region shown on the map below has been the scene of frequent conflict stemming from a variety of sources.

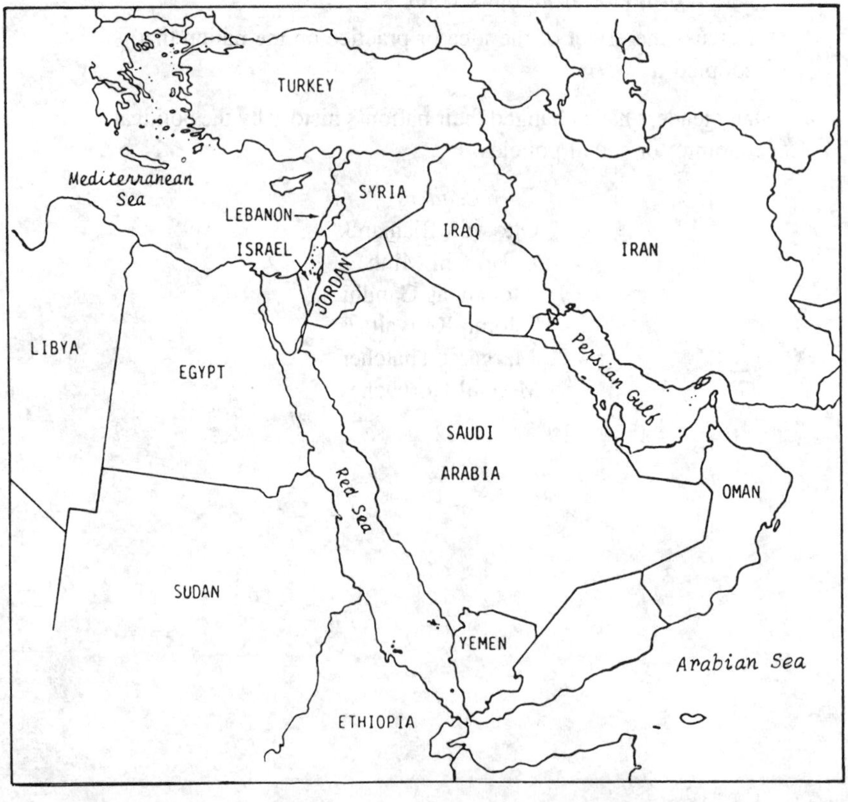

a Select *two* sources of conflict from the list below. Show how *each* source of conflict has influenced a specific nation or nations labeled on the map. [You may use the same or different nations for each source of conflict selected.]

Sources of Conflict
Oil resources
Territorial disputes
Religious differences
Nationalism

b Choose *one* nation labeled on the map. Identify a development that has occurred since World War II that has required a change in United States policy toward that nation. Show how United States policy has changed as a result of the development.

9. Civil wars have occurred in various nations throughout modern history. In each nation listed below, a civil war occurred during the time period indicated.

Select *three* of the nations listed below. For *each* one chosen:

- Identify the opposing forces involved
- Describe a major issue that led to civil war
- State the outcome of the civil war and discuss a change that resulted from it

Nations Experiencing Civil Wars
United States (1861–1865)
The Soviet Union (1918–1922)
China (1927–1949)
Spain (1936–1939)
Greece (1945–1949)
Vietnam (1956–1975)

UNIT 3 Global Society

MAKING CONNECTIONS

As you review each unit, you will find additional information in this column: major ideas, connecting themes, and questions to reinforce your learning. These items are closely tied to the Regents examination. Read this material carefully, and jot down any other facts that you would like to remember in the column's blank spaces. Using this column will **add to your success on the Regents exam.**

Section 1 Africa
Section 2 India
Section 3 Southeast Asia
Section 4 China
Section 5 Japan
Section 6 Latin America
Section 7 The Middle East
Section 8 Western Europe
Section 9 Northern Eurasia and Eastern Europe

The focus of this unit is on the culture of the people within each of the regions of the Global Studies curriculum. **Culture** is defined as the way in which a group of people live. It includes and affects a people's customs, traditions, values, religion, art, music, government, and economic system. Some factors that account for variations or differences in cultures include (1) geographic conditions; (2) isolation; (3) basic values and beliefs; and (4) discovery and invention.

Review the definitions that follow to increase your understanding of this unit.

- **Customs** are rules of behavior, or norms, that affect a people's ordinary ways of doing things such as eating habits and dress. Customs are also called **folkways**. Customs called **mores** are values and behaviors held by a particular society.
- **Cultural diffusion** is the way in which one society borrows aspects or traits from another society and incorporates them into its own culture.
- **Assimilation**, or absorption, is the result of cultural diffusion.
- **Ethnocentrism** is the belief that one's culture is superior to all others. It is important not to judge the culture of another group of people from the viewpoint of your own.

As you read this unit, remember that **social perspective** is concerned with people and their institutions, such as the family, and how their cultures have affected their particular societies and the history of that global region.

SECTION 1 Social Setting: Africa

OVERVIEW

MAKING CONNECTIONS

The continent of Africa has a diversity of cultures. There are over 800 ethnic groups, each with its own language or dialect. An **ethnic group** is a classification of people who share a common racial, national, tribal, religious, linguistic, or cultural origin or background. The Europeans who colonized Africa during the 1800s used the word **tribe** to describe Africa's various ethnic groups. Although textbooks use both terms, "tribe" appears on the Global Studies Regents exam.

A key concept in African studies is **tribalism**, loyalty to one's ethnic group (tribe) rather than to a nation. European imperialism encouraged tribalism. The imperial powers drew political boundaries that disregarded traditional ethnic (tribal) territories. They created nations that divided some ethnic groups (tribes) and artificially drew others together.

AFRICAN SOCIETY

The majority of the people who live in North Africa (the lands stretching from Morocco to Egypt) are Arabs who practice Islam. Most Africans who live south of the Sahara Desert consider themselves members of a particular ethnic group.

Traditional African Families

Most Africans live in **extended families**. These are families in which three or more generations live in one household or near each other. The extended family educates and trains the young, ensuring that they learn traditional customs and ways of life. Most ethnic groups in Africa are **patriarchal**, or male dominated, rather than **matriarchal**, or female dominated. Descent in most traditional family units is **patrilineal**, or passed on from father to oldest son. In matriarchal ethnic groups, descent is **matrilineal**, or passed on from mother to oldest daughter.

MARRIAGE Marriage in traditional African society is seen as the union of two families rather than two individuals. **Polygamy**, the practice of having more than one wife, is permitted. The custom is practiced in northern and western Africa, where Islam allows it, and in sub-Saharan Africa. The custom of **bride-wealth** has tended to limit polygamy today. Bride-wealth is a gift given by the groom to a bride's family to make up for the loss of her work. Africans believe bride-wealth

MAKING CONNECTIONS

brings status to the bride and helps guarantee that the marriage will last.

EMPHASIS ON THE GROUP The traditional African social structure emphasizes the group over the individual. The social hierarchy, or system of social rankings, is illustrated by the diagram on this page.

Social Hierarchy in Africa

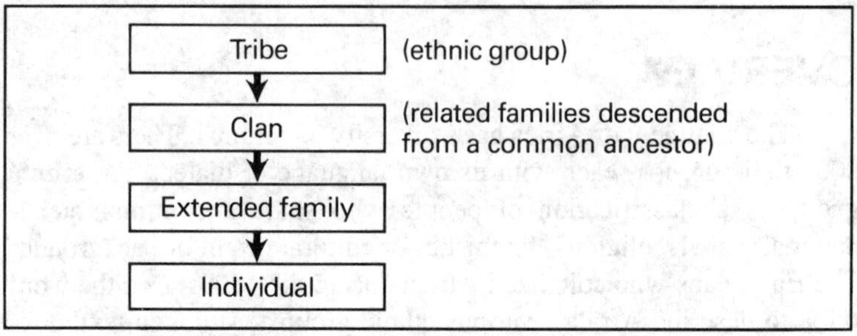

Changes in Traditional African Society

In the past, ethnic groups provided protection and security for their members. However, since independence during the 1950s and 1960s, several forces have changed the role of ethnic groups and traditional families.

- **Tribalism vs. Nationalism** Conflicts have emerged between the interests of ethnic groups and the interests of the nation.
- **Urbanization** The movement of people from rural areas to cities has lessened the traditional influence of both the extended family and the ethnic group.
- **Rapid Population Growth** A high birth rate has led to overcrowding in cities and put a strain on resources in rural areas. Nearly 45 percent of the people in Africa are under 15 years of age. Scarcity of food and lack of good health care have led to famine and disease. Africa has the highest infant mortality rate, or death of infants at or soon after birth, of any continent on earth.

AFRICAN RELIGIONS

Religions in Africa include animism, Islam, and Christianity.

Animism

Traditional African religion is called **animism**. While religious practices differ among ethnic groups, followers of animism share certain beliefs and practices.

- **One supreme God** created the universe.
- **Spirits and forces of nature** exist in all living and nonliving things.
- **Ancestor worship** respects deceased ancestors, whose spirits can affect life in a positive or negative way.

- **Medicine men**, or **diviners**, counsel the people and have special powers, including the power to heal illnesses.

Islam

Islam, founded by Muhammad, spread to northern and western Africa through the process of cultural diffusion. Islam upholds belief in one god, Allah, and in the Five Pillars. At present, Islam is the fastest-growing religion in the world.

Christianity

Like Islam, Christianity came to Africa through cultural diffusion. Coptic Christians in Ethiopia and Egypt trace their roots back to the Byzantine Empire. Other Christian churches in Africa resulted from missionary activities during the age of European imperialism.

MAKING CONNECTIONS

Society and Religion For more information on Islam, see the section on the Middle East in this unit.

Key Concepts: Change Religion can act as an agent of social and political change that is already underway. Many Africans developed their own forms of Christian practice by breaking away from the churches established by European missionaries and creating their own organizations.

AFRICAN ARTS

African arts are a reflection of strong ethnic traditions and religious beliefs.

History and Literature

History and literature are based on an oral, or spoken, tradition. Each ethnic group has a **griot**, or storyteller, who passes the group's oral history onto the next generation. A key theme in modern African literature is the conflict between traditional values and the values of the modern industrial world. Traditional values include:

- Respect for the spirits and forces of nature
- Dominance of group interests over individual interests

Woodcarving

Woodcarving is a popular artistic form in Africa. Woodcarvers carve statues and masks. Traditional Africans believe masks possess spiritual powers when worn during religious ceremonies. The design of African masks has influenced the style of masks worn by goalies in hockey. African masks have also inspired artists such as Henri Matisse and Pablo Picasso.

Key Concepts: Culture Traditional African art is both utilitarian and sacred in nature.

Painting and Sculpture

Styles vary across the continent, but most African artists place special emphasis on the human head because of the importance given to the inner self. Painters emphasize bright, geometric colors. The geometric, abstract styles of African art affected the development of modern art in the United States and Europe. Many of Pablo Picasso's paintings are of a similar style.

Music

African music is **polyrhythmic**, or multirhythmic. Unlike Western music, which usually has a maximum of two rhythms at the same

MAKING CONNECTIONS

time, African music can have as many as five overlapping rhythms. Drums play an important part in African music and in communicating messages between villages. Africans use music for ceremonial purpose and to relieve the drudgery of day-to-day work. African music has influenced contemporary non-African artists such as Santana and Paul Simon.

MAJOR SOCIAL THEMES

1. Ethnic groups (tribes) form the basic social unit in sub-Sahara Africa, and tribalism (loyalty to one's tribe) is stronger among most Africans than nationalism (loyalty to one's nation).
2. In most ethnic groups (tribes), people usually live in extended families, or households made up of three or more generations.
3. Traditional African values are changing as a result of industrialization, urbanization, education, and political revolutions.
4. Most African ethnic groups (tribes) practice animism. Followers of animism believe in one supreme god, respect for the spirits and forces of nature, ancestor worship, and the special powers of diviners.

SECTION 2 Social Setting: India

OVERVIEW

The subcontinent of South Asia includes the nations of India, Pakistan, Bangladesh, and Sri Lanka. The region is home to a diversity of peoples and cultures. For example, India alone has 15 major languages, including English, and more than 800 dialects. Religious diversity also characterizes the region. India is the birthplace of Hinduism, the world's oldest religion, and Buddhism. In nearby Pakistan and Bangladesh, Islam prevails. In Sri Lanka most people follow Buddhism. This section focuses on India because of the length of its ancient civilization and its unique culture.

MAKING CONNECTIONS

Key Concepts: Identity Identity in India is still based more upon cultural groupings than upon national or political loyalty.

INDIAN SOCIETY

Indian society is organized around extended families and the caste system.

Traditional Indian Families

Most Indians live in a type of extended family called the **joint family**. This kind of family structure includes married brothers who live together with their families. They hold all property in common, and younger brothers assume responsibility for educating the children of older brothers.

MARRIAGE Like most African societies, India is **patriarchal**, or male dominated. Traditional marriages in India represent a union between two families rather than two individuals. A wife usually moves in with her husband's family, a custom known as **patrilocal** marriage. Parents often arrange marriages for their children, and most marriages are strictly determined by the caste system.

Society and Politics The village remains central to India's social structure. In many former colonies, adherence to the traditional social order has deterred the national government's efforts to develop a strong sense of national unity and purpose throughout the country.

The Caste System

The **caste system** is a system of social stratification, or the ranking of people. It is based on Hindu beliefs and has long been a part of Indian society. Although the Indian constitution banned discrimination on the basis of caste in 1950, the system still influences many people's lives.

MAKING CONNECTIONS

VARNA Traditional Indian society rested upon four main **varna**, or occupational groupings.

- **Brahmans**, a religious class of priests
- **Kshatriyas**, a warrior class
- **Vaisyas**, a class of landowners, merchants, and herders
- **Sudras**, a laboring class of servants and peasants

The **Harijans** were a group of people outside the caste system known as the "untouchables," or outcasts. They were not considered one of the varna.

EFFECT OF THE CASTE SYSTEM Thousands of subcastes have developed within the four varna. The castes into which people are born affect their occupations, marriage partners, and rights and duties within society. The caste system is an important aspect of beliefs in Hinduism, India's primary religion.

INDIAN RELIGIONS

Key Concepts: Culture
In India religious beliefs and social organization are closely related.

Hinduism is the predominant religion in India. However, a number of other religions exist within Indian society, leading to conflicts among the Indian people.

Hinduism

Hinduism began about 5,000 years ago and is considered the world's oldest religion. Approximately 83 percent of India's population practices Hinduism.

FOUNDING No one person founded Hinduism. It evolved over a long period of time into a flexible, tolerant religion that allows for individual differences in beliefs. Unlike Christianity and Islam, Hinduism does not have one sacred book, such as the Bible or Koran. Instead Hindus have the **Vedas**, collections of prayers and verses, and the **Upanishads**, philosophical descriptions of the origins of the universe.

DEITIES Hindus believe in one supreme force called **Brahma**, whose presence is everywhere and in all things. Hindu gods are considered aspects, or manifestations, of Brahma. Three major deities, or aspects of Brahma, are **Brahma** (the creator), **Vishnu** (the preserver of life), and **Shiva** (the destroyer and re-creator of new life).

REINCARNATION A belief in **reincarnation**, or rebirth of the soul in another body after death, forms the basis of Hinduism and underlies the entire caste system. Hinduism maintains that people's actions in this life determine their reward or punishment in the next life. A person's caste is the reward or punishment for **karma**, deeds committed in a previous life. Acceptable behavior means following the **dharma**, or rules and obligations, of the caste into which a person is born.

MAKING CONNECTIONS

CYCLE OF LIFE Because Hindus believe in reincarnation, they practice **cremation**, or the burning of dead bodies. They see life as a cycle of birth, death, and rebirth. The cycle of reincarnation continues until a person achieves **moksha**, the highest state of being and perfect internal peace.

HINDUISM AND SOCIETY Hinduism is both a religious and a social system. It especially affects the lives of people in rural India, who form the bulk of the population. The untouchables must still drink from certain wells and take jobs no other caste would consider. Recent laws have aimed at improving their lives, but centuries of belief in the caste system have hindered change.

Buddhism

India is also the birthplace of a second great world religion, Buddhism.

FOUNDING The founder of Buddhism was a prince named **Siddhartha Gautama**, who lived in Nepal from 563–483 B.C. Gautama rejected his wealth to search for the meaning of human suffering. He became the **Buddha**, or Enlightened One, after meditating under a sacred bodhi tree.

FOUR NOBLE TRUTHS Buddhism rests upon the **Four Noble Truths**.

- All life is suffering.
- Suffering is caused by desire.
- Desire can be eliminated.
- There is a path, or way, to end desire.

NOBLE EIGHT-FOLD PATH To eliminate earthly desire, a person needs to follow the Noble Eight-Fold Path. The path requires right speech, action, views, intention, livelihood, effort, concentration, and mindfulness. By following this path, a person will move toward **nirvana**, a state of perfect peace and harmony.

CYCLE OF LIFE Buddhism does not have a belief in a supreme being. The goal of life is nirvana. Achievement of nirvana may take many lifetimes, and Buddhists accept the Hindu concepts of karma and reincarnation. However, Buddhism was created in opposition to the Hindu caste system. As a result, all people can achieve nirvana without moving up through the castes.

CULTURAL DIFFUSION Buddhism spread from India to China, Korea, Japan, and Southeast Asia. Peoples outside of India adapted Buddhist beliefs to fit their cultures. Today more than 300 million people follow Buddhism, about 10 percent of whom live in India.

MAKING CONNECTIONS

Key Concepts: Diversity
Religion has worked both to unify and divide the people of India.

Key Concepts: Culture and Change
Differences between the Islamic world and the world view of Hinduism resulted in cultural change when the two philosophies came into contact with each other. These changes are the result of cultural diffusion.

Key Concepts: Change
Urbanization in India has tended to weaken traditional beliefs and life patterns.

Other Religions in India

Although Hinduism and Buddhism are the two largest religions in India, other faiths are also practiced.

JAINISM Jainism was founded in opposition to Hinduism. It preaches nonviolence, refusal to kill all living things, and vegetarianism.

SIKHISM Sikhs follow the beliefs of their founder, **Nanak**. These beliefs include monotheism (one God), rejection of the caste system, and reincarnation. Male Sikhs do not cut their hair and have traditionally belonged to India's warrior class.

CHRISTIANITY European missionaries introduced Christianity to southern India during the age of imperialism.

ISLAM Approximately 11 percent of the Indian population practice Islam, founded by Muhammad (A.D. 570–632). The followers of Islam believe in one God, **Allah**. (Islam means "submit to Allah's will.") They do not eat pork, and pray five times a day facing **Mecca**, the religion's sacred city located in Saudi Arabia. Islam arrived in India in the 700s, and the major concentration of believers lives in the far western and eastern parts of the country. When India won independence, violent clashes between Muslims (followers of Islam) and Hindus led to the creation of West Pakistan and East Pakistan.

Changes in Traditional Indian Society

Indian society has undergone major changes since independence in 1947.

EXTENSION OF THE BRITISH SYSTEM OF EDUCATION British emphasis upon equal education, including the right of untouchables to attend school, has broken down some caste barriers.

CONSTITUTIONAL GOVERNMENT In the campaign for independence, Mohandas K. Gandhi supported increased rights for the untouchables, a demand reflected in the Indian constitution. The constitution also gave women the right to vote (1950) and recognized their right to divorce and inherit property. In 1966 **Indira Gandhi** became the nation's first woman prime minister. However, constitutional changes have been slow to reach the masses of untouchables and women, especially in rural areas.

URBANIZATION The movement of people from rural areas to cities has tended to break down restrictions imposed by the caste system.

INDUSTRIALIZATION The rise of industry and growth of new jobs has blurred caste distinctions and increased social mobility.

INDIAN ARTS

MAKING CONNECTIONS

Indian arts show the strong influence of its three major religions—Hinduism, Buddhism, and Islam.

Architecture

Hindu temples, such as those at **Ellora**, include carvings that tell important Hindu stories that can be understood even by those who cannot read. Buddhist architecture is best illustrated by the carved caves of Ellora. However, the most famous monument in India is the **Taj Mahal**, located in Agra. It was built in the 1600s by a Muslim ruler named Shah Jahan as a tomb for his wife. In accordance with Islamic law, the Taj Mahal contains no carvings or paintings.

Literature

The *Mahabharata* is an epic poem about the influence of a Hindu deity named **Krishna**. It contains the *Bhagavad-Gita*, a poem setting forth correct Hindu conduct. Another famous Hindu epic poem, the *Ramayana*, also expresses Hindu values.

Music

Indian music is centered primarily around its melody and a countless variation of notes called **ragas**. A long-necked stringed instrument named the **sitar** has influenced the music of Western artists such as George Harrison and the Beatles.

Movies

Today India produces more movies than any nation in the world. Adventure films and films with religious overtones are favorites.

MAJOR SOCIAL THEMES

1. Hinduism had significant impact upon Indian society as a religious and social system.
2. Traditional Indian society is based on the joint family and the caste system.
3. The caste system and its beliefs provide a highly organized and structured society in which people believe social mobility comes only through reincarnation.
4. Provisions in the Indian constitution, urbanization, industrialization, and westernization of education have brought some changes to traditional Indian society. However, Hindu belief in the caste system has slowed change.
5. India is the birthplace of two major religions—Hinduism and Buddhism. While Hinduism has stayed primarily an Indian religion, Buddhism has spread throughout Asia as a result of cultural diffusion.

SECTION 3 Social Setting: Southeast Asia

MAKING CONNECTIONS

OVERVIEW

A key social pattern in Southeast Asia is the region's diversity of people. Another pattern is the influence of religion, particularly Buddhism, upon cultural life.

SOUTHEAST ASIAN SOCIETY

The majority of people in Southeast Asia live in rural areas. The region's rain forests, mountains, and string of archipelagoes limit travel. As a result, social and cultural life tends to center on the village and agricultural production of rice.

SOUTHEAST ASIAN RELIGION

Key Concepts: Culture The spread of Buddhism from India through Southeast Asia is an example of cultural diffusion.

Religion has traditionally shaped the cultural life of Southeast Asia. In Cambodia, Hinduism influenced the architecture of Angkor Wat, while Buddhism affected the styles of more modern temples and some dance forms. Because of contact with Arab traders, Islamic culture gained a strong foothold in Indonesia and Malaysia. Roman Catholicism took root in the Philippines after 400 years of colonial rule by Spain.

Buddhism

Society and Religion For more information on Buddhism, see the section on India in this unit.

Buddhism originated in India with the teachings of Siddhartha Gautama. Two hundred years after Gautama died, an Indian ruler named Ashoka embraced Buddhism and sent missionaries to Southeast Asia and China. Today numerous Buddhist temples and statues are the centers of village life.

THERAVADA BUDDHISM The branch of Buddhism that became popular in Cambodia, Laos, and Thailand was Theravada or Hinayana Buddhism. Theravada Buddhism emphasizes release from secular, or worldly, suffering through meditation. Many young men are expected to live at least part of their lives as monks in monasteries or temples.

MAKING CONNECTIONS

MAHAYANA BUDDHISM In Vietnam and northern Asia, many people embraced Mahayana Buddhism. This branch of Buddhism holds that salvation is open to everyone, not just monks, through the achievement of perfect faith. Mahayana Buddhism has split into many sects, or smaller groups, that follow its basic teachings.

MAJOR SOCIAL THEMES

1. The physical geography of Southeast Asia has isolated peoples in the region and produced great cultural diversity.
2. Social life in Southeast Asia centers around the village and agricultural production of rice.
3. Religion, especially Buddhism, has shaped cultural life in Southeast Asia.

SECTION 4

Social Setting: China

MAKING CONNECTIONS

Regents Tip List the advantages and disadvantages to the individual and to society when the five relationships of Confucius are followed.

To the individual

Advantages:

Disadvantages:

To society

Advantages:

Disadvantages:

OVERVIEW

Throughout their long history, the Chinese adopted an ethnocentric world view in which they saw their culture as dominant. At times, they thought of China as a civilization rather than as a nation with distinct physical borders. Fundamental to this world view was a highly structured society based on traditional values that evolved over 3,000 years.

PHILOSOPHICAL INFLUENCES

Various philosophies, or systems of thought, influenced the development of Chinese civilization.

Confucianism

Confucius (551–479 B.C.), the Chinese philosopher and scholar, established his own school. Here he taught a system of thought that helped shape China's history and society.

ORGANIZATION OF SOCIETY Confucius defined the social order on the basis of five key human relationships.

Five Relationships of Confucius

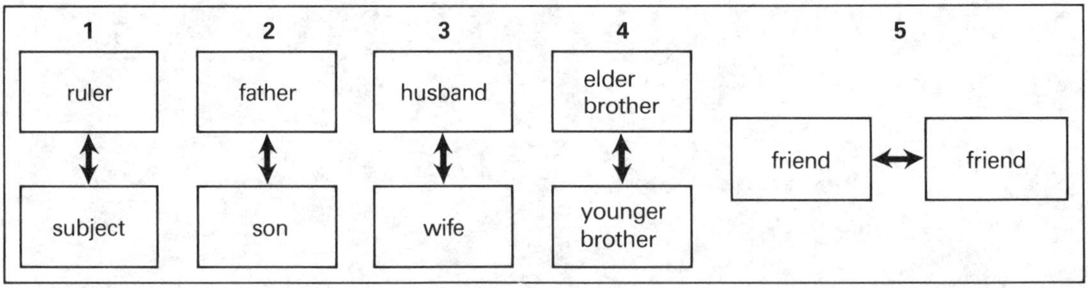

PRINCIPLES OF HUMAN RELATIONSHIPS

1. Confucianism arranged Chinese society according to a hierarchy, or arrangement of ranks. Four of the five relationships cited by Confucius were between superiors and inferiors. Only in the context of friend to friend did Confucius conceive of a relationship between equals.

2. To Confucius, the family was the most important aspect of society. The family taught the young correct human behavior and loyalty. Three of the five Confucian relationships occurred within the family.
3. Confucian society was **patriarchal** and **patrilocal**. Wives moved in with the husband's family and became part of it. Of the five relationships, the only role assigned to women was that of wife. Sister to sister or mother to child were not included among the primary relationships of society.
4. Confucius lived in a time of political upheaval. As a result, he placed special emphasis on the ruler-to-subject relationship. He envisioned a perfect society in which capable ministers served good rulers. Confucius drew many of his followers from China's educated class of administrators, who spread the influence of his teachings.

MAKING CONNECTIONS

SYSTEM OF ETHICS Confucianism was not a religion. Confucius acknowledged "heaven's will," but confined his teachings to questions of ethics and morality. He took an optimistic view of human nature. He thought the outward use of **li**, or ritual, would produce an inner harmony and perfect human character. Confucius supported moral education and taught anyone regardless of their finances. He stressed human society, rather than the individual, and emphasized the social importance of correct behavior.

Key Concepts: Culture and Identity
Confucius valued the family, government, education, and ethics. Confucian thought came to influence Chinese social organization, political structure, and the educational system. In so doing, Confucian thought became the foundation of Chinese civilization.

CONFUCIANISM AND GOVERNMENT By the T'ang Dynasty (A.D. 618–907), Confucianism dominated political life in China. Confucian teachings became the basis of a civil service examination used to recruit able administrators. While any person could take the examination, the necessity of an education limited it to those who could afford schooling. The system provided the emperor with a trained core of administrators schooled in Confucian ideas.

Taoism

Taoism emphasized self-knowledge and contemplation. While Confucianism stressed social conformity, Taoism stressed personal freedom. It taught people to ponder the Tao, or source of life, so that they could find harmony with nature and the universe. Taoism envisioned nature as a marriage of opposites, symbolized by the **yin-yang**, or female-male aspects of life. Taoist teachers saw no conflict with a person practicing Confucianism (conformity) within the family and Taoism (personal freedom) in private meditation. A balance between the two was sought.

Yin-Yang

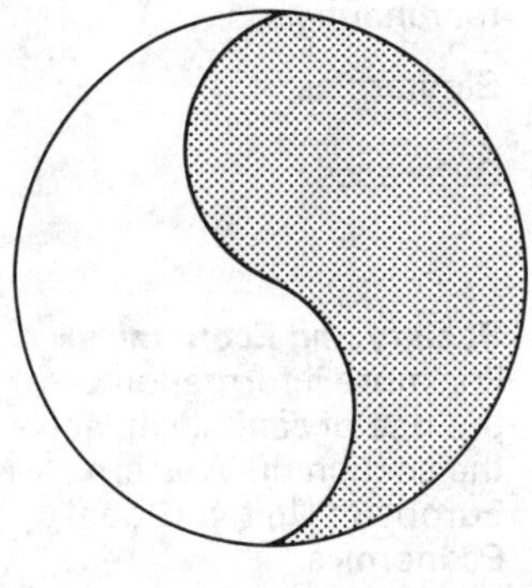

Buddhism

Buddhism was introduced to China by way of India. Like Taoism, it emphasized a denial of worldly goods and a life of meditation.

Society and Religion For more on Buddhism, see the section on India in this unit.

MAKING CONNECTIONS

TRADITIONAL CHINESE SOCIETY

The traditional social order in China reflected Confucian rankings. The emperor held the pivotal position in society, with a hierarchical order beneath him.

Traditional Social Order in China

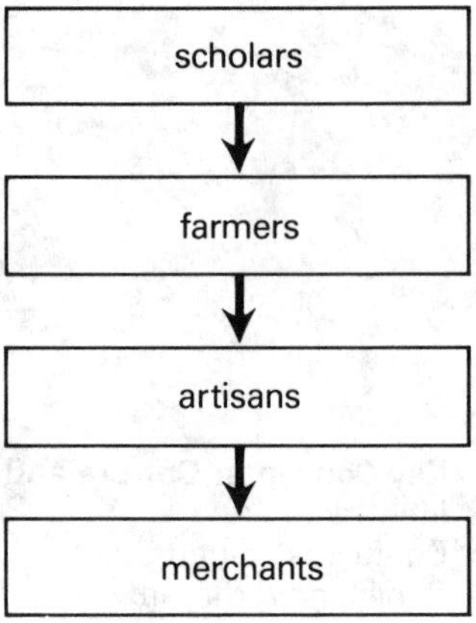

Scholars

Because of the Confucian system of examinations, only scholars held high positions in government. These administrators came from wealthy families who could afford to educate their sons. They used their power to protect the interests of their social class, which became known as the **scholar-gentry**. This class of rich landowners provided officials for the empire while promoting a social order based on Confucian ideals.

Farmers

Confucians ranked farmers second in the traditional social order because of their importance to food production. The majority of the Chinese population was made up of **subsistence farmers** who grew enough food to feed themselves and their own families. Many farmers did not own their own land. Instead, they farmed a part of a large landowner's property in exchange for a share of the crop. Confucianism emphasized **extended families** as the ideal. However, rural poverty often made it impossible for a farmer to support more than a **nuclear family**, or family unit made up of parents and children.

Artisans

Artisans made up the third group in the social order. They represented only a small percentage of the population in agricultural China. Most worked at skilled trades, such as blacksmithing, to produce goods necessary for farmers.

Regents Tip Compare the Chinese and the European merchant class.

Similarities:

Differences:

Merchants

Merchants were the lowest-ranking class in traditional Chinese society. Land formed the basis of wealth in traditional China, and merchants often used the profits from commerce to invest in land. Unlike merchants in Western Europe, merchants in traditional China used their wealth to become members of the scholar-gentry and to educate their male children for positions in government. They never developed the independent power and status of merchant-class investors in Europe which contributed to the rise of capitalism.

Society and Economics For more information on the rise of capitalism, see the section on Western Europe in Unit 4, Global Economics.

CHALLENGES TO TRADITIONAL CHINESE SOCIETY

The traditional social order in China weakened in the late 1800s and finally collapsed under communism.

Arrival of Imperialism

In the 1800s, western imperialists encroached on China's territory. The military and industrial power of the imperialists challenged Chinese ethnocentrism and eroded the power of the scholar-gentry. It also undermined the social order set up by Confucius.

Nationalist Revolution

The Nationalist Revolution of October 10, 1911, overthrew the Manchu rulers of the Ch'ing dynasty. Wealthy landowners supported the rebellion along with an expanding merchant class enriched by contact with the Europeans. A civil war between the Nationalist and Chinese Communist parties prevented the Nationalists from taking firm control of China. Disorder was also heightened by the invasion and occupation of China by Japan (1937–1945) and the outbreak of World War II.

Communist Victory

After World War II, the Communists led by Mao Zedong stepped up efforts to take over the government from the Nationalists. In 1949 they triumphed, and Mao embarked on a plan to remake Chinese society.

END OF THE SCHOLAR-GENTRY The Communists scorned and persecuted the scholar-gentry. They eventually seized private land and redistributed it to the peasants. The ideal of a scholar-gentry was replaced by the ideal of a model farmer working on a large communal tract of land for the good of the state.

ATTACK ON CONFUCIANISM Mao challenged Confucian values, especially by emphasizing the value of manual labor. He specifically targeted Confucianism for destruction during the Cultural Revolution of 1966. He ordered formation of the Red Guard, groups of Communist-trained students, to lead the revolution. They destroyed many cultural relics created by imperial dynasties and attacked white-collar professionals. Many scholars and administrators were ordered to do manual labor. Children were rewarded for loyalty to the state rather than for loyalty to the family. Women, traditionally bound by the Confucian family, received some expanded rights.

CHINA AFTER MAO A few years after Mao's death in 1976, Deng Xiaoping came to power. He ended the disruption that followed the Cultural Revolution and allowed some degree of private ownership. In June 1989, students demonstrated in Tiananmen Square for greater freedom in China. The government, however, brutally crushed the student rebels, leaving the future direction of social policy in China uncertain.

MAKING CONNECTIONS

Society and Economics For more information on land redistribution under the Communists, see the section on China in Unit 4, Global Economics.

Regents Tip List four ways that Mao modified China's social structure. (An example has been listed.)

Elevated the farmer in the social order

MAKING CONNECTIONS

CHINESE ART

Traditional Chinese Art

Chinese artists traditionally favored ceramics, such as the vases of the Ming Dynasty (1368–1644), and paintings done on paper scrolls. Painters often chose three subjects: landscapes, birds and flowers, and portraits. **Calligraphy**, or beautiful handwriting, was considered an integral part of the painting. Taoist painters tried less to duplicate reality than to suggest their feelings about nature.

Communist Art

Communist rulers used art as propaganda to speed transformation of Chinese society. During the Cultural Revolution, all forms of art glorified the goals of Mao. Art was used as propaganda. Since Mao's death, the Communists have relaxed their control of the arts somewhat.

MAJOR SOCIAL THEMES

1. Confucius defined five human relationships as the basis of social organization. These relationships emphasized the family and social conformity.
2. Taoism emphasized self-knowledge and contemplation, seeking knowledge of the Tao, or source of life.
3. The traditional social hierarchy created by Confucianism assured dominance of a scholar-gentry and disdain for commerce.
4. Triumph of the Communists ushered in a period of great social upheaval in which the ideal of peasant-workers replaced the ideal of the scholar-gentry.
5. Traditional Chinese art reflects a Taoist influence while contemporary art has been used for propaganda purposes.

SECTION 5 Social Setting: Japan

OVERVIEW

Japan's society and culture have been shaped by Japan's geographic isolation and by a pattern of selective borrowing. Traditional Chinese culture came to Japan through the process of cultural diffusion. The Japanese then adapted Chinese culture to fit their own society and identity as a people. After the arrival of Commodore Perry, the Japanese also selectively borrowed from the industrialized nations of the West.

JAPANESE SOCIETY

Japan's proximity, or nearness, to China opened the way to cultural contact between the two societies. The Japanese borrowed Chinese writing, imperial court procedures, architectural styles, and Confucian thought. However, the Japanese did not remake their culture in China's image. Instead, they integrated Chinese cultural traits into their society without being overwhelmed by them.

Japanese Feudalism

The Japanese ordered society in much the same way as the Chinese, with one important exception. In China the scholar-gentry occupied the highest class. In Japan the **samurai**, or warrior class, held the highest position in society. This difference was a result of Japanese feudalism.

SYSTEM OF LOYALTIES In Japan feudal principles of loyalty governed society. The traditional political structure rested upon personal loyalties between the samurai (warriors) and daimyo (lord). This differed from China where rulers recruited administrators by civil service examinations. At the top of Japanese society was the **shogun**, who theoretically ruled on behalf of the emperor.

CODE OF HONOR Feudalism limited the influence of Confucianism in Japan. Confucius, for example, considered the family to be the basis of society. Under feudalism, however, a Japanese warrior might place the interests of his lord above those of his family. The code of **bushido**, "way of the warrior," provided the framework for Japanese ideas on honor and proper conduct in society.

MAKING CONNECTIONS

Traditional Social Order in Japan

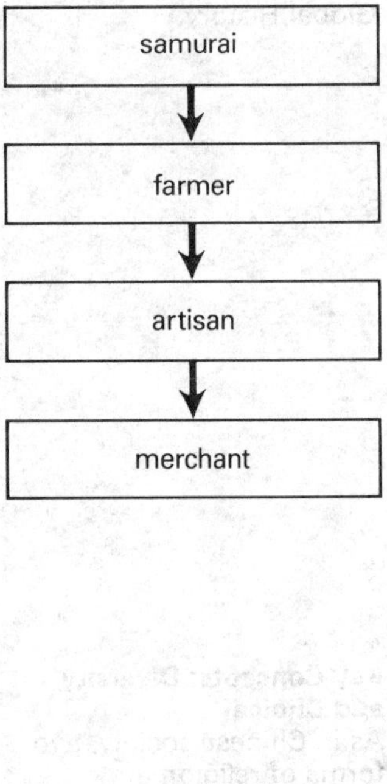

Society and History For more on Japanese feudalism, see the section on Japan in Unit 2, Global History.

MAKING CONNECTIONS

Traditional Japanese Families

Like Confucian families in China, Japanese families were **patriarchal**, or male dominated. Parents arranged marriages, and women occupied a lower status than men. The oldest male in the household, usually the father, looked out for the interests of the family as a whole. Individual desires mattered little. If individuals threatened the family's good name, the family would expel them. Open displays of love between a husband and wife were considered "unmanly" according to the warrior code.

Changes in Traditional Japanese Society

Society and History For more on the Meiji Restoration and United States occupation, see the section on Japan in Unit 2, Global History.

The opening of Japan by Commodore Perry in 1853 brought profound changes to traditional Japanese society. Starting with the Meiji Restoration, Japan became the first nonwestern nation to modernize. Further changes were introduced at the end of World War II when United States troops occupied Japan and introduced a new constitution.

DECLINE OF THE SAMURAI The rise of industry and adoption of western education blurred class lines. The power of the merchant class grew at the expense of the samurai. Also, the start of conscription, or drafted army, opened the military to people of all ranks—even peasants.

NEW FAMILY RELATIONSHIPS Laws imposed during the American occupation ended the special legal privileges given to the male head of household. Individual family members, especially women, gained more rights. The relationship of husband and wife grew in importance as more couples married for love. Although husbands and wives today tend to follow separate lives, they commonly appear together in public. Also, the husband's mother exercises less control over her daughter-in-law than in the past.

Key Concepts: Diversity and Choice
As in Chinese society, two forms of religion are practiced in Japanese society.

JAPANESE RELIGION

Unlike other major religions, Japanese religions allow people to be involved with more than one religion at a time. A person seeking religious fulfillment may look for answers in a blend of religions. The two major religions in Japan are Shinto and Buddhism.

Shinto

Shinto originated in Japan. It has no founder or sacred scriptures. The name Shinto means the way of the **kami**, or spirits. The followers of Shinto believe all things—living and nonliving—possess a kami, or divine spirit. Shinto even gives Mt. Fuji a guardian spirit. According to Shinto, the imperial family possesses a kami that descends from the Sun Goddess. As a result, they are given special reverence.

Buddhism

Mahayana Buddhism arrived in Japan from Korea in the mid-500s. The Japanese selectively borrowed from Buddhism and blended it with Shinto beliefs to form a branch of Buddhism known as **Tendai**. Two of Japan's most popular Buddhist sects—**Jodo** and **Zen**—grew out of Tendai teachings. Jodo offers enlightenment to all people through faith and intervention of a deity known as the Infinite Light. Zen calls for strict discipline, meditation, and humility as the paths to **satori** (the Japanese word for nirvana or enlightenment).

URBANIZATION Industrialization and urbanization went hand in hand. Today more than 75 percent of Japan's population lives in cities. Housing shortages and overcrowding are common problems.

JAPANESE ART

Traditional Chinese art influenced the Japanese through cultural diffusion. Chinese scroll painting, for example, provided the model for Japanese painters. The influence of Zen was also felt, especially in the Japanese preference for subjects from nature. Zen emphasis on ritual and precision led to the highly stylized Japanese tea ceremonies and to landscape gardening. In literature, the Japanese contributed several unique styles including the **haiku**, or brief poem, and two forms of drama, **Noh** and **Kabuki**.

MAJOR SOCIAL THEMES

1. Japan's island location has allowed it to borrow selectively from other cultures without being overwhelmed by them.
2. Traditional Japanese society rested upon a system of feudal relationships, which sometimes limited the influence of Confucianism.
3. Industrialization and United States occupation after World War II dramatically altered the social order in Japan.
4. Japanese religion and art illustrate the process of cultural diffusion and Japanese ability to absorb new ideas without losing their own sense of identity.

MAKING CONNECTIONS

Society and History The novel in the Japanese literary tradition dates back over a thousand years. Noblewomen helped develop a distinctly Japanese literature. *The Tale of the Genji*, written by Lady Murasaki, is considered one of the world's first novels.

SECTION 6 Social Setting: Latin America

MAKING CONNECTIONS

OVERVIEW

The nations of Latin America include a diversity of people and cultures. The current social and cultural characteristics of the region are the result of a complex mix of forces, including a varied physical landscape and interrelations within the region and with other parts of the world.

Key Concepts: Diversity
The racial and ethnic composition of many Latin American countries has resulted in more blending and blurring of racial lines than in North America.

LATIN AMERICAN SOCIETY

The Latin American population is divided by physical barriers and political boundaries. Within the nations of Latin America, a wide range of social differences exists. Ethnic and racial groups include Native American Indians, blacks of African descent, mestizos (people of mixed European and Indian descent), and the descendants of European colonists. The influence of Spain is strongly felt everywhere but Brazil, which was colonized by Portugal. A common language, Spanish, and similar social and religious beliefs help define Latin America as a region.

Traditional Social Order in Latin America

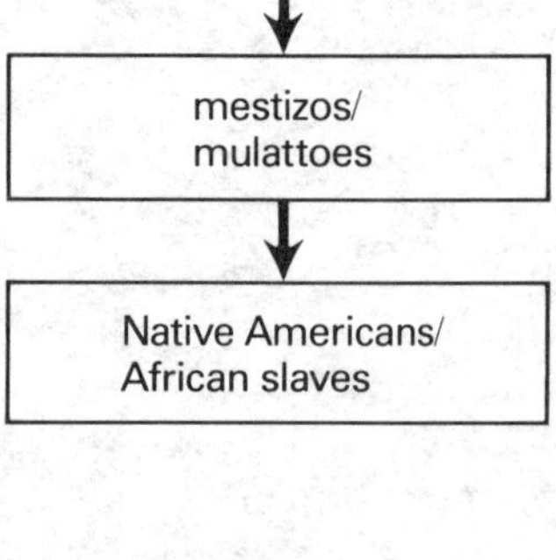

Traditional Social Order

The Spanish conquest of Latin America during the early 1500s resulted in a highly **stratified society**, or society with a strict system of social ranks. The diagram on this page shows the structure of traditional Latin American society after 1500. Social classes ranged from the small group of **peninsulares**, or Spanish-born upper class, to the mass of Native American Indians and black African slaves who formed the base of Latin American society.

Social Mobility

Even after Latin American independence, social mobility was often limited by the colonial class structure. Wealth and family origins remained important criteria for social status. The landed upper class held onto power and still exercises great influence even today. The rise of industry has created and expanded a middle class, drawn mainly from the rank of the mestizos. This group is making inroads in society and using its wealth to gain positions in government. However, class distinctions still remain in Latin American society.

Traditional Latin American Families

Latin American society is family-centered. In the past, Latin Americans favored **extended families** to care for children and the elderly. However, since World War II, increased poverty in rural areas and migration to urban areas has resulted in a great increase in the number of **nuclear families**.

FAMILY ROLES The structure of Latin American families reflects the region's colonial past. Most families are **patriarchal**, or male dominated. Men are influenced by the concept of **machismo**, an attitude that glorifies masculinity. Many men refuse to help in family chores and demand obedience from their wives and children.

MARRIAGE Most Latin Americans still marry in the Roman Catholic Church. Parents play an important role in marriage decisions. They frown upon marriages between couples from different social classes because of the pressures such marriage will bring to the families. Well-to-do couples often keep two surnames, or last names, upon marriage to show the status of their families.

MAKING CONNECTIONS

Key Concepts: Culture
The family represents stability and security in social environments that are politically unstable and economically uncertain.

Key Concepts: Culture
The role of godparents (padrinos) is important to children. Godparents are considered a central part of the family and take part in social occasions.

LATIN AMERICAN RELIGION

Many of the **conquistadores** (Spanish for ''conquerors'') who came to Latin America sought wealth and glory for their nation. However, some came to spread the Christian faith among the Indians. As a result, the Roman Catholic church became an important unifying force in both Spanish and Portuguese colonies.

Indian Religions

Many Indian religions tended to be **animistic**, that is, they believed all objects possessed spirits. These spirits taken together often represented one Supreme Being. The Inca, for example, worshiped a Supreme Being called Viracocha the Creator. Roman Catholic priests used this belief in a Supreme Being to convert Indians to Christian **monotheism**. Some priests turned Indian sacred shrines into Christian holy places. Many conquerors, however, looked down upon the Indian faith and destroyed Indian sacred objects. Because Indians were deeply religious, the loss of these objects often broke their morale. Today some Latin American Indians who live in remote areas still practice ancient religious customs, although others belong to the Roman Catholic church.

Key Concepts: Human Rights
The situation of the Native American Indians, especially in those areas where there is a wide disparity in technology, represents an example of the violation of human rights.

The Role of the Church

Throughout Latin American history, the Roman Catholic church has exerted a major influence on the lives of people. The church acquired vast amounts of land and property, set up schools and universities, kept official records, established hospitals, and served as a gov-

MAKING CONNECTIONS

ernmental agency of Spain. The independence movements of the 1800s created a major crisis for the church. The Roman Catholic clergy had to decide whether to support the independence movements or not. After independence, the church faced another crisis when the new government reexamined the church's power and wealth.

Liberation Theology

Latin America's Roman Catholic clergy has long been split over social policy. Some clergy supported the peninsulares and the Spanish Crown. Others, especially native-born clergy, felt sympathies for the common people. This split has continued into the present. In the 1960s many Latin American priests and nuns spoke out against poverty and advocated political reform.

Supporters of what has become known as **liberation theology** argue that the church has a responsibility to bring about secular, or worldly, change. This position has been controversial. For example, some Roman Catholic clergy have vocally protested human rights abuses by military governments in Latin America.

Evidence of Social Changes

Traditionally three groups—the landed upper class, the military, and the Roman Catholic clergy—have resisted changes in the old social order. They have been aided by a lack of education among many Latin Americans and geographic barriers that have separated peoples. However, in recent years, several forces have combined to bring about change:

- Increasing success of some democratic governments, such as Brazil and Venezuela, and declining influence of the military
- Rise of labor unions and a new industrial middle class
- Huge migration of people from rural areas into the cities
- Desire among many Roman Catholic clergy to relieve poverty among the mass of Latin Americans
- Increased availability of television, spreading new ideas and breaking down cultural barriers among people

LATIN AMERICAN ARTS

Society and History For more information on the accomplishments of the Mayas, Aztecs, and Incas, see the section on Latin America in Unit 2, Global History.

Early pre-Columbian civilizations, such as the Mayas, Aztecs, and Incas, produced major cultural achievements. (See Unit 2, Global History.) Spanish and Portuguese settlers added new traits to these native American cultures. So did black slaves from Africa. This blending of cultures from three continents can be seen in much of the region's art today.

Literature

Intellectuals in Latin American are called **pensadores**, or thinkers. This group produced a tremendous outpouring of literature in the

1900s. Two Chilean poets, Gabriela Mistral and Pablo Neruda, won Nobel Prizes in literature. Another Nobel Prize winner is Gabriel Garcia Marquez. Other major Latin American writers have included Guatemalan author Miguel Angel Asturias and Uruguay prose writer José Enrique Rodo.

MAKING CONNECTIONS

Art and Architecture

Since independence, Latin American artists have experimented with new styles. Often the works are inspired by the rich heritage of Indian art and a desire for artistic freedom. Mexico has dominated styles in painting, especially the murals of Diego Rivera, José Clemente Orozco, and David Alfaro Siqueiros. In architecture, many people look to Brasilia, the capital of Brazil, for spectacular examples of original Latin American designs.

Music

Latin American music clearly shows the blending of racial and ethnic cultures. Composers have drawn upon melodies and instruments used in European, African, and Indian music to create unique works. Leading composers include Brazilian Hector Villa-Lobos and Mexican Carlos Chávez. Latin American music has influenced North American artists, including Stan Getz in jazz and Paul Simon in his album *The Rhythm of the Saints*.

MAJOR SOCIAL THEMES

1. The predominant social institutions in Latin America are the traditional patriarchal family and Roman Catholic church.
2. The class structure present within Latin American society has traditionally favored the landed upper class, military, and Roman Catholic clergy. These groups have dominated the Indians, blacks, and mestizos and restricted social mobility.
3. Societal changes have occurred in Latin American countries through industrialization and urbanization, but are slow to affect the traditionally male-dominated society.
4. The current problems of overpopulation, drug trade, violations of human rights, deforestation, and debt crisis pose many significant obstacles to change within Latin America.
5. Latin American arts reflect a blending of Indian, African, and European cultures.

SECTION 7

Social Setting: The Middle East

MAKING CONNECTIONS

OVERVIEW

The nations of the Middle East span the continents of Europe, Africa, and Asia. Because of the region's strategic location, the Middle East has served as a cultural crossroads. Historically, people in the Middle East have been exposed to many ideas and goods from other lands. Even so, they have retained a sense of regional identity, and traditional social values remain strong.

MIDDLE EASTERN SOCIETY

Key Concepts: Culture and Identity
Religious beliefs and values play a major role in shaping the character and identity of a culture.

Islam, the predominant religion in the Middle East, forms the foundation of Middle Eastern society. Like Hinduism, Islam is a complete way of life. The Islamic sacred book, the *Koran*, summarizes social relationships: "Men are dominant over women . . . and upright women are submissive."

Traditional Middle Eastern Families

Traditional Middle Eastern societies are based upon the **extended family**. According to Islamic custom, families are **patriarchal**. Women and children are expected to practice strict obedience. When a father dies, his brother or eldest son replaces him as the head of the household.

MARRIAGE Courtship is limited or nonexistent in much of the Middle East. Teenage boys and girls are not allowed to socialize, and even in urban, westernized families dating is restricted. As in Africa and India, marriage is seen as a union between two families rather than two individuals. Parents arrange marriages, and the groom's father gives the bride's family a gift to pay for the loss of her labor. The bride's father gives his daughter a dowry, which the husband cannot claim upon divorce. However, Islamic law makes divorce a man's right, and few women initiate it. Islamic law also allows the practice of **polygamy**, or marriage to several women. A man may have up to four wives if he can support them equally.

Key Concepts: Human Rights
Throughout the Middle East, women have not generally achieved equal rights.

ROLE OF WOMEN Women in the Middle East have traditionally had few rights. In some nations, women still wear veils in public and practice **purdah**, or seclusion in the home. Traditional beliefs grant women property inheritance, but it is generally less than men. In the 1920s, the leader of the Turkish Republic, **Mustafa Kemal Atatürk**, announced reforms aimed at westernization. These reforms gave greater rights to women. Other nations followed Turkey's lead. However, in the late 1970s, the rise of Islamic fundamentalism pressured women to conform to traditional customs.

MAKING CONNECTIONS

MIDDLE EASTERN RELIGIONS

The Middle East was the birthplace of three of the world's great religions: Judaism, Christianity, and Islam.

Judaism

Judaism began some 4,000 years ago and is the world's oldest monotheistic religion. It originated with the Hebrews who worshiped a single God called **Yahweh**. The first books of the Bible, or Old Testament, comprise the Jewish holy scripture, or **Torah**. These books tell the history of the Hebrews, including their enslavement by the pharaohs of Egypt.

TEN COMMANDMENTS A prophet named Moses led the Hebrews out of Egypt to the promised land of Canaan around 1300 B.C. During their flight, according to the Torah, Moses gave the Hebrews the **Ten Commandments**. The Hebrews believed these laws formed part of a **covenant**, or solemn agreement, with Yahweh.

DIASPORA For several hundred years, the Jews lived in the kingdom of Israel. Here they built a temple to honor Yahweh in the capital of Jerusalem. Because Israel lay at a crossroads between empires and continents, it was subject to repeated invasions. In 586 B.C., the Babylonians destroyed the Temple of Jerusalem and exiled many Jews. This was the start of the **diaspora**, or dispersion of Jews from their ancient homeland to other parts of the world. Dreams of reclaiming the Hebrew homeland shaped the Jewish identity for many centuries. Today there are approximately 18 million followers of Judaism, four million of whom live in the nation of Israel.

Society and Politics Early theological beliefs helped shape political power and social relationships between Christians and Jews that persisted for centuries.

Christianity

Christianity began in the Middle East with the birth of Jesus about 2000 years ago. Christians believe that Jesus is the son of God and that he ascended into heaven after his crucifixion. Christians accept that Jesus was the Messiah, or savior, spoken of in the Old Testament. The story of Jesus and the basis of Christian religion is contained in the **New Testament** of the Bible. Christians also accept the Old Testament, including the Ten Commandments, as a foundation for their religious and ethical beliefs. A key moral idea in the Christian religion is the Golden Rule: "Do unto others as you would have them do unto you." Today there are over 1.5 billion followers of Christianity.

MAKING CONNECTIONS

Islam

Islam means "submit to God's will." It was founded in Arabia by Muhammad in 622 B.C. The followers of Islam are called Muslims or Moslems. Islam is monotheistic and accepts many of the same prophets as the Jews and Christians. However, Muslims believe that Jesus was a prophet and that Muhammad was the last and greatest prophet of **Allah**, or God. Although the Muslims accept many of the spiritual beliefs of the Bible, they follow a holy scripture called the **Koran**. The basic duties of Muslims are outlined in the **Five Pillars of Islam**.

Society and Religion Muslim prayer takes place at dawn, noon, mid-afternoon, dusk, and after sunset.

1. There is no God but Allah and Muhammad is his prophet.
2. Muslims must bow toward the holy city of Mecca and pray five times a day.
3. Muslims must give **alms** (money) to the poor.
4. Muslims must fast during the ninth month of the Muslim calendar, **Ramadan**, from sunrise to sunset each day.
5. Muslims must make a pilgrimage to Mecca (called the hejira), once in their lifetime.

ISLAM AS A WAY OF LIFE Islam is a way of life for all those who practice it. Muslims are not allowed to eat pork, drink alcohol, or gamble. To prevent idol worship, Islamic law forbids people from drawing images. Therefore, no statues or pictures adorn **mosques**, or Muslim places of worship. Also, as you have read, Islam created a male-dominated society in which women have few rights.

JIHAD *Jihad* is an Arabic word that means "struggle." Muslims justify jihad as a military action for two reasons, the struggle to defend against aggression and the struggle for freedom of religion and justice. Jihad can also take a non-religious form, such as the struggle to get an education.

SPLITS WITHIN ISLAM After Muhammad's death, Islam split into two sects.

- *Sunnis*: The Sunnis are the largest group of Muslims. They believe that the first four caliphs were the successors of Muhammad and that there should be no central authority for enforcing Islamic law. Sunnis also think that all Muslims are bound spiritually regardless of their customs and traditions.
- *Shiites*: The Shiites believe that Muslims should only be led by a descendant of Ali, Muhammad's son-in-law, and that true knowledge can only come from an **Imam**, or religious leader. Shiites are found principally in Iran, Iraq, Lebanon, and Bahrain. In Iran, **ayatollahs** are experts on Islamic law. Today Iran is the only Middle Eastern nation in which Shiite Islam is the official state religion.

Today there are over 850 million followers of Islam, and it is the fastest-growing religion on earth.

Changing Population Base

Traditional life in the Middle East centered upon the agricultural village. Today, however, less than 50 percent of the region's population lives in villages. The majority lives in cities, making urbanization a key force for change in the region.

VILLAGE LIFE Most village people in the Middle East cluster around sources of water. Agricultural lands tend to be overcrowded, and individual plots are small. Rural peasants in Egypt, known as **fellahin**, often do not own their own lands. Like many farmers in the region, they tend to be subsistence farmers.

NOMADIC LIFE Nomads generally live in small groups bound by kinship. Traditionally, the **sheik**, or tribal leader, makes important decisions for the group on the advice of a council made up of representatives from the leading families. Nomadic peoples travel from place to place in search of water and pasturelands. Their possessions are limited by the number of items they can transport by camel. The custom of hospitality is central to their culture.

The nomads who inhabit the Arabian and Sahara deserts are called **bedouin**, the Arabic word for "desert dweller." Other groups include the **Berbers** in northwest Africa and the **Kurds** in western Iran. Because of urbanization and industrialization, only a small number of people follow a nomadic life today.

CITY LIFE Middle Eastern cities such as Alexandria, Baghdad, Cairo, and Istanbul have long been important hubs of economic and social activity. Their location along key waterways has made them century-old gathering places for merchants and artisans. Today, trade takes place on a daily basis in busy Middle Eastern marketplaces called **souks**. Here, according to custom, prices are determined by negotiations between buyers and sellers. The large-scale migration of people into cities in recent years has caused many problems. These include overpopulation, lack of adequate housing, and breakdown of traditional authority over the individual.

MAKING CONNECTIONS

Key Concepts: Change
Urbanization, modernization, and industrialization are among the numerous agents of social change in the Middle East. Many segments of the population are seeking to achieve a balance between traditional culture, including religion, and forces of modernization.

MIDDLE EASTERN ARTS

The Islamic civilization of the Middle East has made many contributions to world culture.

Achievements of the Abbasid Empire

Historically, the Golden Age of Islamic culture existed during the **Abbasid Empire**, which lasted from 750–1258. During this time Muslim scholars accomplished the following:

- Translated Greek texts into Arabic to preserve this knowledge for history
- Introduced the concept of zero; devised Arabic numerals (based on Indian numerals); developed geometry, algebra, and trigonometry

MAKING CONNECTIONS

- Increased astronomical knowledge to calculate the Muslim calendar
- Invented the **astrolabe** (similar to a sextant) to determine direction at sea
- Established the earliest hospitals and pharmacies and determined that diseases can be contagious

Some English Words Derived from Arabic

alcohol	bazaar	magazine	sugar
algebra	coffee	orange	syrup
almanac	cotton	sherbet	

Art and Architecture

Because Islam forbad images and drawings, Muslims found other forms of artistic expression. They developed the art of **calligraphy**, or beautiful writing, and used it to decorate many holy places with lines from Muslim scripture. Muslim artists also created stained glass windows, mosaic tiles, and handwoven carpets. Muslim architecture is best expressed in mosques with tall towers, or **minarets**. Minarets vary in shape and size from the squared towers of North Africa to the rounded domes in Turkey. Two of the most famous architectural structures built by Muslims during their conquests are the **Taj Mahal** in India and the **Alhambra Palace** in Spain.

Literature

A rich oral tradition inspired the works of Arab poets. The most famous Arab epic poem is the *Rubáiyát* written by Omar Khayyám (1048–1122) of Persia (present-day Iran). Among the most widely read Middle Eastern stories are the tales of Aladdin and Sinbad from *A Thousand and One Nights*. Also known as *Arabian Nights*, this collection of tales is drawn from Persia, Egypt, and India.

MAJOR SOCIAL THEMES

1. The Middle East is the birthplace of three great religions: Judaism, Christianity, and Islam. These religions have had a great impact on human culture and have historically been a source of social and political conflict.
2. Islam is among the world's youngest religions. In forming, it incorporated elements of Judaism and Christianity into its main body of beliefs.
3. Islam is a complete way of life, affecting the structure of the traditional families in the Middle East and the roles played by men and women.
4. The use of the Arabic language helped unify Muslim culture. Muslim achievements spread to other parts of the world through the process of cultural diffusion.

SECTION 8 Social Setting: Western Europe

OVERVIEW

Today Western Europe consists of 26 independent nations that differ in terms of geography, language, and culture. However, the people of this region have been bound together through the process of cultural diffusion and economic interdependence. They share a common history based upon Greco-Roman traditions and Judeo-Christian values, which form the basis of Western Civilization.

MAKING CONNECTIONS

Key Concepts: Diversity and Culture
Western Europe is a region of great ethnic and religious diversity; this diversity has helped to define Europe's rich cultural identity.

FAMILY LIFE

The family is the basic unit of western European society. Prior to the Industrial Revolution (1750), most people made their living as farmers, and several generations lived and worked together. The traditional family was **extended** and **patriarchal**, dominated by the eldest male. As western Europe began to industrialize, however, **urbanization** took place. People who lived and worked in cities could only support their immediate, or **nuclear**, family. The increase in women's rights also helped families to become more **egalitarian**, meaning that both husbands and wives took part in decision making.

The family today is valued as the cornerstone of society. It is considered the family's responsibility to instill cultural beliefs and traditions in the children. However, because of social problems such as divorce, the traditional nuclear family is in a state of change. Some believe that the breakup of the traditional nuclear family has made it more difficult to transfer societal values to future generations.

SOCIAL STRUCTURE

Since the Middle Ages, social mobility has increased in western Europe and the power of the traditional upper class has declined.

Effect of Feudalism

The traditional class structure of western Europe was based upon the division of society common during the Middle Ages. Under feudalism, the king and nobles made up the upper class. Their social position

Society and History For more information on feudal society in western Europe, see the section on western Europe in Unit 2, Global History.

MAKING CONNECTIONS

was based on the ownership of land, which was passed down from generation to generation. The majority of people owned no land and made up the broad base of society. These people lacked privileges and status.

Social Changes Since the Middle Ages

The Crusades helped revive an interest in trade, which in turn led to the emergence of a middle class of merchants, professionals, and artisans. They were wealthy and influential and resented their status as commoners. This class pushed for change.

AGE OF REVOLUTIONS Both the French Revolution and the Industrial Revolution helped to bring about greater social equality.

- **French Revolution** The educated middle class, schooled in the ideas of the Enlightenment, led the revolution in France. The violent overthrow of the French monarchy ended the special privileges of the nobility. The ideal of "égalité" (equality) was spread throughout Europe by the armies of Napoleon.
- **Industrial Revolution** Industrialization went hand-in-hand with urbanization. Industrialization concentrated power in the cities, which were populated by the middle and working classes. These groups pressured their governments for **suffrage**, or the right to vote. They used this power to make their countries more democratic and egalitarian.

Regents Tip List some of the characteristics of a nation undergoing industrialization.
(An example has been listed.)
Increased social mobility

SOCIAL SYSTEM TODAY Although societies in several western European nations maintain positions of nobility, this aristocracy is not granted any special power or privileges. As in the United States, all people are provided with equal opportunity. Even so, people with wealth find it easier to attain upward social mobility.

WESTERN EUROPEAN RELIGION

Christianity is the major religion of western Europe. It is a monotheistic religion founded by Jesus during the Roman Empire. Christians believe that Jesus fulfilled the Old Testament promise of the coming of a messiah, or saviour, for the Jews. The basic teachings of Jesus emphasized a love of God and neighbor. The Christian sacred book is the Bible, which contains both the Old Testament and the New Testament. The New Testament tells the story of the life and teachings of Jesus and the work of his Apostles (disciples), or first missionaries.

Since the time of Jesus, the Christian religion has undergone many changes in western Europe.

The Medieval Church

The Roman Catholic church became the dominant religious institution in western Europe during the Middle Ages. It not only took care

Long Range Causes
- Agricultural Revolution
- Population increase

↓

Immediate Causes
- New inventions
- Large pool of workers available
- Access to raw materials and investment capital
- Existence of markets
- Laissez-faire economy

↓

Industrial Revolution

↓

Immediate Effects
- Population explosion
- Development of new financing strategies and an international economy
- Rapid growth of cities
- Rise of a powerful middle class
- Use of child labor

↓

Long Range Effects
- Labor reforms and labor unions
- Growth of democracy
- Rise of socialism
- Romanticism in literature, art, and music
- Realism in literature and art

MAKING CONNECTIONS

of the spiritual needs of the people, but it performed other important political, economic, and social functions as well.

- **Political** The church kept official records of births, deaths, and marriages.
- **Economic** The church amassed great wealth through the ownership of land and the collection of taxes such as the **tithe**, or a 10 percent tax on wealth.
- **Social** The church maintained an educational system and encouraged the development of universities. Monks copied ancient writings of Greece and Rome, preserving classical learning and creating manuscripts that were works of art. Members of the clergy also ministered to the sick and poor.

The Protestant Reformation

Society and History For more information on the Protestant Reformation, see the section on western Europe in Unit 2, Global History.

In 1517 Martin Luther began the Protestant Reformation, which resulted in the formation of different Christian sects and ended religious unity in western Europe. Religious differences often led to conflicts with political or economic overtones.

THIRTY YEARS' WAR (1618–1648) This religious and political conflict involved most of the major nations of Europe. For the most part, Catholic and Protestant nations lined up against each other. Catholic France, however, joined with Protestant nations to get land from Austria.

Society and Religion Religion has served both to unify and to divide the peoples of Europe. Persecution and discrimination against the Jews has recurred throughout European history since the Middle Ages.

CONFLICT IN NORTHERN IRELAND Religious conflicts have continued into the present. The political turmoil and violence in what is now Northern Ireland grew out of the colonization of Ireland by English Protestants. Struggles between Catholics and Protestants led to the division of Ireland in 1921.

Today the Catholic minority in Northern Ireland has been the target of economic and political discrimination. Many Catholics want to reunite Northern Ireland (which is presently part of Great Britain) with the largely Catholic Republic of Ireland in the south. Some Catholics support the outlawed Irish Republican Army (IRA), an organization that uses terrorist tactics to achieve its goals. Since the beginning of "The Troubles" in 1969, steps have been taken to resolve the conflict and end violence. A permanent solution, however, still appears a long way off.

CULTURAL EXPRESSION

Western European art has been built on a heritage thousands of years old.

Ancient Greece and Rome

Classical culture emphasized secular, or worldly, values.

ART AND ARCHITECTURE The art and architecture of the ancient Greeks reflected their love of beauty, perfection, balance, and symmetry. Their sculpture idealized the human body, and they often used their gods as subjects. An example is the sculpture of **Venus de Milo**. The Romans borrowed the style of the Greeks, but became more realistic in style, using ordinary people as models.

The Greeks created well-proportioned buildings using three styles of columns. The Parthenon became the Greek model of perfection. The Romans concerned themselves with more practical, public buildings. They perfected the arch and dome and used these architectural principles to build aqueducts and other massive structures such as the Colosseum.

LITERATURE Ancient literature reflected the history of the people, their heroes, and legends. Examples of Greek classical literature include the *Iliad* and the *Odyssey*. The *Aeneid* is an example of Roman classical literature.

The Middle Ages

Medieval culture centered on religion.

ART AND ARCHITECTURE Artists portrayed religious subjects in an unrealistic, two-dimensional style, to indicate the importance of the soul over the body. Artists concentrated their talents on the construction of cathedrals. **Gothic** architecture, used in many medieval cathedrals, is characterized by vaulted ceilings, stained glass windows, and pointed arches. This style of architecture was used to represent worshipers reaching toward their goal of heaven.

MUSIC AND LITERATURE Much of the music from the time is religious. However, composers also wrote court pieces for kings and lords. Medieval literature is characterized by epic poems such as *Beowulf*, which praises the virtues of chivalry.

The Renaissance

The Renaissance was the rebirth of learning and culture that began in Italy during the late Middle Ages. It then spread to the rest of Western Europe. The spirit of the Renaissance was represented by the philosophy of **humanism**. Humanism was characterized by renewed interest in the classic civilizations of Greece and Rome and a concentration on human beings and their world.

LITERATURE Humanism began as a literary movement. Humanist writers copied classical styles and their topics were secular rather than religious. Although early humanists wrote in classical Latin, later writers made use of the **vernacular**, or language of the people, to reach a wider audience. An important Renaissance writer was William Shakespeare (1564–1616), an English poet and playwright. Shakespeare's unique understanding of human feelings, problems, and relationships is displayed in such works as *Macbeth* and *Romeo and Juliet*.

MAKING CONNECTIONS

Key Concepts: Power
Increased trade created the preconditions for the Renaissance, greater affluence, and the rising power of the merchant class.

Key Concepts: Identity and Culture
Humanism, which emphasized individual identity and the worth of the individual in a secular world, was reflected in the arts and culture of Renaissance Europe.

MAKING CONNECTIONS

ART Artists of the Renaissance were inspired by the works of ancient Greece and Rome. The style of Renaissance art was three-dimensional, realistic, and lifelike. Artists paid great attention to detail and scientifically studied human anatomy. Unlike medieval artists, Renaissance artists painted individual portraits and depicted everyday scenes, including landscapes. Although artists also used religious themes, they portrayed them realistically. The art of the period reflected the humanist idea that man was at the center of creation and the universe and the belief that earthly life was as important as the afterlife. Two famous artists from the period included **Leonardo da Vinci** (1452–1519) and **Michelangelo** (1475–1564). The major paintings of da Vinci include *The Last Supper* and *The Mona Lisa*. Michelangelo, a famous sculptor and painter, created such statues as the *Pietà* and *David*.

Society and History For a description of the style and works of Leonardo da Vinci and Michelangelo, see the section on western Europe in Unit 2, Global History.

Cultural Movements of the Nineteenth and Twentieth Centuries

The development of modern artistic styles was shaped by the intellectual, political, and industrial revolutions of the 1700s and 1800s.

ROMANTICISM Romanticism was a cultural movement that reflected the spirit of the French Revolution (1789–1799). It promoted nationalism and individual freedom. It also was a reaction against the problems of the Industrial Revolution. Romanticism praised beauty, emotion, nature, and past glories.

Leading Romanticists

Literature	English poet John Keats wrote numerous odes and sonnets reflecting a love of beauty and nature, such as "Ode to a Nightingale" and "To Autumn."
Art	French painter Eugène Delacroix produced dramatic scenes filled with color and emotion such as *Liberty Leading the People*, inspired by the Revolution of 1830.
Music	German composer Ludwig von Beethoven produced symphonies, concertos, sonatas, and quartets.

REALISM Instead of reacting against the problems of industrialization, realists confronted them. They drew their inspiration from everyday people and life. Charles Dickens, an English novelist, called attention to social problems during the industrial age. His works include *Hard Times*, *Oliver Twist*, and *David Copperfield*.

IMPRESSIONISM Impressionism was a reaction against realism. Artists attempted to capture their feelings, or impressions, about a particular moment or scene in nature. Impressionists were inspired by the Japanese style of painting. A leading impressionist painter was Claude Monet.

CONTEMPORARY CULTURE In the twentieth century, writers, artists, and musicians have created works that reflect the progress and problems of society. All areas of culture have been affected by science, technology, and politics.

MAKING CONNECTIONS

Key Concepts: Culture
Western culture has to a very large extent been an urban culture.

MAJOR SOCIAL THEMES

1. The traditional family in western Europe has undergone change as a result of industrialization and urbanization.
2. The social structure of western Europe has become more democratic as a result of political, intellectual, and economic revolutions.
3. The Roman Catholic church significantly shaped the cultural development of western Europe.
4. The Protestant Reformation and subsequent religious conflicts played an important role in the political and social evolution of western Europe.
5. The culture of western Europe has reflected the values and beliefs of the people as well as changes in society.

SECTION 9 Social Setting: Northern Eurasia and Eastern Europe

MAKING CONNECTIONS

OVERVIEW

Northern Eurasia is a huge area made up of 15 countries and over 100 ethnic groups that, until 1991, were one nation—The Soviet Union. Eastern Europe is also an area of many cultures and nationalities. As a result, diversity has been a key pattern in the social and cultural development of the two regions.

FAMILY LIFE

Traditional Russian Family

At the time of the Revolution of 1917, most people in Russia made their living by farming. Traditional Russian families were **extended** and **patriarchal**. Several generations lived together and worked the land. The eldest male dominated the family and both women and children were under his strict control. Fathers arranged the marriages of their children.

Changes in the Family Since 1917

Key Concepts: Human Rights
Traces of inequality still remain in many countries of Northern Eurasia and Eastern Europe today.

After the Communists seized control of Russia, great changes took place in society. Rapid industrialization led to **urbanization**. In the cities, the **nuclear** family, consisting of parents and children only, became more commonplace. The creation of collective farms by Joseph Stalin also helped to break up extended families in the countryside. The Communist doctrine of equality was extended to women who took on a greater role in the running of their families. Although at first the Communists tried to weaken the family in favor of communism and the state, they eventually realized the importance of the family as a means of instilling in youth the basic values and ideas of society.

Following World War II, most of the nations in Eastern Europe became Soviet satellites. As a result, traditional extended families also underwent change in this region. However, since most Eastern European nations did not reach the same level of industrialization and urbanization as the Soviet Union, the changes were not as dramatic.

SOCIAL STRUCTURE

MAKING CONNECTIONS

Communist ideology called for a complete restructuring of social classes.

Czarist Russia

Society in Czarist Russia revolved around a rigid system of feudal classes. The upper classes, composed of nobility and Russian Orthodox clergy, were both privileged and powerful. Most peasants were bound to the land as serfs until their emancipation in 1861. Despite achieving freedom, however, they still had limited opportunities to improve their status. During the late 1800s, Russia began to industrialize and two new classes developed, made up of wealthy capitalists and workers. These two classes pushed for changes and helped pave the way for revolution.

Society under the Communists

The Bolsheviks, who seized control in 1917, promised the people a "classless society" in accordance with the theories of Karl Marx. Once in power, they stripped the nobility and clergy of their privileges and wealth and claimed to create a society based on political, economic, and social equality. In reality, special status and benefits were set aside for leaders as well as for those people with unique talents and abilities to devote to the state.

In this poster, Lenin sweeps those he considers exploiters—monarchs and capitalists—off the face of the earth.

MAKING CONNECTIONS

Eastern Europe

After World War II, Communist governments in Eastern Europe set up social systems similar to those in the Soviet Union. In 1989, however, these nations began shaking free of Communist control and took steps to set up more open societies. By 1992, even the Soviet Union no longer existed and the former republics had begun a transition to democracy.

NORTHERN EURASIAN AND EASTERN EUROPEAN RELIGIONS

Northern Eurasia

A diversity of religions has existed in Northern Eurasia: primarily Russian Orthodoxy, Judaism, and Islam.

Society and Religion For more information on the Eastern Orthodox Church, see Unit 2, Global History.

RUSSIAN ORTHODOXY In the tenth century, the Russian czar converted to the Eastern Orthodox religion of the Byzantine Empire and made Orthodox Christianity the official religion of Russia. Under Peter the Great, the Russian Orthodox Church was placed under the control of the czar's government. The church generally supported government policies, and church officials became part of an elite class. The church became a source of comfort and guidance.

Karl Marx called religion the "opiate of the people," a drug that made people satisfied with their lives and unwilling to bring about social change. As a result of the Communist revolution, the Russian Orthodox church lost its land, wealth, and power. Religious worship was strictly controlled and discouraged. When Mikhail Gorbachev instituted the policy of **glasnost**, or "openness," the government relaxed its restrictions on religion. This has resulted in a resurgence of religious activity in the countries of Northern Eurasia.

JUDAISM Jews represent a sizable minority in Northern Eurasia. In czarist Russia, Jews were used as scapegoats, becoming targets for the misplaced anger and frustration of the people. Sometimes this anti-Semitism turned into violent attacks called **pogroms**. Despite the fact that many Jews, such as Leon Trotsky, helped lead the revolution, persecution continued under the Communists. Jews who wished to leave the Soviet Union were often denied permission. Pressure from the United States resulted in periodic easing of restrictions. Thousands of Jews left the Soviet Union after 1970. Recent political changes have brought both freedom and fear to Jews. Some worry that less government control may result in renewed anti-Semitic feelings.

ISLAM As Russia expanded, a number of Muslim territories became part of the empire. Today about 55 million Muslims live in Northern Eurasia. The policy of **glasnost** allowed Islamic fundamentalism to spread. As a result, the republics with large Muslim populations were eager to seek independence.

Eastern Europe

Cultural diversity within Eastern Europe has also led to a diversity of religious beliefs in this region.

ROMAN CATHOLICISM The Roman Catholic religion has strong followings in Poland, Hungary, and the Czech and Slovak Republics. Despite attempts by Communists to limit the influence of the church, it has remained an important force in these countries. In Poland, for example, Roman Catholic officials were outspoken critics of the Communist regime. The church supported the Solidarity movement in Poland and helped end Communist domination of the country.

ORTHODOX CHRISTIANITY AND ISLAM In nations that were once part of the Byzantine Empire and later the Ottoman Empires, Orthodox Christianity and Islam are still practiced. In the former Yugoslavia, most Serbs practice the Eastern Orthodox faith. Islam has a following in Bosnia-Herzegovina as well as Albania.

JUDAISM Prior to World War II, Jews formed a large minority in Eastern Europe. The Nazi Holocaust, however, nearly destroyed Eastern Europe's Jewish population.

MAKING CONNECTIONS

Society and Religion
Religion was seen as an ideological competitor in Communist efforts to obtain the loyalty of the peoples of Eastern Europe.

Key Concepts: Human Rights
In Eastern Europe, discrimination against minorities was a common practice.

CULTURAL EXPRESSION

Artists in Northern Eurasia and Eastern Europe have made many contributions to world culture.

Kievan Russia

The Byzantine Empire exerted a strong influence over Kievan Russia. Both art and architecture reflected the importance of the Eastern Orthodox religion. Artists focused on the creation of **icons**, small religious paintings. Architects adapted Byzantine styles. Distinctive features of their churches include onion-shaped domes and tall, tapering spires.

Czarist Russia

The westernization policies of Peter the Great (1682–1725) and Catherine the Great (1762–1796) led Russian artists to look to Europe for inspiration. However, in the 1800s, a spirit of nationalism motivated many artists to create works focusing on the cultural identity of Russia.

LITERATURE The czarist government did not allow outright criticism of its policies. As a result, Russian authors of the 1800s used their creativity to point out social injustices and the problems of Russian society. Leading writers from the period include:

- **Alexander Pushkin** Pushkin based much of his work on Russian history and folklore. One of his most famous poems, *Boris Gudonov*, was transformed into an opera by Modest Mussorgsky.

Key Concepts: Culture
Throughout the nineteenth and twentieth centuries, artists from various parts of the czarist empire made brilliant contributions to European culture.

MAKING CONNECTIONS

- **Count Leo Tolstoy** Tolstoy is considered one of the greatest novelists of all time. Although a member of the nobility, Tolstoy became part of an intellectual movement to bring social change to Russia. Despite his criticism of Russian society, he had a deep sense of nationalism. *War and Peace*, for example, recounts Napoleon's invasion of Russia in 1812.

MUSIC Russian composers in the nineteenth century created distinctly Russian music. Their work was inspired by a feeling of nationalism and romantic themes of beauty, love, and nature. One of the most important composers was **Peter Tchaikovsky**, who created such works as *Swan Lake*, *The Sleeping Beauty*, and *The Nutcracker*.

Key Concepts: Power
Soviet arts are an expression of Communist ideology and Soviet nationalism or "socialist realism."

Northern Eurasia

The Communists continued the czarist policy of **censorship**. Under Soviet **totalitarianism**, the government controlled everything people read, saw, or heard. Those with creative talents were expected to serve the state and to promote the positive aspects of socialism. Writers who criticized the system faced exile or death. Some of the Soviet Union's most talented artists escaped to find artistic freedom in the West. More recently, the policy of **glasnost** and the end of Communist rule have offered greater opportunity for more original and more open creative expression. Outstanding contributors to Russian culture include:

- **Boris Pasternak** Pasternak won the Nobel Prize in literature in 1958 for his novel, *Dr. Zhivago*. Soviet authorities opposed Pasternak's interpretation of the Revolution of 1917 and banned him from accepting the prize. The novel was not released in the Soviet Union until recently.
- **Alexander Solzhenitsyn** Solzhenitsyn wrote many works criticizing the Soviet system and the rule of Joseph Stalin. *One Day in the Life of Ivan Denisovich* describes life in a Soviet concentration camp. Solzhenitsyn was sent to such a camp for being critical of Stalin. In 1973, *The Gulag Archipelago*, which exposed the Soviet police state, was published in the West. As a result of his work, Solzhenitsyn was deported from the Soviet Union and took up residence in the United States.

Eastern Europe

Like Russia, culture in Eastern Europe was inspired by nationalism and the traditions of various ethnic groups. **Fréderic Chopin**, a Polish composer famous for his piano concertos, expressed nationalist sentiments in his polonaises and mazurkas. After 1945 the Communist governments of Eastern Europe instituted policies of censorship. In 1989, the Soviet satellite nations broke from communism and greater freedom resulted. The attitude of change was evident in Czechoslovakia, for example, where **Vaclav Havel**, a former **dissident** playwright, won election as president.

MAJOR SOCIAL THEMES

MAKING CONNECTIONS

1. Communist leaders dismantled the rigid class structure in Russia and promised a "classless society." Some inequality still existed since Communist Party leaders were given special status and privileges.
2. The forces of industrialization and urbanization in the Soviet Union and Eastern Europe have fostered the growth of nuclear families.
3. Traditional religious beliefs and a spirit of nationalism inspired the work of artists in pre-Communist Russia and Eastern Europe.
4. Communist leaders sharply curtailed religious and artistic expression, leading thousands of people to seek refuge in the West.
5. Communist totalitarianism opposed the influence of religion and restricted artists to glorification of the state. Gorbachev's policy of **glasnost** and political changes in the Soviet Union and Eastern Europe loosened the hold of totalitarianism. Communist rule officially ended in 1991.

Regents Questions for Practice

Review the Test-Taking Strategies section of this book. Then answer the following questions, drawn from actual Regents examinations. Circle the *number* of the word or expression that best completes the statement or answers the question. Write your answers to essay questions on a separate piece of paper. Hints on good ways to approach these questions are provided in the margins.

Test Hint Before answering a multiple-choice question, underline the key words in the question.

1. Cultural diffusion occurs most rapidly in societies that:
   1 adhere to traditional social values
   2 have extended families
   3 come into frequent contact with other groups
   4 have a strong oral history

2. The spread of Islam throughout the African continent is an example of:
   1 national security
   2 socialism
   3 cultural diffusion
   4 self-determination

3. Which was true of food-gathering societies in prehistoric times?
   1 Society was highly industrialized.
   2 The population tended to be small.
   3 The concept of private property was important.
   4 There was a system of mass production.

MAKING CONNECTIONS

Test Hint Remember to read all the choices before you select an answer.

4. The study of culture primarily involves:
1 observing the physical environment of people
2 learning why various peoples live as they do
3 understanding the technology of modern machinery
4 analyzing the personalities of children in the same family

5. Which is a characteristic of a feudal society?
1 rapid social change
2 high literacy rate
3 industrial-based economy
4 rigid class structure

6. Which is the most accurate statement about art and literature in a totalitarian society?
1 Artistic expression is channeled into approved themes.
2 Artistis and writers are subsidized by wealthy patrons.
3 All forms of art and literature are banned by the government.
4 Artists and writers are encouraged to borrow and adapt ideas from other societies.

7. Which situation would probably bring about changes in most traditional societies?
1 existence of cultural isolation
2 establishment of local governments
3 dependence on subsistence agriculture
4 increase in industrialization

8. Historically, which has tended to occur in nations that experience continuing severe political instability and economic depression?
1 easing of social tension
2 growth of the economic base
3 growth of the middle class
4 rise of totalitarian regimes

---

9. Which is usually a characteristic of societies that have the extended family as their basic unit?
1 The society tends to be highly industrialized.
2 The roles of the family members are economically and socially interdependent.
3 The government usually provides incentives to increase family size.
4 The functions of the family unit are defined mainly by the government.

10. The growth of multinational corporations, the establishment of the United Nations, and the exchange of information among scientists of many nations indicate increasing:
1 disillusionment with communism in most countries
2 prosperity and rising standards of living in most developing countries
3 isolationism in United States foreign policy
4 interdependence among nations

11. Cultural diversity in any area of the world is generally the result of:
1 actions by the government of the area
2 the desire of the inhabitants to develop original ideas and styles
3 competition among the people for control of food sources
4 migrations to the area by various groups

12. Which is a major characteristic of traditional African art?
1 African art contains a great deal of symbolism.
2 The human form is represented very realistically in African art.
3 Painting is the primary medium for African art.
4 African art reflects a highly urban culture.

13. The influence of traditional African cultures is best seen today in Western:
1 technological advances
2 art forms
3 family patterns
4 political ideas

14. Tribalism in modern African nations has frequently resulted in political:
1 disunity
2 equality
3 interdependence
4 harmony

15. An African proverb states that "a person without relatives is as good as dead." The most valid conclusion to be drawn from this proverb is that traditional African cultures:
1 reflect the values of an urbanized society
2 stress personal initiative as the means to success
3 emphasize the role of government in caring for people
4 are based on systems of loyalties involving the extended family

16. In traditional India, the caste system and the Hindu beliefs in karma and dharma most directly resulted in:
1 the establishment of a set of rules for each individual in the society
2 the rapid industrialization of the economy
3 a strong emphasis on the acquisition of wealth
4 a strong belief in the importance of education

17. In India, migration of people from rural areas to urban areas has resulted in:
1 an increase in the number of people involved in agriculture
2 the strengthening of the caste system
3 more limitations on the freedom of women
4 a weakening of traditional values

18. In India, the traditional role of women has changed during the 20th century primarily because of the:
1 impact of increased urbanization
2 effects of religious persecution
3 use of passive resistance
4 growth of political unrest

19. In India, the caste system has been weakened most by the:
1 presence of the military to enforce the laws
2 migration of people to the cities
3 incrased productivity of farms
4 strengthened position of the Hindu religion

20. In traditional Chinese culture, which philosophy had the greatest influence on the development of social order and political organization?
1 Taoism
2 Shintoism
3 Confucianism
4 Marxism

21. Which statement best describes the status of women in most traditional Asian societies?
1 Women were encouraged to obtain an education.
2 Women were expected to run for political office.
3 Women were expected to dedicate their lives to their families.
4 Women were encouraged to work outside the home.

22. The philosophies of Confucius and Mao Zedong both emphasized:
1 individual rather than cooperative gain
2 industry rather than agriculture
3 group rather than individual welfare
4 religious values rather than economic profits

23. An analysis of the art of pre-Communist China clearly reveals the traditional Chinese concern for:
1 order and harmony in the natural world
2 material progress
3 political democracy
4 the role of the individual at the center of the universe

24. Which value was common to traditional society in both China and Japan?
1 pacifism
2 family loyalty
3 individualism
4 materialism

25. One factor that accounted for Chinese influence on traditional Japanese culture was the:
1 continuous warfare between the countries
2 geographic location of the countries
3 refusal of Western nations to trade with Japan
4 annexation of Japan into the Chinese Empire

26. An accurate description of life in Japan today is that the Japanese people have:
1 remained a largely rural, agricultural society
2 isolated themselves from Western culture
3 blended traditional ways with Western ways to meet the needs of modern life
4 achieved their goal of a classless society in which all people benefit from economic progress

27. Which statement about Latin America is an opinion rather than a fact?
1 African slaves were imported because there was a scarcity of workers.
2 Roman Catholicism is the dominant religion of the area.
3 Enormous diversity exists in the physical environment of Central and South America.
4 The people of this area are less resistant to change than people in other developing areas.

28. Which group has most frequently opposed social and economic changes in Latin America?
1 landowners
2 students
3 liberation priests
4 peasants

29. Which statement best describes the Roman Catholic Church in most Latin American countries in the 1980s?
1 The activities of the church are controlled by the national governments.
2 The church has confined its activities to religious issues.
3 The church has become active in social and human rights issues.
4 Most people see the church as having little influence in daily life.

30. The Middle East has been a crossroads for trade from Asia, Africa, and Europe. Which is a major result of this fact?
1 Most of the Middle East's natural resources have been exhausted.
2 The Middle East has become a wealthy area with a high standard of living.
3 Many different cultures can be found in the Middle East.
4 The Middle East has experienced a strong sense of national unity.

31. Which generalization is best supported by a study of the Middle East?
1 Illiteracy has become almost nonexistent.
2 Religious differences have led to serious conflicts.
3 Oil wealth has led to economic equality.
4 Industrial development has urbanized the area.

32. In the Middle Eastern society, women have increasingly been at the center of a conflict between the forces of modernization and the:
1 values of traditional Islamic culture
2 pressure for a Palestinian homeland
3 shortage of capital for industrial development
4 need to reduce the birth rate

33. In most of the oil-rich Arab nations, the wealth generated by oil has affected the way of life in that:
1 most people have adopted a Western life-style and given up their traditional ways
2 oil money has been used by the religious institutions, but not for educational and health facilities
3 technological modernization has occurred, but traditional laws and customs continue
4 women have been given political and social rights equal to those of men

34. Which is a valid conclusion based on a study of European art during the Renaissance in Europe?
1 Emphasis on artistic creativity can discourage a society from pursuing reforms.
2 The development of guilds prevented artistic creativity.
3 The presence of a wealthy leisure class contributes to artistic achievement.
4 An economy based on subsistence agriculture encourages artistic development.

35. In most nations of the world, the long-term effect of the Industrial Revolution has been to:
1 strengthen the extended family structure
2 place women in a second-class position
3 encourage education and increase literacy rates
4 increase poverty

36. Which has been a significant cultural aspect of life in many Communist nations?
1 organized social and economic discrimination against women
2 emphasis upon athletics and other forms of non-economic competition
3 restraints upon the development of social welfare programs
4 encouragement of free creative efforts of writers and composers

37. The Romans of ancient times and the English of medieval and modern times made their most significant contributions to the development of Western society in the fields of:
1 law & government
2 religion & science
3 painting & sculpture
4 music & literature

38. Which change in social living patterns has occurred in most industrialized nations since 1900?
1 increased leisure time
2 lower standards of living
3 decreased emphasis on material goods
4 increased emphasis on hereditary status

39. Which was characteristic of life in Europe during the early Middle Ages?
1 The lives of individuals were regulated by a rigid class system.
2 The authority of the Catholic Church was limited to religious matters.
3 Social control was primarily a responsibility of national government.
4 Political power was mainly concentrated in the guilds.

40. In the Soviet Union, which was the major source of conflict in the sourthern and central republics during the 1980s?
1 influence of Chinese ideas
2 discontent of ethnic minorities
3 efforts to establish a capitalist economic system
4 desire of these republics for Russification

41. Which statement is most clearly supported by the situation in Northern Ireland, the position of Jews in the Soviet Union, and relations between India and Pakistan?
1 Society has come to accept differing points of view.
2 The effects of World War II have remained fresh in the minds of society.
3 Religion continues to influence people's actions and behavior.
4 Decisions of political leaders are determined by actions of the United Nations.

42. Global problems of uneven economic development, environmental pollution, and hunger reflect the need for:
1 a return to policies of economic nationalism
2 increased military spending by all nations
3 a reduction in foreign aid provided by industrialized nations
4 increased international cooperation

43. Eighteenth-century Russia and 19th-century Japan were similar in that both countries:
1 began the process of modernization after a long period of isolation
2 developed democratic governments after years under absolute monarchies
3 refused to accept Western technological ideas
4 adopted socialist economic systems after capitalism had failed

44. A major cause of the continued conflicts in Northern Ireland and Lebanon has been:
1 opposing dynastic claims
2 religious differences
3 interference from the superpowers
4 industrial rivallry

45. Feudalism in western Europe was similar to feudalism in Japan in that:
1 power was based on class relationships
2 the national government controlled the nobility
3 social mobility was easily achieved
4 most of the people lived in cities

Essay Questions

1. Human interaction has often resulted in conflict between groups and cultures. Some groups and cultures that have experienced conflict are listed below.

Groups and Cultures
Israelis and Arab Palestinians in the Middle East
Sandinistas and Contras in Central America
Blacks and whites in the Republic of South Africa
Shiite Muslims and Sunni Muslims in the Middle East
Hindus and Sikhs in India
Catholics and Protestants in Northern Ireland

Select *three* of the groups or cultures from the list. For *each* one selected, discuss a major cause of the conflict and the effects of the conflict on the groups involved.

2. Throughout history, both men and women have had an impact on their times. They have played various roles.

Roles
Scientist
Political reformer
Social reformer
Writer
Revolutionary

a Select *two* roles from the list and for *each* role selected, identify one man or woman who played the role in a specific African, Asian, Latin American, Middle Eastern, or European nation. (You must identify a different person for each role.)

b Describe an action, discovery, or work of *each* individual identified in part *a*, and discuss the individual's impact on the political, economic, or social development of his or her nation or society.

3. Nations and regions often adopt ideas and practices from other parts of the world. The nations listed below have experienced cultural diffusion.

Japan from China
Mexico from Spain
Rome from Greece
Europe from Africa
Russia from the Byzantine Empire
Southeast Asia from India

Select *three* of the examples listed and for *each* example:

- Describe one idea or practice that was acquired by the first nation or region from the second.
- Discuss the effect of the idea or practice on the nation or region that adopted it.

4. Religion has often strongly influenced many aspects of culture in societies.

Aspects of Culture
Painting or sculpture
Music
Literature
Architecture
Sex roles
Education
Social class

Choose *three* of the aspects of culture listed. For *each* aspect of culture chosen:

- Identify a religion that has influenced that aspect of culture in a specific society.
- Using specific examples, discuss how the religion has influenced that aspect of culture in that society.

You must use a different religion for each aspect of culture chosen.

5. The human rights of certain groups of people have been violated through official governmental policy and/or by traditional social patterns.

Groups

Blacks in South Africa
Untouchables in India
Inhabitants of Kampuchea (Cambodia)
Jews in Europe
Palestinian refugees in the Middle East
Political dissidents in the Soviet Union

Choose *three* of the groups from the list. For *each* group choosen:

- Describe a specific violation of human rights that the group suffered or is suffering.
- Describe efforts that were made or are being made to overcome or compensate for the violations of that group's human rights.

6. Throughout history, religion has played an important role in the lives of people. Each religion listed below is paired with a cultural characteristic it has influenced.

a Select *three* of the pairs listed below. For *each* one chosen, show how the religion influenced the cultural characteristic in a specific society.

Religon/Cultural Characteristic

Animism—dance
Catholicism—architecture
Hinduism—social structure
Islam—art
Judaism—law
Protestantism—work ethic

b Describe *two* specific examples where religion has been a contributing factor to conflict among peoples.

7. While societal change is a reality in most countries throughout the world, it does not always come easily or without resistance. Societal change can be rapid or slow, widespread or limited, long lasting or temporary.

Identify and describe a societal change that has occurred since World War II in *each* of *two* of the countries listed below. For each of the changes, discuss one force that has acted to promote that change and one force that has acted as a barrier to that change. Use a different change for each country chosen.

Countries
India
Japan
Poland
Republic of South Africa
Soviet Union

8. In various times and places throughout history, differences in philosophies and/or religious beliefs have led to social, economic, and political conflicts. Listed below are pairs of philosophical and/or religious beliefs in the framework of particular times and places.

Pairs
Roman Catholicism—Protestantism in western Europe during the 1600s
Divine right—natural rights in western Europe during the 1700s
Hinduism—Islam in India since World War II
Confucianism—communism in the People's Republic of China since World War II
Roman Catholisism—Protestantism in Northern Ireland since 1960
Islam—Western materialism in Iran since the mid-1970s

Choose *three* of the pairs of beliefs listed above. For *each* pair chosen, show how philosophical and/or religious differences between the beliefs led to social or economic or political conflict in the particular time and place mentioned.

9. Throughout time, humans have expressed certain values by means of various art forms such as architecture, dance, literature, music, and painting.
Select *three* of the areas with their indicated time periods from the list below.

Areas and Related Time Periods
Italy during the Renaissance (1300–1450)
France during the Revolutionary era (1789–1815)
United States during the Gilded Age (1870–1900)
Africa since 1875
People's Republic of China since 1950

For *each* area selected,

a Name and briefly describe at least *two* specific examples of creative expression in *one* art form.

b Indicate how these examples reflect the values of that area during that time period.

UNIT 4 Global Economics

MAKING CONNECTIONS

As you review each unit, you will find additional information in this column: major ideas, connecting themes, and questions to reinforce your learning. These items are closely tied to the Regents examination. Read this material carefully, and jot down any other facts that you would like to remember in the column's blank spaces. Using this column will **add to your success on the Regents exam.**

Section 1 Africa

Section 2 India

Section 3 Southeast Asia

Section 4 China

Section 5 Japan

Section 6 Latin America

Section 7 The Middle East

Section 8 Western Europe

Section 9 Northern Eurasia and Eastern Europe

Each section in the Global Economics unit contains comprehensive coverage of world economic systems. The unit examines the economies within each region and notes ways in which economic interdependence links the world today. Major economic ideas and concepts in the overview of each section help you identify connecting themes.

The effect of industrialization and efforts by developing nations to modernize are explained. The text explores regional and worldwide distribution of economic resources—natural, capital, and human. It also traces shifting global power, including the decline of European dominance and the far-reaching changes brought about through technology. Finally, the unit looks at economic decision making—the ways in which nations have used their scarce resources and reasons they have chosen certain economic systems.

SECTION 1 Economic Setting: Africa

OVERVIEW

Africa's immense size and great variety of climates have resulted in a huge diversity of crops grown for commercial and domestic uses. The continent also possesses vast deposits of minerals—gold, copper, diamonds, cobalt, and phosphates. Despite such valuable agricultural and mineral resources, the developing nations of Africa remain dependent upon the West for trade, capital, and food. This dependency has created bitterness among Africans and contributed to continuing tensions between Africa and the industrialized nations of the **first world** (United States, Western Europe, and Japan). As an agricultural region with developing nations, Africa is considered to be part of the **third world**.

MAKING CONNECTIONS

Economics and Resources Africa is the source of 80 percent of the world's diamond production, and almost 50 percent of the world's gold is mined there. Nigeria is the eighth largest producer of oil and the second largest supplier of petroleum products to the United States. The Congo is one of the largest producers of zinc, and Zambia is fourth in the production of copper. Rubber is grown in substantial quantities in Nigeria, Liberia, and the Congo.

LEGACY OF IMPERIALISM

Much of Africa suffers from restrictive trading patterns established during the age of European imperialism. In the late 1800s and early 1900s, European nations acquired colonies in Africa in order to **exploit**, or take advantage of, the continent's raw materials. For example, imperial powers built zinc mines in the Democratic Republic of the Congo and copper mines in Zambia. They set up tea and coffee plantations in Tanzania and peanut plantations in West Africa. When the nations of Africa became independent in the 1950s and 1960s, they inherited national economies focused on the export of mineral resources and agricultural products. This situtation has created a number of serious economic problems for Africa.

Reliance on the Export of Cash Crops

Because European colonial powers hoped to reap huge profits in Africa, they set up plantations and used African labor to produce high-yield **cash crops**, or products grown only for sale or export. In some cases, Europeans introduced new crops into Africa from the Americas, including the cocoa and cassava plants. Today over fifty cash crops are raised in Africa. However, five products—cocoa, coffee, cotton, peanuts, and items from palm trees—account for 80 percent of the continent's agricultural output. Other plantation crops include bananas, tea, and sisal, which is made into rope.

Africa's Agricultural Exports

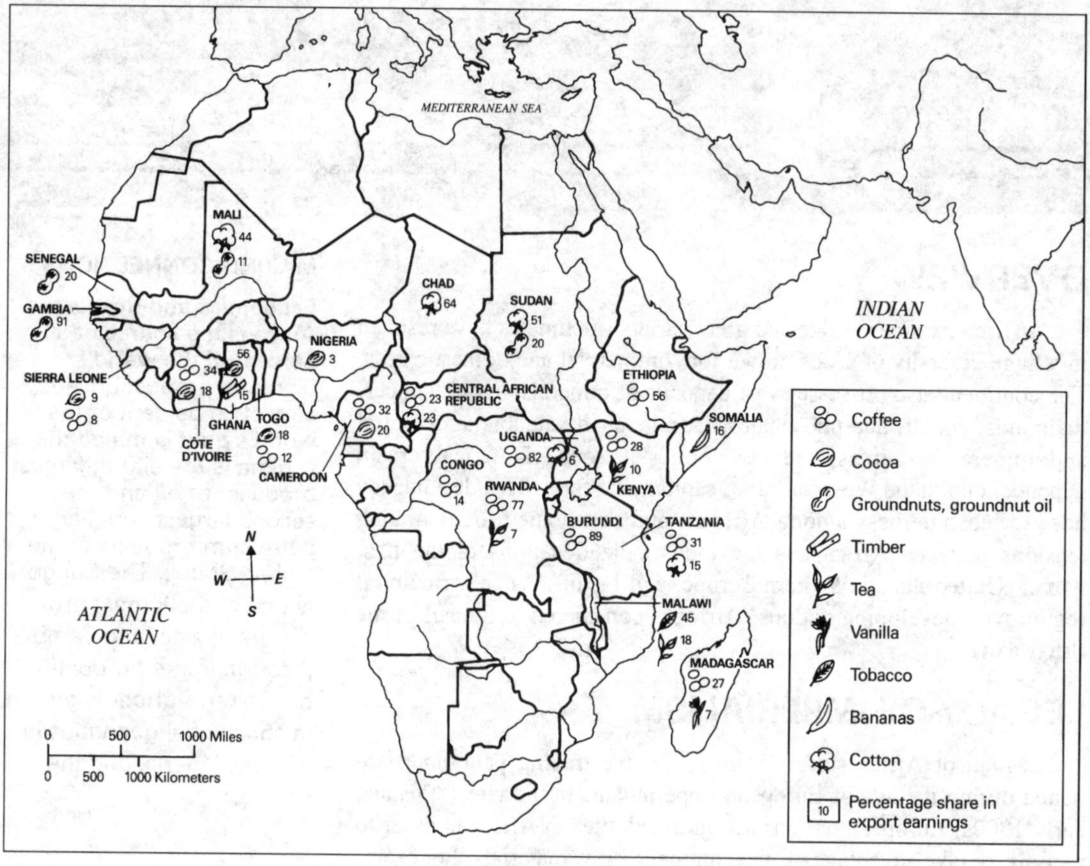

MAKING CONNECTIONS

Regents Tip Study the map to determine which agricultural import earns the highest percentage share in export earnings.

Economics and History Prices for minerals such as copper and agricultural products like coffee have varied a great deal on the international market.

NEOCOLONIALISM The heavy dependence of most African nations upon the export of cash crops has left them unprotected from falling prices in the world market. A nation that relies on the sale of a single cash crop can find its entire economy threatened when international prices drop or when a drought or crop failure occurs. Such a nation cannot accurately predict its future **revenues**, or income. African governments have borrowed money from banks in Europe and the United States, but they are often unable to repay these debts when their income from exports is not as great as expected. This situation has been described as **neocolonialism**, a system in which nations have won their political independence but remain economically dependent upon outside powers.

RESTRICTIVE TARIFFS Africa's dependence upon cash crops has continued, in part, because of the structure of international **tariffs**, or taxes on imports. Industrial nations in Western Europe and North America have often imposed high tariffs on **processed**, or finished, goods from other nations. These tariffs protect their own native industries and the jobs of people who work in them. To ensure the flow of inexpensive raw materials, many industrial nations put low tariffs or no tariffs at all on raw materials. This pattern of tariffs has discouraged African nations from developing industries to process their own raw materials. As a result, African nations receive only a small share of the profits made from African raw materials.

Lack of Industry

During colonial times, foreign companies owned most of the mines and industrial resources of Africa. Upon independence, many of these industries were **nationalized**, or taken over by the new governments. However, most African nations still face serious obstacles to industrialization.

- **Unstable political situations**—civil wars, military coups, and one-party, dictatorial states—have slowed economic development.
- **Outdated transportation systems** reflect colonial patterns of trade. Imperial powers built railroads in Africa for one main purpose—getting raw materials to ports along the coast. As a result, Africa has few international transportation networks to link the continent and encourage the growth of regional trade.
- **A lack of capital** has forced African nations to turn to other nations and the World Bank for the funds to invest in industry. This has increased African indebtedness and strengthened neocolonialism.
- **Shortages of skilled workers and technology** have made it difficult for Africa to develop an industrial base and compete with the more established industrial nations.
- **Limited energy resources** hinder industrial growth in Africa. Despite the continent's large size, it has few coal and oil deposits. Africa's greatest energy source may be its water power. Africa possesses 40 percent of the world's water power potential. But to date, few nations have had the capital to develop hydroelectric energy.

Reliance on Imported Manufactured Goods

Most African nations still import large quantities of foreign manufactured goods much as they did during colonial times. African consumers pay high prices for items processed from raw materials originally shipped out of Africa at a low price. Many African nations have attempted to form regional and international organizations to control the world price of African products so that they can raise the capital to industrialize. But so far they have not been very successful, and Africa remains in an economic pattern established under colonialism.

MAKING CONNECTIONS

Economics and Politics
Industrial development in Africa has favored state corporations. Conflicting ideological and economic goals led to the creation of mixed socialist/capitalist economies in Tanzania, Ethiopia, Kenya, and Nigeria.

Economics and Geography
For more on geographic barriers to transportation, see Unit 1, The Geographic Setting: Africa.

Key Concepts: Culture and Diversity
Cultural and ethnic diversity and nationalism have made it difficult for strong pan-African cooperation.

MAKING CONNECTIONS

A RURAL, AGRICULTURAL ECONOMY

In the 1990s, more than 80 percent of sub-Saharan Africa is still rural and follows a traditional pattern of agricultural production. Most people earn their living by **subsistence farming**, a system in which farmers grow just enough food to feed themselves and their families.

A Food Crisis

Africa's population has grown rapidly in the last decades, while the continent's ability to feed itself has declined. Africans are having increasing difficulty getting an adequate diet. Periodic shortages of food have led to an undernourished population that is prone to disease. Today famine is widespread. This food crisis has been caused by several factors.

COLONIAL TRADING PATTERNS The most fertile land in Africa is often used for growing cash crops. Most cash crops are used for export rather than to feed Africa's people.

Economics and Geography
For more on desertification, see Unit 1, The Geographic Setting: Africa, and Unit 6, The World Today.

DECLINING PRODUCTIVITY Without modern farming methods, African farmers have worn out large tracts of land. Erosion has speeded up the process of **desertification**, or spreading deserts. As a result, many nations have been forced to import large quantities of food.

Economics and Geography
Problems in food production have produced famine in the African nations of the Sahel. In parts of southern Africa, inadequate supplies of food have often resulted in large numbers of people being undernourished.

CLIMATE Over 60 percent of Africa is **arid**, and **recurring droughts** in the 1970s and 1980s have put a strain on the already scarce sources of water, especially in the Sahel (the area south of the Sahara) and Ethiopia. Drought in Africa has greater impact than in developed nations because reservoirs and pumping stations to conserve and distribute water are generally not available.

Climatic conditions have been complicated by overgrazing of cattle by nomadic peoples such as the Masai of Kenya and Tanzania and the Watusi of Rwanda. These people look down on farming and have expanded into the agricultural territories in search of grasslands for their herds. The conflict for land has increased ethnic tensions.

OVERPOPULATION Food pressures are increased by traditional social values that favor large, **extended families**, or several generations of relatives that live together in the same household. The absence of social security and retirement plans in Africa reinforces this pattern. Younger people have large families, in part, to help take care of older generations. However, improved medical care has extended life spans and reduced infant mortality rates. As a result, African nations have some of the highest birth rates in the world. Kenya's annual population increase of 4.1 percent is typical of other African nations. Today overpopulation severely strains food supplies, and many people have moved into urban areas in search of work. This migration has greatly disrupted traditional African society.

Population of Lagos, Nigeria

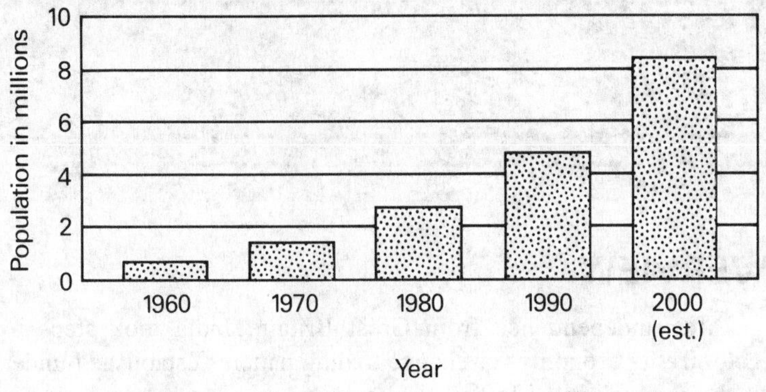

Source: United Nations Department for International Economic and Social Affairs.

MAKING CONNECTIONS

Regents Tip Practice improving your data-based skills. Study the graph to determine how many more millions of people are estimated to be living in Lagos, Nigeria in 2000 than lived there in 1980.

Efforts at Relief

Local and international efforts are being made to relieve the food crisis. Musicians have organized concerts, such as Live Aid, to raise contributions. Nations such as Ethiopia have begun reforestation projects to stop desertification. Sometimes, however, local wars have set back relief efforts and further disrupted food production. In some nations, socialist policies have weakened farmers' incentives to grow more food.

Economics and Politics Conflicts in Ethiopia, Chad, Mozambique, and the Sudan have interfered with food production and relief efforts.

CYCLE OF POVERTY

Standards of living in sub-Saharan Africa remain among the lowest in the world, and people are locked into a cycle of poverty. With low per capita (per person) incomes, people have little or no money to set aside for savings. As a result, Africa suffers from a shortage of capital to invest in equipment to improve production. As a result, the level of production remains low and so do incomes. This vicious cycle makes it difficult for African nations to industrialize and relieve the continent's food crisis.

Cycle of Poverty

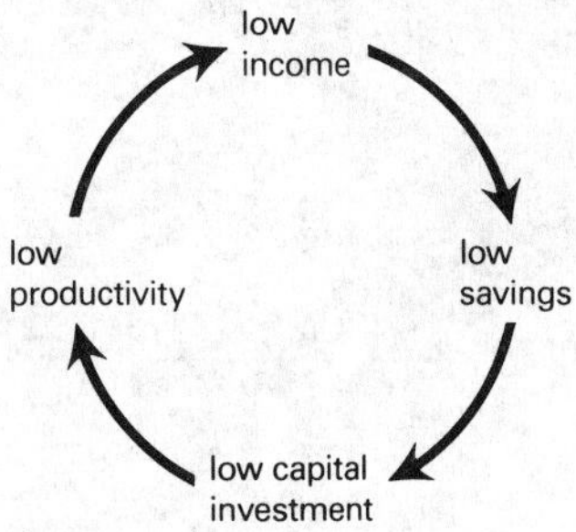

MAJOR ECONOMIC THEMES

1. Upon independence, African nations inherited trading patterns rooted in imperialism. They continued to act as suppliers of raw materials and importers of manufactured goods.
2. Africa's continued reliance upon cash crops has given rise to neocolonialism, a system in which Africans remain economically dependent upon industrialized nations.
3. Africa suffers from a food crisis, caused by such factors as drought, overpopulation, and declining productivity.
4. A cycle of poverty prevents Africa from accumulating the capital necessary to industrialize.

SECTION 2 Economic Setting: India

MAKING CONNECTIONS

OVERVIEW

After independence from Great Britain, India took steps to **decolonize** its economy, or change trading patterns established under British imperial rule. Indian economic planners tried to increase national self-reliance and decrease foreign dependency. In meeting this goal, Indians have developed a **mixed economy** in which some segments of the economy operate according to the principles of capitalism and other segments operate according to the principles of socialism.

TRADITIONAL INDIAN ECONOMY

Prior to the arrival of the British, India had a **self-sufficient economy** based on subsistence farming and the production of hand-woven **textiles**, or cloth. Although Indian merchants established themselves in Southeast Asia during the first century A.D., international trade was limited. Between the eleventh and the fifteenth centuries, India was part of the Muslim trading network, built on the spice trade. India's ports grew in response to outside markets and merchants seeking India's raw materials. In the sixteenth century, Europeans began trading directly with India. British commercial involvement through the East India Company eventually led to British political control of India in 1858.

INDIAN ECONOMY UNDER THE BRITISH

Under British domination, India fell into the typical colonial trading pattern. It exported raw materials and imported manufactured goods. This pattern greatly disrupted traditional Indian commercial activity, especially its local textile industry.

Economics and History
When Mohandas K. Gandhi called for a boycott of British-made cloth, he was not only seeking to challenge British colonial rule but also to revive a **cottage**, or home-based, industry for the benefit of the Indian people.

With the opening of the Suez Canal in 1869, the British could more easily than before ship raw cotton from India to British textile mills. They returned machine-made cloth to sell in India. The selling of imported cloth and later the establishment of textile mills in India undermined the local production of hand-woven cloth, which was more expensive to make than mass-produced cloth. The colonial system put a large number of traditional Indian laborers out of work and hurt local economies. The British also placed a tax on Indian manufactured goods.

However, certain aspects of British colonial rule laid the groundwork for future economic development.

MAKING CONNECTIONS

Improvements Introduced by the British

- Increased the amount of farmland under irrigation
- Revolutionized transportation through the construction of railroads to move goods and people cheaply and quickly
- Brought the Industrial Revolution to India through construction of steel and jute mills near Calcutta and textile mills near Bombay
- Established Western educational institutions and modern medical care
- Set up a modern banking system to handle business transactions within India

INDIA'S ECONOMY SINCE INDEPENDENCE

Since independence in 1947, India has created a **mixed economy** based on government and private investment. This system reflects the diversity of economic thought among India's political and business leaders. Some leaders, for example, favor government intervention in the economy. This **socialist** approach to the economy has led to a succession of **five-year plans**. These plans set broad economic goals, direct government investment according to national priorities, and recommend public policies. Other leaders, however, support **capitalism** and **free enterprise** in which private investors gear production to meet the demands of a free market. Under this mixed economic system, India has achieved some measure of agricultural and industrial progress.

Economics and Politics India's mixed economy evolved from the different views of its leaders. For example, Nehru promoted a socialist economy. Wealthy industrialists and business leaders have favored free enterprise.

Regents Tip What other regions have developed a mixed economy? Where have these mixed economies been most successful and why?

Agricultural Gains

Improved irrigation doubled the amount of available farmland in India and made possible **double cropping**, or the planting of two crops a year on the same land. The Indian government also attempted to apply modern methods of technology to agriculture. This so-called **green revolution** introduced farmers to new fertilizers and high-yield seeds that doubled and tripled agricultural output. India no longer depends on trade and foreign assistance for adequate food. Wheat production has increased in the Punjab region, but the impact on rice production has not been as dramatic due to climate and soil conditions.

Although agricultural production in India has more than doubled, so has the population. As a result, India still faces the challenge of maintaining self-sufficiency in food production. In addition, the distribution of food has been unequal. A significant portion of the population continues to live in poverty.

Key Concepts: Technology Technological progress and industrial growth have had uneven effects on the standard of living of the Indian people.

MAKING CONNECTIONS

Key Concepts: Interdependence
The economic systems of the world's nations have become an interdependent network.

Industrial Gains

India has a well-developed industrial base, including a modern steel industry, textile mills, and jute mills that use natural fibers from Bangladesh. Energy needs are met by domestic reserves of coal and oil. India demonstrated its technological progress by exploding a nuclear device in 1974 and launching space satellites in the 1980s. However, foreign investors still play a heavy role in Indian economic development. In fact, in 1984 a foreign company contributed to one of the world's worst industrial accidents: a pesticide plant in Bhopal accidentally released toxic chemical fumes that resulted in over 2,000 deaths and 150,000 injuries. Four years later, India's Supreme Court ordered the United States corporation responsible for the plant to pay $470 million in damages.

THE ISSUE OF POPULATION

The single largest obstacle to full economic development in India is the nation's huge population. Its **gross national product** (the total monetary value of goods and services produced in a year) is one of the highest in the world. However, India's **per capita GNP** (gross national product divided by population) is about $300 and ranks among the world's lowest. Poverty is widespread, and industrial growth has been uneven.

MAJOR ECONOMIC THEMES

1. The traditional economy of India was largely self-sufficient being based on subsistence agriculture and the production of textiles.
2. Although British rule undermined the textile industry and local economies, it also laid the foundation for future economic development and industrialization in India.
3. After independence, India created a mixed economy in which both government and private investment and ownership play important roles.
4. The green revolution helped India take important strides toward agricultural self-sufficiency, but benefits have been unevenly enjoyed.
5. Population growth and the demands it places on India's resources remain the biggest challenge to future economic progress in India.

SECTION 3 Economic Setting: Southeast Asia

OVERVIEW

Although Southeast Asia is economically underdeveloped, the region's rich agricultural and mineral resources suggest a positive economic future. The biggest obstacles to industrial progress in Southeast Asia include a scarcity of capital, lack of skilled workers, and low incomes.

AGRICULTURAL ECONOMIES

The economies of Southeast Asia are based on agriculture. More than 80 percent of the region's population work at some type of farming. Systems of land ownership vary from nation to nation. In Vietnam, for example, the Communist government encourages collective farms, while in other nations the land is privately owned. Southeast Asians practice basically two types of agriculture.

Subsistence Farming

Most farmers in the region engage in **subsistence farming**, producing only enough food for themselves and their families. On the plains, **wet-field rice** is grown in water-filled paddies. In the uplands, farmers use the **slash-and-burn** technique—that is, they cut down the rain forests and burn the fallen trees during the dry season. Farmers then plant crops of maize, or corn, and use the land until they deplete the soil of its minerals, forcing them to cut down yet more rain forest. This environmentally harmful practice has created international concern over the fate of the earth's rain forests.

Commercial Farming

European imperialism introduced commercial farming to Southeast Asia through the construction of plantations. Here Europeans used Southeast Asian labor to produce **cash crops** for export. Upon independence after World War II, the new governments in Southeast Asia continued to rely on cash crops. For example, Thailand is the world's leading exporter of rice. Malaysia and Indonesia lead in the export of rubber. The region also produces huge quantities of hardwoods, but logging threatens to exhaust forest reserves within the next several decades.

MAKING CONNECTIONS

Key Concepts: Diversity
Different goals and values than those held by the colonizing power have brought about a diversity of economic patterns in Southeast Asia.

Economics and Geography
For more information on deforestation, see Unit 6, The World Today.

Economics and History
Rubber trees were introduced into Southeast Asia from Brazil by the Europeans to be grown on plantations. Rubber is now a major export of Malaysia and Indonesia.

MAKING CONNECTIONS

MINERAL RESOURCES AND INDUSTRIAL GROWTH

Modern industry arrived in Southeast Asia with the Europeans, who processed the region's agricultural and mineral resources for their own profit. Europeans kept tight control of industry and held the highest-paying economic jobs. As a result, few Southeast Asians learned the technical skills necessary to manage industry. Today most Southeast Asian nations still ship their products out in a raw state. Some oil and tin from Indonesia and Malaysia are partially refined before export for final processing abroad.

OBSTACLES TO DEVELOPMENT

Economics and Development Singapore's skilled work force and its economic potential have attracted capital investment from Japan and the United States. In 1985 its per capita income of $6200 was the highest in the region.

Political turmoil within Southeast Asia has prevented governments from developing sound economies. During the 1970s and 1980s, thousands of refugees fled political repression in Laos, Cambodia, and Vietnam. Those who escaped by sea won international attention as the "boat people." Today, nations in the region are seeking to repair war-torn economies. However, low incomes and low standards of living prevail. The exception is Singapore, which has established itself as a **processing nation**; it imports raw materials and exports manufactured goods. Here people enjoy prosperity and an 85 percent literacy rate.

MAJOR ECONOMIC THEMES

1. Most Southeast Asians earn their incomes through subsistence farming methods that may exhaust the rain forests.
2. Southeast Asia reflects colonial trading patterns based on export of raw materials and import of manufactured items.
3. Obstacles to economic progress include lack of capital, low incomes, and a scarcity of skilled workers.

SECTION 4 Economic Setting: China

OVERVIEW

China contains more than one-quarter of the world's population. Agriculture dominates China's economy today as it did in the past, and nearly 80 percent of its people work at some kind of farming. However, Communist leaders are seeking to change this situation. Since the Communist takeover in 1949, they have embarked on an ambitious program of modernization. Their goal is to transform China from a primarily agricultural economy to a primarily industrial economy.

MAKING CONNECTIONS

Key Concepts: Scarcity and Technology
China is attempting to utilize technology to overcome problems of scarcity in both food and consumer goods.

ECONOMIC DEVELOPMENT IN PRE-COMMUNIST CHINA

Although China is a large country, only about 11 percent of its land is suitable for farming. To support a historically large population, China practiced **intensive farming** which used enormous amounts of human labor, assisted by simple aids like foot treadles and water buckets, to irrigate fields and tend terraced hillsides.

A Landed Gentry

A pattern of land ownership emerged early in China's history in which a **scholar-gentry** class controlled most of the land and rented it to a vast number of peasant tenant-farmers. Crop failures, periodic flooding, high taxation, and indebtedness to landlords increased discontent among the peasants. Throughout history, peasants rebelled and overthrew ruling dynasties. In the mid-1900s during the civil war between the Nationalists and the Communists, many peasants turned to the Communists who promised ambitious land reforms.

A Traditional Economy

Although the Industrial Revolution spread throughout much of the world in the 1800s and early 1900s, Chinese emperors resisted Western technology. They saw industry as a symbol of Western imperialism and feared it would undermine traditional Chinese social values. After the fall of China's last emperor, foreign invasions and civil wars slowed industrial progress until the 1950s.

China: Land Use

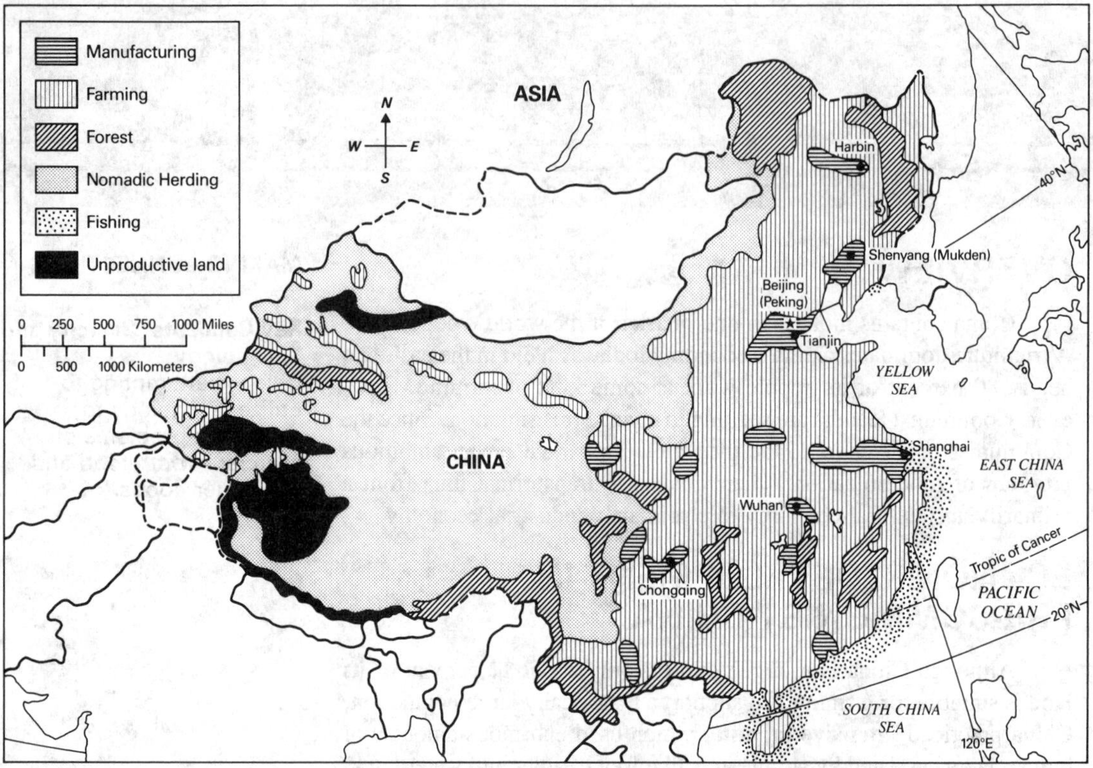

MAKING CONNECTIONS

Regents Tip Read map keys carefully. Which part of China is agricultural?

ECONOMIC CHANGES UNDER COMMUNISM

On October 1, 1949, **Mao Zedong** proclaimed the People's Republic of China. Under his direction, the Communists reshaped China's economy according to Marxist ideology. Through a series of five-year plans, the government laid the framework for a highly centralized system to achieve modernization in a relatively short time.

Modernization Under Mao Zedong

From 1949 to 1953, Mao attacked the old pattern of land ownership. He took land away from large landholders and redistributed it to the peasants. All industry and commerce was **nationalized**, or put under government control. To stop foreign influence, Mao sharply restricted trade with the West.

FIRST FIVE-YEAR PLAN (1953–1957) The first five-year plan sought to turn China into a **command economy**, or an economic system in which government controls and directs all aspects of production. In agriculture, the government abolished privately owned farms and combined them into cooperative farms. On **cooperative farms**, farmers worked the land together but had small private plots near their homes. While farm output increased, the government's share was not enough to feed the growing population.

THE GREAT LEAP FORWARD (1958–1962) Mao's second five-year plan aimed at bringing China even closer to his vision of an ideal Communist society. He reorganized the cooperatives into **communes**, which became the basic political, economic, and social units in China. Family members no longer lived together but in dormitories. Each commune member was paid a wage to do the work assigned by the commune leaders.

Mao used the communes to mobilized China's huge population into massive "production teams." The system split families and assigned people jobs in farming or heavy industry. Communal labor produced steel and built roads, dams, and factories. Peasants resented the loss of their lands and the disruption of family life. Public dissatisfaction, coupled with a series of crop failures and withdrawal of Soviet aid, turned the Great Leap Forward into a disaster. The second five-year plan was canceled and communes were made smaller. Communal living ended and private plots were again given to the farmers.

THE CULTURAL REVOLUTION (1966–1976) Mao blamed failure of the Great Leap Forward on Chinese bureaucrats. He began a campaign to create a society in harmony with his ideology. During the **Cultural Revolution**, ideological purity was more important than technical expertise. This struggle became known as the "red versus expert" controversy.

Mao released Communist-trained students from school and set up the **Red Guard**. He used his student armies to denounce teachers and white-collar workers. Everyone was expected to share in manual labor. Skilled workers were sent to labor in fields and factories. The system of the "iron rice bowl" was created in which workers were all paid the same salary regardless of their individual productivity and responsibilities.

China's economic development during the last decade of Mao's rule was severely limited by the removal of technically qualified personnel and the elimination of higher pay for more productive work. The chaos that resulted from the Cultural Revolution lasted even beyond Mao's death in 1976.

Modernization Under Deng Xiaoping

After a power struggle, **Deng Xiaoping** became head of the Communist Party in China. Deng adopted a more practical approach to industrialization called the **Four Modernizations**, which called for progress in science, education, industry, and agriculture. The program attempted to increase productivity through limited private ownership and trade with the West. Material incentives were introduced by offering higher wages and bonuses for workers who produced more.

FOREIGN INVESTMENT The government ended China's economic isolation and welcomed foreign investment through **joint-venture companies** in which ownership and profits were shared by

MAKING CONNECTIONS

Regents Tip The Regents exam often has questions on reform movements. What were the major focuses of economic reform in each of the following Chinese reform movements?

First five-year plan:

Great Leap Forward:

Cultural Revolution:

Four Modernizations:

Economics and History For more on the Cultural Revolution, see the section on China in Unit 2, Global History.

Economics and History For more on Deng Xiaoping, see the section on China in Unit 2, Global History.

MAKING CONNECTIONS

the Chinese government and the foreign investors. Deng also allowed thousands of Chinese students to study foreign technology abroad.

LIMITED FREE ENTERPRISE To increase worker incentives, the government turned the control of industry over to local factory managers. It also allowed limited **private ownership** of businesses by individuals. In the cities, Chinese entrepreneurs set up restaurants, beauty shops, and other small businesses.

RESPONSIBILITY SYSTEM In rural areas, farmers won long-term leases of land under a program called the **responsibility system**. According to this system, farmers agreed to sell a portion of their crops to the government at set prices. They could then sell their surplus crops privately and keep the profits. This system spurred agricultural production, and the standard of living for many farmers improved.

OBSTACLES TO PROGRESS

Economics and History
For more on Tiananmen Square, see the section on China in Unit 2, Global History.

Economics and Resources
The availability of natural resources can facilitate economic development, but a large population can have such great demands on available resources that little is left for development.

The reform programs instituted by Deng received a setback after the student uprisings in Tiananmen Square in 1989. A number of foreign investors pulled out of China and have only recently resumed a cautious program of economic investment.

China also faces strains from a population that has topped the one billion mark. Leaders have instituted a program called the "one-child family," which offers financial incentives to couples willing to limit their families. While this program has been successful among urban professional couples, rural families still prize large families as a source of labor. Although China's population growth rate of 1.4 percent is well below the world's average, the total yearly increase in China's population is enormous in actual numbers. This increase translates into a tremendous strain on schools, health care, and jobs.

MAJOR ECONOMIC THEMES

1. The economy of China was traditionally based on agriculture, and industrial activity was very limited before 1949 when the Communists took power.
2. Under Mao Zedong, China's Communist leaders set up a strict command economy and sought to industrialize rapidly through implementation of a series of five-year plans.
3. Many peasants resisted Mao's economic policy because it deprived them of land and disrupted traditional family patterns.
4. Communist leaders since Mao's death have sought to increase productivity and speed industrialization through a measure of private ownership and greater contact with the West.
5. China's huge population taxes its resources and limits its economic progress.

SECTION 5 Economic Setting: Japan

OVERVIEW

MAKING CONNECTIONS

Japan has proven that it is not necessary to have a large resource base for economic development. Since Japan opened its doors to Western trade in the 1850s, it has gone through a series of economic transformations that has made it into one of the world's leading exporters of manufactured goods. A key theme in Japanese economic history has been **interdependence**, both with the nations that supply Japan with raw materials and with the nations that buy its manufactured goods.

Key Concepts: Scarcity
Japan's scarcity of raw materials and oil has affected its pattern of economic development. As a **processing nation**, a country that imports natural resources and exports manufactured goods, its prospects for a healthy economy depend on world trading conditions and on its capacity to maintain and expand its exports.

ECONOMIC GROWTH PRIOR TO WORLD WAR II

In terms of physical geography, Japan seems an unlikely candidate to become an industrial giant. Its four main islands occupy a land area that is about the same size as the state of California, while Japan's population is roughly half that of the United States. Japan is the most densely populated country on earth. Its terrain is largely mountainous, and its natural resources are few. For centuries Japan isolated itself from the rest of the world. Yet today it produces nearly 10 percent of the world's manufactured goods. The reasons for Japan's tremendous economic growth can be found in its history.

The Tokugawa Shogunate

Prior to the establishment of the Tokugawa shogunate in the early 1600s, Japan's economy was based on **subsistence agriculture**. After centuries of civil war, the rise of the **Tokugawa shoguns** ushered in nearly 250 years of peace. They maintained control of the country through a **feudal system** in which the daimyo, or lords loyal to the shogun, were placed strategically throughout the land.

Economics and History
For more information on feudalism in Japan, see the section on Japan in Unit 2, Global History.

Early in this period, the Tokugawa rulers expelled all foreign traders and missionaries. This self-imposed isolation helped Japan to avoid the patterns of colonial exploitation that took place elsewhere in Asia. Japan fell behind the West in terms of technological progress. But the long peace stimulated the growth of cities and the rise of a commercial economy based on the production of rice. Expanded literacy among a skilled class of urban workers helped pave the way for future modernization.

MAKING CONNECTIONS

The Meiji Restoration

Japan's isolation ended with the arrival of Commodore Matthew Perry in 1854. Perry's steam-powered "black ships" shocked Japanese rulers and alerted them to the danger of conquest. In 1868 a small group of leaders overthrew the last Tokugawa shogunate and restored Emperor Meiji to power. The emperor and his supporters ushered in a series of economic reforms so that Japan would not fall victim to European imperialism.

TRANSPORTATION The Japanese planned an extensive transportation network. In 1870 work began on the nation's first railroad.

MANUFACTURING Using small domestic coal deposits as an energy source, Japan developed weapons and shipbuilding industries. A few families formed large-scale business enterprises known as **zaibatsu**. These conglomerates helped Japan to industrialize.

TECHNOLOGY Japan sent students abroad to study Western technology. However, while the Japanese borrowed freely from the West, they adapted new ideas to fit their culture. As a result, the Japanese modernized rather than Westernized.

Economics and History
For more information on Japanese imperialism, see the section on Japan in Unit 2, Global History.

IMPERIALISM After modernizing their military, Japan undertook a policy of imperialism. It sought colonies as sources of raw materials and as markets for finished products. By 1941 Japan ruled a vast Asian empire.

World War II and Defeat

Japan's aggressive empire-building led the Japanese into World War II. Defeat by the United States and its allies destroyed Japan's empire and left its economy in shambles. United States occupation of Japan laid the foundations for the rise of a **capitalist** economic system.

POSTWAR ECONOMIC RECOVERY

General Douglas MacArthur, commander of United States forces in the Pacific, helped draft a new democratic constitution for Japan. He also redistributed land more fairly and made efforts to break up the large business monopolies of the zaibatsu. When war broke out in Korea, the United States stimulated Japanese economic growth through its war purchases. After United States occupation ended in 1952, several factors combined to continue that growth.

Selective Borrowing

Key Concepts: Technology
Increasingly Japan has turned to advanced technology to improve its economic position in the world market.

Japan continued its historic pattern of selective borrowing through cultural diffusion. The Japanese borrowed Western technology and then used their own **innovation** and marketing skills to adapt it. Today Japan leads the world in the production of televisions, video cassette recorders, compact disc players, automobiles, and motorcycles. Japan has also invested heavily in research to develop its own supercomputers, superconductors, and biotechnology.

Skilled Work Force

A competitive education system in Japan has created almost universal literacy. Japanese schools train more engineers than any other Western nation, including the United States. Japanese firms organize their work forces much like Japanese families. They expect loyalty, hard work, and discipline. In exchange, most firms rarely fire workers, even when work is slow or new technology is introduced. Managers set up **quality-control circles** to seek worker suggestions on how to improve production.

Capital Funding

Japan's financial structure provides capital for economic growth. The Japanese people save approximately 20 percent of their income and buy little on credit. The high rate of savings enables banks to make loans for investment and for research and development. Four of the five largest banks in the world are Japanese.

Government Cooperation

The Japanese government encourages industry through loans, favorable tax breaks, and a close watch on the value of the **yen** (the basic monetary unit of Japan). Minimal government regulation has favored the growth of large corporations and allowed the zaibatsu (although no longer under single-family ownership) to become extremely competitive. High protective tariffs discourage foreign competition.

MAKING CONNECTIONS

Economics and Society
The Japanese tradition of "wa," or obedience to superiors and team spirit, along with a commitment to high-quality production, has served to make Japanese products successful.

Key Concept: Choice
By limiting its defense spending to about one percent of its GNP, Japan has lower military expenditures than the United States or the Soviet Union and more funds are available for capital investment and economic expansion.

JAPAN AND THE GLOBAL ECONOMY

In today's interdependent world, Japan's economic policies have a far-reaching impact, especially on the United States.

A Trade Imbalance

By keeping the value of the yen down, Japan has been able to sell its goods more cheaply than the United States. This has resulted in a **trade imbalance**, or a situation in which Japan sells more goods to Americans than the United States sells to the Japanese. The trade imbalance with Japan has contributed to the U.S. **trade deficit** in which more money flows out of the United States than flows into it.

Suggestions for Change

Under pressure from the American government, the Japanese have allowed the yen to increase in value. The United States hopes that this will make American products more price-competitive in Japan. However, so far Japanese consumers have remained loyal to Japanese products. As a result, some Americans have suggested more drastic measures, including high protective tariffs against Japanese goods and restrictions against the flow of American technology. In response, Japan has placed quotas on the number of automobiles it ships to the United States. It has also invested capital in building some joint Japa-

MAKING CONNECTIONS

nese-American industries in the United States. However, the trade imbalance promises to remain a key economic issue for the 1990s.

PROBLEMS FOR THE JAPANESE ECONOMY

Japan's economy is not without problems. Most Japanese workers do not work for large corporations and so lack the extensive benefits these corporations provide. Housing and food costs are high, so Japanese purchasing power is only half that of an American with the same relative income. The aging population with inadequate pensions and health-care facilities is also a cause for social concern.

The Japanese have already made an effort to control the air and water pollution that resulted from industrialization, but urban water supplies and sewage need improvement. A better system of roads is needed. The traffic problems of the cities and better housing require urgent attention.

MAJOR ECONOMIC THEMES

1. As Japan's isolationist period ended, the Japanese laid the groundwork for modernization through development of an urban culture and a commercial economy.
2. The leaders of the Meiji Restoration industrialized through a program of selective borrowing and cultural adaptation.
3. Since World War II, Japan has revived its economy through selective borrowing, its skilled workers, high accumulation of capital, and government cooperation.
4. In recent times, the trade imbalance between Japan and the United States has been a cause for concern between the two nations.
5. Today, Japan's economy is being affected by social problems, including an aging population without adequate economic support and problems related to urban living.

SECTION 6

Economic Setting: Latin America

OVERVIEW

MAKING CONNECTIONS

Latin America has had a pattern of economic dependence, first upon colonial powers and then upon the United States. Today Latin America is still primarily an agricultural region. A small group of large landowners controls the economic resources in most Latin American nations, a practice that grew out of the region's colonial heritage.

PRE-COLUMBIAN PERIOD (1500 B.C.–A.D. 1530)

Pre-Columbian societies of Latin America supported large populations through the **development of agriculture**. The Incas, for example, used techniques such as irrigation, fertilization, and terracing to feed the millions of people that made up the empire.

THE COLONIAL HERITAGE (1520–1808)

For nearly 300 years, Spain and Portugal dominated Latin America. They seized the most fertile land and exploited the region's natural resources. Latin America fulfilled the colonial economic role as an exporter of raw materials and an importer of manufactured goods.

Encomienda System

Under the **encomienda system**, established in the Spanish colonies, landowners were given huge estates and control of the labor of Indians who lived on the land. Spanish landlords used Indian labor to build huge plantations or mines. When large numbers of Indians died from European diseases and harsh treatment, the practice of slavery spread to the Americas. Slavery brought landowners enormous wealth, while the rest of the population fell into poverty.

Single-Commodity Economies

Most Latin American colonies specialized in the export of a **single cash crop** or a **single mineral**. The colonial powers stripped Latin America of large quantities of gold and silver. The sale of exports in Europe enriched Spain and Portugal and impoverished Latin America. Under colonialism, the system of **mercantilism** guaranteed trading partners for the colonial nations by limiting the industries and trade of the Latin American colonies.

MAKING CONNECTIONS

Economics and History
For more information on independence movements, see the section on Latin America in Unit 2, Global History.

ECONOMIC DEVELOPMENT AFTER INDEPENDENCE

Colonial exploitation was one cause of the Latin American independence movements of the early nineteenth century. However, political independence did not bring economic independence to the region. Land remained concentrated in the hands of a few, and the gap between the rich and the poor widened. The new governments continued to export raw materials and import finished products. They relied on industrial nations, first England and France and then the United States, for investment capital and a supply of manufactured goods.

By the end of the nineteenth century, **economic imperialism** had replaced mercantilism. Latin America threw off foreign political rule only to fall prey to foreign economic domination. Investment by foreigners helped to bring about some industrialization, but most Latin American countries did not benefit from the profits of these investments. Both colonialism and economic imperialism hindered economic development.

LATIN AMERICA TODAY

Today most Latin American nations have **capitalist economies** in which private individuals own large farms and industries. However, there has not yet been a major redistribution of the wealth, and some **socialist leaders** have gained a foothold in the region.

Agriculture

The topography of Latin America makes farming difficult. Less than one-third of the region is **arable**, or able to be farmed. Even so, the nations of Latin America are largely **agricultural**. Although large numbers of people are engaged in farming or ranching, countries must struggle to feed their populations.

Economic Systems
Commercial farming on large estates produces crops for export. Coffee, bananas, and sugar are the major cash crops.

The legacy of the encomienda system continues in much of Latin America. Millions of poor **tenant farmers** still live on the estates or plantations of the landowning elite. In return for their labor, the farmers receive small plots of land on which they practice **subsistence farming**. Many Latin American countries continue to rely on a single cash crop for export. This practice exposes Latin America to price fluctuations on the world market and severe economic shortages at home. To modernize agriculture, Latin American nations have tried several approaches.

Economics and Politics
With few exceptions, land reform has not been effectively pursued in Latin America. For example, when Brazil opened up the Amazon rain forest to settlers, the land they cleared lost its fertility within two years, and the resulting deforestation may have devastating worldwide effects.

LAND REFORM Several countries have attempted to break up large estates and distribute land more evenly. The method of redistribution depended upon the nation's political and economic philosophies.

In Mexico, about half the large estates, or **haciendas**, were converted into community lands called **ejidos** following the 1910 Mexican

Revolution. This land was worked by the peasants but owned by the village. Ejidos account for about 50 percent of Mexico's farm land.

In Cuba, Fidel Castro seized privately owned lands after the 1959 Communist Revolution and transformed them into state farms and collective farms. This **nationalization** of land was done without compensation and caused many members of the upper classes to flee to the United States.

CROP DIVERSIFICATION Crop diversification has become increasingly important to Latin America. In order to feed their growing populations adequately, countries must use less of their land for cash crops and more for **staple crops**, such as wheat and corn. Those who control the land resist this change because growing staple crops for local consumption is not as profitable as growing cash crops for export.

Overdependence on single cash crops is also very risky. Poor weather conditions, overproduction, or a drop in world demand can mean economic disaster. For example, reduced demand for Colombian coffee depressed its price in the world market. People resorted to growing coca, used in the production of cocaine, to increase their incomes. In an effort to stop this illegal activity, the Colombian government appealed to the government of the United States to increase coffee imports from Colombia.

POPULATION PLANNING As in many rural, developing nations, Latin American farmers still value large families as a source of labor. However, food supplies cannot keep pace with the population of Latin America, which is expected to double in the next 30 years. Some people have called for **family planning**, or limiting the number of children a couple may have. But cultural and religious beliefs have made family planning difficult to achieve.

Industry

Industry in Latin America also suffers from the region's colonial heritage. In the past 30 years, Latin American nations have attempted to produce more of their own manufactured goods, with varying degrees of success. Some nations turned to foreign investors for help. However, many nations—including Chile, Cuba, Nicaragua, and Venezuela—grew to resent outside influence and **nationalized** all or some of the foreign-owned businesses. In 1975, for example, Venezuela nationalized its oil industry. In order to achieve full economic independence, Latin America needs to solve a number of serious problems.

RAPID URBANIZATION Every year, hundreds of thousands of people migrate to urban areas seeking employment. Rapid urbanization places an economic burden on cities to provide jobs, housing, education, medical care, and other services. Economic problems also lead to **emigration**, or the movement of people from their native country to another country, where they hope to find a higher standard of living.

MAKING CONNECTIONS

Economics and Politics
Economic change requires government support and, often, intervention. People must be assured that changes will not decrease their standards of living. Funding is required for the changes in production and for training of workers.

MAKING CONNECTIONS

Foreign Debt of Mexico

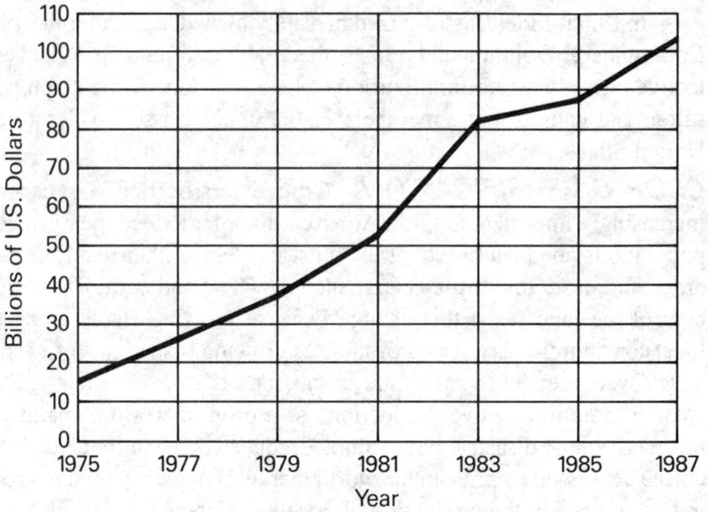

Source: *CIA Handbook of Economic Statistics*

For example, Latin Americans comprise the fastest-growing immigrant group in the United States.

LACK OF CAPITAL To industrialize, Latin Americans need to find new ways to raise capital. Unfortunately, many Latin Americans still invest capital in North America or Europe since profits are more likely there than in Latin America. Potential foreign investors often do not invest in Latin America because of political instability caused by changes in governments or due to fear that their property may be nationalized.

Key Concepts: Interdependence
The multinational corporation embodies the growing interdependence between more-developed and less-developed regions.

COMPETITION FROM MULTINATIONALS In recent years, large **multinational corporations**, or corporations with operations in many nations, have established factories in Latin America. However, these factories sometimes aggravate economic problems because local industries cannot compete with their capital or technological knowledge.

INFLATION Some Latin American nations, such as Argentina, have experienced soaring **inflation**, or rapid price rises and sharp declines in the value of money. Inflation causes workers to demand higher wages, which in turn triggers even greater inflation. Real buying power is reduced, and the standards of living drop.

NATIONAL INDEBTEDNESS Many nations have been unable to pay off bank loans made in the 1960s and 1970s. Mexico, for example, borrowed extensively when the price of its oil reached an all-time high during the oil crisis of the 1970s. However, when the crisis

MAKING CONNECTIONS

eased in the 1980s, the Mexican economy faltered and the government could not pay off its debts. When debtor nations fall behind in payments, foreign banks tighten credit and economic problems deepen.

SOLUTIONS TO ECONOMIC PROBLEMS

The countries of Latin America have tried to find solutions to their economic problems through regional cooperation. Cooperative efforts are difficult because of Latin America's diversity. In order to foster economic development, Latin American governments need to concentrate in three areas.

- **Control population growth** Overpopulation not only taxes available resources, it makes education very costly.
- **Establish fairer systems of taxation** In many Latin American countries, the rich do not pay their fair share of taxes and the nation loses revenue.
- **Generate new sources of capital without increasing foreign debt**

In three separate votes over the course of 1993, the legislatures of Canada, the United States, and Mexico ratified the North American Free Trade Agreement (NAFTA). Supporters portrayed the agreement as an opportunity for greater economic growth for all three countries.

MAJOR ECONOMIC THEMES

1. Latin America has a history of economic dependence upon the industrial nations of the world.
2. Agricultural and industrial problems in the region are rooted in old colonial policies, which caused uneven distribution of wealth and one-commodity economies.
3. Economic independence in Latin America requires finding solutions to such problems as overpopulation, lack of capital, high inflation, and national indebtedness.

SECTION 7 Economic Setting: The Middle East

MAKING CONNECTIONS

OVERVIEW

The Middle East contains the world's largest known reserves of oil but suffers from a scarcity of other resources—especially water. Because of its possession of oil, the Middle East has become a symbol of global **interdependence**. The economic decisions made in the Middle East affect the economic planning of industrial nations around the world.

TRADITIONAL ECONOMIC SYSTEMS

Two main forms of production exist in the Middle East: (1) agriculture centered around villages, and (2) commerce and industry located in the cities. Many agricultural and commercial practices are rooted in the traditional economies of the past.

Economics and Society
The expanding population of the Middle East and its limited amount of agricultural land has caused this region to import more food than it exports.

Agriculture

Agriculture in the Middle East reflects the topography and climate of the region. Because of the arid climate, less than 10 percent of the land is farmed. Scarce supplies of water have led to a concentration of population in river valleys and coastal areas. Here farmers grow crops that originated in the Middle East thousands of years ago—wheat, oranges, cotton, and sugar cane. A small percentage of people live nomadic lives and raise camels, donkeys, and horses for transport.

Commerce

The Middle East was the hub of commerce in the ancient world, and Arab traders developed many business practices used today. The word "check" is Arabic in origin, and Arabs were the first to use checks in their business dealings. The word "bazaar" also originated in the Middle East. It still describes the busy marketplaces of the region and has crept into use in the English language.

Key Concepts: Interdependence
European explorers improved the magnetic compass, a Chinese invention that the Arabs had brought to Europe.

Arab traders borrowed the Hindu number system with its concept of zero. The Hindu-Arabic number system facilitated financial activities and was eventually adopted by the West through cultural diffusion. Arab control of the spice trade caravans in the Middle East motivated Europeans to look for a sea route to the East Indies so that they could share in the wealth available from commerce.

ECONOMIC SYSTEMS TODAY

The economic systems practiced in the Middle East vary from nation to nation. The region as a whole suffers from several problems including a shortage of food and rapid population growth. Today most Middle Eastern nations must import more food than they export. And most nations experience overcrowding in cities and on the region's limited farmlands. Governments have adopted a variety of approaches to solve these problems.

Arab Socialism in Egypt

Upon independence, some Middle Eastern nations nationalized businesses and instituted land reforms. Egypt became the model for what has become known as **Arab socialism**. Under President Gamel Abdel Nasser, who held power from 1954 to 1970, Egypt broke up large estates and redistributed the land to Egyptian peasants known as the **fellahin**. With Soviet aid, Egypt also built the Aswan Dam to control flooding on the Nile and increase farm land. The dam, however, caused unforeseen ecological damage. For example, it blocked accumulation of silt and increased erosion along the Mediterranean coast.

Mixed Economy in Israel

Economic planners in other Middle Eastern nations set up **mixed economies**, or economies that combine features of free enterprise and government planning. Israel became the model for this type of economic system. For example, Israel allows private ownership of some property. However, it has also developed the **kibbutz**, or collectively owned farm, in which people share equally in the work and the profits. Israel has chosen to diversify its agricultural production so that the nation does not rely on a single cash crop. It also has emphasized industrialization over agricultural development.

MAKING CONNECTIONS

Key Concepts: Diversity
Standards of living show great diversity throughout the Middle East.

Economics and Politics
Israel is the most technologically advanced nation in the Middle East, with significant industrial development. However, its political isolation in the region has limited its commercial interaction with neighboring countries.

MIDDLE EASTERN OIL

The discovery of petroleum in the Middle East and the large-scale production of oil after World War II immensely changed the region and the entire global economy.

The Region's Major Resource

The current oil reserves in the Middle East represent two-thirds of the world's known supplies. Leading oil-producing nations include Saudi Arabia, Kuwait, Iraq, Iran, and the Gulf States. Smaller reserves are found in Algeria, Libya, and Egypt.

OPEC Industrial nations—including Western Europe, the United States, and Japan—rely heavily upon petroleum for fuel, lubricants, and the production of synthetics such as plastic. At first, industrial

Oil Regions of the World

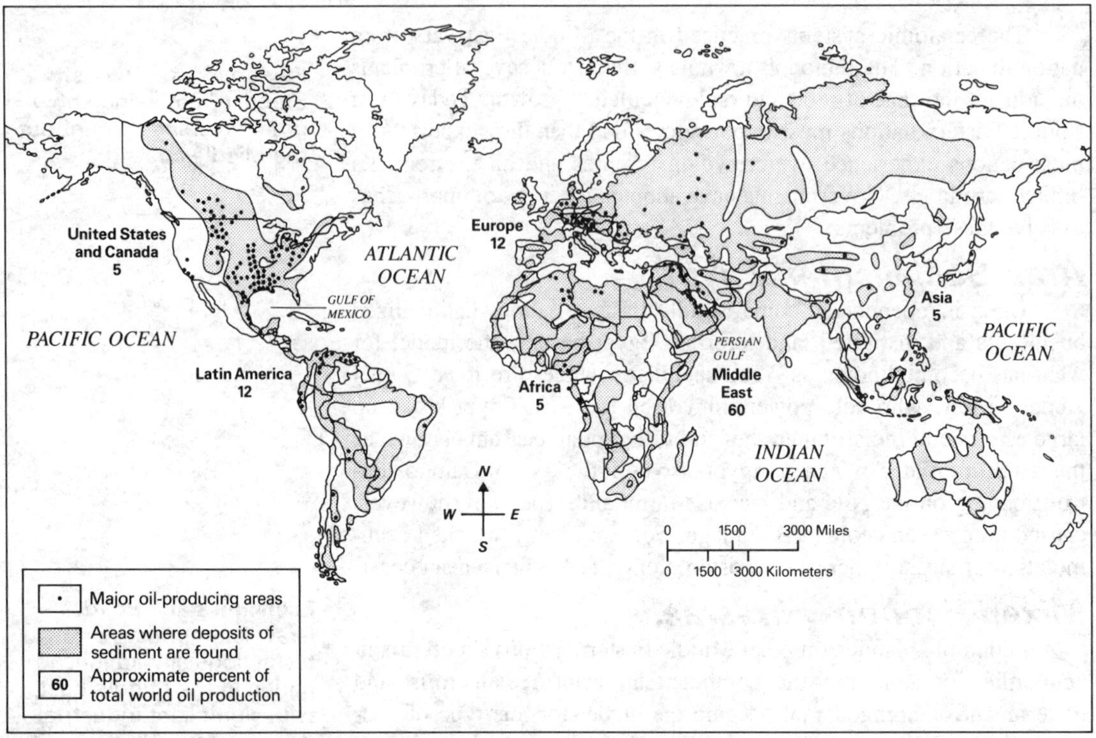

MAKING CONNECTIONS

Regents Tip Note that although North America has many major oil-producing areas, only about 5 percent of the total world oil production takes place there. Looking at both the map and the key carefully can prevent incorrect Regents answers.

Regents Tip What was the major reason for the formation of OPEC?

nations used their economic power to help Middle Eastern nations develop their oil reserves. In exchange, Western oil companies controlled the prices and royalties earned from the region's most valuable resource. To break Western influence, oil-producing nations formed the Organization of Petroleum Exporting Countries, or OPEC, in 1960. Throughout the 1960s, oil companies were able to counter the power of OPEC because they owned the technology and means of producing the oil. Also, the production of oil was larger than the demand, which remained relatively low until the 1970s.

OIL POLITICS As the demand for oil grew, power shifted from the oil companies to the oil-producing nations. During the 1973 Yom Kippur War with Israel, Arab members of OPEC refused to sell oil to nations supporting Israel. Included in the embargo was the United States, which in 1973 imported nearly half its oil from the Middle East. The oil embargo caused global oil shortages and raised the price of oil on the world market. More important, oil-producing nations realized that oil had become a powerful political weapon.

Impact of Oil on the Middle East

The use of oil politics brought many changes to the Middle East. Governments in the region nationalized foreign oil companies, strengthening the move toward Arab socialism. Oil-producing nations used oil profits to fund development projects and to gain influence in the world's financial markets. A few nations, such as Iraq and Libya, bought large inventories of armaments.

SECULARIZATION The wealth from oil created tensions within traditional Arab society. A secular middle class grew up that followed Western ways of life, creating concern among conservative Islamic leaders. Religious tensions and anti-Western hostilities led to the overthrow of the American-backed Shah of Iran in 1979. The spread of Islamic fundamentalism led to tensions in other Arab nations, too.

REGIONAL CONFLICTS Middle Eastern nations did not share equally in the possession of oil and the technological changes that it brought to the region. The wealth from oil increased divisions among the "have" and "have not" nations. Egypt and Turkey, for example, are the most populous nations in the Middle East. But they produce far less oil than they consume and they lack significant reserves. Therefore, both nations have sought friendlier relations with the United States, which has led to conflicts with some of their Arab neighbors.

The Situation Today

A global recession in the 1980s and increased fuel efficiency in industrial nations helped reduce the power of OPEC. But as the prices of oil dropped, conservation efforts declined and fuel consumption again rose. In August 1990, Iraq seized the nation of Kuwait and threatened to invade Saudi Arabia. The United Nations condemned Iraqi aggression, and the United States and other nations sent troops into Saudi Arabia. In January 1990, the United States and its allies bombed Iraq and war began in the Middle East. By the end of February the war ended with the liberation of Kuwait. Hussein, however, remained in power.

MAKING CONNECTIONS

Key Concepts: Interdependence
The relationship of oil prices to global economic growth is a strong one. An increase in the price of oil adds to the costs of many products. Third World nations that lack energy resources find economic progress even more difficult to attain because of increasing fuel costs.

MAJOR ECONOMIC THEMES

1. The traditional economies of the Middle East reflect the region's physical geography and its position as commercial hub of the ancient world.
2. Middle Eastern governments have adopted a variety of economic solutions to the problems of modernization, including Arab socialism and development of mixed economies.
3. Foreign investors helped Middle Eastern nations develop their oil reserves. But a rise in worldwide consumption in oil encouraged oil-producing nations to nationalize the oil fields and to take control of the profits themselves.
4. The wealth of oil has brought far-reaching changes to the Middle East and underscored global interdependence.

SECTION 8 Economic Setting: Western Europe

MAKING CONNECTIONS

Key Concepts: Environment
In spite of a relatively narrow resource base, Western Europe is a highly developed region, although southern Europe remains less economically developed than the north. Dependence on the resources of other regions, such as Middle Eastern oil, affects policy decisions.

OVERVIEW

Western Europe's economic system has evolved over a long period of time. The region was the birthplace of the Industrial Revolution and center of a worldwide trading system based on imperialism. Although Western European dominance has declined in the post-industrial age, the region still plays a key role in the global economic community. Today the nations of Western Europe are moving toward greater regional interdependence. Most nations have struck a balance between market and planned economies, or systems that combine principles of capitalism and socialism.

PRE-INDUSTRIAL EUROPE (27 B.C.–A.D.1750)

Modern Europe has an economic heritage that began over 2,000 years ago under the Roman Empire.

The Ancient World

During the period of political stability known as the **Pax Romana** (Roman Peace) from 27 B.C. to A.D. 180, commerce and trade flourished throughout the Roman Empire. An extensive network of roads, together with Mediterranean sea-lanes, gave people access to raw materials, products, and markets over a wide area. Trade thus contributed to regional interdependence and a higher standard of living.

The Middle Ages (500–1500)

Following repeated invasions by Germanic peoples, the political, economic, and social systems of the Roman Empire collapsed. As warfare raged, roads fell into disrepair. Traders found it too dangerous to travel, and commercial centers disappeared. People tried to bring order into their lives through a social and political system known as **feudalism**.

MANORIALISM The economic system on which feudalism rested was called **manorialism**, a system in which land served as the basis of wealth. A small elite group of nobles, called **lords**, owned the land, and the great mass of peasants, or **serfs**, worked it. The serfs provided a lord with food and services in exchange for protection. All activities centered on the lord's estate, or **manor**. Because of the lack of trade, manors were almost entirely self-sufficient.

REVIVAL OF TRADE In time, greater political stability helped revive trade and commerce. The **Crusades** stimulated an interest in goods from the Islamic and Byzantine worlds. As a result, a lively trade developed between the East and West, with Italian merchants leading the way. Cities again became centers of trade, first in Italy and then in other parts of Europe. A new middle class, made up of merchants and artisans, took shape. Skilled workers formed **guilds**, the forerunners of modern labor unions, to protect themselves from competition. The guilds trained workers, set standards for quality, controlled prices, and provided benefits for members.

THE COMMERCIAL REVOLUTION (1600–1700) The desire to find new trade routes to the East led to the Age of Exploration. By sailing around Africa, Portuguese adventurers found a new way to acquire the riches of India. This all-water route allowed Portugal to break the monopoly on trade held by the Italian city-states. Spain and other European nations entered the race to find new water routes to Asia. Their explorations led them across the Atlantic and to the European discovery of the Americas. The new lands created opportunities for business ventures, which in turn sparked a commercial revolution. The commercial revolution had several important effects.

INTERDEPENDENT TRADE The economies of Europe, Asia, Africa, and the Americas became interconnected through trade. An exchange of goods—and cultures—developed.

CAPITALISM The economic philosophy of capitalism became popular. **Capitalism** is based on the idea of private ownership and private control of property and wealth. New business ventures, as well as the expansion of business, were assisted by banks and by the development of joint-stock companies.

MAKING CONNECTIONS

Regents Tip The need for markets and raw materials was the major reason for the revival of European interest in overseas possessions.

Economics and History Overseas exploration dramatically changed the patterns of world trade.

Principles of Capitalism

Private Ownership	All property, including the means of production, should be privately owned.
Free Enterprise	Individuals should be free from central control so that they can make basic economic decisions, including what, where, how much, and at what price goods will be produced.
Supply and Demand	Prices will be determined by the scarcity of a product; that is, a large supply with reduced demand will bring down prices, while a small supply with increased demand will raise prices.
Competition	Competition will ensure high-quality goods at low prices, thus benefiting consumers.

Atlantic Trade Routes, 1750

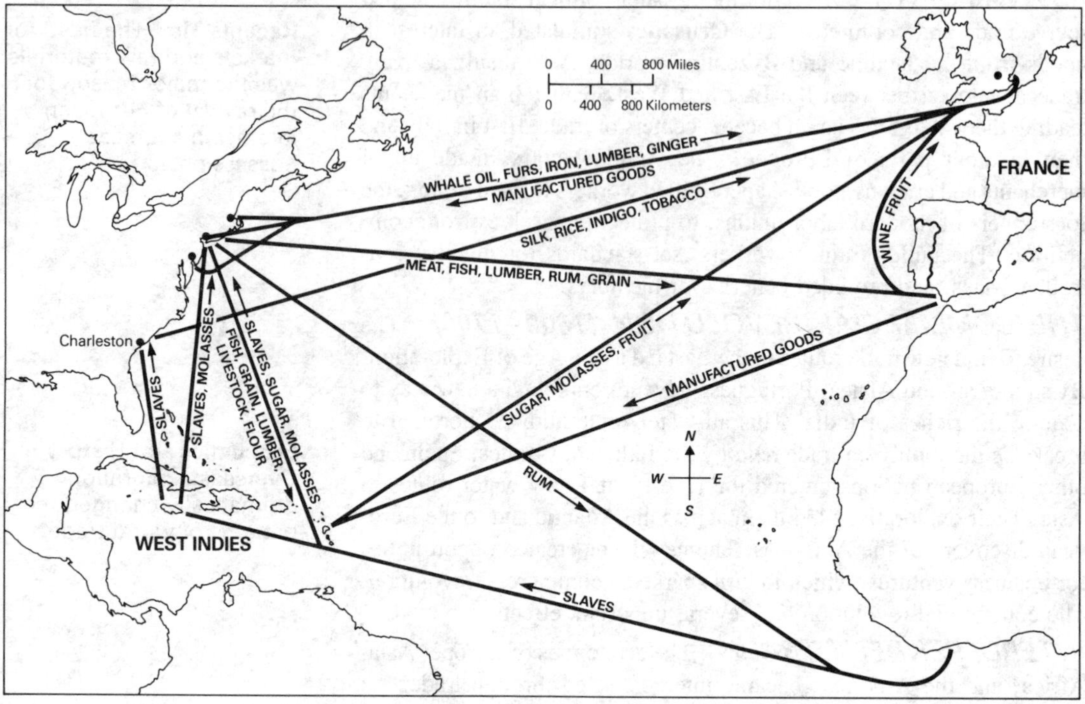

MAKING CONNECTIONS

Regents tip How did the slave trade affect Africa?

Profit Motive Because businesses operate to earn money, they will seek ways to lower costs and increase production so that they can compete more effectively.

MERCANTILISM Many governments at the time adopted an economic policy known as **mercantilism**. This policy measured a nation's wealth in terms of the amount of gold and silver that it possessed. Many European nations tried to fill their treasuries by establishing a **favorable balance of trade**, or situation in which a nation's exports outweigh its imports. To achieve this goal, European nations built colonies as sources of raw materials and markets for manufactured goods. They also levied high tariffs on imported goods. Because mercantile nations believed colonies existed for the benefit of the home country, they exploited the natural resources of the colonies and undermined manufacturing efforts there.

RISE OF BANKING Mercantilism increased money circulation in Europe. Banking services developed to handle the flow of hard cash. Banks issued paper bank notes, which helped make business transactions easier.

THE INDUSTRIAL REVOLUTION (1750–1914)

In the mid-1700s, English inventors developed ways to produce textiles, or cloth, by machine instead of by hand. At first, the machines were powered by water. But in the mid-1700s, James Watt developed the steam engine, which freed humans from dependence on animal, wind, and water power. This switch from handmade to machine-made production has been called the **Industrial Revolution**. The technological developments of this period brought sweeping cultural changes.

MAKING CONNECTIONS

Economics and Society As a result of the industrial revolution, the structure of European society changed to include a growing middle class.

New Methods of Manufacturing

From England, the Industrial Revolution spread to the rest of Europe and the United States. The textile, mining, and metal industries were the first to industrialize. Next came the expansion of the transportation and communication industries, which developed out of the need to get raw materials to factories and finished goods to market. Over time, several important principles of industrial production emerged.

Principles of Industrial Production

Factory System	All means of production are housed in one place.
Interchangeable Parts	Parts of machines or tools are made alike so that one part can be exchanged for another.
Division of Labor	Workers specialize in one task to speed up completion of an entire product.
Mass Production	Large quantities of identical goods are produced through the use of interchangeable parts and a division of labor.
Assembly Line	A conveyor belt carries a product from worker to worker so that each worker may add a part.

Laissez-Faire Capitalism

The Industrial Revolution encouraged new economic ideas. During the reform movement known as the Enlightenment, a Scottish philosopher and economist named **Adam Smith** challenged mercantilism. In his book, *The Wealth of Nations*, Smith rejected the idea of government regulation of the economy because it stifled economic growth. He promoted a **laissez-faire**, or "hands-off," policy. Smith argued that the "invisible hand" of the market would spur individuals to seek profit for their own good. That is, consumer demand would guide producers to supply only the best and cheapest goods, which in turn would benefit the general welfare of the nation. Smith's ideas formed the basis of **laissez-faire capitalism**.

Laissez-faire capitalism became the prevailing economic system. As the theories of Adam Smith were accepted, governments assumed less responsibility for economic matters and allowed the **business cycle** to operate with virtually no interference.

MAKING CONNECTIONS

The Business Cycle

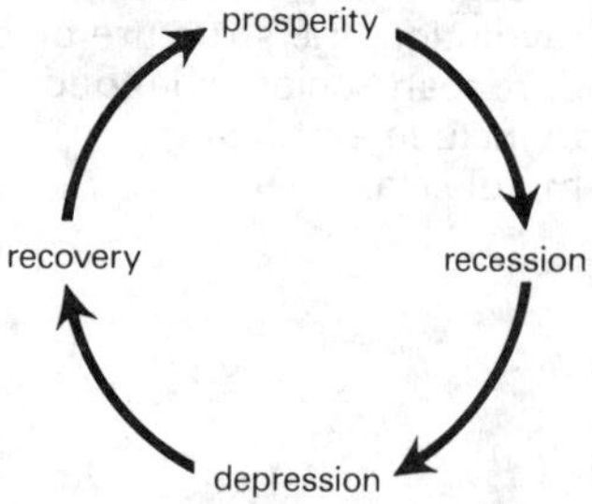

Economics and Politics In 1832, the Sadler Commission of the British Parliament investigated conditions in factories. The resulting legislation included child labor laws and safety and sanitation codes.

Economics and Politics The adoption of Marx's ideas by such people as Lenin, Mao Zedong, and Fidel Castro helped to bring about revolutions in Russia (1917), China (1949), and Cuba (1959). Adherence to Marxist doctrine had profound economic, political, and social impact on those countries and the world.

The theory of the business cycle predicted that **prosperity** (economic good times) would be followed by a **recession** (an economic slowdown). The recession would be followed by a **depression** (a severe economic stagnation characterized by business failures and high unemployment). The depression would be followed by a **recovery** and a gradual return to prosperity.

Reactions to Laissez-Faire Capitalism

The Industrial Revolution created a number of hardships that led people to challenge the idea of limited control of business. Workers faced repetitive tasks at long hours and low pay, and often under dangerous conditions. Several responses to laissez-faire capitalism emerged.

LABOR UNIONS Workers organized labor unions to win better working conditions and higher wages. They developed the technique of **collective bargaining**, in which union representatives negotiated with factory owners on the behalf of workers. Unions also organized **strikes**, or work stoppages. Governments, when pressured by the public, passed regulations curbing the power of big business, thus limiting laissez-faire capitalism.

ALTERNATIVE ECONOMIC SYSTEMS Two new economic systems also developed as alternatives to capitalism.

- **Socialism**: Early socialists proposed public ownership of some industries such as mines, banks, and railroads. They believed these industries should be operated for the general welfare of the people rather than for the profit of individuals. In general, socialists proposed evolutionary change rather than revolutionary change.
- **Marxism**: **Karl Marx**, a German writer and economist, and **Friedrich Engels**, a German socialist, developed the idea of "scientific socialism." Two important books outlined this theory—the *Communist Manifesto* and *Das Kapital*.

Principles of Marxism

Economic Determinism	The course of history is primarily determined by economic conditions; those with economic power are generally those with political power.
Class Struggle	The history of the world is a series of conflicts between rich and poor (for example, master vs. slave, feudal lord vs. serf, capitalist vs. proletariat)
Overthrow of Capitalism	Continued exploitation of workers would lead to more frequent depressions and eventual overthrow of the capitalists by the workers, who would seize the means of production.
Dictatorship of the Proletariat	The workers would assume political as well as economic power. The economic system would be based on

Individual Contributions public ownership. A "classless society" would emerge, there would be no need for government, and the state would just "wither away." Each person would contribute to Communist society "according to his ability and receive according to his needs."

WORLD WAR I TO THE PRESENT (1914–present)

During the late nineteenth century, the nations of Europe began to concentrate their economies on the buildup of military armaments. The atmosphere of militarism made war almost inevitable.

World War I

The Industrial Revolution triggered a race for empire and the aggressive policies of imperialism. Competition for new sources of raw materials and markets for finished goods fueled nationalism and international rivalries. This competition led to the outbreak of World War I, which had a devastating effect on all participating nations. It began the decline of European economic dominance.

MAKING CONNECTIONS

Economics and History
The effect of World War I on the economy of Germany was severe. The Treaty of Versailles forced Germany to pay an enormous amount in reparations. Unemployment and inflation hit Germany in the early 1920s, but U.S. loans aided economic recovery by 1925.

The Great Depression and World War II

The Industrial Revolution increased global interdependence as trading networks spanned the world. In 1929 a stock market crash in the United States began the Great Depression of the 1930s. The shattering of the United States economy had global repercussions. Unemployment and business failures occurred in many industrial nations.

Widespread economic despair paved the way for the rise of fascism in Germany, Spain, and Italy. The fascists supported total state control of all aspects of life, including the economy. The government dictated what, how, and for whom goods would be produced. Because the fascists opposed communism and allowed private ownership, they won support among the middle class. The aggressive nationalism of fascist dictators led to World War II, which nearly destroyed Europe.

The Cold War and Recovery

After defeat of the fascist powers, Western European nations faced enormous obstacles to rebuilding.

THREAT OF COMMUNISM The Soviet Union took steps to protect its borders against future attacks by turning Eastern European nations into Soviet **satellites**, or nations with Communist-backed governments. The United States believed economic recovery was essential to the future freedom of Western Europe. So it approved the **Marshall Plan**, a massive package of economic aid aimed at **containment**, or stopping the spread of communism. Europe thus became caught up in the **Cold War**, or war without bullets, between the Soviet Union and the United States.

MAKING CONNECTIONS

Key Concepts: Change
At present, many countries of Western Europe have adopted some aspects of socialism.

Key Concepts: Power
As single sovereign nations, the countries of Western Europe cannot compete with the U.S. and Japan, but united they become a major economic power.

ECONOMIC INEQUALITIES Many European nations adopted certain aspects of socialism to correct economic inequalities among their citizens. However, they combined elements of socialism with elements of capitalism to set **mixed economies**. This approach led to evolutionary, rather than revolutionary, economic change in Europe.

Great Britain's social welfare state provides a case study of a mixed economy toward socialism after World War II. In 1945, the British Labor Party won control of the parliament and instituted socialist policies. It nationalized key industries and increased taxation of the wealthy. The government also increased the amount of tax money used for social programs.

WEAKENED NATIONAL ECONOMIES World War II broke the global dominance of Western Europe. Most of Europe's former colonial holdings sought and won independence during the 1950s and 1960s. The end of imperialism greatly reduced Europe's resource and market base. In order to counterbalance the new **superpowers**—the United States and the Soviet Union—six nations banded together in 1957 to form the **European Economic Community (EEC)**, or **Common Market**. Today the European Community includes almost all Western European nations. The EEC has acted to lower trade barriers among member nations and to promote uniform economic policies. It has also encouraged the sharing of industrial technology.

Toward a United Europe

In 1991, leaders of the European Community held a summit in Maastricht, the Netherlands to discuss future plans. The Maastricht Treaty, agreed to at the Summit, commits member nations to a closer union. Its goals include the development of common foreign and defense policies as well as the creation of a single European currency by 1999. Great Britain and Denmark were given the option of maintaining their own currencies so as to remove a nationalistic stumbling block to ratification of the Treaty. In general, the European Union is an example of greater political, economic, and social interdependence in the region.

MAJOR ECONOMIC THEMES

1. The extensive trading networks developed during the Pax Romana, Commercial Revolution, and Age of Imperialism all promoted interdependence between Western Europe and other parts of the world.
2. Western Europe's Industrial Revolution dramatically changed human culture.
3. Despite the loss of empire and the devastation of two world wars, Western Europe has rebuilt through regional cooperation.
4. In spite of Western Europe's narrow resource base, the application of technology has enabled the region to create some of the highest standards of living in the world.

SECTION 9 Economic Setting: Northern Eurasia and Eastern Europe

MAKING CONNECTIONS

OVERVIEW

Unlike Western **market economies**, which rely on the independence of many producers, until 1991 the Soviet Union had a national economy based on a rigid central plan. This type of **command economy** was introduced after the 1917 takeover by the Bolsheviks. Only recently did Soviet leaders reform and dismantle the nation's planned economy, and, ultimately dissolve the Soviet Union itself.

PRE-COMMUNIST ECONOMY

Under the czars, the Russian economy was based on a **feudal, agricultural system**. Following the emancipation of the serfs, or peasants, in 1861, Russia began to industrialize. Since Russia lagged behind Western Europe, its efforts to modernize became more intense during the late nineteenth and early twentieth centuries. Russia's industrial revolution was supported by its abundant supply of natural resources and its huge population, which could provide the necessary workers for its factories. Despite the growth of industry, Russia remained primarily agricultural. The poverty of workers and peasants led both groups to support movements for change.

THE BOLSHEVIK REVOLUTION

In 1917 the **Bolsheviks** toppled the czar from power. Inspired by the ideas of **Karl Marx**, Bolshevik leaders implemented what was known as **war communism**. Two goals became top national priorities: (1) rapid industrialization, and (2) control of agricultural resources. To achieve these goals, the Bolsheviks, under the leadership of **Nikolai Lenin**, took charge of the government and the economy.

A Command Economy

Under capitalism, private individuals own businesses and industries, or what the Communists call the means of production. Capitalist governments rely upon the free operation of the law of supply and demand to regulate the market. In a **Communist state**, the government owns industry and controls economic decisions. The Bolsheviks introduced this system to Russia when they nationalized all privately owned

Regents Tip What are the two major differences between a command economy and a market economy?

MAKING CONNECTIONS

businesses. Under war communism, economic planners decided what, where, how many, for whom, and at what price goods should be produced. In this way, the Bolsheviks set up a **command economy** rather than a capitalist **market economy**.

Lenin's New Economic Policy

Peasants and workers soon became disillusioned by war communism. To revitalize the spirit of revolution, Lenin modified Marxist ideology to fit conditions in the Soviet Union. He announced the **New Economy Policy** (NEP) in 1921. Under this plan, Lenin allowed some private ownership and individual profit-making. Although the government still controlled most of the economy, a degree of freedom helped the Communists to rebuild a nation ravaged by civil wars, revolution, and World War I.

SOVIET ECONOMY UNDER STALIN

The death of Lenin signaled a sharp redirection in Communist leadership. In 1927 **Joseph Stalin** assumed sole control of the Communist Party. Stalin shared Lenin's desire to industrialize rapidly. However, he replaced the NEP with **centralized economic planning**. The **Politburo**, or inner circle of the Communist Party, appointed an economic agency called **Gosplan** to oversee a series of **five-year plans**. These plans set production standards for industry and agriculture by assigning quotas to every factory and farm.

Key Concepts: Scarcity and Empathy
Due to the scarcity of resources in Russia, it was impossible for Stalin to satisfy all the needs of the country. He chose to concentrate on "guns," or heavy industry, while paying little attention to "butter," or light industry (consumer goods). He gave the needs of the state priority over the needs of individuals.

Forced Industrial Development

Stalin's early five-year plans emphasized development of heavy industry, particularly military goods and machinery. Consumer goods fell in short supply. But Stalin expected the Soviet people to accept shortages and poor quality as a necessary sacrifice for the good of the nation. By 1940 Stalin had turned the Soviet Union into an industrial and military giant. However, he achieved this goal at great human cost, especially in eastern portions of the Soviet Union. Here political prisoners worked in forced labor camps. Stalin showed little empathy for individual lives. Attainment of economic goals was all-important.

The Failure of Agriculture

In agriculture, Stalin aimed to produce enough food for trade surpluses. Stalin hoped to trade food for foreign machinery, but his agricultural reforms were unsuccessful.

COLLECTIVIZATION The 1917 Revolution promised the Russian peasants land, and for a while the Communists gave it to them. But Stalin viewed individual farms as inefficient. Under his direction, the Communists created large government-owned farms called **collectives**. Here peasants worked under government direction and received a share of the produce and profits. Stalin also set up factory-like **state farms** on which workers received wages.

MAKING CONNECTIONS

RESISTANCE Many peasants, especially more affluent peasants known as **kulaks**, resisted collectivization. Some killed their livestock and destroyed their machinery rather than turn them over to the government. Stalin struck back with executions and exiles to Siberia numbering in the millions. The failure of collectivization was demonstrated by the success of the small **garden plots** that Stalin allowed farmers to work for themselves. These small parcels of land consistently outproduced the collectives and state farms. This situation testified to the importance that individual farmers placed on private ownership.

SOVIET ECONOMY AFTER STALIN (1954–1985)

For 30 years after Stalin's death, Soviet leaders followed in his footsteps. They continued to emphasize heavy industry and development of the nation's rich natural resources. They consistently allocated a significant amount of the country's gross national product (GNP) to the manufacture of military goods.

Beginning in the 1960s, the government allowed increased production of consumer goods. Even though the Soviet standard of living increased, it still compared unfavorably to other industrialized nations.

Agriculture continued to be the weakest part of the economy. Even with 25 percent of the labor force engaged in farming, the Soviet Union was unable to feed its population. Lack of economic incentives for farmers, poor weather conditions, and inefficient central planning led to food shortages. By the early 1960s, the Soviet Union was forced to import foreign grain to feed its people. Despite these setbacks, the Soviets made gains in other areas.

Technology

Soviet leaders encouraged scientific research to catch up with the West. They placed top priority on military weapons. In 1949 Soviet scientists exploded the nation's first atomic bomb, an event that triggered a nuclear arms race with the United States. In 1957 the Soviets launched the first space satellite, *Sputnik I*, setting off the space race. Soon both the United States and the Soviet Union were sending humans into space. Since the 1960s, the Soviets have made progress in lunar exploration, telecommunications, and the establishment of **Salyut** space stations.

Trade

In 1949 the Soviet Union organized governments in Eastern Europe into the **Council for Mutual Economic Assistance**, or COMECOM. Other Communist nations, including Cuba and Vietnam, later joined the organization. The Soviet Union used COMECOM to promote regional interdependence. However, the Soviets still fell short of their economic goals. Food shortages and a desire for Western tech-

Economics and Politics Eastern European nations under the political and economic dominance of the Soviet Union came to be called "satellite" nations.

MAKING CONNECTIONS

nology led them to seek limited trading relations with capitalist nations such as the United States. The Soviets also turned to the Middle East for oil. In many cases, the Soviets traded weapons for oil, increasing tensions in the Middle East.

ECONOMIC REFORMS (1985–present)

In 1985 Mikhail Gorbachev came to power. He inherited an economy on the verge of collapse. Soviet citizens waited in long lines for almost everything—even bread and milk. Poor central planning, corruption among bureaucrats, and lack of worker incentives had taken their toll. Empty shelves and poor living conditions attested to the failure of central economic planning.

Perestroika

Regents Tip List three conditions that led the Soviet Union to adopt perestroika. (An example has been listed.)
Failure to reach agricultural self-sufficiency

Gorbachev introduced a series of economic reforms called **perestroika**—"restructuring." Perestroika focused on a shakeup of the Soviet bureaucracy and a gradual shift in power to the regional and local levels. It affected all facets of the economy.

INDUSTRY Under Gorbachev, the Soviet government ended its total control over production and the distribution of profits. The goal was less dependence on central planning and more responsibility for managers and workers. Perestroika called for greater competition and the closing of unproductive, outdated factories. It also offered worker incentives—pay raises, promotions, and the threat of firing. Outside the factories, the government encouraged individuals to set up small businesses, or **cooperatives**, which paid taxes to the government based on the profits that they earned. To capture their share of the market, the privately owned cooperatives tended to offer better-quality goods than state-run businesses.

AGRICULTURE Here, too, perestroika reduced central planning and increased control by individual farmers. Gorbachev endorsed the idea of granting 50-year leases to farmers on collectives in an effort to increase production. In this way, he hoped to encourage collectives to match the output of garden plots.

TRADE The Soviet Union sought to expand trade through increased contacts with the West. It also opened the door to joint ventures with foreign investors.

Setbacks to Reform

Gorbachev encountered many obstacles to perestroika.

CONSERVATIVE BACKLASH Conservative members of the Communist Party accused Gorbachev of moving too fast and too far from their Marxist roots. They criticized his diversion of money from military spending to other areas. They also charged that Gorbachev's liberal attitudes encouraged national unrest.

MAKING CONNECTIONS

RADICAL ATTACK Radicals, led by **Boris Yeltsin**, president of the Russian Republic, pointed to the slow pace of economic improvement and urged even bolder action.

BUREAUCRATIC CAUTION Government planners, reluctant to give up their former privileges, resisted perestroika. There was similar resistance within the military.

FEAR AMONG WORKERS While many workers looked forward to reform, some feared the end of guaranteed job security. Workers in outdated industries faced the highest risks.

CONSUMER FRUSTRATION Consumers expected to see an immediate flood of goods and an end of shortages. Instead, they witnessed a growing number of homeless people and continued empty shelves. Also, some people genuinely supported the Communist ideals of shared wealth and equal distribution of goods. Such people resisted the prospect of competition in the marketplace and fluctuating prices.

A New Era Begins

The failure of the political coup in August 1991 (see page 175) led to an acceleration of the economic and political changes in the Soviet Union. All the republics sought greater freedom to determine their own economic and political policies. By 1992, the dissolution of the Soviet Union was complete. In Russia, President Boris Yeltsin has faced many problems in his pursuit of a free market economy for his country. Yeltsin has sought economic assistance from the United States in order to solve problems such as inflation and unemployment. In 1994, Russia gained inclusion in the G-7 group of industrialized nations. It is hoped that cooperation with major economic powers will help Russia complete the transition to free market economy.

EASTERN EUROPE SINCE 1985

The rise of Gorbachev loosened Soviet control over Eastern Europe. Generally, the 1989 elections in the region marked a revolution as voters elected democratic governments in several key Eastern European nations. In general, communism has been abandoned throughout Eastern Europe as nations turn to democratic governments and market economies.

Key Concepts: Change
Although the standard of living of the average Soviet citizen has risen since the revolution, it is below that of many Eastern European nations.

Case Study: Poland

Poland was the first satellite to cut ties with communism and Moscow. **Solidarity,** the trade union formed in 1980 under the leadership of **Lech Walesa,** swept the first free elections held in Poland since World War II. In December of 1990, Walesa became Poland's first freely elected President. He was the first non-Communist in forty years to hold that position.

MAKING CONNECTIONS

The Solidarity-led **coalition** government embarked on a radical course to change Poland to a market economy by ending price fixing and canceling subsidies to industries. As expected, this new course caused inflation and high unemployment in the short term. The government urged voters to be patient until the reforms took effect. But the pain caused by these policies cost the government public support, and in 1995 a former Communist defeated Lech Walesa in the race for president.

Case Study: Germany

In November 1989, the world watched in disbelief as pressure from East German citizens led to the dismantling of the Berlin Wall. This development paved the way for the reunification of East and West Germany, an event that became official in October 1990. A unified Germany has the advantage of a strong West German economy being able to absorb a crumbling East German economy.

East Germany's break with communism and its economic system had the following results:

- Exchange of East German currency for that of West Germany
- Joint ventures between East German industries and privately owned West German firms
- Encouragement of **entrepreneurship**, or the opening of privately owned and operated businesses and economic assistance from West Germany that helped East Germans cope with the difficulties of economic change
- Social and political problems brought on by the economic hardships generated by the merger of the two countries

Germany's liberal immigration policies were criticized as incidents of violence against foreigners increased. Some Germans viewed immigrants as threats in the job market.

MAJOR ECONOMIC THEMES

1. An abundance of natural resources helped in the rapid industrialization of the Russian economy.
2. The Bolsheviks set up a command economy in which economic planners made all decisions about production of goods.
3. Stalin's approach to economic development concentrated on central planning and farming collectives.
4. Food shortages and failure to meet industrial objectives led Mikhail Gorbachev to institute perestroika, a restructuring of the economy that helped accelerate changes leading to the dissolution of the Soviet Union in 1991.
5. Since the late 1980s, most Eastern European countries have moved away from communism and are making the difficult transition to capitalism or mixed economies.

Regents Questions for Practice

Review the Test-Taking Strategies section of this book. Then answer the following questions, drawn from actual Regents examinations. Circle the *number* of the word or expression that best completes the statement or answers the question. Write your answers to essay questions on a separate piece of paper. Hints on good ways to approach these questions are provided in the margins.

1. The main features of a capitalistic economic system are
1 powerful labor unions and fixed prices
2 export quotas and state ownership of basic industries
3 private ownership and the profit motive
4 central planning by government and full employment

2. The basic characteristic of subsistence agriculture is that farmers
1 produce mostly staple crops to sell
2 sell large portions of their crops at the market price
3 produce crops mainly for their own immediate use
4 produce crops according to government orders

3. "A group of planners makes all economic decisions. The group assigns natural, human, and capital resources to the production of those goods and services it wants. The group decides how to produce them and to whom to distribute them." This description best applies to the
1 manorial economy of feudal Europe
2 mercantile economy of 18th-century Europe
3 command economy of the Soviet Union
4 market economy of the United States

Base your answers to questions 4 and 5 on the statements below and on your knowledge of social studies.

Speaker A: Increased contact among nations and peoples is characteristic of our times. A single decision by OPEC, or a multinational corporation, can send ripples of change throughout our global society.

Speaker B: If the last 500,000 years were divided into lifetimes of years, there would be 800 such lifetimes. Humans spent the first 650 of these in caves, and the most important changes occurred only during the final lifetime.

Speaker C: If we are to survive, all passengers on our Spaceship Earth must participate in efforts to solve the issues that threaten mankind—poverty, resource depletion, pollution, violence, and war.

MAKING CONNECTIONS

Test Hint Question 1 asks you to select the answer with the "main features." Some answers may contain unessential features, so read all choices carefully to select the correct answer.

Test Hint Question 2 is similar to question 1. Read all the answer choices carefully to select the "basic characteristic."

MAKING CONNECTIONS

Test Hint When several questions are about the same material, take the questions one at a time. Reread the material before you answer each question.

Speaker D: We must understand that no single culture's view of the world is universally shared. Other people have different value systems and ways of thinking and acting. They do not see the world as we do.

4. Which concept is discussed by both Speakers A and C?
1 self-determination
2 nationalism
3 conservation
4 interdependence

5. Which statement *best* summarizes the main idea expressed by Speaker B?
1 Humans have always had to deal with many changes during their lifetime.
2 The rate of change has increased rapidly during the 20th century.
3 Throughout history there has always been great resistance to change.
4 Conditions in the modern world are better than in any prior era.

6. A nation has a favorable balance of trade if it
1 sells all of the products it manufactures
2 buys most of its products from friendly nations
3 exports more than it imports
4 heavily taxes its exports

Base your answers to questions 7 and 8 on the graph below and on your knowledge of social studies.

Population and Food Production Growth

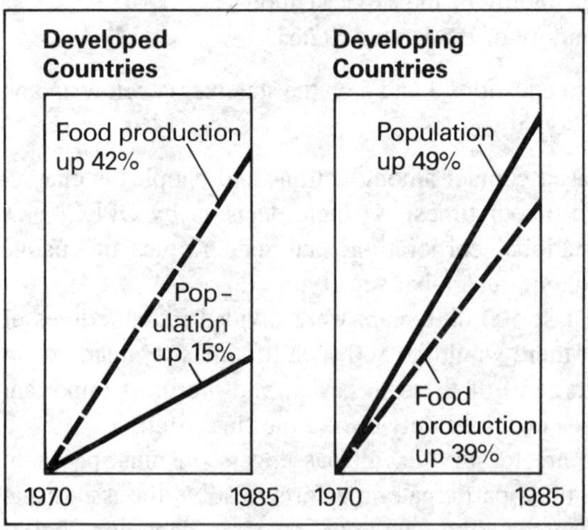

7. Which statement is *best* supported by the data in the graphs?
 1 Food production is rising in both developed and developing countries.
 2 Food production is rising at a faster rate in developing countries than in developed countries.
 3 Population is rising at a faster rate in developed countries than in developing countries.
 4 Population is rising at the same rate in both developing and developed countries.

8. If the trends shown in the graphs continue, it is *most* likely that developing countries will
 1 be able to feed their populations and export food to developed countries
 2 narrow significantly the gap between their population growth and their food production
 3 have a lower birth rate than developed countries
 4 need to import food

9. Future economic development of sub-Saharan Africa will most likely be centered around Africa's
 1 handicraft traditions
 2 mineral resources
 3 rich agricultural soil
 4 highly developed transportation systems

Base your answer to question 10 on the chart below and on your knowledge of social studies.

What Americans Buy From Africans*
*1982 U.S./sub-Saharan Africa trade
($ value in millions)

Crude petroleum	$9,900
Coffee beans	$599
Platinum	$352
Aluminum	$292
Diamonds (non-industrial)	$286
Uranium	$200
Cocoa beans	$137
Iron alloys (for steel)	$119

10. Most of the exports from Africa to the United States can be described as
 1 high-technology components
 2 consumer goods
 3 raw materials
 4 agricultural products

11. A chronic problem facing most African and Asian countries since World War II has been a shortage of
 1 natural resources
 2 investment capital
 3 unskilled labor
 4 markets for their agricultural products

12. Which is *most* characteristic of a nation whose economy is dependent on the production of one commodity?
 1 The economy is self-sufficient.
 2 The nation has a subsistence economy.
 3 Economic well-being is closely tied to world market prices.
 4 Industrialization makes it possible to export a variety of goods.

13. During the 1980s, a major goal of China was to
1 accelerate economic growth
2 encourage the growth of traditional religions
3 establish a federal system of government
4 protect individual liberties

14. The recent encouragement of private enterprise in the People's Republic of China is a shift from that country's practice of
1 mercantilism
2 laissez-faire
3 imperialism
4 Marxism

15. In Japan, a major economic problem has been the lack of
1 natural resources
2 investment capital
3 skilled labor
4 experienced management

16. In the period since World War II, Japan has dealt with its shortage of natural resources mainly by following a policy of
1 becoming an agriculturally oriented nation
2 enforcing a program of austerity for its civilian population
3 attempting to take over nearby resource-rich nations
4 developing many industrial products for export

17. Which is the *best* explanation for Japan's current success?
1 need to support heavy military expenses
2 vast reserves of raw materials and fossil fuels
3 the government's role in setting and supporting national goals
4 emphasis on individual achievement rather than group effort

18. Which has been an important factor that has discouraged investment in the economic development of many Latin American nations?
1 lack of natural resources
2 history of colonial dependence
3 declining birth rate
4 political instability

19. Which was an economic development in Caribbean countries during early European colonial rule?
1 Employment was limited to Spanish-speaking citizens.
2 Scarcity of labor led to the importation of African slaves.
3 Plantations were owned in common by two or three villages.
4 Machine production generally replaced manual labor.

20. A major problem for many Latin American countries has been the
1 payment of their debts to foreign countries
2 shortage of water
3 rapidly decreasing population
4 shortage of labor in agricultural areas

21. The Organization of Petroleum Exporting Countries (OPEC) was formed primarily to
1 give member nations more influence in world markets
2 force developing countries to abandon policies of nonalignment
3 help Middle Eastern nations form alliances with Western powers
4 allow the Soviet Union to develop greater influence in the Middle East

22. Which was a result of the Industrial Revolution in England during the 19th century?
1 The number of farmers increased as the demand for wool in the textile industry rose.
2 Democratic principles were weakened as the power of the working class increased.
3 Workers became more secure in their jobs and less dependent on employers.
4 The structure of society changed to include a growing middle class.

23. The theory of laissez-faire capitalism advocates
1 government control of the economy
2 noninvolvement of the government in the economy
3 government regulation of big business
4 government sponsorship of labor union

24. "The average worker can never obtain more than a minimum level of living. The worker is deprived of the wealth he himself has created. The state is a committee of the bourgeoisie for the exploitation of the people." The ideas in this quotation would most likely be expressed by a
1 Christian humanist
2 mercantilist
3 laissez-faire capitalist
4 Marxian socialist

25. Which action is *most* consistent with the practices of 17th-century mercantilism?
1 expanding the export of goods from the colonies to other nations
2 reducing the shipments of manufactured goods from the home country to the colonies
3 increasing the supply of raw materials from the colonies to the home country
4 prohibiting the importation of slaves to the colonies

26. A major immediate goal of the European Common Market has been to
1 develop a single monetary system among member nations
2 improve the military defense of Western Europe
3 encourage trade among member nations
4 eliminate national political boundaries

27. The increase in trade and commerce during the Middle Ages resulted in
1 lower living standards for workers
2 increased growth of towns and cities
3 increased power for feudal lords and the clergy
4 less rivalry among European nations

28. Which development in Europe contributed *most* to the revival of European interest in overseas possessions during the second half of the 19th century?
1 political revolutions
2 need for social reform
3 emergence of trade unions
4 need for markets and raw materials

29. The belief that colonies exist for the good of the home country is a characteristic of which system?
1 mercantilism
2 capitalism
3 communism
4 feudalism

30. An advocate of mercantilism would most likely have agreed with the idea that government should
1 abandon the policy of colonial expansion
2 raise tariffs on imported goods
3 impose export duties on manufactured goods
4 encourage manufacturing in its colonies

31. During the 1980s, the Soviet Union experimented with modifications of its command economy by
1 eliminating central planning
2 allowing private ownership of major industries
3 introducing some market economy strategies
4 legalizing independent trade unions

32. During the 1980s in the Soviet Union, a major element of the economic policy of **perestroika** was
1 increased collectivization of farms
2 more reliance on local and regional decision making
3 the expanded use of national five-year plans
4 an emphasis on the redistribution of wealth

33. The economy of the Soviet Union has differed most from the economy of the United States in the
1 emphasis placed on technological development
2 need for skilled workers
3 manner of deciding which goods will be produced
4 importance given to production of military weapons

Essay Questions

1. Throughout history, societies have attempted to solve the problem of scarcity of food and/or manufactured goods.

Systems/Policies
Manorial system in medieval Europe
Guild system in medieval Europe
"Great Leap Forward" in China
Green Revolution in Asia
Marshall Plan in Europe
Gorbachev's perestroika in the Soviet Union

Select *three* of the systems or policies listed. For each system or policy selected:

- Describe the conditions that led the society to adopt the system or policy
- Describe the main features or characteristics of the system or policy
- Discuss the extent to which the system or policy was successful in solving the problem of scarcity for that society

2. Developing nations in Africa, Latin America, and the Middle East have been faced with many problems that have restricted their economic development.

Problems
One-crop economy
Overpopulation
Foreign debt
Illiteracy
Poverty
Topography
Lack of natural resources

Choose *three* of the problems listed. For *each* one chosen:

- Identify a developing nation in Africa, Latin America, or the Middle East that is facing the problem
- Describe specific conditions that the problem has caused in the nation

- Explain how these conditions restrict the nation's economic development
- Describe *one* specific attempt that has been made by the nation to overcome the problem

You must use a different nation for each problem chosen.

3. Today, developing nations seek to improve the lives of their people through economic development. To reach this goal, developing nations face decisions of whether to move toward a command economy or toward a market economy.
   a Explain how *two* characteristics of a command economy might enable developing nations to achieve this goal.
   b Explain how *two* characteristics of a market economy might enable developing nations to achieve this goal.
   c Few nations choose to follow an absolute command economy approach or an absolute market economy approach. Identify a nation that has sought to develop its economy in the 20th century. Show, by using specific historical examples, how the nation has used a characteristic of each of these economic systems in this attempt.

4. The majority of the people in Africa, Asia, and Latin America live in poverty. Some of these people contend that their poverty is the result of the actions of industrialized nations.
   a Cite *two* factors that may lead to people living in poverty. For *each* factor mentioned, describe *one* way in which that factor may have helped to cause the poverty of the people in Africa, Asia, or Latin America.
   b Describe *one* action taken by either the people of Africa, Asia, or Latin America, or an action taken by the people in some other area of the world, to raise the standard of living of the people.
   c Tell how *one* action taken by the leaders or people of Africa, Asia, or Latin America to improve the standard of living of the people in their area affected the area's relations with one or more of the industrialized nations.

UNIT 5 Global Politics

MAKING CONNECTIONS

As you review each unit, you will find additional information in this column: major ideas, connecting themes, and questions to reinforce your learning. These items are closely tied to the Regents examination. Read this material carefully, and jot down any other facts that you would like to remember in the column's blank spaces. Using this column will **add to your success on the Regents exam.**

Section 1 Africa
Section 2 India
Section 3 Southeast Asia
Section 4 China
Section 5 Japan
Section 6 Latin America
Section 7 The Middle East
Section 8 Western Europe
Section 9 Northern Eurasia and Eastern Europe

This unit focuses on the ways in which people organize themselves into particular units for representation and for governing their nations. In many of the countries that you have studied, this experience of self-government is a relatively new one and one in which age-old traditions have come into conflict with current political realities. The study of **politics**, therefore, is concerned with the **structure** and the **organization** of government. How a nation rules its people, what its laws are, what freedoms it allows, and how it interacts with other countries all reflect its political system.

Factors that affect a nation's political system are:

1. its **geography** and **topography**. Land surfaces have served to protect and isolate nations from hostile neighbors. Japan and the Soviet Union are two such nations.
2. its **culture**. Common customs, languages, and history unify people with a sense of **nationalism**—love and devotion to one's country.
3. its **economy**. The economy of a nation must be stable in order to prevent social upheaval, revolution, and the rise to power of totalitarian regimes.
4. its **legal system** and **political philosophy** or ideas about governing. During the Enlightenment, the ideas of Montesquieu, Rousseau, and Voltaire heavily influenced the people and political events in France.
5. its **ability to protect its borders** with an adequate defense. The inability of Kuwait in August 1990 to protect itself from the invasion by Iraq's military forces is one example.

SECTION 1 Political Setting: Africa

PRE-WORLD WAR II

The present-day political boundaries of the nations of Africa resulted from the nineteenth-century colonization of the continent by the nations of Europe, particularly Great Britain and France. Nationalistic feelings grew among black Africans in reaction to the effects of imperialistic rule, which included the following:

1. The many years of exploitation of raw materials and natural resources of the African continent.
2. The arbitrary division of tribal (ethnic) lands by the Europeans without regard for traditional territories or tribal rivalries.
3. The experience of the European educational system, which valued equality and democratic rights. Many African nationalistic leaders who had been educated in universities and colleges in Europe and the United States started nationalistic movements against their colonial rulers.

Prior to World War II, the tribe (ethnic group) was the traditional political unit. Through the tribe, the basic necessities of life and social order were achieved. In some colonial systems, notably the British system of indirect rule, African tribes were used as intermediaries to pass on the rules and requirements of the colonial regime to their own people.

MAKING CONNECTIONS

Politics and History For more information on colonialism in Africa, see the section on Africa in Unit 2, Global History.

POST-WORLD WAR II

Many Africans served in the military forces of their colonial regimes during World War II. This military service, in addition to the following factors, increased the desire among Africans for **Pan-Africanism** (Africa for the Africans): the provisions of the **1941 Atlantic Charter**, signed by Franklin Roosevelt and Winston Churchill on August 14, which advocated **self-determination**, or the right to choose one's government; the formation of the United Nations in 1945; and the achievement of independence in a number of Asian countries, including India and Pakistan.

With the weakening of Britain and France as a result of World War II, the first African country to receive its independence from Great

Politics and History "Pan" means common to all. For information on Arab nationalism (Pan-Arabism), see the section on the Middle East in Unit 2, Global History.

MAKING CONNECTIONS

Britain was the Gold Coast, which became **Ghana** in 1957 under the leadership of Kwame Nkrumah. Felix Houphouet-Boigny led independence for the **Ivory Coast** from France in 1960. **Jomo Kenyatta** achieved independence in 1963 for Kenya. Between 1960 and 1970 there were over 30 revolutions and independence movements throughout the African continent. With the achievement of independence for the nation of **Namibia** in 1990, the colonial period for the African continent ended.

Some of the political problems that have persisted since the independence of the African nations have been:

1. **Tribalism v. Nationalism**
   The loyalties toward the tribe (ethnic group) still remain stronger than the feelings toward the new nation. This has made it difficult to govern these nations. Civil wars such as that in Zaire (1965) and Nigeria (Biafran War 1967-70) have resulted. In 1994 a bloody conflict erupted between rival ethnic groups in Rwanda—the Hutus and the Tutsis—resulting in the deaths of thousands of civilians.
2. **Single Political Party Governments**
   The lack of adequate preparation and transition for independence from the European colonial powers resulted in the rise of single-party governments. A strong political leader would emerge, many times representing the largest tribe (ethnic group) or major region with economic resources. Once established in office, the leader would ban the existence of other political parties. Often this would continue until the military seized power in a **coup d'état**, or overthrow of the government. The cycle of the overthrow of governments by military strongmen and the rise of dictators was a pattern found during the last ten years in many of the newly independent nations of Africa, including Uganda, Liberia, and Ghana. Protests for political **pluralism**, or allowing for different groups, have increased today within many African nations, including Senegal, Ivory Coast, Benin, and the Democratic Republic of the Congo.

Key Concepts: Power
For more information on the role of the military, see the section on Latin America in this unit.

3. **Apartheid**
   In 1948, the policy of racial separation and segregation, called **apartheid**, was established in the Republic of South Africa. Four major racial groups were designated: whites, blacks, coloreds (mixed races), and Asians. The black Africans today make up approximately 70 percent of the population, with the whites being 15 percent. Under the former system of apartheid total power was held by the white population of South Africa.
   The system of apartheid classified people according to their race, set up separate living areas for non-whites, and restricted the job and educational opportunities for the majority of South Africa's population. Although the Afrikaner government established four black homelands within the Republic of South Africa, the inability of the residents of these homelands to survive on the impoverished land forced them to find work outside of these territories.

Winds of Change

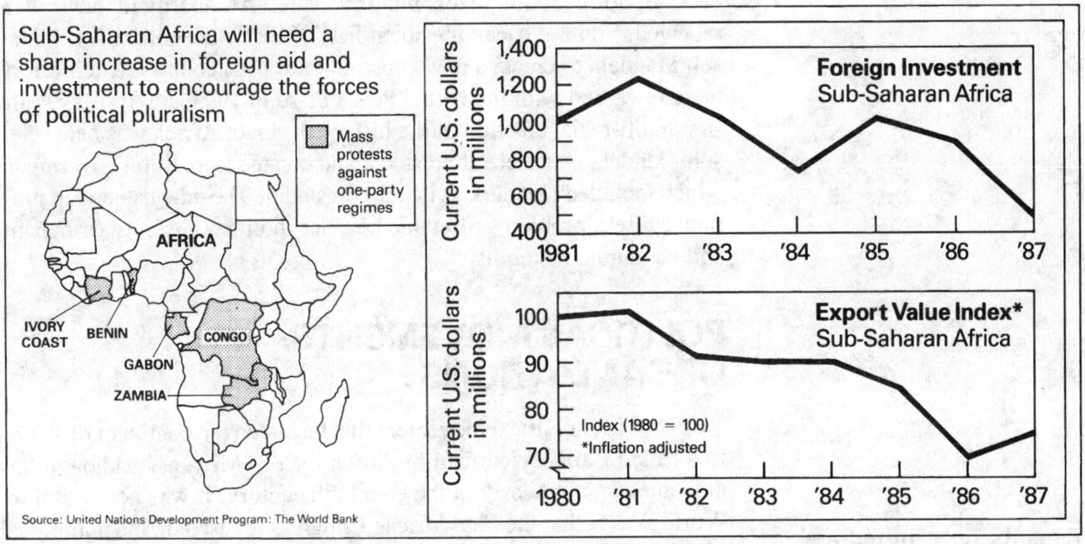

The formation of the **African National Congress (ANC)** in 1912 represented the first group to advocate fundamental rights for black Africans. The ANC launched boycotts and practiced nonviolent civil disobedience during the period following World War II. In 1960, the Afrikaner government declared the ANC illegal and imprisoned its president **Nelson Mandela**. For 27 years Mandela remained in jail. During his detention, demonstrations against the Afrikaner government continued. They included a 1960 demonstration at Sharpeville, which resulted in the death of 69 people; a 1976 uprising at Soweto against the requirement of students to learn the Afrikaans language; and the 1983 riots in Sharpeville, which resulted in thousands of deaths. During the next several years, the struggle against the racist policy of apartheid intensified. Black activist **Steven Bikko** was killed in 1977 during police interrogation in jail. Archibishop **Desmond Tutu** advocated nonviolent approaches to bring about change in the apartheid system. In 1984, he received the Nobel Peace Prize.

MAKING CONNECTIONS

Regents Tip Practice your data-based skills. In what year shown on the graph was foreign investment in sub-Saharan Africa highest? What was the export value for that year?

With the release of Nelson Mandela in 1990 and the recognition of the black trade unions, the apartheid system began to change. The huge cost of building parallel (similar) institutions for each of the four racial groups has made apartheid economically difficult to sustain. In addition, the effects of **trade sanctions** on South Africa by various nations, including the United States, have begun to change apartheid. The United States lifted these sanctions in July, 1991. In March 1992, white South Africans voted for an end to minority rule, thereby ending apartheid.

The decision to end apartheid marked the beginning of a process to bring about black majority rule. As apartheid laws were repealed, South African president F.W. DeKlerk negotiated with Nelson Mandela to create a new constitution for the country. Their efforts were rewarded with the Nobel Peace Prize in 1993. In April 1994 the first multi-racial election in the history of South Africa was held. Nelson Mandela was elected president and created a coalition government which included DeKlerk as deputy president. The new leadership must now address problems of ethnic conflict, political disunity (tribalism) and economic instability.

POLITICAL MOVEMENTS/ ORGANIZATIONS

The first political movement that began on the continent of Africa was called **Pan-Africanism** or Africa for the Africans. Although this movement started early in the twentieth century, it was not until after World War II that the Pan-African Congress focused on the major goal of achieving independence for each African country. Now that the African countries have achieved independence, the Pan-Africanism movement works to unite all of Africa politically.

Regents Tip For more information on the Organization of American States (OAS), see the section on Latin America in this unit. How is the role of the OAS similar to the role of the OAU?

In 1963, the **Organization of African Unity (OAU)** was formed. Its purposes were to eliminate colonial control over any African territory, to safeguard independence, and to ultimately unify all of Africa. One of the founders of the OAU was Jules Nyere, the president of Tanganyika (Tanzania) from 1961, when it achieved independence, until 1985.

FOREIGN RELATIONS

Regents Tip List one region or nation you have studied that has followed a policy of nonalignment since its independence.

The foreign policy (how one nation deals with another) of most African nations since their independence has been **nonalignment**. They have attempted to stay neutral and not be too heavily influenced by either superpower, the United States or the Soviet Union.

Key Concepts: Culture These ties are examples of cultural diffusion.

Most African countries, however, still maintain close cultural and economic ties with their former European colonial ruler. French and English are spoken throughout Africa; some African countries have adopted them as their official language. The bulk of African trade is with the countries of Europe, and this is likely to continue in the future.

MAKING CONNECTIONS

Since the African countries make up about one-third of the United Nations, they have had a large impact upon that organization. South Africa relinquished its occupation of Namibia as a result of the protests of the African countries in the UN voting as a bloc.

MAJOR POLITICAL THEMES

1. Nationalism on the continent of Africa developed as Pan-Africanism and received its greatest boost from the African and European experiences during World War II.
2. Many of the political problems that the newly independent countries of Africa face today are conflicts that have resulted from their cultural traditions and the effects of many years of colonial rule.
3. For nonwhites, the racial policy of apartheid produced a system of legalized discrimination and segregation within the Republic of South Africa. In 1992, white South Africans voted to end minority rule, effectively ending apartheid policies.
4. Nonalignment with either the United States or the Soviet Union was the basis of the foreign policy of most newly independent African nations.

SECTION 2 Political Setting: India

MAKING CONNECTIONS

PRE-WORLD WAR II

Given India's diversity in its people, religions, languages, and regions, nationalism developed slowly. The first attempt at organized opposition to British colonial rule was the formation of the **Indian National Congress** in 1885. Many of its Indian leaders were college educated in Europe. Mohandas Karamchand Gandhi, the group's best-known leader, broadened the support of the Indian National Congress by appealing to the masses. Gandhi led an extensive nationalist movement, nonviolent in nature, which eventually gained India independence from Great Britain after World War II.

Regents Tip How did Gandhi's tactics influence the civil rights movement in the United States during the 1960s?

POST-WORLD WAR II

Like the Africans who served in the military forces of their colonial powers, many Indians served in the British armed forces during World War II. The experience of Great Britain in World War II left it unable to continue to control the Indian subcontinent. The land was, therefore, partitioned into two areas based upon the concentrations of its two religious groups: India for the Hindus and East and West Pakistan for the Muslims. In 1947, the British granted these areas independence from colonial rule. Yet bloody riots broke out between Hindus and Muslims. Thousands were killed, millions left homeless. Religious conflicts continue to be a part of political life in India to this day.

Politics and Society For more information on religion in India, see the section on India in Unit 3, Global Society.

Jawaharlal Nehru became the first prime minister of independent India. He had been a close associate of Gandhi during the independence movement. Nehru's daughter, **Indira Gandhi** (no relation to Mohandas Gandhi) became prime minister of India in 1967. Many of her policies, such as mandatory birth control, were controversial. In 1975, she declared a ''state of emergency,'' suspended many democratic rights, and jailed outspoken critics of her government. As a result, she was voted out of office in 1977. She returned as prime minister following the 1980 election. In October of 1984, Indira Gandhi was assassinated by two of her Sikh bodyguards. The attack in June by the Indian army on the Sikh Temple at Amritsar, their holiest shrine, was directly related to her death.

Indira Gandhi's son Rajiv assumed the office of prime minister and ruled India until 1989, when corruption toppled his government. The first two prime ministers to follow were **V. P. Singh** and **Chandra Shekhar.** Due to caste and religious upheavals, Singh's government lasted only eleven months. In 1990, Chandra Shekhar succeeded him. Rajiv Gandhi was assassinated in 1991, and P. V. Rao became prime minister after Shekhar's government collapsed.

Rao's government collapsed after the 1996 elections, in which the **Congress Party,** which had ruled India since independence, failed to capture a majority of seats in the parliament. The party that won the most seats in that election was the Hindu nationalist Bharatiya Janata Party (BJP). This party, however, was unable to assemble a majority in parliament. As a result, a coalition (union of several political groups) including the Congress Party formed a new government.

MAKING CONNECTIONS

Regents Tip List another nation or region you have studied that practices parliamentary democracy.

POLITICAL MOVEMENTS

India is the world's largest democracy. It is a parliamentary democracy, consisting of many political parties. The Congress Party, India's largest and oldest political party, has been affiliated with several other political parties. These coalitions reflect the various regional and religious differences that affect political life in India.

FOREIGN POLICY

India has become the leader of the developing nations of the world in following a foreign policy of **nonalignment**. India has followed this policy since Nehru became its first prime minister in 1947. Since that time, the country has received large amounts of technical and financial aid from the Soviet Union, as well as food and economic assistance from the United States. Indian relations with the Soviet Union were strengthened when India adopted central planning for its industries. However, Indian relations with the United States suffered due to American support for Pakistan during the India-Pakistan War of 1971, which resulted in the creation of Bangladesh (formerly East Pakistan) as an independent nation. Diplomatic relations between India and the United States have since improved.

Pakistan has never coexisted peacefully with India. Conflicts include religious differences between Pakistani Muslims and Indian Hindus and territorial disputes, particularly over the Indian state of Kashmir whose population is mostly Muslim.

China, India's neighbor to the north, strained its foreign relations with India when it invaded Tibet in 1950. In 1959, China violently put down the Tibetan revolt, forcing the Dalai Lama (the religious ruler of Tibet) to flee to India for his safety.

Politics and Geography How has the geography of India affected its foreign policy?

When China took territory bordering India in 1962 and supported Pakistan in the 1971 **Bangladesh War**, it further eroded diplomatic

MAKING CONNECTIONS

relations with India. The change in the Chinese leadership under Deng Xiao-ping improved the relationship between India and China.

In 1998, India abruptly changed world politics by conducting five nuclear tests. Two weeks after the India tests, Pakistan retaliated by setting off nuclear devices of its own. Both countries drew worldwide condemnation and ignited a storm of concerns over the impact of a South Asia arms race. After the India tests, the United States placed economic sanctions on India and pleaded with Pakistan to restrain from responding in kind. Immediately following the Pakistan tests, the United States placed similar economic sanctions on Pakistan.

MAJOR POLITICAL THEMES

1. The diversity of the people on the Indian subcontinent and their different religious beliefs have created problems and divisions throughout history.
2. India achieved independence from Great Britain through Mohandas Gandhi's political philosophy of nonviolence and civil disobedience.
3. Democracy in India continues to represent the changes reflected in various coalitions or unions of many of its diverse ethnic groups.
4. Indian foreign policy has been characterized by nonalignment with the superpowers and by choosing each action with regard to its effect on India's future.

SECTION 3 Political Setting: Southeast Asia

PRE-WORLD WAR II

MAKING CONNECTIONS

Prior to World War II, almost all of Southeast Asia was under foreign control. Only Thailand retained its independence in this period.

POST-WORLD WAR II

The post-World War II era was a period of growing nationalist sentiment. Throughout Southeast Asia, the wartime Japanese conquest of much of the region developed nationalist aspirations for self-rule. Violent struggles brought independence to the former French colonies in Indochina (Vietnam, Cambodia, and Laos) and to the former Dutch colony of Indonesia. The Philippines and most of the British colonies achieved independence in a largely peaceful transition of power.

THE VIETNAM WAR

In Vietnam during World War II the alliance of nationalist and Communist groups formed the Viet Minh. Led by Ho Chi Minh, the Viet Minh successfully fought the Japanese military forces that occupied their country. The Viet Minh received military assistance from the United States in their efforts against the Japanese. With the Japanese defeat in 1945, France wanted to resume control over its colonies of Vietnam, Laos, and Cambodia (Indochina). Ho Chi Minh declared Vietnam to be an independent country. This action resulted in the **French Indochina War** (1946–1954). Great Britain and the United States supported the efforts of the French; China and the Soviet Union allied with the forces of Ho Chi Minh.

The Viet Minh practiced guerrilla warfare in their war against the French. Guerrilla warfare, in addition to the strong nationalistic feelings among the Vietnamese, resulted in the French defeat at the Battle of Dienbienphu in 1954.

Regents Tip In what other revolution was guerrilla warfare successfully practiced?

The Geneva Conference set down the terms and conditions of the **Geneva Accords**, the treaty that ended the French Indochina War. The treaty called for the temporary division of Vietnam into North Vietnam (Communist) and South Vietnam (non-Communist). Free elections were to be held in 1956 to unite the country under one government. The elections were never held. In 1960, the Communists formed the

MAKING CONNECTIONS

National Liberation Front in South Vietnam. Known as the Viet Cong, the National Liberation Front conducted a systematic campaign of armed resistance against the government in the South, which was supported by the United States. The number of military advisors that the United States had in South Vietnam rose to approximately 15,000 by the end of 1963.

In 1964, after North Vietnamese boats reportedly attacked two U.S. ships in the Gulf of Tonkin, the U.S. Congress adopted the **Gulf of Tonkin Resolution**. It authorized President Lyndon Johnson to take all necessary means to stop North Vietnamese aggression. The result was an expansion of U.S. role in South Vietnam. By 1968, the number of American troops was increased to over 500,000 for large-scale military action against the Communists.

Representatives from North and South Vietnam, the United States, and the National Liberation Front signed a peace treaty in Paris in 1973, ending the longest war in U.S. history. After American troops were withdrawn, the fighting between North Vietnam and South Vietnam continued. The result was the April 30, 1975, Communist victory establishing control over all of Vietnam. Hundreds of thousands of Vietnamese fled their country as ''boat people'' seeking another place to live. Economic problems, including indebtedness, are major problems facing the government of Vietnam today. See the map ''War in Southeast Asia'' in Unit 2, Section 3.

Key Concepts: Human Rights
What other groups of people became refugees because of political oppression in their countries?

Cambodia (Kampuchea)

Cambodia had been involved in the Vietnam War as a storage area and hideaway for North Vietnamese and Viet Cong troops. After the 1975 victory of the Communists in Vietnam, fighting resumed in Cambodia, which was under the rule of Pol Pot. During his authoritarian regime, approximately two to four million Cambodians were killed. Pol Pot was overthrown in January of 1979 by Vietnamese forces, which occupied the country until a negotiated settlement ended the civil war in Cambodia in 1990.

Regents Tip List other examples of genocide (systematic extermination of an entire people or national group).

Indonesia

In 1927, the Indonesian Nationalist Party was formed under the leadership of Achmed Sukarno. Its purpose was to achieve independence for Indonesia from the Netherlands. During World War II, the Japanese controlled the islands of Indonesia. Upon the defeat of Japan in World War II, the Dutch reestablished control. After Sukarno declared independence from the Dutch, war broke out between Indonesia and the Netherlands. In 1949, the Netherlands granted independence to Indonesia. Sukarno remained in office until 1967 when General Suharto took control of the government after an attempted Communist coup d'état.

Suharto remained in power as Indonesia's president until 1998. After his seventh re-election, student protesters led a nationwide movement demanding his resignation. When the legislature joined students in calling for him to step down, Suharto resigned and turned over the presidency to his vice president, B. J. Habibe. Indonesia's new president faced major economic challenges, including inflation, food shortages, and bankruptcies.

Philippines

The first country to gain its independence after World War II was the Republic of the Philippines, which was controlled by the United States since 1899. The Philippines were ruled by Ferdinand Marcos from 1965 until 1986. Marcos was a dictator who established martial law (control of the government by the military) in 1972, which lasted until 1981. In 1983, opposition leader Beningno Aquino was assassinated upon his return to the Philippines. This event produced widespread protests and demonstrations, ultimately driving Marcos into exile. Corazon Aquino, the widow of Beningno Aquino, assumed the presidency until 1992. She was succeeded by a former defense secretary, Fidel V. Ramos.

MAKING CONNECTIONS

Politics and Geography Explain how the geographic location of the Philippines has made it important throughout history.

POLITICAL MOVEMENTS/ ORGANIZATIONS

The major political organization within the countries of Southeast Asia is the **Association of Southeast Asian Nations (ASEAN)**, which was formed in 1967 to develop economic and social cooperation among the non-Communist nations of Southeast Asia. At its headquarters in Jakarta, Indonesia, the organization coordinates policies among its member states.

Politics and History What organizations were formed after World War II to unite the free European countries and those under Soviet domination?

MAJOR POLITICAL THEMES

1. Throughout the history of Southeast Asia, local nationalist movements have prevailed over foreign control and domination.
2. The independent nations of Southeast Asia have followed separate policies of economic and political development, reflecting a diversity of political systems.

SECTION 4 Political Setting: China

MAKING CONNECTIONS

PRE-WORLD WAR II

Prior to World War II, the **Kuomintang**, or Nationalist Party, ruled China under **Chiang Kai-shek**. The Chinese Communist Party, under the leadership of **Mao Zedong** (Mao Tse-tung), challenged Chiang Kai-shek's government by waging civil war. A full-scale invasion of China by Japan (1937–1945) led to a suspension of the fighting, but the civil war resumed after Japan surrendered in 1945.

Key Concepts: Power Guerrilla warfare was a major reason for the success of the Communists over the Nationalists.

POST-WORLD WAR II

By 1949, Chiang Kai-shek and his forces had retreated to the island of Taiwan. In October of that year, Mao Zedong established Communist control of mainland China by proclaiming the founding of the **People's Republic of China**.

POLITICAL MOVEMENTS

Politics and History Deng Xiaoping, leader of China from 1978 until his death in 1997, was imprisoned during the Cultural revolution.

Since 1949, the Communist Party has ruled mainland China. Mao Zedong, who headed the party until his death in 1976, instituted a radical program for economic and social transformation, which culminated in the **Cultural Revolution** (1966–1969). Mao's Cultural Revolution emphasized his teachings and ideas as the ''correct'' political attitude at the expense of professional or academic expertise. Chinese government officials, teachers, and other professionals were denounced and forced to do manual labor.

Recognizing the setbacks caused by the Cultural Revolution, China's leaders since Mao have sought economic and technological progress through the **Four Modernizations** program. This ongoing program allows greater economic incentives for industry and labor while opening up China to greater contact with western nations, including the United States. In 1989, student demands for political freedom as a part of the modernization process were violently repressed by the Chinese government when masses of students gathered in May and June in Tiananmen Square, Beijing. On June 4, they were attacked by Chinese troops, resulting in the deaths of approximately 500 to 1,000 Chinese students.

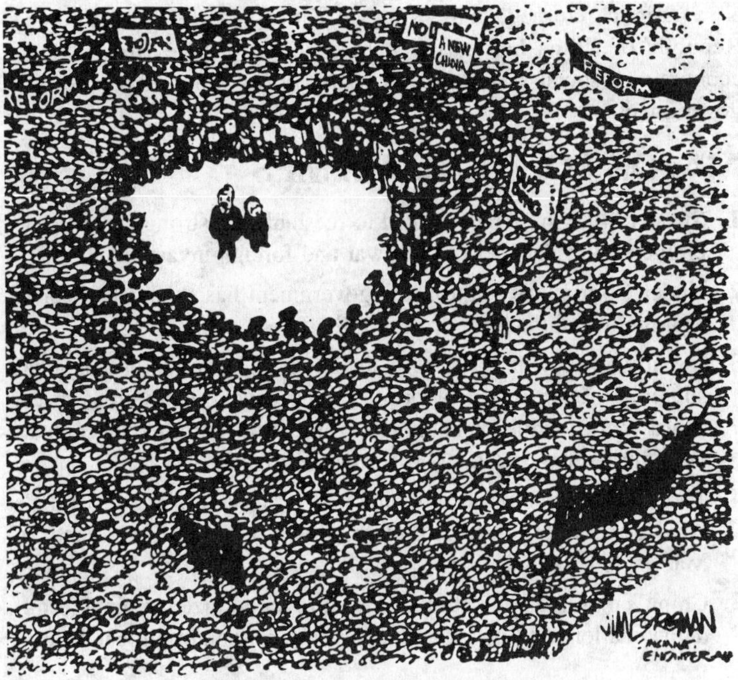

"OH SURE, YOU'LL ALWAYS HAVE A FEW HOTHEADS..."

MAKING CONNECTIONS

What does this cartoon of Tiananmen Square convey regarding the attitude of the Chinese leaders toward student demands for political reform?

FOREIGN RELATIONS

After the Communists came to power in 1949, they formed an alliance with the Soviet Union and received a significant amount of foreign aid. From 1950 to 1953, Chinese troops fought United States troops and other United Nations forces during the Korean War. The Communists resented the continuing United States support for the Nationalist Party rule on the island of Taiwan. By 1960, ideological disputes between the USSR and Communist China led to a withdrawal of Soviet aid. In 1969, border clashes erupted along their mutual frontier.

As China began to expand its contacts with the West, President Nixon visited the People's Republic of China in 1972. The Communist government of mainland China replaced the Nationalist government of Taiwan as the legitimate representative of China to the United Nations. In 1979, the United States and the People's Republic of China established full diplomatic relations, which led to greater commercial ties between the two nations. In 1984, China and Great Britain agreed to the return of Hong Kong to mainland China in 1997. Following the 1989 political repression of Chinese students by their government, the United States temporarily restricted trade and financial aid to China.

Britain returned Hong Kong to China in 1997. The People's Republic of China had earlier agreed not to change Hong Kong's economic or social system for 50 years and to allow its people self-government.

MAKING CONNECTIONS

MAJOR POLITICAL THEMES

1. Since 1949, China has worked to reestablish a strong central government after decades of civil war and foreign invasion.
2. Under Communist control, the government has established China as a major political power in world affairs.
3. Initially allied with the USSR, the People's Republic of China has sought a greater role as a leader among developing nations of the Third World, while expanding its political and commercial contacts with the United States and other western nations.
4. The cultural revolution in China had negative effects on China's educational and industrial growth, which lasted until the death of Mao in 1976.
5. China's massive population and need to modernize remain a formidable challenge to its economic development and political future.

SECTION 5 Political Setting: Japan

PRE-WORLD WAR II

Prior to World War II, military leaders in Japan dominated government policy. Although the emperor was regarded as a divine symbol of the nation, he did not have substantial influence in the decision-making process. This policy was a continuation of the practice by which military rulers (shoguns) prior to 1868 wielded political authority, theoretically on behalf of the emperor. Although the shogunate was abolished in 1868, this practice reasserted itself as leaders of Japan's armed forces made the political decisions, apparently in keeping with the emperor's wishes. The emperor did intervene in August of 1945 and gave support to a faction that favored ending Japan's resistance in World War II. In September of 1945, Japan formally surrendered to the United States and Allied forces in Tokyo Bay.

MAKING CONNECTIONS

Politics and Society For more information on the system of loyalties in Japanese society, see the section on Japan in Unit 3, Global Society.

POST-WORLD WAR II

The United States occupation of Japan from 1945 to 1952, under the command of General Douglas MacArthur, changed the nature of Japan's government. The emperor, Hirohito, was required to renounce his divine status, but he was retained as a symbol of the nation. In 1947, Japan adopted a new constitution that guaranteed civil liberties and free elections and established a bicameral legislature (two houses), the **diet**. The constitution included an article by which Japan renounced war and the use of force. While the constitution also limited Japan's armed forces, the politics of the cold war between the United States and the Soviet Union led to the establishment of Japan's limited self-defense forces. In the 1990 Persian Gulf crisis, calls for the deployment of Japanese troops in a support role in Saudi Arabia were denied in view of Japan's reluctance to establish an overseas military presence.

Politics and History Emperor Hirohito died in 1989, having served as Japan's longest reigning monarch.

POLITICAL MOVEMENTS/ ORGANIZATIONS

For most of Japan's post-war history, the Liberal-Democrats have been the dominant political party. Conservative in outlook, this party has favored Japanese business interests and economic expansion in the world market.

MAKING CONNECTIONS

FOREIGN RELATIONS

In 1952, the United States ended its occupation of Japan, and Japan joined the United Nations. The United States is an ally of Japan by treaty and maintains military bases there. In 1972, the United States restored Okinawa to Japanese control, but the Soviet Union has continued to occupy four Japanese islands that it seized at the end of World War II. While commercial contacts have expanded between the USSR and Japan, the Japanese lay claim to these islands as an integral part of their nation.

Japan's greatest impact since World War II has been as an economic power rather than as a political power. Japanese penetration of the American market and its role in international trade and finance have given it significant influence in the global economy.

MARLETTE'S VIEW

Answer these questions about the cartoon: (1) what is the cartoonist's point of view? (2) How have Japanese products affected the market in the United States?

MAJOR POLITICAL THEMES

1. Following World War II, Japan has established a democratic government that presided over a period of substantial economic expansion.
2. Japan's economy is now one of the largest in the world, yet Japan's political impact on global affairs has been limited.

SECTION 6 Political Setting: Latin America

PRE-WORLD WAR II

Since Latin American countries gained independence in the early nineteenth century, their politics have been affected by the establishment of national governments, the control of military dictatorships, and the influence of the Roman Catholic Church. Regional differences, the concentration of large land holdings in the hands of a few, and the rise to power of *caudillos* (dictators) continue to define the political life in Latin American countries today. Although Latin American nations received political independence from European control, they remained economically dependent upon the Europeans for loans, investments, and trade. The fear that any instability in Latin American governments would adversely affect United States and European business investments in them helped to maintain support for the dictators in power.

MAKING CONNECTIONS

Politics and History For more information on Latin America before World War II, see the section on Latin America in Unit 2, Global History.

Regents Tip At what other time in world history was the role of the Roman Catholic Church especially significant?

POST-WORLD WAR II

Cuba

After World War II, Latin American countries experienced many political changes. One of the most significant events was the **1959 Cuban Revolution** in which **Fidel Castro** overthrew the military dictator **Fulgencio Batista**. After Castro nationalized American businesses and industry in Cuba, the United States refused to recognize his government. Thereafter, Castro sought and received financial and military aid from the Soviet Union. With this continuing aid, Cuba has amassed a debt to the Soviet Union of over $20 billion. Throughout his authoritarian rule, Castro has attempted to support communism in other countries, including Ethiopia, Angola, Grenada, and Nicaragua.

Regents Tip Identify another region in which European influence is still on-going despite the area's independence.

Argentina

In 1946, **Colonel Juan Perón** rose to power with the support of the army as well as the working classes. He and his wife, Eva Duarte, initiated many social welfare programs, which resulted in a large debt for the nation. Because of opposition from large landowners, the military, and the Roman Catholic Church, Perón was ousted by the military in 1955. After spending 18 years exiled in Spain, Perón returned in 1972 and was reelected president. When he died nine months later, his new wife, Isabel, became president. Argentina's internal problems

MAKING CONNECTIONS

Regents Tip List several other dictators who practiced authoritarian rule. (An example has been listed.)
Mussolini

under Isabel Perón's leadership led to her 1976 overthrow by the military. From 1976 to 1983, Argentina has had a series of military dictatorships.

In 1982, after Argentina's disastrous invasion of the British-ruled **Falkland Islands** and its subsequent defeat by Great Britain, Argentina's military dictator, General Galtieri, was forced to resign. In 1983, the election of President Raúl Alfonsin restored civilian rule. In 1989, widespread inflation and a foreign debt of over $45 billion resulted in Alfonsin's resignation and the installation of **Carlos Menem** as the new president.

Nicaragua

Since it gained independence in 1838, Nicaragua experienced a succession of leaders. In 1912, at the request of the Nicaraguan government, United States troops occupied the country to protect American business interests there. From 1926 to 1933, Nicaraguan guerrillas, under the leadership of General Augusto Sandino, tried to force the United States military to leave Nicaragua. Sandino was murdered in 1934 under the command of Anastasio Somoza, the head of the Nicaraguan army. Somoza became president in 1937 and ruled Nicaragua as its dictator until his assassination in 1956. Thereafter, Somoza's two sons, in turn, replaced him as president. With the 1967 rise to power of his son Anastasio, the opposition of the Sandinista guerrilla forces began.

Rule under the Somoza family had concentrated the wealth of the country in the hands of a few landowners and business people. The strong authoritarian regime retained few civil liberties for its citizens. In 1979, the Sandinistas led a revolution that seized control of the Somoza government. The Soviet Union and other countries supported the Sandinista government led by **Daniel Ortega**. Indications that Nicaragua was becoming a Communist stronghold led the United States government to cut off aid to the country and back the **Contras**, a Nicaraguan group fighting to overthrow the Sandinista government. After years of fighting, the Sandinistas and Contras agreed to a ceasefire in 1988. Nicaragua's continuing economic problems of high inflation, an ever-growing debt, and widespread unemployment resulted in the defeat of Sandinistas and the election of president **Violeta Chamorro** in 1990.

Regents Tip List other women who have headed their nations in the twentieth century.

El Salvador

Throughout the history of El Salvador, a series of military governments resulted in conflicts concerning land reform. Between 1979 and 1984, a violent civil war broke out between government troops and rebel guerrilla forces. Although José Napoleón Duarte was elected president in 1984, the fighting continued. Both the rebels and hard-line conservatives opposed Duarte's political and economic reforms. Economic issues and dependence upon United States aid remained ongoing problems. Terrorist acts continued, and the 1988 election of **Alfredo Christiani**, representing the right wing, created further problems for an already troubled El Salvador. In 1992, the government signed a peace treaty with guerrilla forces that formally ended the civil war. Pledging to continue the peace process, Armando Calderón Sol, of the same right-wing party as Christiani, became president in 1994.

MAKING CONNECTIONS

Key Concepts: Political System
As political terms, "right-wing" means very conservative and "left-wing" means very liberal.

Brazil

Brazil is the fifth largest nation in the world and occupies almost half the continent of South America. Portugal colonized Brazil, while Spain principally colonized the rest of Latin America. Rule of Brazil in the early nineteenth century was by King João VI, acting for Portugal. Following Brazil's independence in 1822, a monarch continued to rule Brazil until the **military coup** (overthrow) of 1889. Eventually, Brazil became a republic with an elected president. In 1930, army officers again took over and installed Getúlio Vargas, a *caudillo* (dictator backed by the army and wealthy landowners) who ruled the country on and off for the next 25 years. When the army took over the government in 1954, Vargas committed suicide. A succession of military leaders followed until 1985 when José Sarney became president. A foreign debt of $93 billion and an inflation rate of 600 percent resulted in the election of **Fernando Collor** to the presidency in 1990. Collor resigned in 1992 after he was impeached for corruption. In 1994, Fernando Henrique Cardoso was elected president.

Regents Tip List two ways in which inflation affects a country.

POLITICAL MOVEMENTS/ ORGANIZATIONS

The **Organization of American States (OAS)** is a group of Latin American nations and the United States that work together on common issues. The organization was formed in 1948 to promote trade and peaceful settlements of disputes in the Western Hemisphere. The Pan-American Union of the 1880s was the forerunner of the OAS. The major difficulties of the member nations of the OAS are the dominating role of the United States and the appeal of communism to populations that lack economic stability.

FOREIGN POLICY

The foreign policy of most Latin American nations has been affected by their relations with the United States. In 1823, the United States issued the **Monroe Doctrine**, warning European nations not to interfere with nations of the Western Hemisphere. This doctrine asserted that the United States would protect the independent nations from European colonization.

In 1898, the United States became deeply involved in the **Spanish-American War**, a war in which the United States supported independence for Cuba against Spain, its colonial ruler. The defeat of Spain gave the United States influence over Cuba and ownership of the Philippine Islands and Puerto Rico.

MAKING CONNECTIONS

Key Concepts: Power How might the return of the Panama Canal to Panamanian control affect Latin American nations?

Regents Tip List another example of the Cold War between the United States and the Soviet Union after World War II.

In 1903, the United States supported Panama's fight for independence from Colombia. As a result of Panama's victory, the United States obtained rights to build the **Panama Canal**, a waterway linking the Atlantic Ocean with the Pacific Ocean. In **1977**, U.S. President Carter and Panamanian President Torrijos signed a treaty transferring control of the Canal to Panama on **December 31, 1999**. In the treaty, the United States retains the right to use military force to keep the canal open.

President Franklin D. Roosevelt's 1933 ''Good Neighbor Policy'' promised that the United States would consult with Latin American countries prior to intervening in their affairs. This policy ultimately led to the **1961 Alliance for Progress** under President John F. Kennedy, a ten-year plan to provide economic assistance to raise living standards in Latin American countries by instituting major social reforms. The Nixon administration abandoned the ''Good Neighbor Policy'' in the 1970s.

Perhaps the greatest threat to United States and Latin American relations was the **Cuban Missile Crisis** of 1962. The Soviet Union had installed nuclear missiles in Cuba, and President Kennedy ordered a blockade of Cuba that required the Soviet Union to dismantle and remove those weapons. Ultimately, the Soviet Union complied, thus avoiding a nuclear confrontation between the two superpowers.

A number of other events have involved the United States with various Latin American nations. In 1973, the United States supported the military **coup d'état** that overthrew **Salvador Allende's** Marxist government in **Chile**. Allende came into office in a democratic election. After his death, Chile was under the military regime of **General Augusto Pinochet** who ruled until his 1989 defeat in an election won by **Patricio Aylwin**.

In 1983, thousands of United States troops invaded the Caribbean island of **Grenada**, aided by a small military force of members of the **Organization of Eastern Caribbean States**. Prime minister Maurice Bishop, a Marxist with strong ties to Castro's Cuba, was overthrown and killed in a military coup d'état. In 1984, Herbert Blaize was elected prime minister of the island.

In 1989, United States military forces invaded **Panama** and overthrew the government of **General Manuel Noriega**. Noriega was arrested, removed from Panama, and indicted in the United States on charges of drug trafficking. **Guillermo Endara** was installed as the president of Panama in 1990.

Politics and Geography
How has geography affected the foreign policy of Latin America?

In addition to these conflicts and interventions by the United States, the foreign policy of Latin American nations has included border disputes involving Ecuador v. Peru (1981); Belize v. Honduras (1981); and Chile v. Argentina (1985).

Despite a regional history in which the military has played a significant role, many countries in Latin America have adopted democratic forms of government. Civilian-controlled governments have come to power in Chile, Argentina, Peru, and Bolivia. In Haiti the attempt to break from military domination required extensive help from the United States and the United Nations. Father Jean-Bertrand Aristide was elected president of Haiti in 1990 but was unable to maintain order. Less than a year later, he was arrested by the military and forced to leave the country. The United Nations responded with economic sanctions in the form of a strict embargo. Stronger measures were taken when military leaders reneged on a deal to allow Aristide back into power. As economic conditions worsened, thousands of Haitians attempted to flee to the United States by boat. Many died en route. In July, 1994, the United Nations Security Council authorized an invasion of Haiti by a multinational force. With U.S. forces already on the way, the invasion was called off when military leaders agreed to step down. With the help of thousands of U.S. troops, Aristide returned to Haiti and was restored to office in the fall of 1994. In 1995, Haiti held another election, and presidential power was transferred to Rene Preval.

MAJOR POLITICAL THEMES:

1. Throughout the history of Latin America foreign countries have greatly influenced its political development. First, Europeans colonized Latin American nations, and then the United States intervened in their internal affairs.
2. The tradition of **authoritarian rulers** in Latin America grew out of the experience of Spanish colonization. The role of the *caudillos* (dictators) and the respect for the military are examples of this.
3. The growth of a middle class, comprised primarily of Mestizos (mixed European and Indian), has contributed to the development of democracy in the region. Most Latin American countries today have democratic governments.
4. Post-World War II conflicts within the Latin American nations have involved the two superpowers—the United States and the Soviet Union. The United States wanted to stop the spread of Communist governments; the Soviet Union wanted to increase them.
5. The Latin American nations face the prospect of continued political instability due to their indebtedness to United States and European banks, their rapid population growth, and their social poverty.

SECTION 7 Political Setting: The Middle East

MAKING CONNECTIONS

PRE-WORLD WAR II

Prior to the beginning of European imperialism in the nineteenth century, the predominant political power was based in Turkey with the Ottoman Empire (1453–1918). The Ottomans had overthrown the Byzantine Empire and extended their control of territory into the Balkans, Egypt, and parts of Russia. By the 1800s, the Ottoman Empire was losing its ability to control this territory. Amid various wars for land and independence, the Ottoman Empire was collapsing. The Ottomans were allies of Germany and Austria-Hungary (Central Powers) in World War I. Following World War I, France and Great Britain divided the Ottoman Empire. Syria and Lebanon were under French mandate; Palestine, Iraq, and Transjordan (now Jordan) were controlled by Great Britain.

Politics, History, and Geography Can you cite another nation or region whose strategic location has made it important throughout history?

The European nations were concerned with the Middle East primarily because of its strategic location. The building of the Suez Canal in 1869 guaranteed the Europeans quick access to their colonies in Asia.

During the 1900s, nationalist movements resurfaced in the Middle East. Mustafa Kemal (Atatürk) established a republic in Turkey in 1923 after the fall of the Ottoman Empire. Theodore Herzl had established the Zionist movement in Europe to restore a Jewish homeland in Palestine for Jews throughout the world. In the early 1900s, Zionist communities were established in Palestine, and the issuance of the 1917 Balfour Declaration by Great Britain supported their cause. In this document the British promised to favor the establishment of a Jewish homeland in Palestine while preserving the rights of the Palestinian Arabs living there. The beginnings of **Pan-Arabism** (or the unification of all Arabs into one nation) emerged as a nationalist movement. In the future Pan-Arabism would be in direct conflict with the nationalist movement of Zionism over the land of Palestine.

POST-WORLD WAR II

The end of World War II brought a number of changes for the nations of the Middle East. Lebanon and Syria were granted independence from France, while Jordan gained independence from Great Britain. Growing unrest developed between the Arabs and Jews in

Palestine, each claiming rights to the area as their own homeland. Unable to reach a compromise between these two groups, Britain referred the question of Palestine to the United Nations. The Holocaust, the Nazi extermination of six million European Jews during World War II, resulting in a new wave of Jewish immigration to Palestine highlighted the need to resolve the problem.

In 1947, the United Nations partitioned Palestine into two states, one Jewish and one Arab. The Arabs rejected the UN decision; the Zionists reluctantly accepted it. Upon the British withdrawal from Palestine in 1948, the Palestine Jews proclaimed one part of the land the State of Israel. Israel's Arab neighbors immediately rejected the new nation.

Egypt, Jordan, Syria, Lebanon, and Iraq attacked Israel on May 14, 1948. Although the United Nations arranged a truce, the Arab states refused to negotiate a peaceful settlement. The Arabs vowed to drive the Jews out of Israel and restore Palestine as an Arab nation. The 1948 war had major consequences. Israel seized half the area assigned to the Arabs by the United Nations. Jordan and Egypt divided the rest of Palestine between them. Jordan got the West Bank, and Egypt received the Gaza Strip. Thus, the proposed Palestinian state was lost and its Arabs had no homeland.

Hundreds of thousands of Palestinian refugees fled to Jordan, Syria, and other neighboring Arab states. Arab countries continued their threats to destroy Israel. Other Arab-Israeli wars occurred in 1956, 1967, and 1973.

A major proponent of Arab nationalism was General Abdul Nasser, who had overthrown King Farouk of Egypt in 1952. In 1956 his Egyptian forces seized control of the Suez Canal from England and France. Israeli, French, and English troops attacked Egypt. The intervention of both the United States and the Soviet Union brought about a cease-fire. Thereafter, United Nations troops stationed between the borders of Egypt and Israel kept peace between these two nations. However, Arab raids on Israel continued along its borders with other Arab states.

In May of 1967, Nasser demanded the removal of the UN troops from the Suez, occupied the Gaza Strip, and closed the Gulf of Aqaba to Israeli ships. Israel attacked Syria, Jordan, and Egypt on June 5, 1967, and defeated these Arab nations by June 10. In the Six-Day War, Israel had considerably increased the size of its territory. Israel gained control of the West Bank of Jordan, Egypt's Sinai Peninsula and Gaza Strip, and Syria's Golan Heights. The Israelis also annexed Jordan's half of Jerusalem.

On October 6, 1973, the military forces of Egypt and Syria attacked Israel during the Jewish high holy day of Yom Kippur to regain lost territory. After suffering initial losses of territory, Israel declared a ceasefire, and a United Nations peace-keeping force was assigned to the area.

MAKING CONNECTIONS

Politics and History What other nation that you have studied has been partitioned?

Politics and History Why would the Arab nations refuse to recognize Israel?

MAKING CONNECTIONS

Although Israel recovered lost territories, the 1973 war is considered one in which Arab pride and nationalism was restored by Anwar Sadat of Egypt. The 1973 war was also the first use of oil as a political weapon. By cutting off oil shipments to those countries that supported Israel, the oil-producing Arab nations tried to force them to pressure Israel to withdraw from its occupied territories.

Politics and History The actions of Sadat and Begin resulted in their being awarded the Nobel Peace Prize in 1978.

In 1977, Anwar Sadat declared his desire to travel anywhere for peace. Accepting the invitation of Israel's prime minister Menachem Begin, Sadat spoke to the Israeli parliament, the Knesset. On March 26, 1979, Sadat and Begin signed the **Camp David Accords**, an agreement to end the state of war between Israel and Egypt and return the Sinai Peninsula to Egyptian control. U.S. President Carter negotiated this historic treaty between the two leaders, the first of its kind between Israel and an Arab state. Because he signed this treaty with Israel, Anwar Sadat was assassinated in 1981 by Muslim extremists.

POLITICAL MOVEMENTS/ ORGANIZATIONS

At a 1964 meeting of Arab states, the **Palestine Liberation Organization** (PLO) was founded to regain the land of Palestine as an Arab state, and to eliminate the nation of Israel. **Yassir Arafat** leads the PLO in planning its strategies and attacks. The 1975 civil war raging in Lebanon between Christians and Muslims gave the PLO the opportunity to set up bases there. Aided by Syrian troops and Soviet ammunition, the PLO launched guerrilla attacks on Israel from southern Lebanon. In retaliation, Israeli forces launched a massive assault on Lebanon in 1982. Although an international peace-keeping force arranged a ceasefire in 1983, Israeli forces remained in Lebanon until 1985. The PLO survived but was driven out of Southern Lebanon and its capital city, Beirut. Currently, war between Lebanese Christians and Muslims continues with Syrian forces playing a major role in the conflict.

Politics and History In 1983, 241 United States marines and sailors, who were part of the international peacekeeping force, were killed in a terrorist attack on their headquarters in Beirut, Lebanon.

Organization of Petroleum Exporting Countries (OPEC)

The **Organization of Petroleum Exporting Countries** was formed in 1960. This 13-nation organization joined forces to promote and influence the world market price in oil. Their use of oil as a political weapon during the 1973 Yom Kippur War allowed the organization to greatly increase the price of crude oil. Profits from the dramatic price increases resulted in vast social changes, particularly among the Persian Gulf nations.

Iranian Revolution of 1979

In 1941, the **Shah of Iran, Mohammed Riza Pahlavi**, was installed as a figurehead after his father was forced to resign. In a 1953 coup supported by Great Britain and the United States, the Shah

Israel's Changing Borders

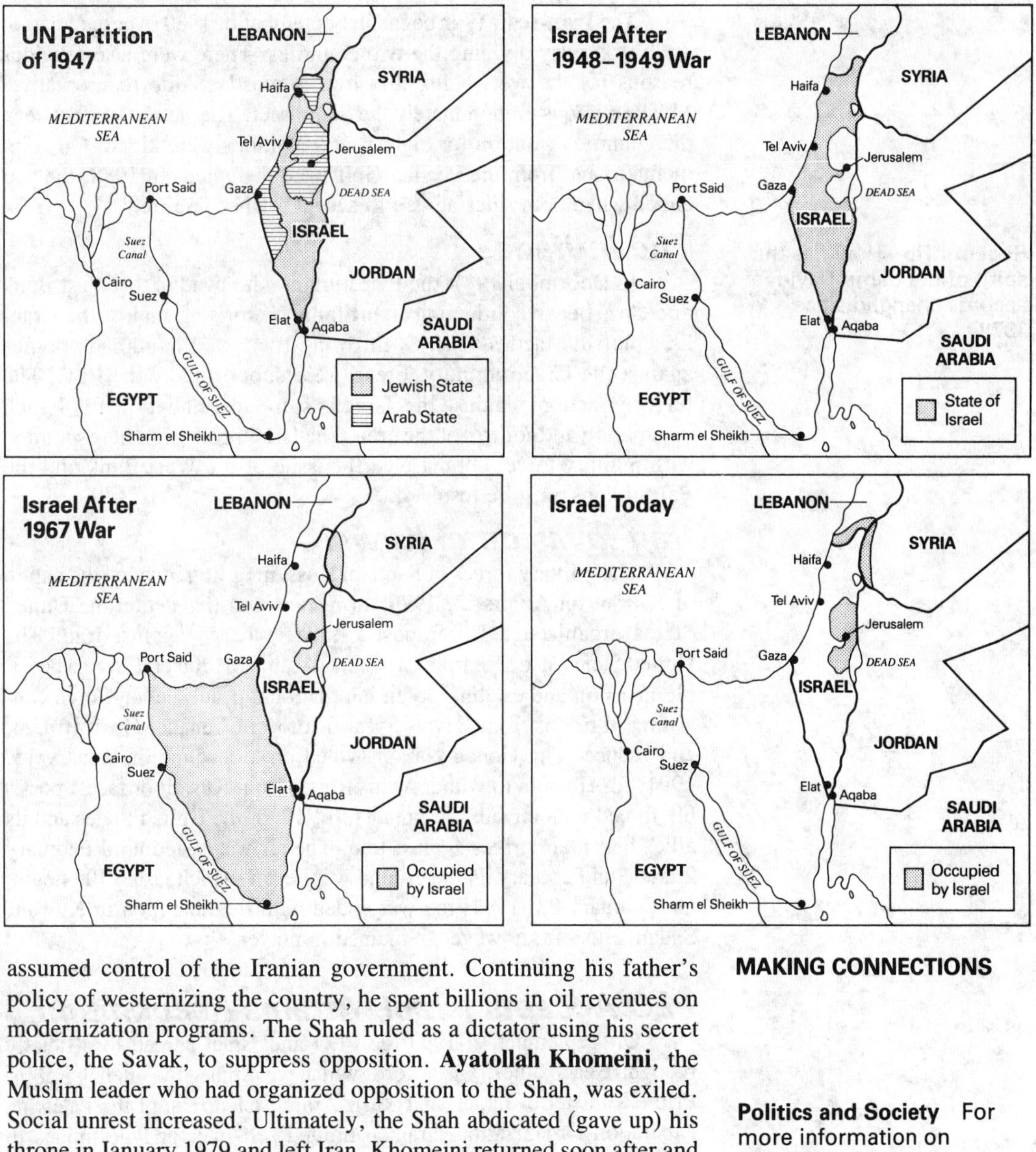

assumed control of the Iranian government. Continuing his father's policy of westernizing the country, he spent billions in oil revenues on modernization programs. The Shah ruled as a dictator using his secret police, the Savak, to suppress opposition. **Ayatollah Khomeini**, the Muslim leader who had organized opposition to the Shah, was exiled. Social unrest increased. Ultimately, the Shah abdicated (gave up) his throne in January 1979 and left Iran. Khomeini returned soon after and declared Iran as Islamic republic. The rise of **Islamic fundamentalism** (the strict adherence to Muslim religious traditions) swept the nation, and pro-Western policies were banned.

In November 1979 Iranian militants seized the American embassy in Tehran and took American hostages. Among other demands, the militants insisted on the return of the Shah from the United States. The Shah never returned to Iran and died in Egypt in 1980. After being held captive for 444 days, the 52 Americans were released on January 21, 1981.

MAKING CONNECTIONS

Politics and Society For more information on Islamic fundamentalism, see the section on the Middle East in Unit 3, Global Society.

MAKING CONNECTIONS

Regents Tip How has the spirit of the Camp David accords changed since 1979?

Iran-Iraq War

The **Iran-Iraq War** began in September of 1980 over the Shatt-al Arab waterway dividing the two countries. There were also religious reasons for the war, being that Iran is mostly Shiite [conservative] Muslim; Iraq is predominately the Sunni sect. The savage war between the countries went on for eight years. Millions were killed. Oil shipments to and from the Persian Gulf were disrupted. In 1988, the war ended when both sides agreed to accept a UN ceasefire.

The Intifada

In December 1987, the Palestinians who lived in the West Bank and Gaza began conducting an **intifada**, or uprising against the Israelis. Guerrilla tactics, such as throwing rocks and handmade bombs against the Israeli military forces, were supported by the PLO. The terrorist actions against the Israelis were in retaliation for Israeli occupation and control of the area. The Israeli government responded with military force. Ultimately , the issue of the West Bank and the Palestinians must be resolved.

Iraq Invasion of Kuwait

The military forces of Saddam Hussein of Iraq invaded the nation of Kuwait on **August 2, 1990**. In response to this action the United States organized a UN-imposed trade embargo against Iraq. The United States also sent troops to Saudi Arabia to protect it from a possible invasion and established an international peacekeeping force consisting of troops from Egypt, Syria, Morocco, Canada, Great Britain, and France. The United Nations voted on a deadline of January 15, 1991, for Hussein to withdraw his troops from Kuwait or face a possible forced withdrawal. On January 16, 1990, the United States and its allies began air strikes against Iraq. The air war lasted until February 23, and on February 24 the ground war began, which lasted 100 hours. On February 28, 1991, the war ended with the liberation of Kuwait. Sadam Hussein, however, remained in power.

PLO Accepts Israel, Attains Recognition

On September 9, 1993 the PLO and Israel agreed to officially recognize each other. The accord, which was signed by Yitzhak Rabin, Prime Minister of Israel, and Yasir Arafat, Chairman of the Palestine Liberation Organization, granted limited self-rule for Palestinians in the Gaza Strip and the West Bank town of Jericho. This historic agreement calls for a five-year period of limited autonomy for Palestinians, the withdrawal of Israeli forces from Gaza and Jericho, and the election by Palestinians of a municipal council. Ongoing negotiations will determine the future of Jerusalem, the 200,000 Palestinian refugees, and settlement disputes.

FOREIGN POLICY

After World War II, the Middle East was an extension of the Cold War between the United States and the Soviet Union. Each side allied itself with various nations within the region. The United States has been a consistent ally of Israel. The Iraqi invasion of Kuwait was the first major post-World War II conflict in which the United States and the Soviet Union simultaneously supported the same side (Kuwait). Their mutual condemnation of the invasion was one indication that the Cold War had ended.

Historic divisions among Arabs have prevented the dream of unifying all Arabs in one nation (Pan-Arabism). Territorial disputes among Arab States, the rise of Islamic fundamentalism in Iran and Arab nations, and conflicts between oil-rich Persian Gulf states and neighboring poor Arab countries have prevented Arab solidarity. Even the potentially unifying factor of the Islamic religion is a source of division because of the opposing beliefs of many of its sects.

MAKING CONNECTIONS

What event is depicted in this cartoon? What does the cartoon lead you to conclude?

MAJOR POLITICAL THEMES

1. Because of its strategic location, the Middle East has been an area that other countries have tried to control.
2. The movement of Pan-Arabism has the unifying aspects of language and religion, but local conflicts and historical rivalries have prevented it from becoming an important force.
3. The Arab-Israeli conflict still remains as the most difficult and important conflict to be resolved in the Middle East.
4. The rise of Islamic fundamentalism has threatened the order and stability of nations within the Middle East.

SECTION 8 Political Setting: Western Europe

MAKING CONNECTIONS

Politics and History For information on ancient Rome, see the section on western Europe in Unit 2, Global History.

The political history of western Europe until the twentieth century was primarily of autocratic rule. An **autocracy** is a government in which power is concentrated in the hands of one person or a small group. The majority of people have no voice in their government, and their rights are frequently abused or denied. Examples of autocratic rule include monarchies, feudal lords, and dictatorships.

The social and political upheavals of the nineteenth and early twentieth centuries led to the fall of autocracy and the establishment of democracy in many countries in western Europe. A **democracy** is a government in which power is held by the people. It promotes the idea of equality, and guarantees basic civil liberties. The democratic traditions of western Europe may be traced to ancient Greece and Rome. The **Athenians** of ancient Greece practiced direct democracy, in which all citizens directly participated in decision making for the city-state. Romans of ancient Rome also had democratic rule. During the time of the **Roman Republic**, representatives were chosen to run the state under a set of codified laws known as the **Twelve Tables**, which protected the rights of all Roman citizens.

PRE-WORLD WAR II

Politics and History Democracy developed in England in an evolutionary way. How did the Industrial Revolution contribute to this growth of democracy?

In 1918, at the end of World War I, democracy became the dominant form of government in western Europe. Most countries were either republics or constitutional monarchies. Democracy had developed differently in each of the countries.

Case Studies

GREAT BRITAIN The evolution of English democracy began in 1215 when King John was forced to sign the **Magna Carta**, which put limits on his power. The power of the monarchy continued to decline over the centuries as the power of Parliament increased. During the nineteenth and twentieth centuries, **suffrage**, or the right to vote, was extended until all adults were able to exercise this power. In 1911, the House of Lords, symbol of the privileged position of the nobility, was stripped of almost all its power. The House of Commons, which represented the majority, became the dominant branch of Parliament, signifying the democratic transfer of power to the people.

FRANCE Democracy developed in France as a result of a number of violent uprisings. The **French Revolution of 1789** was aimed at establishing "Liberty, Equality, Fraternity," but was only partially successful. Subsequent revolutions in 1830 and 1848 finally led to the permanent adoption of a **republican** form of government and further growth of democracy.

ITALY The movement for Italian unification during the nineteenth century was led by **liberals** who favored a limited democracy. In 1861, they proclaimed the establishment of the Kingdom of Italy, a **constitutional monarchy** under King Victor Emmanuel II.

GERMANY German unification was brought about by conservatives who established an autocratic, militaristic government in 1871. Kaiser Wilhelm II, an absolute monarch, followed policies that helped to bring on World War I. At the close of the war, with Germany facing surrender, the Kaiser abdicated and fled the country. In 1918, the democratic **Weimar Republic** was established in Germany.

MAKING CONNECTIONS

Politics and History For more information on the unification of Germany and Italy, see the section on western Europe in Unit 2, Global History.

German Unification, 1871 – 1990

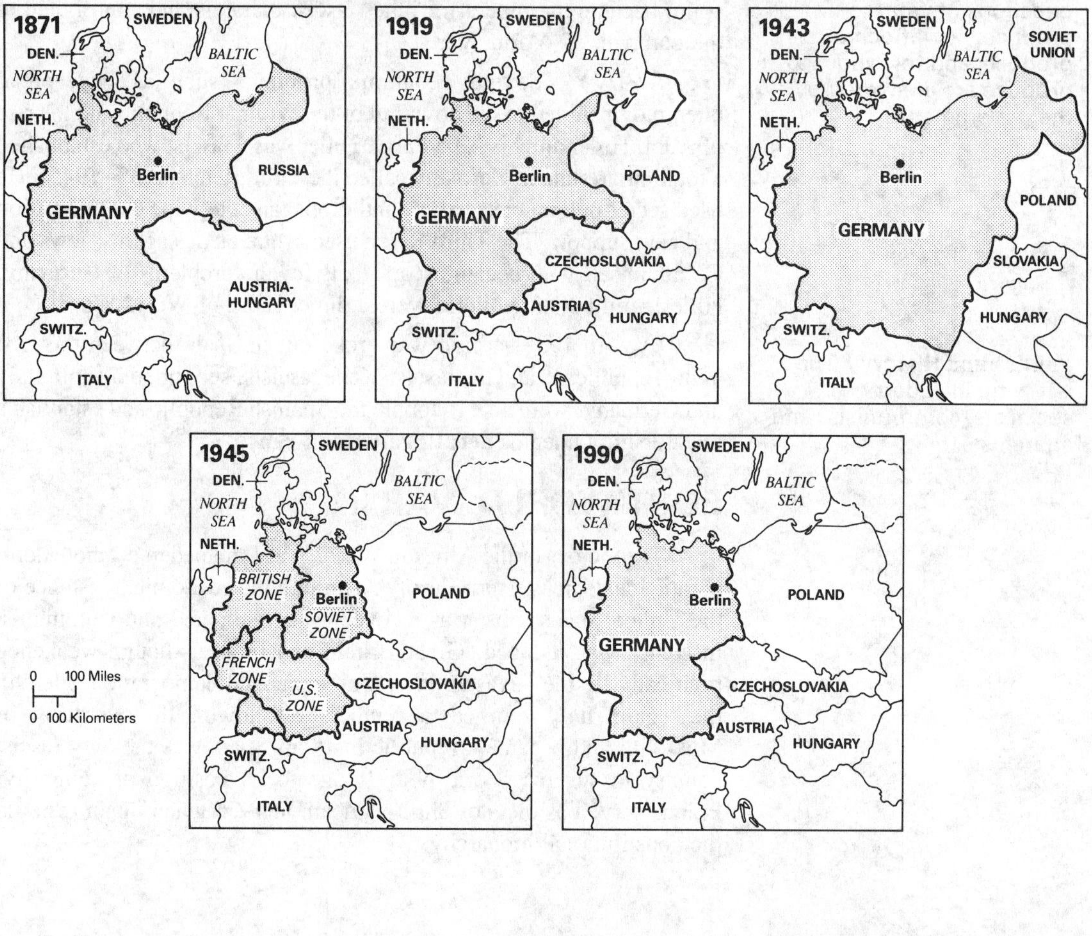

MAKING CONNECTIONS

The Rise of Totalitarianism

In part, the economic and social problems created by the devastation of World War I led to political instability for many countries in Europe. The onset of the Great Depression in 1929 compounded existing problems and caused various countries to turn to strong leaders who promised solutions. During the 1920s and 1930s, totalitarian regimes were established in Italy, Germany, and Spain.

Case Studies

ITALY In 1922, **Benito Mussolini** set up a fascist dictatorship in Italy. **Fascism** is a political philosophy that is **totalitarian**. It favors rule by a dictator who controls all aspects of life. It promotes extreme **nationalism**, encouraging people to make sacrifices, especially of their freedom, for the good of the state. Many Italians had been disappointed at the gains made in World War I and favored Mussolini because he promised to create an Italian empire by means of aggression. Since post-war economic problems made middle-class businessmen fearful of Communist influences, they supported the fascists, who advocated a command economy but allowed private ownership. Mussolini became the model for other fascist dictators and contributed to the outbreak of World War II.

Politics and Economics In a command economy, questions of what to produce, how much to produce, and for whom to produce are answered by the government.

GERMANY Severe economic problems such as widespread unemployment led to the downfall of the Weimar Republic and the rise of Adolf Hitler and his Nazi Party. Hitler was a fascist who established a totalitarian state in Germany called the Third Reich (1933–1945). He used secret police, censorship, and propaganda to wipe out opposition and gain support. The Third Reich used brutal tactics against Jews and Communists, who became scapegoats for the problems of Germany. Hitler's militaristic policies were a direct cause of World War II.

SPAIN In 1936, a civil war broke out in Spain between the Left Wing republicans and the fascists. The fascists, supported by both Italy and Germany, were able to topple the Spanish Republic and establish a dictatorship under **General Francisco Franco**.

Politics and History The left wing included socialists, communists, and anarchists.

POST-WORLD WAR II

The victory of the Allies in World War II helped to promote democratic ideals in Western Europe. Through the economic assistance of the United States, post-war recovery was facilitated and Communist influence was reduced. Great Britain and France, though weakened politically by the devastation of war, remained democratic leaders in the region. Italy returned to democracy following the overthrow of Mussolini and became a republic in 1946. Spain was the only fascist country to survive World War II due to its position of neutrality. Franco served as dictator until his death in 1975 when Spain restored the constitutional monarchy.

Special Case Study: Germany

As a result of agreements made among the Allies at the close of World War II, Germany and its capital of Berlin were divided into zones of occupation. This division resulted in the creation of two Germanies: West Germany and East Germany. West Germany, which had been occupied by Great Britain, France, and the United States, became a democratic, capitalist nation. East Germany became a Communist satellite of the Soviet Union. Berlin remained a divided city. In 1961, the Communists built the Berlin Wall, which physically and psychologically separated the people of the free world from those of the Communist world. The Berlin Wall remained until November 1989 when the people of East Berlin tore down the wall and thus began a movement that would lead to unification.

The actions of the East Germans became possible due to the policies of **Mikhail Gorbachev** who became leader of the Soviet Union in 1985. In his own country, Gorbachev promoted the ideas of "glasnost" and democratization, which gave the people greater rights and freedoms. He subsequently began to encourage the satellites to adopt similar reforms and implied that they were free of Soviet domination. This atmosphere of change led the East Germans to bring down their Communist government as well as the wall.

Soon after the fall of the East German Communist leadership, the people voted to join with West Germany. Unification was achieved as a result of extensive negotiations among the former Allies, Great Britain, France, the United States, and the Soviet Union, and the Germans. The Soviets agreed to gradually withdraw their troops from East Germany and to allow the united country to be part of **NATO**, the Western defense alliance. On October 3, 1990, the formal unification took place amid huge celebrations. In December 1990, the first all-German elections since 1932 took place. Chancellor **Helmut Kohl**, former head of West Germany, became the first leader of a united Germany since Adolf Hitler. German unification has brought mixed reactions. There is happiness for the German people and for what seems to be the end of the Cold War. There is also fear, however, that a united Germany will come to dominate Europe and that it may return to its prewar policies of militarism and aggression. German leaders have assured the world that the democratic traditions established in West Germany over the past 45 years will make a united Germany a force for good.

MAKING CONNECTIONS

Regents Tip How did the Marshall Plan affect the division of post-World War II Europe? How was the Truman Doctrine an example of the new diplomatic relations between the United States and the Soviet Union?

Key Concepts: Change
For more information on glasnost, see the section on the Soviet Union and Eastern Europe in this unit.

POLITICAL MOVEMENTS/ ORGANIZATIONS

The cooperation forged among the Allies during World War II continued after the war through the formation of various organizations.

MAKING CONNECTIONS

The United Nations (1945)

At the end of World War I, an international peace-keeping organization called the **League of Nations** was formed. The United States, which feared becoming entangled in future European conflicts, refused to become a member. The absence of American participation, as well as the nationalistic goals of member nations, helped to weaken the League and make it ineffectual in dealing with the acts of aggression that led to World War II. In 1942, the World War II Allies pledged to create a new and stronger organization to take the place of the League. The **United Nations** was formally established in 1945.

Regents Tip List another international organization in another region whose purpose is to promote peace.

PURPOSE The purpose of the United Nations is to provide a place where countries can discuss common problems, develop solutions, and settle disputes without resorting to war. The UN is designed to promote peace, human rights, and economic and social welfare around the world. It is also empowered, through the votes of its membership, to take actions against those who threaten world peace.

STRUCTURE There are six main bodies that make up the United Nations, two of which are most important. The **General Assembly** includes representatives from all member nations and provides a forum for discussion. The **Security Council** contains fifteen members, five of whom are permanent: Great Britain, France, the United States, the Soviet Union, and China. The Security Council is most responsible for dealing with threats to peace.

KOREAN CONFLICT (1950–1953) In 1950 Communist forces from North Korea invaded South Korea. Prompted by the United States, the Security Council voted to use military force to stop the North Korean aggressors. This use of a multinational UN force was possible only because the Soviet Union had been boycotting the UN at the time of the vote. The war ended in a stalemate, the North Koreans withdrew and the country today is still divided.

Key Concepts: Power The embargo was an attempt to isolate Iraq by halting trade between Iraq and other countries.

IRAQI INVASION OF KUWAIT (1990) On August 2, 1990, Iraqi troops invaded Kuwait out of a desire to seize control of the nation's oil fields. International outrage led the United Nations to authorize an **embargo** against Iraq to force withdrawal. **Saddam Hussein**, leader of Iraq, demonstrated an unwillingness to withdraw peacefully from Kuwait, despite the embargo. The UN Security Council subsequently voted to allow the use of military force against Iraq if troops were not withdrawn by January 15, 1991. On January 16, 1991, the United States and allied forces began to use force against Iraq, thus acting on the U.N. Security Council vote.

WEAKNESSES The success of the United Nations is dependent upon the cooperation of its members. Often the UN is hampered by the tendency of countries to pursue goals of national interest rather than achieve what is best for the global community. The UN has in the past been divided into **blocs**, groups of countries that vote the same way (Western Bloc, Communist Bloc, and the Developing Nations Bloc),

The United Nations

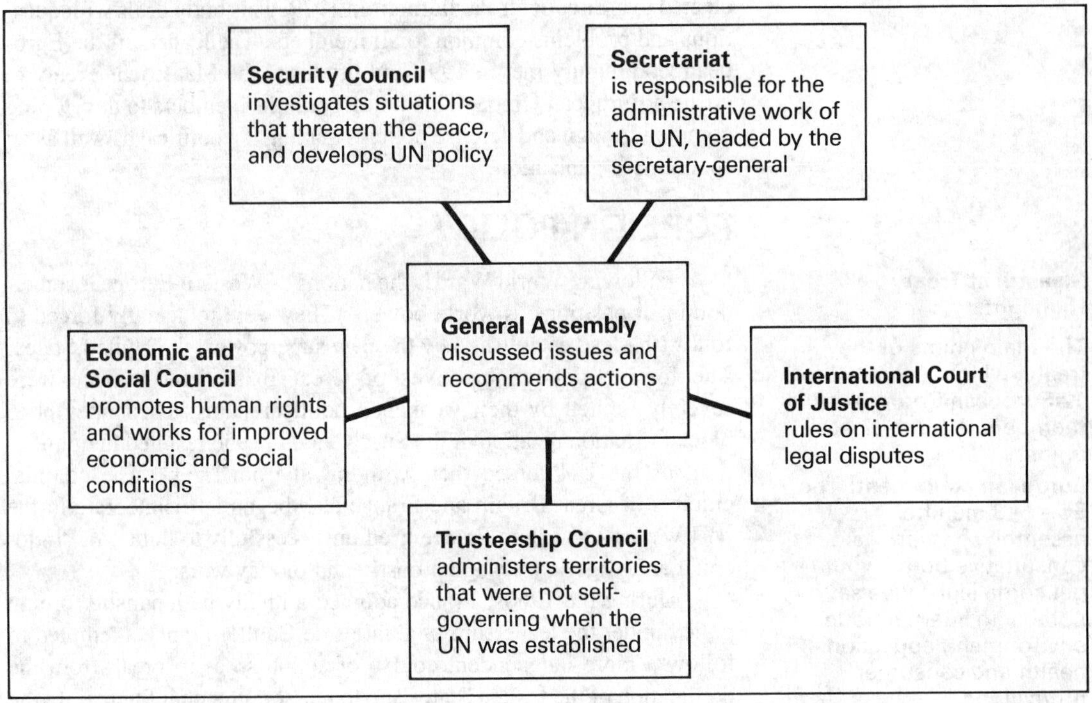
Security Council
investigates situations that threaten the peace, and develops UN policy
Secretariat
is responsible for the administrative work of the UN, headed by the secretary-general
General Assembly
discussed issues and recommends actions
Economic and Social Council
promotes human rights and works for improved economic and social conditions
International Court of Justice
rules on international legal disputes
Trusteeship Council
administers territories that were not self-governing when the UN was established

which serve as an obstacle to effectiveness. The changes in Eastern Europe and the Soviet Union have caused much of the Communist Bloc to dissolve, as evidenced by the recent vote in the Security Council. Such cooperation among the major powers will help to make the UN more powerful.

MAKING CONNECTIONS

NORTH ATLANTIC TREATY ORGANIZATION (NATO)

The **collective security agreement** known as NATO was formed in 1949. Its members include most of the nations of Western Europe, as well as Canada and the United States. It is a defensive military alliance that was organized following the Berlin Blockade, when the former Allies realized they could no longer trust the Soviet Union. Its purpose has been to protect the Atlantic region from Communist aggression by means of an international military force and through a coordinated defensive strategy. The recent changes in Eastern Europe and the Soviet Union have brought the purpose of NATO into question.

Regents Tip What other organization has a purpose that has to do with collective security?

THE EUROPEAN ECONOMIC COMMUNITY (1967)

The European Economic Community developed from earlier efforts at European cooperation—the European Coal and Steel Community, the European Economic Community (the Common Market), and the European Atomic Energy Community. Its members include twelve countries of Western Europe. These organizations were originally formed to bring about recovery from World War II and a return of economic prosperity to the region. In the 1970s, a movement for greater economic

MAKING CONNECTIONS

and political integration began. For example, representatives were elected to a **European Parliament** in 1979. This body deals with questions and problems common to all members. The leaders of the European Community met in 1991 and produced the Maastricht Treaty to create a European Union. This union commits members to developing common foreign and defense policies making it a political as well as an economic organization.

Maastricht Treaty Highlights

The main points of the treaty, which commits the 12 European Community members to forge closer union.

European parliament: The EC's 518-member assembly, primarily a consultative body, would get some legislative say, notably in internal trade, environment, education, health and consumer protection.

Immigration: Would set goal of common rules on immigration from outside the EC, movement of immigrants within the Community, and increased immigration law enforcement. Decisions would need unanimity.

Citizenship: Would introduce "Citizenship of the Union," guaranteeing free movement within the Community, granting after 1994 the right to vote and run in municipal elections in any EC nation, and giving EC nationals the right to diplomatic protection by all Community embassies abroad.

SOURCE: Associated Press

FOREIGN POLICY

Following World War II, the nations of Western Europe lost their dominant positions as world powers. They were reluctantly forced to follow the lead established by the new superpower, the United States. The foreign policy objectives of Great Britain and France were severely limited by their weakened political status. Their attempt to block the nationalization of the Suez Canal in 1956 resulted in humiliation, as the UN forced their withdrawal from Egypt. The colonial empires of Great Britain and France also began to disintegrate in the post-war era, although France tried unsuccessfully to hold on to Indochina and Algeria by waging costly and bloody wars.

During the 1960s, France adopted a highly nationalistic foreign policy under the leadership of Charles de Gaulle. France attempted to follow a more independent course of action so as to break from the domination of the United States and to reassert French influence. In the 1980s, Margaret Thatcher also encouraged policies that promoted British prestige and global importance. The 1982 Falklands War against Argentina helped to preserve what was left of the empire. Unlike de Gaulle, Thatcher consistently supported the United States and proved to be an important American ally. Her domestic policies, as well as her nationalistic stand against some of the plans for European integration, helped lead to her downfall in December 1990. John Major, her successor, was less conservative regarding the European Community, but continued support of the United States. In 1997, the Conservative Party was voted out of power, and Labour Party leader Tony Blair became Prime Minister.

MAJOR POLITICAL THEMES:

1. Democracy in western Europe had its roots in ancient Greece and Rome.
2. A key element of democracy is the guarantee of basic civil liberties.
3. Totalitarianism developed in western Europe during a period of economic distress and political instability.
4. The United Nations is an international peace-keeping organization that also promotes human rights and social and economic welfare.
5. Following World War II, Europe was divided between the democratic West and the Communist East. Changes that began in 1989 are helping to bring the entire region together.
6. The goal of Europeans today is greater economic and political integration as well as increased power and prestige.

SECTION 9 Political Setting: Northern Eurasia and Eastern Europe

SOVIET UNION

MAKING CONNECTIONS

The people of the Soviet Union had little experience with democracy. Their political history was distinguished by a tradition of **authoritarianism**. The Russian Empire was controlled by czars—absolute monarchs who ruled with complete power. The czars believed the great size of Russia required a strong autocratic ruler to maintain order and stability. Through strict laws, secret police, and harsh punishment, the czars promoted ''Nationality, Orthodoxy, and Autocracy''—devotion to Russian culture, the Russian Orthodox Church, and the rule of the czar. Eventually, the injustice and inefficiency of absolute rule drove the people to revolt in 1917 when Czar Nicolas II was forced to abdicate.

Regents Tip List another authoritarian regime that you have studied.

PRE-WORLD WAR II

Following the Revolution of 1917, **Nikolai Lenin** attempted to establish a Communist state in Russia. According to the theories of **Karl Marx**, the revolution was to bring about a ''dictatorship of the proletariat'' (workers), which would rule temporarily during the transition from capitalism to communism. Once that was accomplished, the state would ''wither away.'' In a society where everyone would be truly equal and contribute according to his ability, there would be no need for government. Lenin felt that a core of educated and dedicated leaders was necessary to make the revolution a success. He adapted Marx's theories, and the ''dictatorship of the proletariat'' became the dictatorship of the Communist Party.

In 1922, the Russian Empire became the Union of Soviet Socialist Republics, which operated according to a constitution drawn up by the Communists. Although it outwardly appeared to be a democracy, the constitution was open to the interpretation of the Communist leaders and in reality, it was the Communists, not the people, who held power.

Key Concepts: Political System
Having a constitution does not necessarily mean having a democracy.

The Role of the Communist Party

- The Communist Party was the only political party allowed to exist. Only loyal Communist Party members or sympathizers were permitted to run for public office.

MAKING CONNECTIONS

- Membership in the Communist Party was restricted. Only a small percentage of the entire population belonged to the Party.
- The **Politburo**, or inner circle of the Communist Party, consisted of fifteen men who were responsible for making policy.
- The **general secretary**, or leader of the Communist Party, was the most powerful man in the Soviet Union.

The Role of the Government

- Voting was considered to be a responsibility required by law. The people had no choice but to vote for candidates promoted by the Communist Party.
- The organization of the government mirrored that of the Communist Party, but its leaders and bodies had no real power.
- The legislature, called the **Supreme Soviet**, was merely a rubber stamp for policies made by the Communist Party.

The Rise of Totalitarianism

Regents Tip How were the tactics of Stalin similar to those of Hitler and the Nazis?

As premier of Russia, Lenin ruled as a dictator. It was **Josef Stalin**, however, who created the Communist totalitarian state of the Soviet Union. Stalin combined brutality with modern technology to efficiently control all phases of Soviet life. The needs of the state were always considered more important than the needs of individual citizens. He used **indoctrination, propaganda**, and **censorship** to encourage loyalty to the government and support for Communist ideas. Stalin would not tolerate opposition. Even within the Party, purges were carried out to get rid of those he suspected of disloyalty. It is believed that Stalin was responsible for the deaths of millions of people who were obstacles to his rule.

POST-WORLD WAR II

Politics and Economics For more information on perestroika, see the section on Northern Eurasia and Eastern Europe in Unit 3, Global Economics.

Although the successors of Stalin were not as brutal in dealing with opposition, they nonetheless continued to maintain the Communist monopoly on power and the totalitarian control over the people. In 1985, however, **Mikhail Gorbachev** was named general secretary. Faced with the reality of a crumbling economy, Gorbachev began to take steps to reform the entire Soviet system. The Soviet economy was dependent upon centralized state planning. **Perestroika** was Gorbachev's plan to restructure and decentralize the economy. In order for economic reform to work, Gorbachev realized that it was necessary for political and social changes to take place as well.

GLASNOST **Glasnost** referred to a policy of greater "openness" within Soviet society and with other countries. This policy included a willingness on the part of the government to admit past mistakes and to recognize the excesses of previous regimes. Dissidents received much better treatment and Soviet citizens have more freedom to speak out or demonstrate against government policies.

DEMOCRATIZATION President Gorbachev instituted these three major changes in the Soviet political system to make it more democratic:

1. The creation of the **Congress of People's Deputies**. This new body was elected by the people. Anyone could run; it was not restricted to Communist Party members. The Congress met annually to discuss important issues. Although it was designed to be "window dressing," it became very influential.
2. The end of the Communist Party's monopoly of power. Other political parties were allowed to exist and function in the Soviet Union.
3. The establishment of new executive powers for the president. Eventually, the head of the government would replace the general secretary as the most powerful person in the Soviet Union.

MAKING CONNECTIONS

Problems Fractured the Soviet Union

Gorbachev's policies of fewer restrictions and greater political and economic freedom caused the Soviet leader serious problems, including ethnic unrest and secessionist movements and, eventually, the breakup of the Soviet Union itself.

ETHNIC UNREST The Soviet Union was a country that contained over one hundred different ethnic groups, each having a distinct language and culture. In the past, a policy of Russification was used to encourage a feeling of unity and nationalism. In the absence of government restraints, however, various ethnic groups promoted their own nationalism, which contributed to the disunity that tore the country apart. In addition, rival ethnic groups renewed old conflicts and violence broke out in several republics (*e.g.*, Moslems of Azerbaijan and the Christians of Armenia).

Regents Tip Explain why secessionist movements appealed to the republics of the Soviet Union.

SECESSIONIST MOVEMENTS As the Eastern European satellites began to break from the Soviet Union and remove their Communist governments, some of the Soviet Republics attempted to do the same. By the middle of 1990, the large and powerful republics of Russia, Ukraine, and Byelarus, joined by the Baltic republics and several smaller republics, had declared independence from the Soviet central authority. By 1992, the dissolution of the Soviet Union was complete. The 12 republics of Russia, Ukraine, Moldova, Uzbekistan, Turkmenistan, Armenia, Azerbaijan, Kazakhstan, Georgia, Tajikistan, Kyrgyzstan, and Byelarus are independent countries that are members of a new Commonwealth of Independent States. Three other former republics—Latvia, Estonia, and Lithuania—although newly independent, will not be a part of the new commonwealth. They have officially declared their sovereignty and have been accepted as members of the United Nations.

Regents Tip Cite an example of a nation or region that has many ethnic groups.

MAKING CONNECTIONS

What was the result of Gorbachev's democratic reforms?

Bob Englehart, Hartford Courant

Politics and History For more information on the Soviet Union as a superpower, see the section on Northern Eurasia and Eastern Europe in Unit 2, Global History.

POLITICAL MOVEMENTS/ ORGANIZATIONS

Following World War II, the Soviet Union emerged as a superpower and helped to create the United Nations. Soviet post-war cooperation with the Allies quickly changed to competition with them. With the onset of the Cold War, the Soviets sought to protect themselves from the West. In 1949, the Western powers formed NATO as a alliance against Soviet aggression. In response, the Soviet Union organized the **Warsaw Pact** with its Eastern European satellites. It was a defensive alliance designed to protect Eastern European satellites. It was a defensive alliance designed to protect Eastern Europe and the Soviet Union from an attack by the West. The Warsaw Pact was dismantled in 1991, as the East and the West moved closer together and embraced common values of democracy and capitalism.

Politics and History For more information on the Cold War, see the section on Northern Eurasia and Eastern Europe in Unit 2, Global History.

FOREIGN POLICY

From 1945 to 1990, the foreign policy of the Soviet Union focused on the **Cold War**, the struggle between the democratic West and the Communists. Although it was a war of words, the Cold War created an atmosphere of hostility and fear that negatively affected both sides. The tensions of the Cold War were heightened by the following:

The Berlin Blockade (1948–1949): The Soviet attempt to drive the Allies from Berlin. The blockade failed due to the Allied airlift.

The U-2 Incident (1960): A United States spy plane was shot down over the Soviet Union. Although the United States claimed it was a weather plane, the Soviets produced the pilot and proved the U.S. was lying. As a result of this incident, a summit between **Nikita Khrushchev** and **President Eisenhower** was cancelled.

MAKING CONNECTIONS

The Cuban Missile Crisis (1962): The United States discovered that the Soviets were constructing missile sites in Cuba, 90 miles from the coast of Florida. **President Kennedy** ordered a blockade of Cuba, forcing a showdown with **Khrushchev**. The Soviet leader backed down and removed the missile sites.

Invasion of Afghanistan (1979): Soviet troops invaded Afghanistan in an attempt to prevent the fall of a friendly Communist government. In response, the United States refused to approve the SALT II arms reduction treaty, stating that the Soviets could not be trusted. The United States also placed a grain embargo on the Soviet Union and boycotted the Summer Olympic Games in Moscow.

Regents Tip Explain how the experience of the Soviet Union in Afghanistan was similar to that of the United States in Vietnam.

The End of the Cold War

The mounting buildup of nuclear arms during the Cold War led to apprehension that an incident might spark a nuclear World War III. During the 1970s, the United States and the Soviet Union pursued a policy of **détente**, or easing of tensions. Détente resulted in the nuclear arms treaties known as **SALT I** and **SALT II**, which limited production of nuclear weapons. Although the United States never approved SALT II, it adhered to it in principle. During the late 1980s, the "glasnost" policies of **Mikhail Gorbachev** led to a major improvement in relations with the United States. Summits between Gorbachev and President **Ronald Reagan** resulted in the **INF Treaty**, the first agreement to eliminate some types of existing nuclear weapons. Continued negotiations brought about more reductions in nuclear arsenals as well as conventional weapons in Europe. In November 1990, the Cold War was proclaimed officially over.

OVERVIEW: EASTERN EUROPE

Since most of Eastern Europe is made up of flat plains, it lacks the geographic barriers that might deter invasion. Throughout history, the countries of Eastern Europe have been dominated by foreign powers.

Key Concepts: Environment
Geography affects the historical development of an area.

PRE-WORLD WAR II

In the early twentieth century, the people of Eastern Europe gained their freedom from various empires, and independent countries emerged in the region. Poland, for example, was formed in 1918 from land taken from Russia, Germany, and Austria-Hungary. In the years between World War I and World War II, authoritarian regimes developed in most countries of Eastern Europe. Czechoslovakia alone was able to maintain a democracy.

POST-WORLD WAR II

During World War II, Eastern Europe fell under the control of Nazi Germany. Following the Battle of Stalingrad (1942), the Soviets went on the offensive against the Nazis, driving them west. As they

MAKING CONNECTIONS

pushed the Nazis toward Germany, the Soviet troops occupied most of the countries of Eastern Europe. At the **Yalta Conference** (1945), the Allies agreed that the Soviets would occupy Eastern Europe until free elections could take place. Stalin made certain that Communist regimes were installed in each of the countries under his control. By 1948, the Eastern European nations were transformed into "satellites" of the Soviet Union. Soviet leaders in Moscow directed policy for the satellites, binding them politically and economically to the USSR. Yugoslavia was the exception. Although it was a Communist nation, it never became a satellite. **Marshall Tito**, leader of Yugoslavia, was able to maintain a policy of **nonalignment**, meaning he did not side with either the Soviets or the West.

Regents Tip What famous leader of Great Britain used the phrase the "Iron Curtain"?

The Iron Curtain

Soviet leaders from 1945 to 1985 would not tolerate any movement toward freedom or reform among the satellites. The two most dramatic attempts at change—the Hungarian Revolt of 1956 and the Prague Spring Reform Movement in Czechoslovakia in 1968—were stopped with the use of military force. It was as if an "Iron Curtain" separated these countries from the free world and there was nothing that could be done to alter the situation. In 1985, Mikhail Gorbachev became head of the Soviet Union and began a series of reforms. He encouraged the satellites to do the same, and eventually allowed them to go their own way, free of Soviet domination.

The End of the Iron Curtain

The countries of Eastern Europe followed different paths to freedom and democracy.

POLAND In the 1970s and 1980s, there was widespread unrest in Poland due to poor economic conditions. **Solidarity,** a trade union formed in 1980, pressured the government for changes that would improve living standards. Led by **Lech Walesa,** Solidarity promoted strikes and demonstrations to achieve its goals. Although the government outlawed Solidarity and declared martial law, the public continued to press for reform. Encouraged by the policies of Gorbachev, the government eventually legalized Solidarity and allowed free elections in 1989. The new government was dominated by Solidarity, including Walesa, who became president in 1990. The government undertook bold reforms to create a market economy. These reforms caused widespread short-term suffering, which led many Polish voters to back former Communists in later elections. In 1995 Aleksander Kwasniewski, a former Communist, became president.

CZECHOSLOVAKIA Public protest brought about a nonviolent revolution, which led to the downfall of the Communist government in Czechoslovakia. As an indication of the dramatic changes taking place, **Vaclav Havel**, a playwright and former dissident was chosen president. Czechoslovakia had in its favor economic stability and experience in democracy. However, different ideas on economic reform caused the people of Czechoslovakia to democratically choose to separate into two countries. The Czech Republic and Slovakia officially became independent nations in January 1993.

ROMANIA In December 1989, violent revolution brought down the Communist regime in Romania. When police fired on a group of protesters, Romanians became enraged and overthrew their dictator, Nicolae Ceausescu who was subsequently tried and executed. Romania has had difficulty making the transition to democracy.

Regents Tip Note the different ways in which revolutions can occur.

YUGOSLAVIA Formed after World War I, Yugoslavia was made up of many ethnic and religious groups. A Communist government was established after World War II by dictator Josip Tito, who kept the country under strict control until his death in 1980. After the fall of communism, tensions among the peoples of Yugoslavia began to tear the nation apart. In June 1991, after the Yugoslav republics of Croatia and Slovenia declared independence, civil war began. In 1992 Bosnia-Hercegovina also attempted to break away, leading to intense fighting among Bosnia's Muslims, Serbs, and Croats. The bloody Bosnian conflict included human rights violations by all sides. The worst such atrocity was "ethnic cleansing," in which Serbs killed or terrorized thousands of Muslim civilians in order to drive them out of the region. Ethnic cleansing has been labeled genocide and has been compared to the actions of Nazi Germany against European Jews.

Politics and History: It is ironic that the Serbs have been accused of genocide. During World War II the Croats, allied with the Nazis, tried to wipe out the Serbs.

Early United Nations involvement failed to halt the suffering in Bosnia. In 1995, NATO warplanes bombed Serbian positions to try to force a settlement. Later that year, in a meeting in Dayton, Ohio, the warring sides finally agreed to a cease-fire. Foreign troops, including many Americans, were sent to Bosnia to keep the peace. Yet tensions among the peoples of Bosnia remained extremely high, and many obstacles remained in the path of a lasting settlement.

MAJOR POLITICAL THEMES

1. The political history of the Soviet people has been influenced most by authoritarian regimes.
2. Stalin refined the methods of the czars to create a totalitarian police state in the Soviet Union.
3. Gorbachev's policies resulted in greater individual freedom and led to the dissolution of the Soviet Union.
4. The 45-year-old Cold War was eased by détente, but ended by "glasnost."
5. Eastern Europe, long dominated by foreign powers, has finally broken free and is now pursuing policies of democracy and capitalism.

Regents Questions for Practice

MAKING CONNECTIONS

Review the Test-Taking Strategies section of this book. Then answer the following questions, drawn from actual Regents examinations. Circle the *number* of the word or expression that best completes the statement or answers the question. Write your answers to essay questions on a separate piece of paper. Hints on good ways to approach these questions are provided in the margins.

1. Which statement about nationalism is most accurate?
1 It becomes a unifying force among a people.
2 It encourages diversity within nation-states.
3 It prevents the rise of militarism.
4 It eliminates the ethnic identities of different groups.

2. Nationalism is most likely to develop in an area that has
1 land suited to agriculture
2 adequate industry to supply consumer demands
3 a moderate climate with rivers for irrigation
4 common customs, language, and history

Regents Tip Questions 1–3 all deal with nationalism. Which answer choices can you eliminate right away in these questions?

3. To develop a sense of nationalism, a group of people must:
1 share the control of an important natural resource
2 believe in the value of democracy
3 have some beliefs and values in common
4 develop a strong military force

4. A totalitarian government would most likely develop in a country where
1 economic prosperity has been increasing
2 people are unwilling to form alliances with other nations
3 concern for human rights is an important value
4 economic and social stability is rapidly declining

Regents Tip Remember that a totalitarian government is one of total authoritarian rule by one party or group of people.

5. Which is a belief shared by totalitarian governments?
1 Written constitutions and free elections are necessary for the proper functioning of society.
2 The rights of dissenters must be respected.
3 Human rights should be guaranteed to all citizens.
4 The requirements of the state are more important than the rights of individuals.

6. "All great nations . . . have desired to set their mark upon barbarian lands, and those who fail to participate in this great rivalry will play a pitiable role in time to come." This quotation supports the concept of
1 socialism
2 human rights
3 revolution
4 imperialism

MAKING CONNECTIONS

7. The centralization of governmental power within a developing nation would probably be most opposed by
1 leaders of minority groups
2 business leaders
3 military leaders
4 foreign investors

8. Which is the most common characteristic of societies that have stable governments?
1 a single language
2 two-party political system
3 general respect for law
4 mandatory military service

Regents Tip The words "the most common" are key in this question.

---

9. Jomo Kenyatta and Kwame Nkrumah were African leaders opposed to
1 militarism
2 socialism
3 nationalism
4 colonialism

10. In the Republic of South Africa, the government's apartheid policy has been based primarily on the concept of
1 justice under the law
2 nativism
3 racial segregation
4 economic specialization

11. The term "Pan-Africanism" can best be defined as a movement whose purpose is to
1 promote African unity
2 support cultural diversity
3 encourage European investment in Africa
4 advocate a return to colonial conditions

12. During the 19th century, the African continent was affected most by
1 the Commercial Revolution
2 the introduction of socialism
3 the Crusades
4 European imperialism

13. Many modern-day African nations have had difficulty uniting their people because the people
1 have strong tribal ties
2 are still loyal to the former colonial power
3 do not wish to remain in Africa
4 are unwilling to accept authority figures

14. Which statement best describes the significance of awarding the 1985 Nobel Peace Prize to Bishop Desmond Tutu of South Africa?
1 The world community was endorsing the apartheid practices of the government of South Africa.
2 The European policy of remaining neutral in regard to human rights issues was reaffirmed.
3 The separation of church and state was promoted as a universal concept.
4 Nonviolence was recognized as a way to bring about change in South Africa.

15. Which was a major reason for the creation of the separate nations of India and Pakistan in 1947?
1 India was economically dependent on Great Britain, while Pakistan was economically self-sufficient.
2 The two nations favored vastly different forms of government.
3 The religious and cultural patterns of the two areas were in serious conflict.
4 Natural geographic features of the Indian subcontinent divided the two areas.

16. Which development was a result of the other three?
1 West Pakistani government administrators being appointed in East Pakistan
2 the creation of the nation of Bangladesh
3 the existence of cultural and economic differences between East and West Pakistan
4 rioting in East Pakistan in 1971

17. Which is a result of India's policy of nonalignment?
1 India has kept its defense spending at a low level.
2 The Indian government has been successful in limiting population growth.
3 The Indian government has worked to reduce religious conflicts.
4 India has accepted aid from both the United States and the Soviet Union.

18. Dr. Martin Luther King, Jr's ideas on nonviolence were most directly influenced by the
1 sayings of Confucius
2 teachings of Buddha
3 principles of Mohandas K. Gandhi
4 philosophy of Socrates

19. Which generalization best explains the creation of the nations of India and Pakistan in 1947?
1 Armed conflict is necessary for independence movements to succeed.
2 Religious conflicts may have a strong influence on political events.
3 Industrialization needs to reach a high level before a nation can become independent.
4 Similar geographical and historical conditions may promote unity between nations.

20. In the 20th century, most nations of Southeast Asia have been characterized by
1 struggles for independence
2 a high standard of living
3 political stability
4 tolerance of ethnic minorities

21. A major problem faced by Southeast Asian nations today is that
1 increased immigration has created high levels of employment
2 industrial development has hindered democratic reform
3 rapid modernization has led to a shortage of agricultural products
4 economic growth has not kept pace with population growth

22. The division of Korea in 1945 and of Vietnam in 1954 are decisions that were
1 made as direct results of popular elections
2 reached by Korea and by Vietnam without the interference of other nations
3 worked out as compromise political solutions reflecting Cold War realities
4 based on the principles of national self-determination

23. The Boxer Rebellion in China in 1900 and the Iranian Revolution in 1979 were similar in that both
1 blamed foreigners for the erosion of traditional cultures
2 were led by young radicals who wished to modernize their country
3 spared the rights and property of foreign diplomats
4 were successfully suppressed by foreign military intervention

24. Soon after coming into power, the government of the People's Republic of China tried to make significant changes in the traditional Chinese family. This policy was adopted because the traditional family
1 was seen as an obstacle to Communist plans for modernization
2 gave too much decision-making power to women
3 had become too similar to the family in Western societies
4 did not encourage sufficient respect for China's cultural history

25. Which segment of Chinese society gave the most support to the Communists during the Revolution?
1 peasants
2 religious leaders
3 landowners
4 bureaucrats

26. Which was a major justification used by Japan for empire building in the 1930s and 1940s?
1 revenging attacks by aggressive neighbors
2 promoting immigration of foreigners
3 spreading the Buddhist religion
4 obtaining food and raw materials

27. Since the early 1970s Japan's foreign policy has become independent of United States policies because
1 Japan opposes the United States policy of détente with Communist countries
2 Japan has emerged as an economic superpower
3 the United States has failed to honor its commitments to defend Japan
4 Japan is so militarily strong that it no longer needs United States help to protect itself

28. The best evidence that Japan has been greatly influenced by Western values and ideas is Japan's:
1 strengthening of the old family system
2 efforts to increase the power of landlords
3 insistence upon rigid job definitions and work rules
4 adoption of parliamentary democracy

29. Japan's current position as a world power is most directly based upon Japan's:
1 economic strength
2 abundance of natural resources
3 diversity of cultures
4 military superiority

30. Which is the main purpose of the Good Neighbor policy, the Alliance for Progress, and the Organization of American States (OAS)?
1 to establish democracy among newly independent Latin American nations
2 to provide mutual military support for Latin American nations
3 to develop cooperation among nations of the Western Hemisphere
4 to eliminate all barriers to trade between member nations

31. Many governments in developing countries are controlled by the military because the military is
1 usually in favor of rapid change
2 supported by democratic political parties
3 usually the most organized and efficient institution
4 dominated by officers who are members of the wealthy class

32. Since Fidel Castro assumed control in 1959, many nations have considered Cuba a threat because the Castro regime
1 overthrew a democratic Cuban government when taking control
2 has seriously hindered trade among countries of the Western Hemisphere
3 has supported revolutions in various parts of the world
4 has refused to sell sugar or tobacco to industrialized nations

33. Which factor has served as a bond among Arab countries in the Middle East?
1 similarity of government
2 unity under a military leader
3 reliance on the United States for aid
4 hostility toward Israel

34. Which has been a serious problem for many nations of the Middle East since World War II?
1 renewed colonial conquest by Europeans
2 cutbacks in foreign aid from the United States
3 increased world demand for oil
4 conflicts between traditionalists and modernists

35. The primary goal of the Palestine Liberation Organization (PLO) has been to
1 establish a home state for Palestinian Arabs
2 eliminate Communist influence in the Arab nations
3 bring about a peaceful settlement of the conflicts between Egypt and Palestinian Arabs
4 control the Organization of Petroleum Exporting Countries (OPEC)

36. In the 1980s, the major source of the conflict between Israel and Palestinian Arabs has been
1 the presence of Israeli ships in the Suez Canal
2 the interference of Libya in Middle Eastern affairs
3 the demand of Palestinian Arabs for their own homeland
4 Soviet support of radical Arab groups in occupied territories

37. Which statement best describes the Middle East during the 1980s?
1 Palestinians in the occupied territories want greater integration into Israeli society.
2 The nations of the Middle East have adopted a common foreign policy.
3 Arab unity has not been achieved.
4 International cooperation has brought about an era of peace.

38. Which statement concerning the Islamic world is most accurate?
1 Religious unity has led to political unity among Islamic nations.
2 The only Islamic nations of the world are found in the Middle East.
3 All Islamic nations are totally committed to the destruction of Israel.
4 Significant religious and political differences exist among Islamic sects.

39. Which statement best describes the result of the Crusades?
1 Europeans maintained a lasting control over much of the Middle East.
2 Islamic influence dominated Europe.
3 Europeans developed tolerance of non-Christian religions.
4 Trade between Europe and the Middle East was expanded.

40. The writers and philosophers of the Enlightenment believed that government decisions should be based on:
1 fundamental religious beliefs
2 the concept of divine right of kings
3 laws of nature and reason
4 traditional values

41. Which situation contributed to Adolf Hitler's rise to power in Germany after World War I?
1 support of Hitler's radical policies by the Social Democrats in the Reichstag
2 strong feelings of resentment and nationalism built up by economic and political crises
3 refusal by the League of Nations to admit Germany as a member
4 violence and terrorism promoted by Germany's former enemies

42. Which has been a major change in the political situation in Western Europe in the last half of the 20th century?
1 Nationalism has increased rivalry between Western European nations.
2 Western European nations have gained power through control of world oil resources.
3 Western European nations have worked cooperatively for security and prosperity.
4 Powerful dictatorships have emerged throughout Western Europe.

43. The political reorganization of Russia after the Communist Revolution of 1917 resulted in
1 the establishment of a two-party political system
2 increased political power to ethnic minorities
3 a limited monarchy with the Czar as a figurehead
4 a federation of socialist republics

44. European imperialism promoted the development of nationalism in Asian and African countries by
1 unintentionally uniting people to oppose foreign domination
2 promoting free trade associations among the colonies
3 establishing Christianity as the common religion
4 discouraging patriotic feelings toward the mother country

45. The primary aim of the concept of balance of power in Europe during the 19th century was to
1 eliminate war as a foreign policy
2 prevent domination by any one country
3 create equal land and sea forces within each nation
4 divide Europe under two equal military powers

46. "Heretofore, philosophers have only interpreted the world differently; the point is, however, to change it and change it rapidly."
A person holding this point of view would most likely be considered a
1 reactionary
2 conservative
3 moderate
4 revolutionary

47. Balance of power in international relations is achieved when
1 all nations have armies and navies
2 the strength of the aristocracy and proletariat is about the same
3 no nation is powerful enough to defeat other countries or groups of countries
4 nations have transferred their military forces to an international organization

48. Which characteristic is most essential to a democratic society?
1 a respect for individual rights
2 a federal structure of government
3 a strong two-party system
4 a written constitution

49. Which is the major reason that the United Nations has often been unsuccessful in solving international disputes?
1 The United Nations does not have sufficient funds to act.
2 The disputing nations are usually not members of the United Nations.
3 National sovereignty stands in the way of international cooperation.
4 The United Nations Charter does not provide a means to settle disputes.

50. Which term best describes the political system in Russia before the 20th century?
1 constitutional republic
2 absolute monarchy
3 parliamentary democracy
4 military dictatorship

51. Which statement best describes the political situation in the Soviet Union immediately after Lenin's death in 1924?
1 The nation adopted a constitutional monarchy.
2 Trotsky and his followers assumed full control of the Communist Party.
3 Popular elections were held to choose a new General Secretary.
4 A power struggle developed among Communist Party leaders.

52. The events that took place in Hungary in the 1950s and in Czechoslovakia in the 1960s demonstrated the Soviet Union's
1 support of nationalism among satellite nations
2 influence on the economies of developing nations
3 determination to maintain political control over Eastern Europe at that time
4 attempts to promote its artistic and literary achievements in Western Europe

53. The main purpose of the many purges and public trials that took place in the Soviet Union in the 1930s was to
1 force the Jewish people to leave the Soviet Union
2 eliminate opposition to Joseph Stalin and his government
3 establish a free and independent court system in the Soviet Union
4 reform the outdated and inadequate agricultural system

54. A study of Yugoslavia, the People's Republic of China, and the former Soviet Union would best indicate that Marxism
1 had achieved its goal of a classless society
2 had been formally discontinued by all three countries
3 was often reshaped to meet the particular needs of the government
4 was practiced strictly in accordance with Karl Marx's idea

55. Gamal Abdul Nasser, Mao Zedong, and Simon Bolivar were similar because they
1 promoted nationalism among their people
2 believed in Marxist principles
3 modeled their political actions on religious doctrine
4 encouraged terrorism and violence in their revolutions

56. Giuseppe Garibaldi, Thomas Jefferson, and Simón Bolívar were similar in that each
1 encouraged a spirit of nationalism in their people
2 denied voting rights to the citizens after gaining control of their nation
3 opposed the territorial expansion of the United States
4 followed the ideas of Marx in establishing a government

57. A study of the causes of the American, French, and Russian Revolutions indicates that revolutions usually occur because the
1 society has become dependent on commerce and trade
2 society has a lower standard of living than the societies around it
3 existing government has been resistant to change
4 lower classes have strong leaders

58. The Committee of Public Safety in France and the Khmer Rouge in Kampuchea (Cambodia) are similar in that they
1 were loyal to the monarchies in their countries
2 used terror to further their revolutionary goals
3 were intellectuals who promoted moderate reforms in their countries
4 sought to establish democratic institutions in their countries

59. For much of Asia and Africa, the three decades following World War II may be best described as a period of
1 economic independence
2 cultural isolation
3 social unification
4 political instability

Essay Questions

1. Some of the principal aims of the United Nations are listed below.

Maintaining international peace and security
Fostering and promoting human rights
Promoting social progress and better standards of life

For *each* aim listed:

- Describe a specific action taken by the United Nations between 1945 and the present to achieve this aim
- Describe a major obstacle the United Nations has faced in trying to achieve this aim
- Discuss the extent to which the United Nations has been successful in achieving this aim

2. A strong leader acts decisively not only to influence events within his or her nation but also to influence relations with other nations.

Leaders

Corazon Aquino	Fidel Castro
Peter the Great	Napoleon Bonaparte
Ayatollah Khomeini	Indira Gandhi
Deng Xiaoping	Jomo Kenyatta

Select *three* leaders listed and for *each* leader:

- Identify the nation in which the leader acted
- Discuss one domestic policy or one foreign policy of the leader
- Discuss a method used by the leader to put his or her policies into effect

3. Since World War II, the 20th century has been a period of increased interdependence. International organizations reflect this interdependence.

International Organizations

European Economic Community (EEC)
North Atlantic Treaty Organization (NATO)
Warsaw Pact
Organization of Petroleum Exporting Countries (OPEC)
United Nations
Organization of African Unity (OAU)

Select three of the organizations listed and for each organization:

- Describe the organization
- Identify a major goal of the organization
- Discuss a problem faced by the organization in attempting to achieve this goal

4. Below are listed foreign policies that have been important throughout history.

Foreign Policies

Imperialism	International cooperation
Neutrality	Intervention
Militarism	Assuring human rights
Collective security	

Select *three* of the foreign policies listed above. For *each* one chosen:

- Identify a specific nation that adopted the policy and indicate a specific time period of its adoption
- Describe a basic goal of the policy and how the nation attempted to achieve it
- Describe one effect of the policy on another nation or nations

UNIT 6 The World Today

MAKING CONNECTIONS

As you review each unit, you will find additional information in this column: major ideas, connecting themes, and questions to reinforce your learning. These items are closely tied to the Regents examination. Read this material carefully, and jot down any other facts that you would like to remember in the column's blank spaces. Using this column will **add to your success on the Regents exam**.

Key Concepts: Culture
How is the growth rate of the population in Latin America affected by the religious beliefs of the people?

This unit focuses on several major problems affecting the nations of the world today. We are all part of the global arena in which these problems exist. Therefore, it is vital to understand how the problems developed, where they occur, and how the solution of these interdependent problems requires the cooperation of all nations. Only then can we fully address these problems and find solutions to them.

WORLD ISSUE: OVERPOPULATION

Overpopulation refers to the overabundance of people in a region or area that lacks sufficient resources to adequately provide its people. China, India, and many other countries face severe problems of overpopulation now and in the future. The population of the **People's Republic of China** ranks first in the world with over 1.2 billion (1,200,000,000) people. **India** ranks second with over 900 million (900,000,000) people. Since **Africa** and **Latin America** have the highest birth rates, they are also experiencing major problems with overpopulation. Projections for the future indicate that China, India, Nigeria, Indonesia, Pakistan, Bangladesh, Brazil, and Mexico will continue to experience rapid population growth.

The reasons for overpopulation in various countries include the following:

1. **Religious beliefs**—the belief that procreation (bringing children into the world) is essential.
2. **Cultural factors**—the need to have large families to carry on the family name and provide for the parents in old age.
3. **Economic factors**—large numbers of children to help their working families.
4. **Lack of knowledge**—facts about reproduction and birth control are lacking or misunderstood.

The world's population has increased more rapidly in the twentieth century than at any time in the past. By 2070, it is expected to reach 10 billion, double its 5 billion total in 1988. Various solutions to the problem of overpopulation have been proposed, foremost among which is family planning. The governments of some countries actively

Cycle of Overpopulation

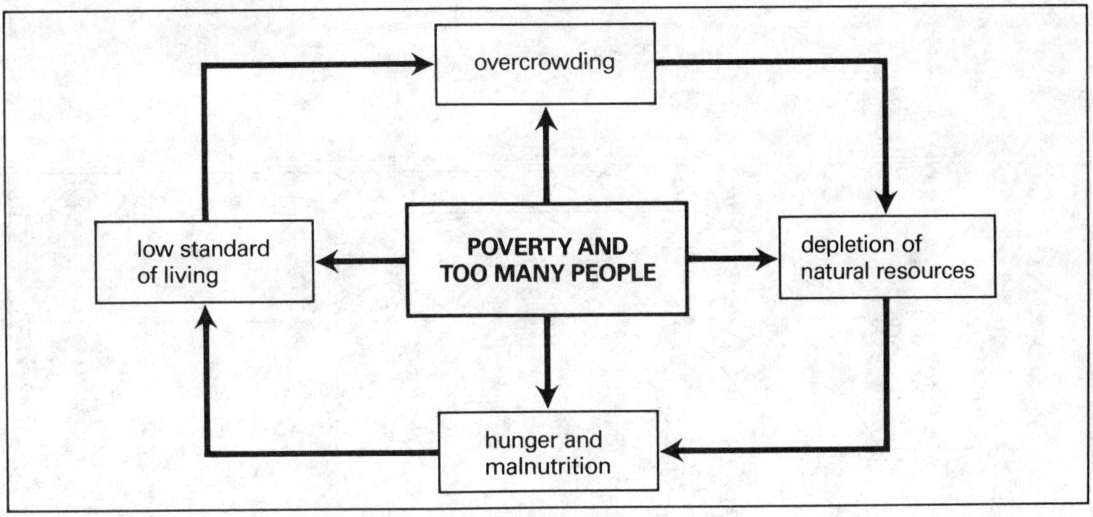

sponsor birth control programs in an effort to control the spiraling birth rate. The Chinese government provides birth control information as well as financial incentives to couples who limit their offspring to one child. However, this program has had only limited success. In China and throughout the world, family planning is difficult to achieve wherever cultural traditions or religious beliefs encourage large families.

Some people believe that improved farming methods can solve the problem of overpopulation by increasing food production to keep pace with population growth. Others believe that the world contains enough food for everyone but that it must be distributed more equitably to feed the growing population.

MAKING CONNECTIONS

DESERTIFICATION

Desertification means the change of arable (farmable) land into desert land. The expansion of deserts is primarily the result of human intervention. Two major causes of desertification are the overgrazing of cattle and the cutting down of trees. Widespread overgrazing eliminates the grass that holds the soil together to prevent erosion. Cutting down trees robs the land of another of its natural barriers to soil erosion. As the grass and trees are eliminated, the soil loses its nutrients and vitality and turns into dry land unable to sustain plant life.

Regents Tip How does overpopulation contribute to desertification?

The most dramatic example of desertification is Africa's Sahara Desert, the world's largest desert, which is expanding at the rate of approximately 50 miles per year. Countries whose fertile land once bordered the Sahara are now becoming part of the desert. These areas comprise what is called the **Sahel**, a dry region characterized by peri-

World Problems Today

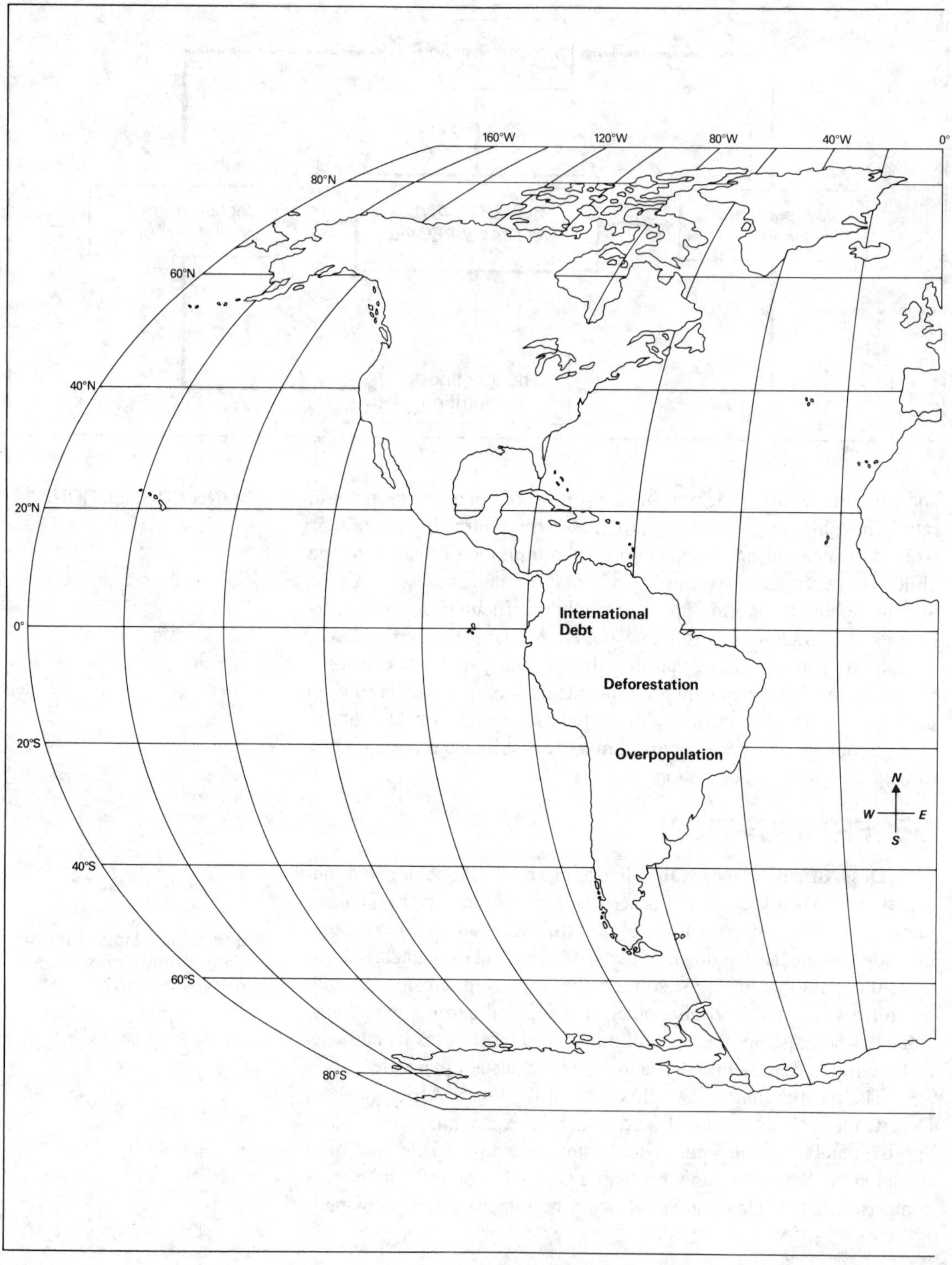

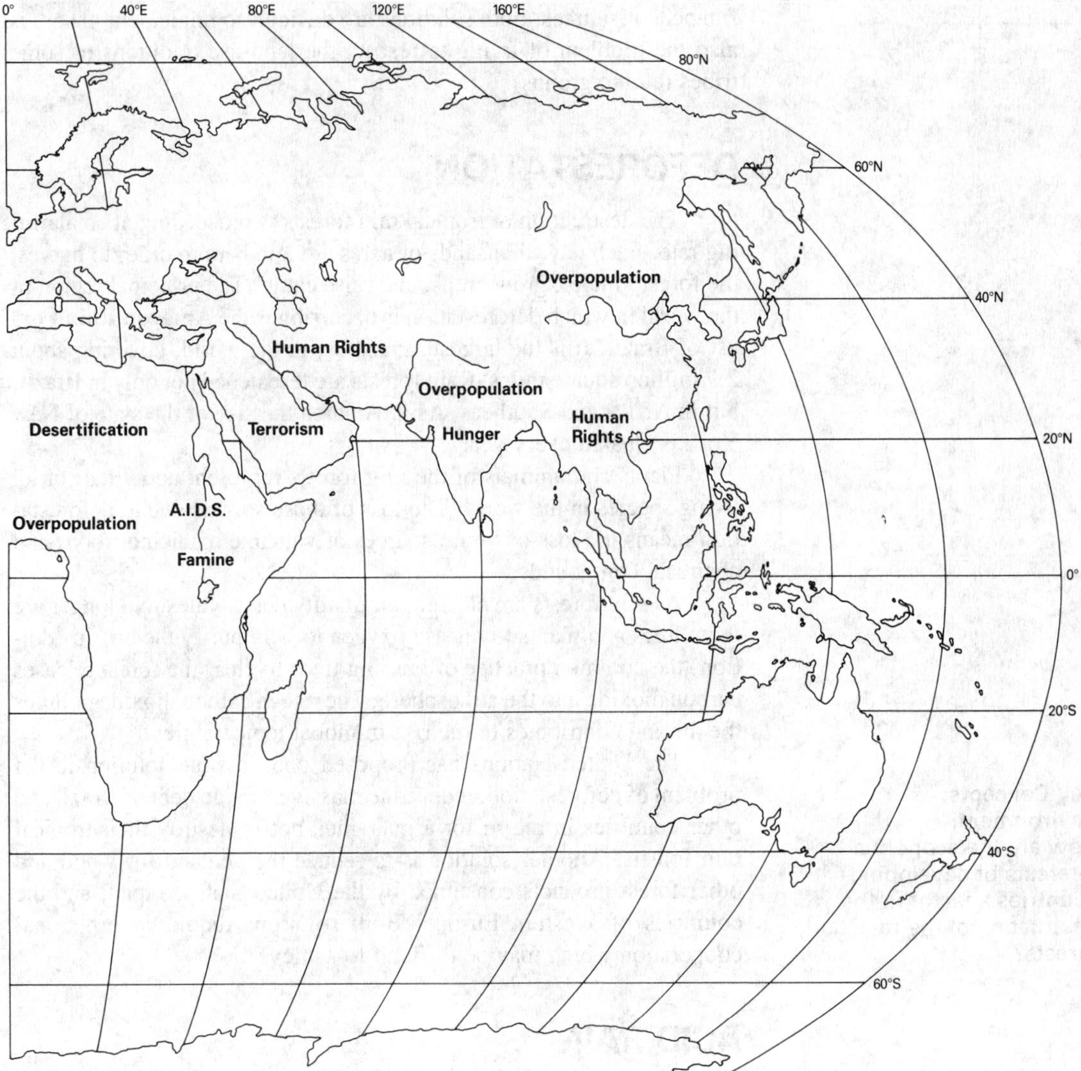
0°
40°E
80°E
120°E
160°E
80°N
60°N
40°N
20°N
0°
20°S
40°S
60°S
80°S
Overpopulation
Human Rights
Overpopulation
Human Rights
Desertification
Terrorism
Hunger
A.I.D.S.
Overpopulation
Famine

MAKING CONNECTIONS

odic droughts. In the 1970s and 1980s, a long-lasting drought in the Sahel caused wide-spread famine.

Controlling desertification involves undoing the very factors that caused it: planting trees to act as a natural barrier against soil erosion and restricting cattle from overgrazing the land. Since most African countries affected by the spread of the Sahara are nations with limited financial resources, both solutions are difficult to implement. There is also the problem of trying to restrict the land-use traditions of some tribes (ethnic groups).

DEFORESTATION

The destruction of tropical rain forests is proceeding at an alarming rate. Each day, thousands of acres are laid bare in order to harvest the forest lumber, grow crops, and raise cattle. The principal region of the world in which deforestation is occurring is the **Amazon Rain Forest** of Brazil. It is the largest rain forest in the world, covering about 2.7 million square miles. Rain forests are threatened not only in Brazil, but in Africa and Southeast Asia. An area the size of the state of New York is cleared every year.

Plants and animals of the rain forests represent about half of all living species in the world. The loss of these species due to deforestation means the loss of future sources of valuable medicine, food, and chemical compounds.

As rain forests are cleared, air quality deteriorates. No longer are there trees and plants to release oxygen to help purify the air. In addition, the common practice of burning trees to clear the forest releases carbon dioxide into the atmosphere. The rise in carbon dioxide pollutes the air and contributes to the rise in global temperatures.

Key Concepts: Environment
How are the economic interests of developing countries a factor in the destruction of the rain forests?

The United Nations has proposed one possible solution to the problem of deforestation: reduce the massive foreign debt of Brazil and other countries in return for a guarantee not to destroy their tropical rain forests. Another solution is to reduce the demand for wood and other forest products consumed by the United States, Japan, and the countries of Western Europe. Both solutions require international cooperation which may be difficult to achieve.

ACID RAIN

Acid rain is rain that contains a high concentration of acids and pollutants. The burning of fossil fuels—coal, oil, and natural gas—by factories, automobiles, and other sources releases chemical pollutants into the air. These pollutants combine with water vapor in the air to form acid rain. Scientists believe that acid rain is responsible for considerable harm to the environment. It may damage plants and animals as well as buildings.

MAKING CONNECTIONS

Since air currents that carry pollution have no boundaries, acid rain is not confined to the industrialized nations where fossil-fuel pollution originates. Acid rain is a global problem affecting many countries. In Western Europe, the destruction of large areas of Germany's Black Forest is attributed to acid rain. It is also the probable cause of the destruction of fish and other aquatic life in lakes, rivers, and streams. The same effects of acid rain are prevalent in other nations, including Canada, the United States, Great Britain, Czechoslovakia, and Poland.

Possible solutions to acid rain include restricting the amount of chemical pollutants released into the air by coal-burning industries. International agreements, such as the 1979 Convention on Long Range Trans-boundary Air Pollution, have set emission controls. Additional international agreements are needed to solve the problem of acid rain.

Key Concepts: Interdependence
How does international cooperation illustrate the concept of interdependence?

GREENHOUSE EFFECT

The **greenhouse effect** is the warming of the earth and its atmosphere caused by the build-up of carbon dioxide. Although some scientists dispute the existence of the greenhouse effect, many others believe it is a reality. Like the glass in a greenhouse, carbon dioxide traps the heat of the sun and prevents it from escaping. The rising levels of carbon dioxide in the atmosphere are due primarily to the burning of fossil fuels. Widespread burning of the rain forests and the use of chlorofluorocarbons (CFCs) in aerosol cans and refrigerators contribute to the problem. Some scientists predict that the level of carbon dioxide in the atmosphere will double by the late 2000s. This increase would raise the earth's average temperature, resulting in climatic changes that might have disastrous results.

There are several solutions to the problem of the greenhouse effect. Encourage cleaner forms of energy that are not fossil fuel based; place stricter controls on automatic emissions; and restrict the use of all chlorofluorocarbons. These solutions require international cooperation to achieve.

AIR AND WATER POLLUTION

Air and water pollution include the release of radioactive particles into the atmosphere and into the ocean and other bodies of water. In 1986, an explosion and fire at the Chernobyl nuclear plant in the Soviet Union released great amounts of radioactive particles into the air. The radiation was dispersed (spread out) into many areas of the Northern Hemisphere. That same year a fire at a chemical plant in Switzerland resulted in the spilling of 1,000 tons of toxic chemicals into the Rhine River. In the Philippines, so much cyanide has been dumped into the ocean that its coral reefs have been severely harmed.

The effects of pollution reach even the upper layers of the atmosphere. In 1974, scientists discovered a hole in the **ozone layer**, which

MAKING CONNECTIONS

lies 15 miles above the earth. The ozone layer protects the earth from the dangerous ultraviolet rays of the sun. Many scientists have concluded that people's use of chlorofluorocarbons (CFCs) and other chemical pollutants has damaged the ozone layer. Further research continues about what is causing holes in the atmosphere at both the North and the South Poles. The breakdown of the ozone layer could lead to an increase in skin cancer and eye disease as well as damage to crops and marine life.

Since the problems of air and water pollution are worldwide, solving them will take international cooperation. In 1989, an international conference was called to halt production of chlorofluorocarbons by the year 2000. In the Marpol V Treaty, several countries prohibited the dumping of plastics into the oceans by international law.

AIDS

Acquired Immune Deficiency Syndrome, or AIDS, is a disease that damages the body's natural immune system, severely limiting its ability to fight off infections. AIDS is caused by a virus for which there is no known cure. Since the 1970s, when AIDS cases were first identified in central Africa, the disease has become a global epidemic. AIDS represents one of the most serious health problems facing the world today. Possible solutions include increased research to find a cure for AIDS and educational programs to stop the spread of the disease.

SPREAD OF NUCLEAR WEAPONS (PROLIFERATION)

Key Concepts: Technology
How has the existence of nuclear weapons affected the foreign policy of nations?

Since the United States first used atomic (nuclear) weapons in 1945 to end World War II, many other nations have developed them. They include the Soviet Union, Great Britain, France, and China. India successfully tested a nuclear device in 1974, becoming the sixth nation on earth to have nuclear weapons. It is widely believed that Israel and the Republic of South Africa also possess nuclear devices. The following countries are working to develop them: Brazil, Argentina, Libya, Iran, and Iraq. Given the social and political problems of these countries, the prevention of nuclear proliferation is of vital concern for the future of the world. This issue drew worldwide attention in 1998 when India and Pakistan launched a series of nuclear tests, raising the spector of an arms race in South Asia.

After decades of engaging in a nuclear arms race, the United States and the Soviet Union began to address the problem of the spread of nuclear weapons. The two nations developed the **1963 Nuclear Test Ban Treaty** prohibiting the testing of nuclear weapons in space, above ground, and under water. This treaty was followed by the **1967 Outer Space Treaty**, the **1968 Non-proliferation of Nuclear Weapons**

Treaty, and the 1972 SALT I and 1979 SALT II treaties. The SALT (**Strategic Arms Limitation Talks**) treaties limited the numbers of offensive nuclear missiles. In 1991 the superpowers signed the **Strategic Arms Reduction Treaty** (START I), making further cuts in nuclear missiles. Two years later, the United States and Russia signed START II, which called for even deeper reductions in Russian and American nuclear forces.

MAKING CONNECTIONS

HUMAN RIGHTS

Human rights are the social, political, and economic freedoms that each individual has a right to possess. Among these are the freedoms of speech, religion, press, and assembly. People also have the right to have a decent standard of living.

Prime examples of human rights violations include the **Holocaust** committed by the Nazi's during World War II; the **pogroms** in the Soviet Union under the czars; and the **African slave trade** between Africa and the Americas. Examples after World War II include the systems of **apartheid** in South Africa, the "Death Squads" in El Salvador, the "Gulag" system in the Soviet Union, and the killing of student demonstrators in Tiananmen Square in China.

Regents Tip List two additional examples of human rights violations.

The United Nations has consistently condemned human rights violations. In 1974, the United States passed the **Foreign Assistance Act**, which cut aid to any government guilty of violating human rights. An organization called **Amnesty International** monitors human rights violations worldwide and puts pressure on governments to release their political prisoners.

TERRORISM

Terrorism is the systematic use of violence to achieve a political goal. Bombings, assassinations, and kidnappings are tactics of terrorist groups. Several groups have used terrorism to attempt to achieve their political goals. They include the **Palestine Liberation Organization** (P.L.O.), which used terrorism in an effort to eliminate the nation of Israel and create a Palestinian state; the **Irish Republican Army** (I.R.A.), Catholic groups whose purpose is to drive the British out of Northern Ireland and unify the country; and the **Islamic Jihad,** whose mission is to spread Islamic fundamentalism by attacking and kidnapping its opponents. Terrorist acts by these groups have often resulted in similar retaliatory responses. Therefore, the cycle of violence has been difficult to control.

Regents Tip List an example of how terrorist actions have produced revolutionary changes in a nation or region you have studied.

International efforts to stop political terrorism have included increasing security at airports and sharing information about terrorists through INTERPOL (the International Police Network).

MAKING CONNECTIONS

HUNGER AND FAMINE

Hunger and famine are the result of overpopulation, inadequate natural resources, and desertification. In some cases, political conflicts also contributed to the problem. For many years the African continent has experienced major famines. In 1973 and 1984, widespread famine occurred in Ethiopia. Efforts to raise money for the thousands of starving Ethiopians led to worldwide fundraising efforts in the form of the July 1985 Live-Aid concerts. International help has been provided by the United Nations, C.A.R.E., and many other relief agencies, but their efforts have not solved the problems. The answer lies with government efforts to balance population growth with proper management of the natural resources.

INTERNATIONAL DEBT

Regents Tip Give an example of how economic problems have affected the government of a particular nation.

Many of the nations of Latin America, Africa, and Eastern Europe face large and growing international debts. Much of the debt was incurred as these nations tried to pay for the drastic increase in the price of oil during the 1973 oil crisis. Since that time, these nations' debts have grown—along with their rates of inflation. Some countries have had yearly inflation rates of well over 1,000 percent. Their dependence on foreign oil also makes them vulnerable to future oil price rises. A return to political stability in all debt-ridden countries, together with some debt forgiveness for them, may be the only workable solutions to the debt problem.

Regents Questions for Practice

Essay Questions

Test Hint Question 1 requires you to use a different area for each problem chosen. Failure to follow instructions like these can result in lack of credit for an otherwise correct answer.

1. Since World War II, many areas of the world have been affected by the problems below.

Problems

Deforestation	Air and water pollution
Desertification	Nuclear proliferation
Terrorism	Human rights violations

Choose *three* of the problems from the list. For *each* problem chosen:

- Select an area from Latin America, Africa, Asia, or Europe and explain how the problem is, or has been, a concern in that area since World War II.
- Explain *one* specific way the problem has had global effects.

You must use a different area for each problem chosen.

MAKING CONNECTIONS

2. Problems in one area of the world often affect other parts of the world.

Problems

AIDS (Acquired Immune Deficiency Syndrome)

Terrorism	Hunger
Pollution	International debt
Nuclear proliferation	

Choose *three* of the problems from the list. For *each* problem chosen:

- Explain how the problem affects a particular nation or area of the world.
- Explain how the problem has become global.
- Discuss a specific effort that has been made to deal with the problem.

3. Below is a list of violations of human rights that have occurred throughout history.

Test Hint Note that question 3 has two parts, a and b. Plan your answer for each part before beginning to write. For part a, select the three human rights violations for which you can provide the best response.

Violations of Human Rights

Repression of dissidents	Forced relocation
Genocide	Denial of civil and legal rights
Destruction of cultural heritage	

a Select *three* of the violations of human rights from the list above. For *each* one chosen, describe a specific historical example of that violation, including approximate time period and place. Use a different example for each violation chosen.

b Show how a specific group or organization, public or private, has promoted the cause of human rights.

4. History has shown that certain groups have been denied fundamental human rights on the basis of their:

- race and/or religion and/or ethnicity.
- political beliefs.
- socio-economic status.

Test Hint Look at question 4, part a. What requirement does your answer have to follow?

a Select *one* of the elements above and discuss *three* specific examples of human rights violations related to the element selected. In *each* example, identify both the oppressed group and the oppressing group. Do not use the same group more than once in your answer.

b United States foreign policy decisionmakers are often faced with problems of political, economic, or military relationships with countries that violate human rights in one way or another.

Discuss briefly one such foreign policy problem between the United States and a specific country within the last ten years.

WORLD PROBLEMS TODAY

Use the facts you have learned to fill in the chart.

Problem	Where Found	Causes	Effects	Solutions
Overpopulation	China Africa India Latin A.	-Religious beliefs -lack of education -cultural factors -economic factors	-Food shortages -overcrowding -depletion of natural resources -law of standard living	-family planning -improved farming methods
Desertification	Africa-Sahara	-overgrazing -cutting trees erosion	-less farmland (Famine) -	-terrace
Deforestation	Brazil-Rain Forest	-cutting down trees for farming	-loss of O_2 -plant and animal species gone	-legislation -economic aid
Acid Rain				
Greenhouse Effect				
Air & Water Pollution				

Problem	Where Found	Causes	Effects	Solutions
AIDS				
Spread of Nuclear Weapons (Proliferation)				
Human Rights				
Terrorism				
Hunger/Famine				
International Debt				

GLOBAL REGIONS REVIEW CHART

Copy this chart and fill one out for each of the nine global regions. As you complete each chart, you will be creating a useful tool for complete Regents preparation.

Global Region:

	Major Facts
Geographic Features	
History	
Social	
Economic	
Political	

Themes	Examples
Imperialism	
Nationalism	
Traditional	
Contemporary	
Pre WW I	
Post WW I	
Pre WW II	
Post WW II	

Nationalist Groups

Organization	Purpose	Effects
Young Italy	Organization founded by Jospeph Mazzini in 1831 to work for unity and democracy in Italy. Used pamphlets, speeches, rallies to encourage unity.	*Risorgimento* (the reawakening of Italian nationalism). Mazzini wanted all Italians to be united together in one goverment. He influenced the entire Italian unification movement.
Red Shirts	Army of Joseph Garibaldi that fought for Italian unity. Began revolution in the two Sicilies.	Italy became a united country by 1871. Government was a limited monarchy under King Victor Emmanuel.
Black Hand	Serbian nationalist group that assassinated the Archduke Franz Ferdinand of Austria in an effort to get freedom and unity for the Slavic people.	Austria declared war on Serbia, thus starting World War I. The Austro-Hungarian Empire eventually was broken up, and Yugoslavia and Czechoslovakia were created.
Bolsheviks	Communist group led by Lenin that helped bring about the Russian Revolution of 1917. Executed the Tsar and his family; nationalized land and businesses.	Created the first Communist system in the world and tried to spread its philosophy. Under Stalin, Russia became a world power in competition with the U.S.
Fascist Party	Mussolini's Fascist political party (1922–1945) in Italy promised the Italians a rebirth of the Roman Empire. Followed policies of militarism, aggression, and imperialism.	Together with Hitler's Nazis, Fascists were responsible for World War II. Caused downfall of Italy; were driven from power, and Mussolini was executed.
Nazis	Hitler's fascist party were extreme nationalists who believed in the superiority of the German-Master Race. Tried to get rid of "undesirables" (e.g., Jews) and rule the world seeking *lebensraum,* or living space: ideas found in *Mein Kampf.*	"Final Solution": attempted extermination of the Jews (the Holocaust; genocide). World War II, which ultimately led to Germany's defeat and division by the Allies.
Irish Republican Army (IRA)	Catholic terrorist group from Northern Ireland, uses violence to try to end Protestant discrimination against them. Also wants the unification of Northern Ireland with the rest of Ireland.	2000 people have died in violence since 1969. Problem is nowhere near a solution. British have troops there to try to keep peace.

Nationalist Groups

Organization	Purpose	Effects
Solidarity	10 million member labor union formed in Poland in 1980. Led by Lech Walesa, it demanded economic and political reforms. It used strikes and peaceful protest. It was outlawed, and Walesa was jailed. After 1983 it became legal again and Walesa pushed for change.	Free elections were held in Poland in 1989, and Solidarity members won many seats, as well as the office of Prime Minister. Democratic and capitalistic reforms have been made. Walesa was elected President of Poland in December 1990.
Boxers	Secret Chinese society rebelled against Western influence in China in 1900. They violently attacked foreigners and their property.	An international army put down the rebellion and the European spheres of influence (economic privileges) remained intact.
Mau Maus	Secret society of the Kikuyu Tribe of Kenya. Used brutal tactics against British settlers to retain their land.	12,000 people were killed in over 10 years of violence, but Kenya was eventually given independence under the leadership of Jomo Kenyatta.
Palestine Liberation Organization (PLO)	Group that has represented the Palestinian refugees. In the past, terrorism was used to achieve the goal of a Palestinian homeland. This method failed to achieve the desired result and the PLO ultimately abandoned terrorism and recognized Israel's right to exist.	Although many Palestinians remain in Israel's occupied Arab lands (e.g. the West Bank), an agreement signed by Israel's Yitzhak Rabin and PLO leader Yasir Arafat has resulted in Palestinian self-rule in Jericho and the Gaza Strip.

Nationalist Leaders

Leader/ Country	Actions	Political/Social/ Economic Changes
Jomo Kenyatta Kenya	Leader of the nationalist movement among the Kikuyu tribe after WWII. He was a leader of the Mau Mau revolt against the British and was imprisoned by them.	He became the first President of Kenya after its independence in 1963. He ruled Kenya until his death in 1978. He removed foreign ownership and influence in Kenya, and set up a democratic government.
Nelson Mandela South Africa	Leader of the African National Congress (ANC) who was imprisoned for 28 years by the Afrikaner government for his actions against apartheid. He was released from prison in February 1990. He and F.W. DeKlerk received the Nobel Peace Prize in 1993.	Mandela was elected the first black President of the Republic of South Africa in April of 1994. He achieved his life-long goal of establishing a democratic government. Economic, ethnic and political problems remain to be solved in his coalition government.
Kwame Nkrumah Ghana	Ghana was the former British colony of the Gold Coast. Kwame Nkrumah studied at Lincoln University in Pennsylvania. After World War II he helped organize the first Pan-African Conference held in England. Nkrumah returned to the Gold Coast to lead demonstrations, and in 1957 led his country to independence. The name was changed to the traditional name—Ghana. This was the first African country to gain its independence.	Nkrumah continued to work at trying to unite the African countries together. He began to rule Ghana autocratically as economic problems continued. He only allowed one political party, and trial by jury was not present. He was a Marxist allied with China and the Soviet Union.
Jules Nyerere Tanzania	Jules Nyerere was the leader of the Tanganyika African National Union. He led the independence movement, which was achieved in December 1961. Tanganyika and Zanzibar later merged in 1964 to form the nation of Tanzania. Nyerere remained as President until 1985.	Nyerere established a single party government in Tanzania. His belief was that a one-party country could function democratically. He also practiced a system of economic socialism in his country. In 1978 a war broke out with Uganda against its leader, Idi Amin. This lasted until 1981. Nyerere left the office of President in 1985.
Leopold Senghor Senegal	Senegal became an independent country in 1960. Senghor was a leading literary figure in Africa who led the independence movement against France. He ruled Senegal as its first President from 1960 to 1980.	Leopold Singhor is most closely associated with the movement known as "negritude." Negritude is a form of African nationalism, and was a reaction to imperialism and prejudice. As a poet and a philosopher his writings all dealt with the themes of greater pride in the feelings and accomplishments of blacks in their African history.

Nationalist Leaders

Leader/ Country	Actions	Political/Social/ Economic Changes
Desmond Tutu Republic of South Africa	Tutu is the Anglican Bishop of South Africa who has advocated a nonviolent and peaceful solution to change the apartheid system in his country.	Desmond Tutu received the 1984 Nobel Peace Prize for his activities in speaking out and peacefully organizing against the system of apartheid.
Benazir Bhutto Pakistan	Benazir Bhutto, the daughter of the former Prime Minister of Pakistan who was executed in 1979, was elected to that office in 1988.	Benazir Bhutto became the first woman to head an Islamic country. In August of 1990 her opponents made charges of corruption against her, and she was dismissed by the President of Pakistan. In 1993, she returned as Pakistan's leader when she was elected prime minister a second time.
Indira Gandhi India	The daughter of Nehru, who became Prime Minister of India in 1966. Her mandatory birth control program and her 1975 "state of emergency" led to her being voted out of office in 1977. She was re-elected in 1980, and was assassinated by her Sikh bodyguards in 1984.	Indira Gandhi took steps to improve India's economy, but her authoritarian rule grew and democratic expression was limited. She was assassinated in retaliation for the assault on a Sikh holy place. Her son, Rajiv, took over after she was killed. He was assassinated in 1991.
Mohandas Gandhi India	Gandhi's policy of civil disobedience and passive non-violence created a mass movement against the British control of the Indian subcontinent. He was responsible for achieving independence for India and Pakistan from Great Britain after World War II in 1947.	Gandhi's philosophy resulted in his actions against British rule in South Africa. He left South Africa and returned to India to lead boycotts and offer non-violent resistance to British troops (e.g., the Salt March), and was jailed for his actions. He affected the civil rights movement in the U.S., led by Dr. Martin Luther King Jr. Gandhi encouraged unity among all people regardless of caste or religion.
Mohammed Ali Jinnah Pakistan	An organizer of the Muslim League, which demanded the creation of a separate Muslim state, on the subcontinent of India. Pakistan received its independence in 1947, and Jinnah became its first leader.	Jinnah was a central figure in the union of the Muslim League and the Congress Party in India that fought for independence from Great Britian. After WWII he insisted on a separate nation for Muslims, and East and West Pakistan were created.
Jawaharial Nehru India	Nehru was a key member and leader of the Indian National Congress. He was a close associate of Gandhi, and became India's first Prime Minister when it achieved its independence.	Nehru restored peace after the religious riots after independence, and set up a constitution and government similar to that of the U.S. He ruled India from 1947 until 1964. Two years later his daughter, Indira, became Prime Minister.

Nationalist Leaders

Leader/ Country	Actions	Political/Social/ Economic Changes
Fidel V. Ramos Philippines	Current leader of the Philippines, who was elected president in May 1992. Ramos served as defense secretary under former President Corazon Aquino. A retired general, he was a leader of the coup that helped oust President Ferdinand Marcos in 1986 and is credited with foiling six coup attempts against Aquino's regime.	The Philippines were ruled for 21 years (1965–1986) by dictator Ferdinand Marcos. The assassination of B. Aquino set the stage for Marcos's loss of power. Corazon Aquino tried to establish democracy and control over the enormous economic problems in the Philippines. Ramos inherited those economic problems including widespread unemployment and poverty.
Ho Chi Minh Vietnam	Ho Chi Minh was the founder of the Viet Minh, a nationalist group whose guerrilla warfare fought against the Japanese during WWII, and succeeded in defeating the French in 1954. As the leader of the Viet Cong (Vietnamese Communists), he continued until his death in 1969, to lead the armed resistance against the government in South Vietnam that was supported by the United States.	The nationalist desire of the Vietnamese to rid their country of foreign control under the leadership of Ho Chi Minh ultimately led to the collapse of the South Vietnamese government and the takeover of the country by the Communists in 1975.
Achmed Sukarno Indonesia	Sukarno was the first President of Indonesia, after it received its complete independence from the Netherlands in 1954. Sukarno was a leader of the Indonesian Nationalist Party. He declared Indonesia independent after the Japanese defeat in WWII. Fighting erupted, and agreement for independence was reached in 1949.	Sukarno started a program of "guided democracy" during his rule of Indonesia. He retained most of the power, but he depended on the army and the Communists to support him. The economic takeover failed. In 1967 General Suharto, backed by the military, took over as president. In 1998 Suharto resigned following a nationwide movement calling for him to step down. He turned over his office to his vice president, B. J. Habibe.
Chiang Kai-shek China	Military leader of the Nationalist Party (Kuomintang) in China following his father-in-law's, Sun Yat-sen, death. He fought the Communist forces led by Mao Zedong, and lost. He retreated to the island of Taiwan where he set up Nationalist China.	Chiang ruled China from 1928 until the Communist victory in 1949. Japanese imperialism in China resulted in both the Nationlists and the Communists fighting the Japanese. After WWII they resumed their civil war. Corruption, inflation, and guerrilla warfare brought about the defeat of Chiang and the Nationalists.
Sun Yat-sen China	Led a popular revolt against the Manchu dynasty. He was the founder of the Nationalist party (Kuomintang) and believed in three Principles of the People: Nationalism, Democracy, and Livelihood. He was elected President of China in 1911.	Sun Yat-sen's impact upon China is that he led a nationalist movement that ended thousands of years of rule by dynasties. He is known as the "Father of the Chinese Republic."

Nationalist Leaders

Leader/ Country	Actions	Political/Social/ Economic Changes
Deng Xiaoping China	Originally a successor to Zhou Enlai, Deng was purged during the Cultural Revolution. By 1978 Deng had become the leader of China. Deng's policies included modernization in industry, elements of capitalism, and attempts at a "one child" family policy. With his death in 1997, he was succeeded by Jiang Zemin.	Deng Xiaoping brought about many reforms for China. The Responsibility System, allowing private plots of land, and the lessening of government controls over industries was implemented. His Four Modernizations strove for improvement in industry, science, agriculture, and technology. Deng's violent crackdown on the students in Tiananmen Square in June of 1989 stopped many of the democratic reforms in China.
Mao Zedong China	Founded the Chinese Communist Party in 1921. Fought against the Japanese occupation of China during WWII, and resumed the civil war against the Nationalists. He was victorious in 1949. The People's Democratic Republic of China was ruled by Chairman Mao from 1949 until his death in 1976.	Mao's Little Red Book and the Cultural Revolution produced many changes in Chinese life. Mao's rule of China enforced traditional Communist ideas, and during his Cultural Revolution, China's economy and educational system fell behind. Mao's death marked the end of an era.
Emperor Meiji Japan	The Meiji Period was from 1869 until 1912. The Meiji Restoration was marked by the emperor's position being re-established, by the end of the shogun system and feudalism, and by constitutional reforms that called for a parliament, the Diet.	The Meiji government ended the unequal foreign treaties that existed in Japan, began industrialization, and created a new educational system. As it modernized, Japan's needs to acquire more resources led to a policy of imperialism against China and Russia, and ultimately, into World War II.
Simon Bolivar Venezuela	Called "the Liberator" for gaining independence for Venezuela, Columbia, Ecuador, and Panama from Spanish rule in 1819.	Bolivar was influenced by the ideas of the Enlightenment. He encouraged the formation of a democratic and a united Latin America under one government.
Fidel Castro Cuba	Fought against Cuban dictator, Batista, using guerrilla warfare. In January 1959 Castro and his guerrilla forces overthrew Batista's government.	After failure to obtain aid from the United States, Castro nationalized foreign sugar plantations, oil refineries, and other businesses, most of which were U.S. owned. He then aligned Cuba with the Soviet Union. He has been heavily dependent for financial and military aid from the Soviet Union, and he has attempted to export communism to other Latin American and African countries.
Violetta Chamorro Nicaragua	Owner of an opposition newspaper to the Sandinista regime, she led a coalition against the government of Daniel Ortega in 1990 and won.	Chamorro ended 11 years of Sandinista rule in February 1990. The Sandinista government was supported by the Soviet Union. High unemployment, inflation, and a national debt are all issues that Chamorro's democratic government must deal with.

Nationalist Leaders

Leader/ Country	Actions	Political/Social/ Economic Changes
Toussant L'Overture Haiti	A former slave, led the people of Haiti in a revolution against French rule in 1801. Complete independence was achieved by Haiti in 1804.	L'Overture led the African slaves who worked on the sugar plantations to fight against the French in the first war for independence in Latin America. He was captured and jailed in France, and died in 1803. Haiti became the first Latin American country to gain its independence.
Daniel Ortega Nicaragua	Was the leader of the Sandinistas, a guerrilla group who had fought against the government of dictator Anastasi Somoza. He ruled Nicaragua from 1967 until he fled the country in 1979.	Daniel Ortega established a Marxist government, heavily supported by the Soviet Union. During his term in office he helped the Communist guerrilla forces in El Salvador, prompting the United States to fund the Contras, in order to overthrow the Sandinistas. Massive economic problems brought about the change in government in 1990, with Ortega being voted out of office.
José de San Martín Argentina	He helped to win independence for Argentina from Spain in 1816. Along with Bernardo O'Higgins, San Martín joined their military forces together in 1817 and by 1818 Chile had declared its independence from Spain. The Spanish were defeated in 1821 in Peru and this was their last colony in South America.	The countries of Latin America were free and independent due in large measure to the efforts of Bolívar, San Martín, and O'Higgins. Independence for most of these countries brought local rule by a *caudillo* and a series of dictatorships until the present day.
Yasir Arafat Middle East	Chairman of the Palestine Liberation Organization (PLO). The PLO was formed in 1964 to advocate the rights of the Palestinians and to establish a Palestinian state.	Under Yasir Arafat the PLO has attempted to control Jordan, been involved in numerous terrorist attacks against Israel, and used Lebanon as a base of operations. In 1988 Arafat declared an independent Palestine, recognizing the state of Israel. In September of 1993 the PLO and Israel signed an historic treaty recognizing each other and granting autonomy to the Palestinians in Jericho and the Gaza Strip.
Mustapha Kemal-Atatürk Turkey	Mustapha Kemal led a movement to first drive the Greeks out of Turkey, and then to establish a republic. In 1923 the Ottoman Empire, with its sultan, was abolished, and Kemal set up a secular state. He was called "Atatürk" the father of the Turks.	Atatürk sought to make Turkey a republic secular state that was mostly Turkish. He required all Greeks to leave Turkey, and Western clothes, laws, and the alphabet were introduced to his people. He favored separation of religion (Islam) and the state, and he industrialized Turkey, making it a modern nation.

Nationalist Leaders

Leader/ Country	Actions	Political/Social/ Economic Changes
Golda Meir Israel	Golda Meir was an early Zionist leader in Palestine, and served as Israel's foreign minister and labor minister before being elected Prime Minister (1969 – 1974).	Golda Meir, as an early founder of the state of Israel, sought to protect the territories that she acquired in the 1967 Six-Day War. Due to the controversy over Israel's unpreparedness in the surprise attack by the Arabs in the 1973 Yom Kippur War, and the high rate of inflation, she resigned in 1974. She died on December 8, 1978. Golda Meir was known internationally as a strong leader who preserved the borders of Israel.
Gamal Abdel Nasser Egypt	Helped to lead a military coup against King Farouk in 1952. He took over the office of Egypt's President in 1954 and served until 1970. His dream was to create a unified Arab state. This movement was known as Pan-Arabism.	Nasser instituted land reform for the fellahin (farmers), set up state controls over industry, and nationalized the Suez Canal in 1956 that led to a war with Israel, Britain, and France. Egypt received a large amount of financial assistance from the Soviet Union, especially in building the Aswan Dam. Nasser died in 1970, and Anwar Sadat was elected President.
Anwar el-Sadat Egypt	Sadat was President of Egypt from 1970 until October of 1981 when he was assassinated. He had been vice president under Nasser, and with his expulsion of Soviet advisors in 1972 and the historic Camp David Accords (March 1979), he and Menachem Begin won the 1978 Nobel Peace Prize.	Sadat's attack on Israel, along with Syria in October 1973 gave Egypt some gains in the first days of fighting, and were attempts at re-creating Arab nationalism. He made a historic visit to Jerusalem in 1977 and signed a peace treaty with Israel in 1979. As a result of this, Egypt was alienated from other Arab nations, and forced to leave the Arab League. Fundamental Muslims assassinated him in October 1981 because of the treaty he signed with Israel.
Muammar Quaddafi Libya	Quaddafi took power in a coup in 1969 overthrowing Libya's monarchy. He followed Islamic fundamentalism and set up a religious state. Quaddafi nationalized the foreign oil companies, allowed one political party, and has supported terrorist groups in many countries.	Muammar Quaddafi has used the oil wealth of Libya to build up his country. The government controls the economy, and he has aligned Libya with the Communist nations. His financial support and training of terrorist groups in his country has led to conflicts with the United States.
Menachem Begin Israel	Prime Minister of Israel from 1977 until 1983. He signed the Camp David Accords with Egypt's President Sadat and President Jimmy Carter on March 26, 1979. He had been an early Zionist and a member of the Irgun, an underground Jewish terrorist group, which fought against the British in Palestine.	The Camp David Accords ended over 30 years of war between Egypt and Israel and established diplomatic relations between the two countries. Although this was a historic treaty and there were no new hostilities between Israel and Egypt after Sadat's assassination, Israel had continued difficulties with Lebanon, domestic inflation, and the building of settlements in the West Bank.

Nationalist Leaders

Leader/ Country	Actions	Political/Social/ Economic Changes
David Ben-Gurion Israel	Israel's first Prime Minister. Considered the "Father of Israel." Israel was proclaimed a nation on May 14, 1948. Ben-Gurion was from Poland and was an early Zionist leader. He was a founder of the Heganah, an underground army whose purpose was to obtain a Jewish state.	David Ben-Gurion served the new nation of Israel for the first 15 years of its existence. During that time he led its survival against an Arab attack the day after Israel was created and again in 1956. Israel experienced economic growth and democratic stability under his leadership.
Ayatollah Khomeini Iran	An Islamic jurist, or mullah, who was driven into exile by the Shah of Iran. When the Shah left Iran in January 1979, he returned and by April had declared Iran to be an Islamic republic, a theocracy, or a government based upon and ruled by religious leaders. "Ayatollah" means a reflection of God. Khomeini died on June 4, 1989.	Khomeini set up a strict Islamic (Shiite) republic in which dress, schooling, and all aspects of culture conformed to Islamic law. Fifty-two American hostages were kept for 444 days in Iran after the Shah was allowed into the U.S. for medical treatment. Under Khomeini, terrorist activites were supported, and they fought to a stalemate an eight-year war with Iraq.
Saddam Hussein Iraq	President of Iraq since 1979. Hussein came to power in a military coup in 1968, but officially assumed the presidency in 1979. He had been involved in the unsuccessful coup in 1956 to over-throw King Faisal II, and the 1958 coup against General Kassem. He studied law in Egypt and was influenced by Gamal Nasser.	Hussein killed 30 of his own party members upon assuming the presidency in 1979. He launched an attack on Iran in 1980 over the Shattal-Arab waterway, and fought to a stalemate over the next eight years. Israeli planes destroyed a nuclear reactor in 1981, and in August 1990 he invaded Kuwait. This triggered off an international crisis, with the U.S. sending over 400,000 troops to Saudi Arabia, and with the United Nations giving Hussein until January 15, 1991 to withdraw from Kuwait.
Otto Von Bismark Western Europe	Prime Minister of Prussia in 1861, under King William I, who pursued a policy of unifying the German states through "Blood and Iron" — militarism and war. He wanted to make Germany the most powerful nation in Europe.	Bismark followed a policy of "Realpolitik," taking whatever political steps were necessary to achieve his goal of a united Germany. He defeated Austria and later France in wars leading to King William I being proclaimed kaiser (emperor) of Germany in 1871. Bismark's changes and efficiency in the running of the government earned him the title of the "Iron Chancellor."

Nationalist Leaders

Leader/ Country	Actions	Political/Social/ Economic Changes
Napoleon Bonaparte France	He was a military hero during the French Revolution who seized power in a coup d'état. He centralized all power and by 1804 proclaimed himself to be "Emperor of the French." Napoleon kept France in a state of war between 1792 and 1815 with the nations of Europe, and his empire extended to Russia.	The Napoleonic Code, which recognized the equality of all before the law, and which guaranteed freedom of religion, was an achievement that would affect France and all of Napoleon's Empire. He abolished serfdom, reduced the power of the Catholic Church, lowered taxes, and drafted soldiers in his conquered lands. His invasion of Russia in 1812 failed, and in 1814 he fled to Elba, only to return to France in 1815 to be defeated in the Battle of Waterloo.
Camillo Cavour Italy	Cavour was named Prime Minister in 1852 under King Victor Emmanuel of Sardinia. Cavour was an advocate of the nationalist movement for the unification of Italy called *Risorgimento.* He was considered the "brains" of Italian unification.	He had used land reforms and had brought about rapid economic growth for Sardinia, which made it a power. Cavour united Italy under the rule of Sardinia following the Crimean War, a war with Austria, and France. Cavour died in 1861 with the last of the unification coming in 1870.
Winston Churchill Great Britain	Churchill was Prime Minister of Great Britain from 1940 through World War II until 1945. Churchill asked his citizens to offer their "blood, toil, tears, and sweat," to defeat Hitler and the Nazis.	Churchill succeeded in rallying his people during World War II, and the Battle of Britain (German bombardment of British cities) marked a turning point for the British in the war. In 1941, Churchill and Franklin Roosevelt signed the Atlantic Charter to support the right to self-determination for all countries. After the war and the Soviet takeover of Eastern Europe and East Germany, Churchill proclaimed an "Iron Curtain" had been erected in Europe. Churchill served again as England's Prime Minister between 1951 and 1955.
Charles de Gaulle France	General Charles de Gaulle had led the Free French Forces in World War II against the Nazis. He became the President of France in 1958 under the Fifth French Republic. De Gaulle remained in power until 1969.	Charles de Gaulle ended the War in Algeria in 1962, giving it independence. De Gaulle followed nationalist policies and believed that France should be a world leader. In 1966 he withdrew France from NATO, developed atomic weapons, and voted to keep Great Britain out of the European Common Market.
Queen Elizabeth I Great Britain	Leader of England from 1558 until 1603. She restored unity over England's religious disputes, making it a Protestant country with the monarch as the head of the Anglican Church.	During the reign of Elizabeth I, England became a world power with the defeat of the Spanish Armada in 1588. Elizabeth encouraged trade and nationalistic feelings. She kept England united and stable during her reign.

Nationalist Leaders

Leader/ Country	Actions	Political/Social/ Economic Changes
Guiseppe Garibaldi Italy	Garibaldi and his army of Red Shirts fought for Italian unification in Sicily in 1860.	Garibaldi led a revolt in the kingdom of the Two Sicilies and then joined forces with Cavour and Sardinia, and by 1870 unifed Italy under King Victor Emmanuel.
Adolf Hitler Germany	Hitler and his National Socialist German Workers' Party rose to power in 1933 as he became Chancellor of Germany. He established a totalitarian regime that was both nationalistic and anti-Semitic. The plans of Hitler for more "living space" (lebensraum) produced World War II.	Hitler's occupation of Czechoslovakia and invasion of Poland produced the beginnings of World War II. Hitler's Final Solution, or the Holocaust, with his massive extermination of Jews in concentration camps and his attempts at expansion (invasion of Russia) ultimately brought about the end to the brutal authoritarian regime of the Third Reich.
Guiseppe Mazzini Italy	Organized a secret society in 1831 called Young Italy, whose goal it was to work for a unified, democratic Italy.	Mazzini used pamphlets, speeches, and rallies to encourage the reawakening of Italian nationalism — *Risorgimento.* He influenced the entire Italian unification movement.
Benito Mussolini Italy	Mussolini's Facist Party rose to power in 1922. The Fascists were opposed to democracy, favored a one-party system, and supported aggressive nationalism. This meant that the state was supreme, and a totalitarian government was set up.	Mussolini's "Black Shirts" used force to stop criticisms of "Il Duce's" (Mussolini's) rule. He annexed Ethiopia in 1935, and allied Italy with Hitler's Germany. He was executed in 1945 at the end of WWII.
Margaret Thatcher Great Britain	Margaret Thatcher was elected as Britain's first female Prime Minister, and she remained as the longest elected head of Great Britian in the twentieth century until her resignation in 1990.	Margaret Thatcher was known as the "Iron Lady" for her tough positions and policies. She was a Conservative Party member, and moved Britain away from socialist practices. She removed government ownership of companies in favor of capitalism and privatization. Thatcher had been a strong supporter of nationalism and had been the first Western leader to see Gorbachev as a different kind of Soviet leader whose reforms would be drastically different. Ultimately, she lost the support of her own party, had many economic problems, such as the poll tax, and refused to go along with a single European currency as part of the European Economic Community (EEC). Her Chancellor of the Exchequer, John Major, became Prime Minister in December 1990.

Nationalist Leaders

Leader/ Country	Actions	Political/Social/ Economic Changes
Mikhail Gorbachev Soviet Union	Mikhail Gorbachev, the youngest man to take over the post of General Secretary since Stalin, took over in 1985 at the age of 54. Gorbachev began the policies of "glasnost" (openness), democratization, and "perestroika" (economic reform). Gorbachev won the 1990 Nobel Peace Prize for his part in bringing about the end of the Cold War.	Gorbachev's policies have resulted in events such as the reunification of Germany and democratic elections in Eastern Europe occurring faster than expected. The end of the Cold War was primarily brought about by the drastic need to reform the Soviet economic system. Domestic problems and republics, such as Lithuania, declaring their independence present many problems for Gorbachev's government. In December 1987, Reagan and Gorbachev signed an agreement limiting intermediate nuclear weapons.
Nikolai Lenin Russia	Lenin was the leader of the Bolsheviks, who helped to bring about the Russian Revolution of 1917. Lenin and the Bolsheviks capitalized on the slogans of "bread, land, and peace" to rally support against Czar Nicholas II. The Bolsheviks were successful in their revolution on November 9, 1917.	Lenin set up the first Communist government, and defended it against a civil war that broke out after the Bolsheviks came to power. Lenin withdrew Russia from World War I. In 1921 Lenin started his New Economic Policy with some elements of capitalism to help the economy damaged by the civil war. The government still controlled the railroads, and heavy industries under a socialist system. Lenin died in 1924, and was succeeded by Stalin, who would lead the Soviet Union on a different course.
Vaclav Havel Czecho-slovakia	Vaclav Havel, a prominent playwright in Czechoslovakia, who was active in Charter 77, a Czech human rights organization of intellectuals, was arrested in February 1989. His arrest and that of others in his group brought international protest on the Czech government for their release. They were released, and the strong governmental suppression of a protest march on November 17 led to massive protests against the Husak regime. Members of the opposition formed the Civic Forum, who pushed for democratization.	Vaclac Havel was elected President of Czechoslovakia on December 29, 1989. In 1992, Czech and Slovak leaders agreed on a plan to peacefully divide Czechoslavakia into two independent states. The country split into two separate states, the Czech Republic and Slovakia, in January 1993. Havel was elected president of the Czech Republic later that month.
Peter the Great Russia	Czar of Russia in 1682 until his death in 1725. Peter became the first Czar to leave Russia when he travelled through western Europe. Upon his return to Russia, he set up programs to westernize his country. He established schools, required nobles to serve in the government or military, and sought to expand Russia's borders.	Peter the Great obtained a warm-water port on the Baltic Sea after he defeated the Swedes in 1709. He built St. Petersburg as his new capital and "window to the west," at the cost of 30,000 peasants' lives. Because of Peter the Great, Russia would always be involved in European affairs.

Nationalist Leaders

Leader/ Country	Actions	Political/Social/ Economic Changes
Catherine the Great Russia	Catherine became czarina of Russia in 1762. She had been the wife of Czar Peter III. She ruled Russia autocratically for 34 years until her death in 1796.	Although Catherine was German by birth, she converted to the Eastern Orthodox faith when she married. She put an emphasis on education and learning that encouraged the ideas of the Enlightenment. Nobles enjoyed rights under her reign, but the conditions of both peasants and serfs worsened. Russian borders expanded, taking over Poland under Catherine's rule.
Joseph Stalin Soviet Union	Ruled from 1924 after Lenin's death until 1953. Stalin means "man of steel," and he ruled the Soviet Union autocratically, becoming an absolute dictator.	Stalin's Five-Year Plans aimed to increase the growth of industry and agricultural production. He collectivized agriculture (government run), and forced labor camps were the result for those who resisted. Stalin's totalitarian state controlled everything. He purged millions of people, who were either executed or sent to labor camps. Stalin aligned the Soviet Union at the end of the war with the Allies, and expanded Soviet control over the countries of Eastern Europe (satellites) after World War II.
Boris Yeltsin Russia	Economic and political reformer who, as president of the Russian Republic, denounced the coup d'etat attempted against Mikhail Gorbachev in August 1991. Following the resignation of Gorbachev in December 1991 and the subsequent dissolution of the Soviet Union, Yeltsin emerged as the leader of the new Russia. He has vigorously pursued economic reform with the goal of a free market economy.	Despite the autonomy of the newly independent countries of the former Soviet Union, Russia under Yeltsin has emerged as the dominant power in the group. He has continued the policy of better relations with the West begun by Gorbachev (e.g. nuclear arms reductions). Economic reforms have led to slow improvement but the country is plagued by old problems such as shortages, and new problems such as unemployment, homelessness, and crime. Opposition to his policies (e.g. devaluating the currency) resulted in an unsuccessful coup d'etat in October of 1993. Yeltsin has looked to the West for both aid and cooperation in completing the transition to free market economy.
Lech Walesa Poland	Lech Walesa was the leader of the trade union, Solidarity, that the Polish government recognized in 1980. Walesa was elected to be Poland's first freely elected President in December 1990.	Lech Walesa led the early strike of the Gdansk shipyard workers. In 1981 Solidarity pressed the government of General Jaruzelski for more demands. He jailed 10,000 people, including Walesa. With the rise to power in 1985 of Gorbachev in the Soviet Union, Jaruzelski legalized Solidarity in 1989. Free elections were held and Solidarity candidate Tadeusz Mazowiecki became Poland's first non-Communist Prime Minister. Poland was the first country in Eastern Europe to hold free elections. Lech Walesa ran against Stanislaw Tyminski in 1990 and won. Poland's economy and large debt are major problems for Walesa to solve.

Regents Examinations

This section contains additional Regents exams for you to take for practice. These are actual Regents Examinations in Global Studies that have been given in New York State.

Circle your answers to Part I in all of these exams and write your answers to essay questions on separate sheets of paper. Be sure to use the blocking technique you learned about in the Test-Taking Strategies section of this book as you prepare to answer essay questions.

Part I (55 credits)

Answer all 48 questions in this part.

Directions (1–48): For each statement or question, write on the separate answer sheet the *number* of the word or expression that, of those given, best completes the statement or answers the question.

1 One result of the Neolithic Revolution was

1 an increase in the number of nomadic tribes
2 a reliance on hunting and gathering for food
3 the establishment of villages and the rise of governments
4 a decrease in trade between cultural groups

2 One reason the cultures of North Africa developed differently from the cultures of the rest of Africa was that these areas of Africa were separated by the

1 Congo River Basin
2 Great Rift Valley
3 Sahara Desert
4 Arabian Sea

Base your answers to questions 3 and 4 on the poem below and on your knowledge of social studies.

. . . , you, African, suffered like a beast
Your ashes strewn to the wind that roams the desert,
Your tyrants built the lustrous, magic temples
To preserve your soul, preserve your suffering.
Barbaric right of fist and the white right to whip,
You had the right to die, you could also weep.

— Patrice Lumumba, "Dawn in the Heart of Africa"

3 This African poem is discussing the evils of

1 imperialism
2 communism
3 nationalism
4 regionalism

4 The tyrants referred to in the poem were

1 communist revolutionaries who took over the newly independent African governments
2 the European governments that had divided the continent of Africa into colonies
3 tribal chieftains who fought each other to control African lands
4 merchants who sought to expand the drug trade in colonial Africa

5 Mansa Musa's journey to Mecca in the 1300's is evidence that

1 the Crusades had a great influence on western Africa
2 most African leaders were educated in the Middle East
3 European culture was superior to the cultures of western Africa
4 Islam had a major influence on the Mali Empire

6 • Rebellion in the Congo during the 1960's
• Civil war in Nigeria from 1967 to 1970
• Fighting in the Sudan in the 1980's
• Massacres in Rwanda in the 1990's

Which factor was the main reason for these conflicts?

1 poor food distribution systems
2 communist interference
3 demands for land reform
4 ethnic rivalries

7 In which way has the end of apartheid had a positive economic effect on South Africa?

1 Black South African managers have increased industrial productivity throughout the nation.
2 The introduction of communism has led to a more equal distribution of income.
3 Many foreign companies have resumed trading and investing in South Africa.
4 All profits of South Africa's industries are now reinvested out of the country.

8 In China, the development of ethnocentrism was most influenced by

1 its historic reliance on foreign nations
2 a long history of democratic government
3 a strong belief in Christianity
4 its geographic isolation

Base your answer to question 9 on the cartoon below and on your knowledge of social studies.

9 What is the main idea of the cartoon?

1 Labor camps remain China's primary method of punishing political prisoners.
2 The Chinese consider the United States an imperialistic power.
3 Economic development in modern China has sometimes been achieved by ignoring human rights issues.
4 The Chinese believe that human rights abuses are also an issue in the United States.

---

10 The Confucian view of government and the Chinese Communist view of government were similar in that both stressed

1 loyalty to the government
2 the need for filial piety
3 a civil service system
4 equality of men and women

11 The results of the Opium War (1839–1842) indicate that China was

1 still a major military power
2 not strong enough to resist Western demands
3 rapidly building a modern industrial economy
4 accepting Western nations as equal trading partners

12 The Tiananmen Square massacre in China was a reaction to

1 Deng Xiaoping's plan to revive the Cultural Revolution
2 student demands for greater individual rights and freedom of expression
3 China's decision to seek Western investors
4 Great Britain's decision to return Hong Kong to China

13 Taoism and Shintoism are similar in that both religions stress

1 adhering to the five Confucian relationships
2 following the Eightfold Path
3 developing harmony between humans and nature
4 believing in one God

14 In Japan between 1603 and 1868, the most notable action taken by the Tokugawa Shogunate was the

1 military conquest of China
2 development of extensive trade with the Americas
3 formation of cultural links with Europe
4 virtual isolation of the country from the outside world

15 Between the Meiji Restoration and World War II, Japan tried to solve the problem of its scarcity of natural resources by

1 exporting agricultural products in exchange for new technology
2 establishing a policy of imperialism
3 building nuclear power plants
4 cooperating with the Soviet Union to gain needed resources

16 In the past decade, Japanese automobile manufacturers have sought to improve Japanese-American trade relations by

1 drastically lowering the price of Japanese automobiles for American consumers
2 allowing an unlimited number of American automobiles to be sold in Japan
3 importing most spare parts from Mexico
4 building an increasing number of Japanese automobiles in the United States

17 Which of these nations is located closest to the Philippines, Malaysia, and Indonesia?

1 Korea
2 Vietnam
3 Somalia
4 Pakistan

18 In India, which aspect of society has been most heavily influenced by religious beliefs, tradition, and the division of labor?

1 caste system
2 policy of neutrality
3 urbanization
4 parliamentary government

19 The "homespun movement" and the Salt March promoted by Mohandas Gandhi in India are examples of his policy of

1 industrialization
2 isolationism
3 nonalignment
4 nonviolent protest

20 Which statement best explains why India was partitioned in 1947?

1 The British feared a united India.
2 One region wanted to remain under British control.
3 Religious differences led to political division.
4 Communist supporters wanted a separate state.

21 From the perspective of the North Vietnamese, the war in Vietnam in the 1960's was a battle between

1 fascism and liberalism
2 nationalism and imperialism
3 republicanism and totalitarianism
4 theocracy and monarchy

22 One similarity between the Five Pillars of Islam and the Ten Commandments is that both

1 support a belief in reincarnation
2 promote learning as a means to salvation
3 encourage the use of statues to symbolize God
4 provide a guide to proper ethical and moral behavior

Base your answer to question 23 on the cartoon below and on your knowledge of social studies.

23 This 1994 cartoon suggests that peace in the Middle East will

1 never be achieved
2 put a stranglehold on the region's politics
3 occur only with the assistance of the United States
4 be accomplished only through negotiation and compromise

Base your answer to question 24 on the map below and on your knowledge of social studies.

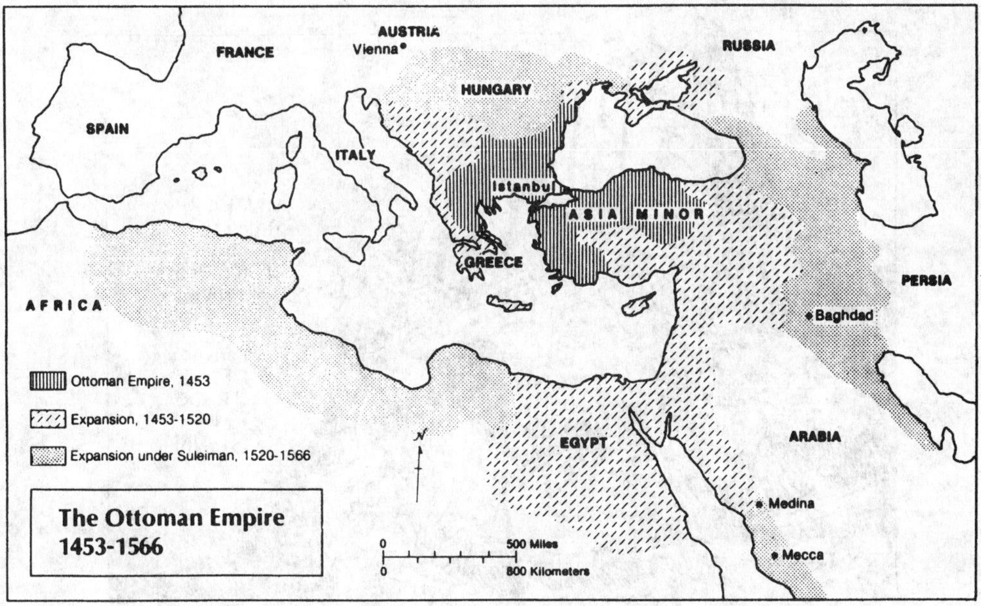

24 An observation about the Ottoman Empire in the 15th and 16th centuries is that the Empire

1 originated in Hungary
2 had a strategic location between Europe and Asia
3 was totally landlocked
4 had control over most of western Europe

---

25 One major result of the Crusades was the

1 permanent occupation of the Holy Land by the Europeans
2 long-term decrease in European trade
3 conversion of most Muslims to Christianity
4 spread of Middle Eastern culture and technology to Europe

26 One way in which the civilizations of the Sumerians, the Phoenicians, and the Mayas were similar is that each

1 developed extensive writing systems
2 emphasized equality in education
3 established monotheistic religions
4 encouraged democratic participation in government

27 One reason the Spanish conquistadores were able to conquer the Aztec and Inca Empires rapidly is that

1 these empires had no standing armies
2 the Spanish had better weapons than the Aztecs and Incas did
3 the Spanish greatly outnumbered the Aztecs and Incas
4 the Aztecs and Incas joined together to fight the Spanish

28 Which type of government has resulted from the changing political trends in much of Latin America during the 1990's?

1 monarchy
2 military junta
3 democracy
4 fascism

Base your answer to question 29 on the cartoon below and on your knowledge of social studies.

NAFTA
WHATEVER HAPPENED TO THE MAYANS ANYWAY?
I THINK IT WAS FREE TRADE WITH SPAIN...
DANZIGER

29 What is the main idea of this cartoon?

1 Ancient ruins and artifacts are often destroyed by modern technology.
2 Trade agreements are sometimes used to reestablish direct colonial rule.
3 Trade agreements sometimes have negative consequences.
4 The civil rights of native peoples are usually recognized by industrialized nations.

---

30 A major contribution of the Roman Empire to Western society was the development of

1 gunpowder
2 the principles of revolutionary socialism
3 monotheism
4 an effective legal system

31 • Man is born free and everywhere he is in chains.
• Everyone has the natural right to life, liberty, and property.
• Slavery, torture, and religious persecution are wrong.

During which period in European history would the ideas in these statements have been expressed?

1 Pax Romana
2 Age of Exploration
3 Enlightenment
4 Age of Imperialism

32 The growth of feudalism in Europe during the Middle Ages was primarily caused by the

1 rivalry between the colonial empires
2 suppression of internationalism
3 decline of the Roman Catholic Church
4 collapse of a strong central government

33 Which idea about leadership would Niccolò Machiavelli most likely support?

1 Leaders should do whatever is necessary to achieve their goals.
2 Leaders should fight against discrimination and intolerance.
3 Leaders should listen to the desires of the people.
4 Elected leaders should be fair and good.

34 European society during the Renaissance differed from European society during the Middle Ages in that during the Renaissance

1 the Church was no longer influential
2 the emphasis on individual worth increased
3 economic activity declined
4 art no longer contained religious themes

35 A major result of the Industrial Revolution was the

1 concentration of workers in urban areas
2 increased desire of the wealthy class to share its power
3 formation of powerful craft guilds
4 control of agricultural production by governments

36 According to the theories of Karl Marx, history can be viewed as a

1 succession of famines that result in the destruction of civilizations
2 repeating cycle of imperialism and colonialism
3 listing of the accomplishments of the ruling classes
4 continuous struggle between economic classes

37 • Congress of Vienna redraws map of Europe.
• Triple Entente is formed to combat the Triple Alliance.
• Treaty of Versailles calls for the creation of the League of Nations.

These events are similar in that each reflects

1 the aggressiveness of dictators
2 an effort to establish a balance of power
3 the rivalry between France, Germany, and Greece
4 the concept of mercantilism

38 After the breakup of the Austro-Hungarian Empire and the Soviet Union, new nations were formed. Which generalization accurately reflects the effect of the breakup on these new nations?

1 New nations are generally too poor and weak to become active members of the United Nations.
2 New nations rarely use their limited resources to wage war.
3 National and ethnic differences often lead to instability and violence in new nations.
4 Self-determination generally leads to democratic forms of government in new nations.

39 Which series of events is arranged in the correct chronological order?

1 The Treaty of Versailles is signed.
Adolf Hitler becomes Chancellor of Germany.
German troops invade Poland.

2 German troops invade Poland.
The Treaty of Versailles is signed.
Adolf Hitler becomes Chancellor of Germany.

3 Adolf Hitler becomes Chancellor of Germany.
The Treaty of Versailles is signed.
German troops invade Poland.

4 The Treaty of Versailles is signed.
German troops invade Poland.
Adolf Hitler becomes Chancellor of Germany.

Base your answer to question 40 on the cartoon below and on your knowledge of social studies.

40 Which conclusion can be drawn from this cartoon?

1 Many nations are interested in buying nuclear technology from the former Soviet Union.
2 Developing countries are looking to the former Soviet Union for investment capital.
3 Soviet nuclear scientists are looking for jobs in the Middle East.
4 The nations of the Middle East are spending millions of dollars on nuclear disarmament.

Base your answers to questions 41 and 42 on the map below and on your knowledge of social studies.

Eastern Europe in 1960

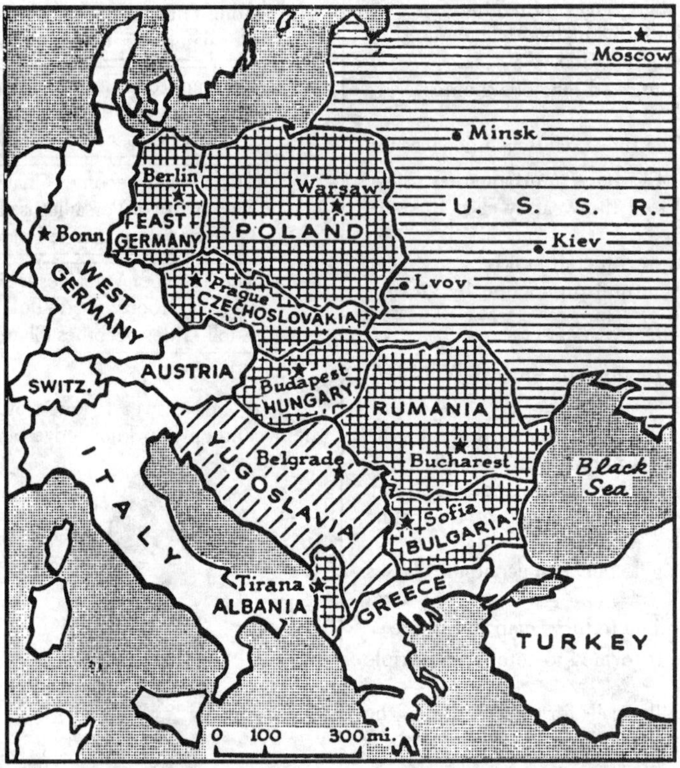

41 Which symbol is used on this map to identify nations that were considered satellites of the Soviet Union?

(1) 

(2) 

(3) 

(4) 

42 The reason that Ukraine, Lithuania, and Belarus are not included on this map is that they were

1 located outside the geographic area shown
2 republics of the Soviet Union and not considered independent nations
3 provinces in Poland and Rumania
4 members of the North Atlantic Treaty Organization (NATO)

43 When Russia was under Mongol domination, the effect on Russia was to

1 end feudalism
2 convert the Russian people to Hinduism
3 keep Russia isolated from western Europe
4 reunite the Eastern Orthodox Church with the Roman Catholic Church

44 Which headline concerning the Soviet Union refers to a Cold War event?

1 **"Yeltsin Assumes Power"**
2 **"Trotsky Forms Red Army"**
3 **"Germany Invades USSR"**
4 **"Warsaw Pact Formed"**

45 In the 1980's, the governments of both Brazil and Malaysia supported the cutting of timber in their rain forests as a means of

1 achieving economic prosperity
2 increasing the national debt
3 controlling rebellions of indigenous peoples
4 preventing exploitation by imperialist nations

46 **"Germany Will Make Reparations For WWI"**
"OPEC Supports Oil Embargo Against Western Nations"
"UN Imposes Sanctions on Iraq"

Which conclusion can be drawn from these headlines?

1 Economic measures are often designed to achieve political goals.
2 Communism as an economic system has failed.
3 Economic policies are often formulated to encourage investment.
4 Nationalism plays a small role in economic decisionmaking.

47 The code of bushido of the Japanese samurai is most similar to the

1 belief in reincarnation and karma of Hindus
2 practice of chivalry by European knights
3 teachings of Judaism
4 theory of natural rights of the Enlightenment writers

48 One similarity between the leadership of the Meiji emperors of Japan, Peter the Great of Russia, and Shah Reza Pahlavi of Iran was that they all supported policies that

1 increased the power of the aristocracy
2 introduced new religious beliefs
3 kept their nations from industrial expansion
4 westernized their nations

Answers to the following questions are to be written on paper provided by the school.

Students Please Note:

In developing your answers to Part II, be sure to

(1) include specific factual information and evidence whenever possible
(2) keep to the questions asked; do not go off on tangents
(3) avoid overgeneralizations or sweeping statements without sufficient proof; do not overstate your case
(4) keep these general definitions in mind:
(a) discuss means "to make observations about something using facts, reasoning, and argument; to present in some detail"
(b) describe means "to illustrate something in words or tell about it"
(c) show means "to point out; to set forth clearly a position or idea by stating it and giving data which support it"
(d) explain means "to make plain or understandable; to give reasons for or causes of; to show the logical development or relationships of"

Part II

ANSWER THREE QUESTIONS FROM THIS PART. [45]

1 Geographic features have influenced the historical, economic, political, and social development of many nations and regions of the world. Several of these nations and regions and a geographic feature in that area are listed below.

Nations/Regions—Geographic Features

Egypt—Nile River
Japan—Island location
Poland—Northern European Plain
Roman Empire—Mediterranean Sea
Russia—Frozen rivers
South Africa—Gold and diamond mines

Select *three* nations or regions and the geographic feature with which each is paired. For *each* one selected, discuss several specific ways that this feature has influenced the historical, economic, political, or social development of the nation or region. [5,5,5]

2 Throughout history, the ideas of leaders have affected historical events within their own nation or region. The ideas of some leaders are reflected in the quotations below.

> I cannot and will not recant anything, for to go against conscience is neither right nor safe. . . . Here I stand. I cannot do otherwise.
>
> **Martin Luther**

> The position of the inhabitants of the American hemisphere has been for centuries purely passive. Politically they were nonexistent. We have been molested by a system which has not only deprived us of our rights but has kept us in a state of permanent childhood with regard to public affairs.
>
> **Simón Bolívar**

> Dear comrades, soldiers, sailors and workers, I am happy to greet in you the victorious Russian revolution, to greet you as the advance guard of the international proletarian army. . . .
>
> **V. I. Lenin**

> Extremes must be fought by extremes. Against the infection of [Marxism], against the Jewish pestilence, we must hold aloft a flaming ideal. And if others speak of the World and Humanity, we must say the Fatherland—and only the Fatherland!
>
> **Adolf Hitler**

> [British rule] has impoverished the dumb millions by a system of progressive exploitation. . . . It has reduced us politically to serfdom. It has sapped the foundations of our culture . . . and degraded us spiritually.
>
> **Mohandas Gandhi**

> A revolution is not a dinner party, or writing an essay, or painting a picture or doing embroidery; it cannot be so refined, so leisurely and gentle, so . . . kind, courteous, restrained, and generous. A revolution is an insurrection, an act of violence by which one class overthrows another.
>
> **Mao Zedong**

> . . . did the former regime not use the radio and television to render religious beliefs valueless and ignore national traditions and customs? In any case, . . . courage, patience, virtue, . . . avoiding dependence on the powers, and . . . sensing responsibility toward the masses, have revived the [leaders] and rendered them steadfast and popular.
>
> **Ayatollah Khomeini**

Select *three* of the quotations above and for *each* one selected:

- Explain the main idea of the quotation
- Describe the historical circumstances related to the quotation
- Explain the role or the action of the leader in the historical event [5,5,5]

GO RIGHT ON TO THE NEXT PAGE. ⇨

3 Turning points are events or key developments that change a nation's history.

Nations

Cuba
Egypt
France
Ireland
Kenya
Korea
Turkey

Select *three* nations from the list and for *each* one selected:

- Identify and describe a turning point in that nation's history
- Explain why that event or development was a turning point in that nation's history [5,5,5]

4 Religion often has significant effects on different aspects of culture.

Aspects of Culture

Architecture
Dietary laws
Dress
Justice
Painting and sculpture
Social relationships

Select *three* of these aspects of culture and for *each* one selected:

- Identify a specific religion that has influenced that aspect of culture [You must use a different religion for each aspect of culture selected.]
- Discuss how the religion's teachings or beliefs have influenced that aspect of culture [5,5,5]

5 Throughout history, technological developments have had a major impact on the global community and on specific nations. Several technological developments are listed below.

Technological Developments

Atomic energy
Chemical fertilizer
Computer
Genetic engineering
Gunpowder
Printing press
Steam engine

Select *three* of the technological developments and for *each* one selected:

- Discuss one specific positive *or* one specific negative impact of the technological development on the global community or on a specific nation [Do *not* use the United States in your answer.]
- Discuss why the technological development had a positive *or* a negative impact [5,5,5]

6 Swedish inventor Alfred Nobel established a peace prize to be awarded annually ". . . to the person [or group] who shall have done the most or the best work for fraternity [brotherhood] between nations . . . and promotion of peace. . . ." In some years, the award has been shared by several individuals or groups who have worked toward a common goal.

Nobel Peace Prize Winners

Amnesty International (1977)
Mother Teresa (1979)
Lech Walesa (1983)
Elie Wiesel (1986)
Mikhail Gorbachev (1990)
Rigoberta Menchú (1992)
Nelson Mandela and F. W. de Klerk (1993)
Yasir Arafat, Yitzhak Rabin, and Shimon Peres (1994)

Select *three* winners (or group of winners) from the list and for *each* one selected:

- Identify and describe the issue for which the Nobel Peace Prize was given that year
- Discuss the specific contributions or actions of the winners in dealing with this issue [5,5,5]

7 Every society must answer basic economic questions in order to survive.

Nations

France (1200–1500)
Belgian Congo (1890–1960)
Soviet Union (1917–1985)
Israel (1949–present)
Japan (1950–present)
Brazil (1950–present)

Select *three* nations from the list and for *each* one selected:

- Explain how these basic economic questions have been answered during the time period given:
  – What shall be produced?
  – How shall goods be produced?
  – Who will use the goods produced?
- Discuss the nation's economic system in that time period [In your discussion, identify who controls the resources and who makes the major economic decisions.] [5,5,5]

Part I (55 credits)

Answer all 49 questions in this part.

Directions (1–49): For each statement or question, write on the separate answer sheet the *number* of the word or expression that, of those given, best completes the statement or answers the question.

1 Revolutions have most often occurred in nations in which

1 the majority of the people are economically prosperous
2 social mobility is encouraged
3 citizens can participate in the political process
4 social, political, or economic dissatisfaction exists

2 "This was the last morning he would have to light the fire. . . . Now father and son could rest. There was a woman coming to the house. Never again would Wang Lung have to rise summer and winter at dawn to light the fire. He could lie in his bed and wait, and he also would have a bowl of water brought to him. . . ."

— Pearl Buck, *The Good Earth*

Which type of society is portrayed in this reading?

1 ethnocentric
2 matriarchal
3 monotheistic
4 patriarchal

3 Take up the White Man's burden —
Send forth the best ye breed —
Go bind your sons to exile
To serve your captives' need;
To wait, in heavy harness,
On fluttered folk and wild —
Your new-caught, sullen peoples,
Half-devil and half-child.

—Rudyard Kipling
"The White Man's Burden"

The phrase "White Man's burden" in this excerpt refers to the

1 negative attitude of Europeans toward peoples of the non-Western world
2 advantages Europeans would gain by colonizing Africa, Asia, and Latin America
3 positive role of the Roman Catholic Church in Africa and Asia
4 challenges non-Europeans faced when trading with the Europeans

4 Which situation best illustrates a traditional practice of women in Masai society?

1 a young woman leaving her village to attend a university in the capital city
2 an educated woman returning to her village to become leader of her tribe
3 a young woman marrying and her husband giving cattle to her family as a wedding gift
4 a young mother discouraging her children from practicing animism

Base your answer to question 5 on the cartoon below and on your knowledge of social studies.

© 1994 TREVER – ALBUQUERQUE JOURNAL

5 This 1994 cartoon suggests that in South Africa

1 both the black majority and the white minority have been denied the right to vote
2 inefficient voting methods lead to lengthy delays at election time
3 only the black majority should now enjoy the full privileges of citizenship
4 recent political changes have given the black majority the right to vote

6 **"The Very First Thing You Should Know About South African Stocks and Bonds"**
"Two Leading Financial Institutions Show You Around South Africa's Banking World"
"Amalgamated Banks of South Africa: Everything You'd Expect From An International Banking Partner"

The titles of these pamphlets, available in 1994 from an American business and financial publication, reflect

1 a continuation of the international trade sanctions imposed on South Africa in 1985
2 a renewed interest in investing in South Africa's economy
3 the hazards associated with overseas economic investment
4 a belief that the banks and the bond market in South Africa are inferior to those in Europe

7 A study of the Maya, Aztec, and Inca civilizations of Latin America would show that these civilizations

1 developed advanced and complex societies before the arrival of the Europeans
2 established extensive trade with Pacific Rim nations
3 were strongly influenced by their contact with Asian and African civilizations
4 were relatively large, but not well organized

8 In Latin America during the early period of Spanish colonialism, the deaths of large numbers of the native people led to

1 a decline in Spanish immigration to the Americas
2 the removal of most Spanish troops from the Americas
3 the importation of slaves from Africa
4 improved health care in the colonies

9 One similarity in the leadership of Latin Americans José de San Martín, Toussaint l'Ouverture, Bernardo O'Higgins, and Pedro I was that each leader

1 opposed United States intervention in Haiti
2 led a struggle to gain freedom for the people of his nation
3 opposed membership of his nation in the League of Nations
4 established an absolute monarchy in his nation

10 Which statement best reflects the effect of mercantilism on the colonies in Latin America?

1 Markets in the colonies were closed to manufactured goods from the mother country.
2 Land was distributed equally between the social classes.
3 Industries in the colonies manufactured the majority of finished goods for the mother country.
4 The wealth of the colonial power increased at the expense of the colony.

Base your answer to question 11 on the graph below and on your knowledge of social studies.

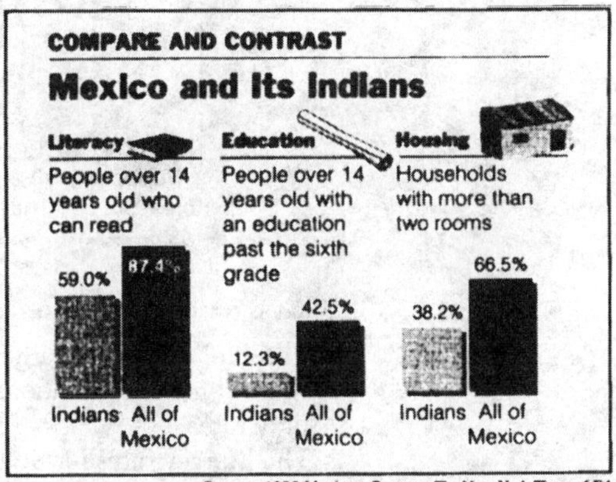

Source: 1990 Mexican Census, *The New York Times*, 6/94 (adapted)

11 According to the graph, a major problem facing Mexico is the

1 increasing infant mortality rate
2 increasing rate of homelessness
3 inequality in educational and economic opportunities
4 lack of foreign investment capital available to Indians

12 Which factor is most directly responsible for the decline in the importance of the caste system in India?

1 India's membership in the United Nations
2 disputes between Hindus and Muslims
3 India's relations with China
4 rapid urbanization

Base your answer to question 13 on the graph below and on your knowledge of social studies.

Selected Asian Countries: Fertility vs. Literacy

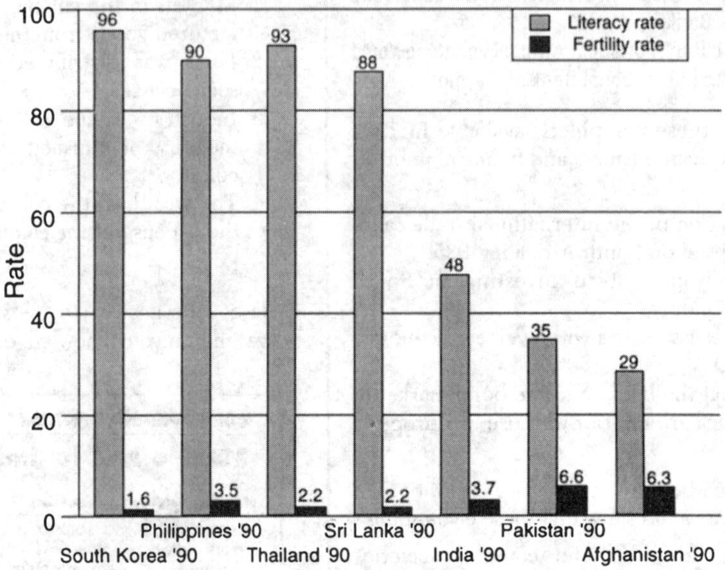

Source: *Statistical Brief*, U.S. Department of Commerce, Bureau of the Census, SB/93-18, November 1993

13 What is a valid conclusion based on the information provided in the graph?

1 The Philippines had a higher fertility rate than Afghanistan did.
2 In most instances, nations with higher literacy rates tend to have lower fertility rates.
3 The literacy rates for South Asian nations are higher than the literacy rates for Southeast Asian nations.
4 Southeast Asian nations have a higher rate of population growth than any other region in the world.

---

14 During India's independence movement, Mohandas Gandhi's boycott of British-made products was effective because the British considered India a major

1 shipping center
2 industrial center
3 market for manufactured goods
4 source of mineral resources

15 Disputes over India's control of Kashmir, Jammu, and Punjab are examples of the continuing problem of

1 territorial claims based on religion
2 Chinese claims to this region
3 terrorist actions by Serbian refugees
4 the policy of nonalignment

16 One similarity between the cultures of traditional China and traditional Japan was that

1 the educated class was held in high esteem
2 religion played a minor role in society
3 social mobility was encouraged
4 the people elected the political leaders

17 The arrival of Commodore Matthew Perry in Japan in 1853 signaled the end of Japanese

1 cultural contacts with the West
2 policies of isolationism
3 militarism in Southeast Asia
4 trade relations with the United States

Base your answer to question 18 on the map below and on your knowledge of social studies.

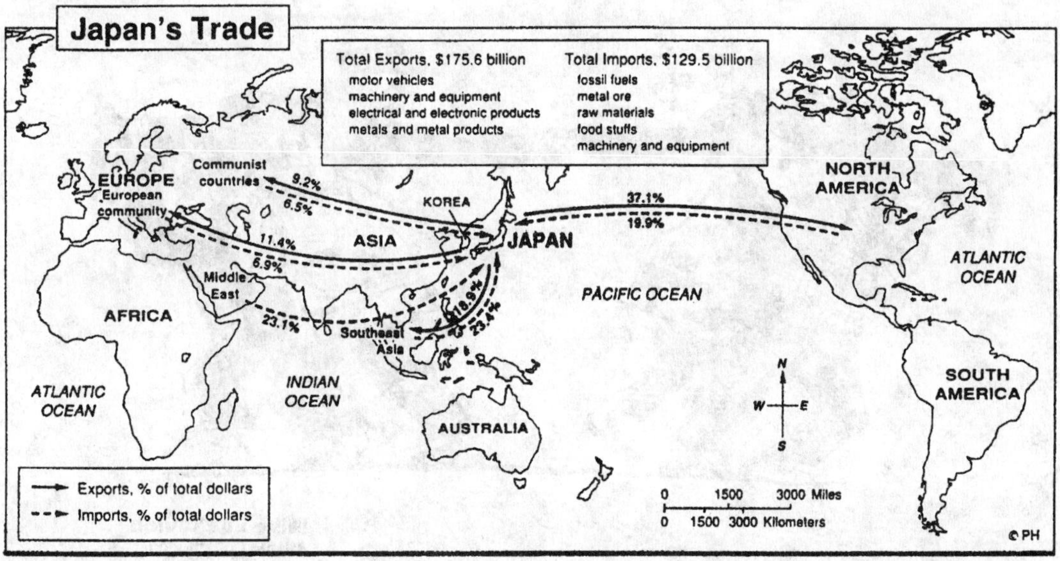

Source: *Pageant of World History*, 1990

18 Based on the information provided by this map, what is a valid conclusion about Japanese trade?

1 Japan had a favorable balance of trade.
2 Japan imported more goods than it exported.
3 Japan exported more fossil fuels than any other nation.
4 Japan traded more goods with Europe than with any other region.

19 Both Japan and China decided to limit trade with Europe during much of the 16th and 17th centuries because the Japanese and the Chinese

1 had few products to sell to the Europeans
2 held religious beliefs that prohibited contact with foreigners
3 thought European technology would hinder any effort to modernize
4 believed they would receive no benefit from increased contact with the Europeans

20 A major reason for the success of the Communist revolution in China was that the Communists

1 stressed Buddhism in their military training
2 included important businessmen in their ranks
3 promised land and power to the peasant class
4 fought successfully against the United States during World War II

21 In China, the Great Leap Forward and the Cultural Revolution promoted by Mao Zedong were similar in that both plans

1 ended dynastic rule
2 disrupted industrial development
3 encouraged capitalism
4 guaranteed human rights

22 One reason North Korea has been the focus of worldwide attention in the mid-1990's is because of its

1 nuclear weapons development programs
2 commitment to increasing political freedoms
3 development of a strong and expanding economy
4 efforts to revive communism in Eastern Europe

Base your answer to question 23 on the cartoon below and on your knowledge of social studies.

Mike Luckovich
Atlanta Constitution

23 What is the main idea of this political cartoon about the Middle East?

1 Peace between Israelis and Palestinians has little chance of succeeding.
2 Israeli and Palestinian leaders strongly oppose peace talks.
3 Israeli and Palestinian extremists have joined forces to bring peace to the Middle East.
4 The peace efforts of Middle Eastern leaders are hindered by radical groups on each side.

---

24 "If a seignior (noble) has knocked out the tooth of a seignior of his own rank, they shall knock out his tooth. But if he has knocked out a commoner's tooth, he shall pay one-third mina of silver."

— Code of Hammurabi

Which idea of Babylonian society does this portion of the Hammurabi code of law reflect?

1 All men were equal under the law.
2 Fines were preferable to corporal punishment.
3 Divisions existed between social classes.
4 Violence was always punished with violence.

25 Which type of government was established by Ayatollah Khomeini as a result of the Iranian Revolution in 1979?

1 constitutional monarchy
2 fundamentalist Islamic state
3 democratic republic
4 radical Marxist regime

26 One similarity in the leadership of Kemal Atatürk, Gamal Nasser, and Shah Reza Pahlavi is that all these leaders

1 sought to modernize their nations
2 came to power as a result of democratic elections
3 encouraged their people to convert to Hinduism
4 led invasions into Israel

27 The Middle East is of global importance today because it

1 has become a model of economic and political equality
2 allows major European powers to retain their spheres of influence
3 provides much of the petroleum used by industrial nations
4 remains a primary source of uranium

Base your answers to questions 28 and 29 on the map below and on your knowledge of social studies.

Trade Routes (13th – 15th centuries)

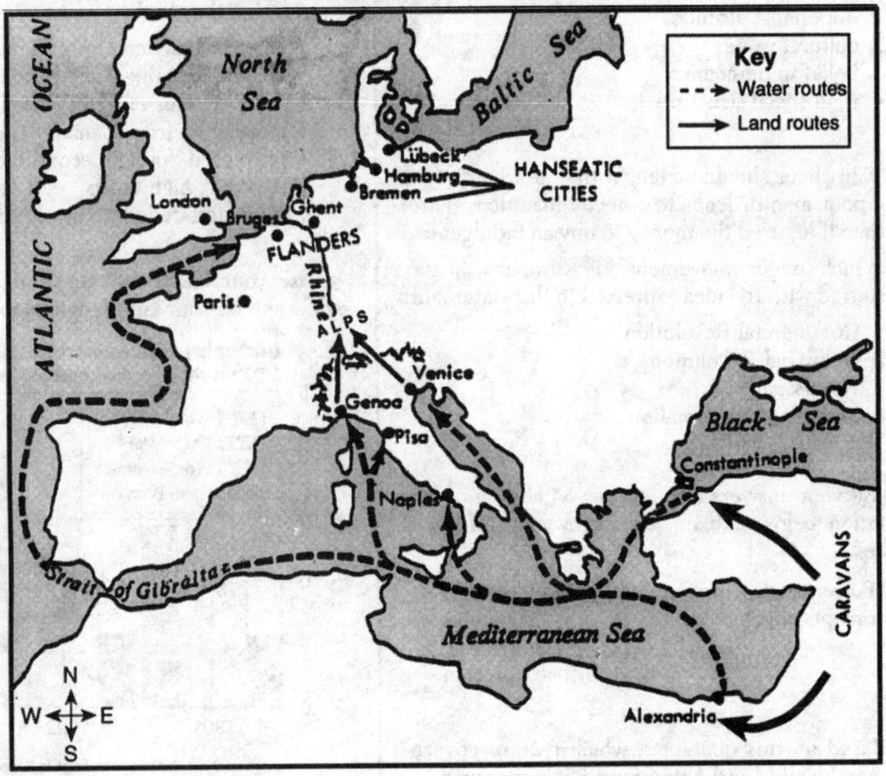

28 One reason Italian city-states were able to dominate the trade pattern shown on the map was that they were

1 centrally located on the Mediterranean Sea
2 situated north of the Alps
3 unified by the Hanseatic League
4 located on the trade routes of the North Sea

29 The development of trade along the routes shown on the map led to the

1 decline of the Greek city-states
2 start of the Renaissance in Italy
3 beginning of the Crusades to the Middle East
4 first religious wars in Europe

30 In European feudal society, an individual's social status was generally determined by

1 birth
2 education and training
3 individual abilities
4 marriage

31 After the fall of Rome, the eastern portion of the Roman Empire became known as the

1 Persian Empire
2 Byzantine Empire
3 Mongol Empire
4 Gupta Empire

32 Buildings such as the Gothic cathedrals in western Europe and the Parthenon in ancient Greece reflect each society's

1 imperialist attitudes
2 cultural values
3 belief in democracy
4 rigid social structure

33 "Christians should be taught that he who gives to a poor man or lends to a needy man does better than if he used the money to buy an indulgence."

Which major movement in European history started with the idea expressed in this statement?

1 Commercial Revolution
2 Industrial Revolution
3 Renaissance
4 Protestant Reformation

Base your answers to questions 34 and 35 on the quotation below and on your knowledge of social studies.

"Power tends to corrupt; absolute power corrupts absolutely."

— Lord Acton,
British historian

34 Based on this quotation, which type of government would Lord Acton most likely support?

1 dictatorship
2 absolute monarchy
3 totalitarian state
4 representative democracy

35 Which individual would most likely agree with this quotation?

1 Louis XIV
2 Niccolò Machiavelli
3 John Locke
4 Joseph Stalin

36 The harsh conditions imposed by the Treaty of Versailles after World War I helped lay the foundation for the

1 rise of fascism in Germany
2 uprisings during the French Revolution
3 division of Korea along the 38th parallel
4 Bolshevik Revolution in Russia

37 One similarity between V. I. Lenin's New Economic Policy of the early 1920's and Mikhail Gorbachev's perestroika policy of the late 1980's was that they both

1 stimulated agricultural and industrial production by implementing some elements of capitalism
2 reduced Russia's trade deficit by importing more grain from Canada
3 prevented foreign economic competition by imposing high tariffs
4 expanded trade into newly acquired colonies

Base your answer to question 38 on the graph below and on your knowledge of social studies.

Unemployment Rate in Germany (1991–1993)
Data is shown for the former East and West Germany

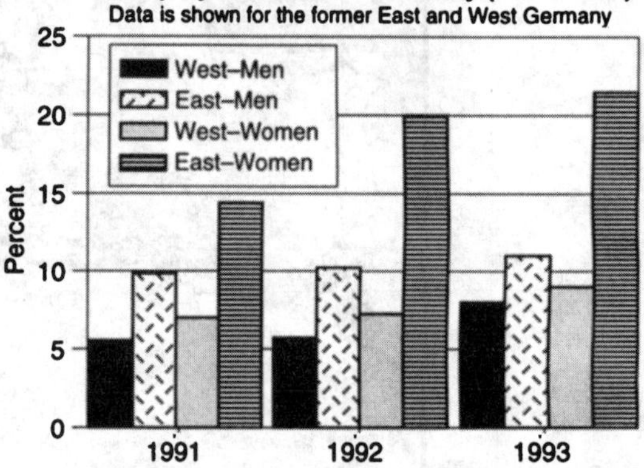

Source: *The Week in Germany* - September 10, 1993 (adapted)

38 This graph shows data on unemployment in Germany after reunification in 1990. Which conclusion can be reached, based on this information?

1 Prior to reunification, East Germany was economically stronger than West Germany.
2 Women in East Germany were poor workers.
3 A reunified Germany has had problems with steadily increasing unemployment rates.
4 The unemployment rate for women was declining in West Germany.

39 Before a nation can begin to industrialize, that nation must first develop

1 a democratic government
2 a rigid class structure
3 a strong religious foundation
4 an adequate food supply

Base your answer to question 40 on the cartoon below and on your knowledge of social studies.

(adapted)

40 In this cartoon, the cartoonist expresses his view of the United Nations policy on the situation in Serbia in 1994 and 1995. Which foreign policy would the cartoonist most likely have represented in a similar way?

1 mercantilism in the late 1700's
2 appeasement in the late 1930's
3 nonalignment in the 1960's
4 détente in the 1970's

41 One similarity between the actions of Mao Zedong, Adolf Hitler, and Pol Pot was that they all used

1 military force to build colonial empires
2 free and open elections to gain power
3 communism as a basis for their governments
4 intimidation and terror to control people

42 The Sepoy Rebellion, the Boxer Rebellion, and the Mau Mau uprising were reactions to

1 rapid industrialization
2 European imperialism
3 Mongol domination
4 World War I

43 A major purpose of the Organization of African Unity (OAU), the Organization of American States (OAS), and the European Union (EU) is to

1 encourage political and economic cooperation between member nations
2 end colonialism in member nations
3 control overpopulation in member nations
4 provide military assistance to member nations

44 Many scientists believe that the "greenhouse effect" is the result of

1 overgrazing on land in developing nations
2 using large amounts of gasoline, oil, and coal in developed nations
3 testing nuclear weapons in violation of the Nuclear Test Ban Treaty
4 using natural fertilizers to increase crop production

45 The Treaty of Tordesillas (1494), concerning Latin America, and the Berlin Conference (1884–1885), concerning Africa, were similar in that each agreement

1 provided for self-government by the native peoples
2 declared that in these areas monarchs rule by divine right
3 divided each area into European-controlled segments
4 suppressed revolts by native peoples against European imperialists

Base your answer to question 46 on the graph below and on your knowledge of social studies.

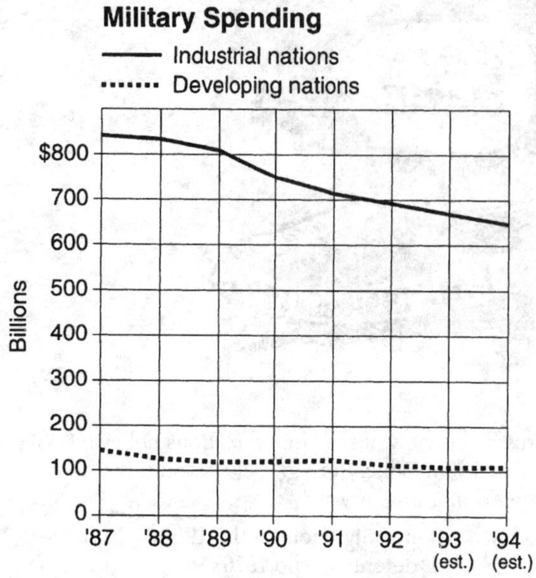

USN&WR—Basic data: United Nations Development Program (adapted)

46 Which statement is a valid conclusion based on the information provided in the graph?

1 Industrial nations increased military spending by $100 billion from 1992 to 1994.
2 Industrial nations sold $100 billion in weapons and military goods to developing nations in 1993.
3 Developing nations decreased military spending by $100 billion between 1987 and 1989.
4 Military spending in industrial nations decreased more than in developing nations from 1987 to 1994.

47 "United States Adopts Economic Sanctions Against South Africa"
"Chinese Dissidents Imprisoned After Student Protest"
"Kurds Forced To Flee Northern Iraq"

These headlines are similar in that each refers to the issue of

1 imperialist expansion
2 peasant revolts
3 human rights violations
4 isolationist policies

48 Which religious belief is shared by the followers of Shinto in Japan and of animism in Africa?

1 Only one universal, all-powerful God exists.
2 Social status in a subsequent life depends on behavior in this life.
3 Spirits are found in all natural things.
4 Waging holy wars is an appropriate way to spread religious beliefs.

Base your answer to question 49 on the cartoon below and on your knowledge of social studies.

Dilemma

Edmund Valtman. © Hartford Times.

49 After 1956, strained relations between the Soviet Union and the People's Republic of China were often caused by

1 disagreements over the meaning and goals of communism
2 difficulties encountered in constructing the trans-Siberian railroad
3 technological differences between the two nations
4 China's reluctance to admit Russian workers into Manchuria

Answers to the following questions are to be written on paper provided by the school.

Students Please Note:

In developing your answers to Part II, be sure to

(1) include specific factual information and evidence whenever possible
(2) keep to the questions asked; do not go off on tangents
(3) avoid overgeneralizations or sweeping statements without sufficient proof; do not overstate your case
(4) keep these general definitions in mind:
(a) discuss means "to make observations about something using facts, reasoning, and argument; to present in some detail"
(b) describe means "to illustrate something in words or tell about it"
(c) show means "to point out; to set forth clearly a position or idea by stating it and giving data which support it"
(d) explain means "to make plain or understandable; to give reasons for or causes of; to show the logical development or relationships of"

Part II

ANSWER THREE QUESTIONS FROM THIS PART. [45]

1 Nations often seek economic assistance from the International Bank for Reconstruction and Development (World Bank). Several nations which may seek assistance are listed below.

Nations

Albania
Bangladesh
Brazil
Haiti
Russia
Somalia
Vietnam

Select *one* nation from the list. Assume that you are a representative from that nation and your task is to write a proposal to the World Bank for economic aid.

Write a proposal that includes:

a a discussion of a specific economic or social problem faced by your nation [3]
b a description of the current political conditions, economic conditions, and/or social conditions that affect the problem [9]
c an explanation of how economic aid from the World Bank would solve the specific problem you identified in part *a* [3]

2 Throughout history, citizen protests have led to change in specific nations.

Citizen Protests

Storming of the Bastille — France (1789)
Bread Riots — Russia (1917)
Amritsar Revolt — India (1919)
Sharpeville demonstrations — South Africa (1960)
Irish Republican Army insurrections - -
Northern Ireland (1969–1990's)
Intifada uprisings — Israel (1987–1997)
Tiananmen Square demonstrations — China (1989)

Select *three* of the citizen protests from the list and for *each* one selected:

- Explain the historical circumstances that led to this protest
- Describe the extent to which the protest led to change in the nation with which it is paired [5,5,5]

3 Nations have specific reasons for entering wars. These wars often have various results.

Wars — Nations

Russo-Japanese War — Russia
World War I — Austria-Hungary
World War II — Japan
Six-Day War — Israel
Vietnam War — South Vietnam
Persian Gulf War — Iraq

Select *three* wars from the list and for *each* one selected:

- Discuss *one* specific reason the nation with which it is paired entered the war
- Explain *one* specific result of the war on that nation [5,5,5]

4 Cultural diffusion often takes place as empires conquer and establish contact with other areas or people.

Empires (centuries)

Ancient Roman (1st–3rd)
Islamic (7th–12th)
Mongol (13th)
Mali (14th)
Spanish (15th–17th)
Manchu (17th–20th)
Russian (18th–19th)

Select *three* empires from the list and for *each* one selected:

- Identify *one* area or people the empire conquered
- Identify *one* specific example of cultural diffusion that resulted from this contact
- Discuss the impact of this contact on the people or areas affected [5,5,5]

5 Geographic factors are often an important influence on specific events.

Events

Industrial Revolution in England
Catherine the Great's decision to conquer Ukraine
Napoleon's invasion of Russia
Bolívar's attempt to create a United Grand Colombia
Building the Suez Canal in Egypt
European efforts to colonize Africa
Japan's decision to invade Manchuria

Select *three* events from the list and for *each* one selected:

- Identify *one* or more geographic factors related to the event
- Explain how that geographic factor or factors influenced that event [5,5,5]

6

UNIVERSAL DECLARATION OF HUMAN RIGHTS

Article 2: Everyone is entitled to all the rights and freedoms set forth in this declaration, without distinction of any kind, such as. . .colour, sex, language, . . . national or social origin, property, birth or other status.

Article 5: No one shall be subjected to torture or to cruel, inhuman or degrading treatment or punishment.

Article 9: No one shall be subjected to arbitrary arrest, detention or exile.

Article 13: Everyone has the right to leave any country, including his own, and to return to his country.

Article 18: Everyone has the right to freedom of thought, conscience and religion. . . .

Article 20: Everyone has the right to freedom of peaceful assembly and association.

Article 21: Everyone has the right to take part in the government of his country, directly or through freely chosen representatives.

— United Nations
December 10, 1948

Since the proclamation of the *Universal Declaration of Human Rights* in 1948, violations of these stated rights have occurred in several nations.

Nations

Bosnia
Cambodia
Cuba
India
Iran
Rwanda/Burundi
Soviet Union/Russia

Select *three* of the nations from the list and for *each* one selected:

- Describe a specific example of the way in which *one* article of the *Universal Declaration of Human Rights* has been violated since 1948 in that nation [Use a different article for each nation selected.]
- Discuss *one* action that has been taken by a specific group, government, or organization to correct this human rights violation [5,5,5]

7 Religion and philosophy have played important roles in the development of a nation or region.

Religions/Philosophies — Nations/Regions

Buddhism — Southeast Asia
Confucianism — China
Hinduism — India
Islam — Middle East
Protestantism — Western Europe
Roman Catholicism — Latin America
Russian Orthodoxy — Russia

Select *three* of the religions or philosophies from the list and for *each* one selected:

- Describe *one* major belief or practice of the religion or philosophy [You must use a different belief or practice for each religion.]
- Explain how this belief or practice has affected the social, economic, or political development of the nation or region with which the religion or philosophy is paired [5,5,5]

Part I (55 credits)

Answer all 48 questions in this part.

Directions (1–48): For each statement or question, write on the separate answer sheet the *number* of the word or expression that, of those given, best completes the statement or answers the question.

1 Censorship, mass arrests, and a secret police force are most characteristic of

1 parliamentary democracies
2 republics
3 totalitarian regimes
4 constitutional monarchies

2 On a map of the world, Asia is to Japan as Europe is to

1 Great Britain
2 the Netherlands
3 Austria
4 Italy

3 Which factor most limited the development of African nationalism?

1 European support of an educational system based on local traditions and language
2 the prior experience of Africans with economic self-sufficiency
3 political boundaries imposed by Europeans that had little relationship to African tribal boundaries
4 the European practice of making decisions based on local customs

4 Which situation would best encourage economic development in most African nations today?

1 increasing the population growth rate
2 attracting investment capital
3 reducing the number of skilled workers
4 depleting their natural resources

5 In the Republic of South Africa, the slogans "Freedom In Our Lifetime" and "New South Africa" changed from promises to reality after

1 Frederik W. de Klerk took over the radical white police force
2 United Nations troops occupied the Transvaal
3 Nelson Mandela was elected President
4 the majority of white South Africans returned to Europe

Base your answer to question 6 on the map below and on your knowledge of social studies.

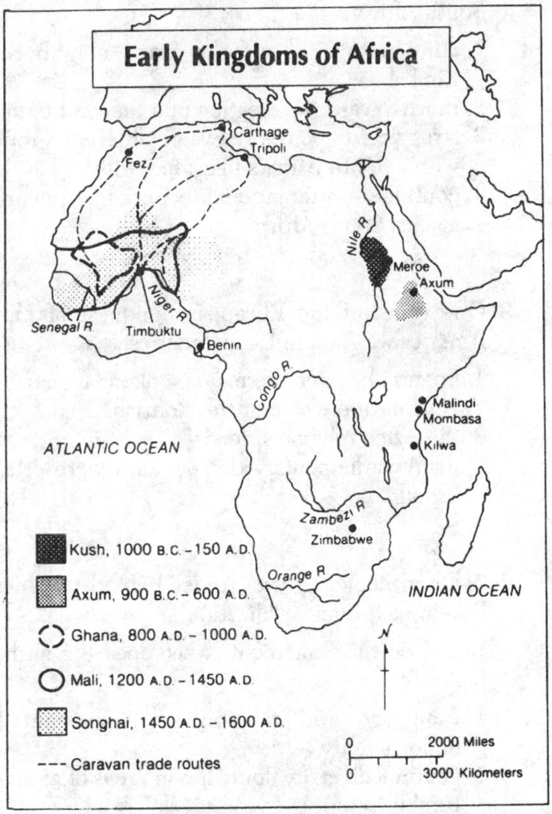

6 Which conclusion regarding early African trade is supported by the information provided by this map?

1 The kingdom of Zimbabwe grew rich from trade with Egypt.
2 The kingdoms of western Africa traded with the city states of eastern Africa.
3 The Congo and Zambezi Rivers played an important role in Africa's early trade.
4 The west African kingdoms had trading contacts with the cities of the Mediterranean.

7 Which activity is the best example of cultural diffusion in Africa?

1 weaving kente cloth in Ghana
2 using masks in traditional African ceremonies
3 discovering bronze sculptures from Benin
4 practicing of Islam in Nigeria

8 A major problem currently facing the Republic of South Africa is the

1 continuation of attacks from neighboring Zimbabwe
2 move toward the creation of a theocratic state
3 struggle for power between different groups within South Africa's black majority
4 continued international economic embargo against South Africa

9 One result of the European conquest of Latin America was that in Latin America

1 Spanish became the major spoken language
2 Native American cultures flourished
3 the Aztec religion spread
4 many parliamentary democracies were established

10 "The challenges of the Andes helped the Incas develop a thriving civilization."

Based on this statement, what does the author believe?

1 Language and religion are important to national unity.
2 Cultural diversity flourishes in areas of agricultural prosperity.
3 People can overcome the limitations of their environment.
4 Natural resources are necessary for economic independence.

11 In colonial Latin America, the main purpose of the encomienda system was to

1 insure that the Indians were humanely treated
2 provide a steady labor supply for early colonists
3 prevent slavery in Spain's New World colonies
4 build and maintain forts to repel foreign invaders

12 The major reason the Mexican Government strongly supported the North American Free Trade Agreement (NAFTA) was that this agreement would

1 raise tariffs on United States products entering Mexico
2 reduce Mexico's economic dependence on Europe
3 promote investment and economic growth in Mexico
4 stimulate trade between Asia and Latin America

13 A major problem facing many Central American nations is that their nation's wealth is

1 generally invested in consumer industries
2 controlled by a small group of landed elite
3 distributed throughout the large middle class
4 held mainly by government agencies

14 Which statement about India is a fact rather than an opinion?

1 Most Indians are happy with the Hindu practice of arranged marriages.
2 India is fortunate to have a multiparty system of government.
3 The Moguls ruled India for more than 100 years.
4 The partition of British India in 1947 helped India prosper.

Base your answer to question 15 on the cartoon below and on your knowledge of social studies.

Source: Nicolielo, 1992 Cartoonists & Writers Syndicate

15 What is the cartoonist's point of view about events in India since independence?

1 Violence has been the best way to achieve political and social goals.
2 Gandhi's beliefs have resulted in a divided India.
3 The destruction of historic monuments has been the goal of radical groups.
4 Many political activists in India have not followed Gandhi's ideas of nonviolence.

---

16 The caste system is still practiced in India today primarily because it is

1 encouraged by village customs and traditions
2 enforced by the military
3 supported by Christian and Muslim teachings
4 mandated by law

17 Korea greatly influenced the development of early Japan by

1 acting as a bridge for ideas from China
2 providing Japan with the technology for industrialization
3 serving as a barrier against Chinese aggression
4 protecting Japan from early European exploration

18 A major goal of the Meiji government in Japan was to

1 isolate Japan from other nations
2 achieve political union with China
3 establish Japan as an industrial power
4 encourage colonization of Asia by Western nations

19 After World War I, Japan attempted to solve some of its economic problems by

1 establishing extensive trade with the Soviet Union
2 expanding its influence in Asia
3 practicing the principles of Marxism
4 refusing to rely on Western technology

Base your answers to questions 20 and 21 on the cartoon below and on your knowledge of social studies.

(adapted)

20 In this 1989 cartoon, the cartoonist is expressing the view that

1 students hunger for the writings of Mao, Deng, and Marx
2 China's Government is meeting the needs and wants of its students
3 China's educational system attempts to maintain Communist ideology
4 Communist ideals have eliminated poverty

21 In this cartoon, the student is asking for information about

1 socialism
2 communism
3 nationalism
4 democracy

---

22 The outcome of the Opium War showed that in the 19th century,

1 the Chinese Army was the most highly disciplined army in the world
2 China was no longer strong enough to resist Western demands for trading rights
3 the Chinese people were successful in eliminating foreign influence
4 the Chinese Government preferred to continue the opium trade

23 Which statement best explains China's economic shift toward capitalism in the 1980's and early 1990's?

1 China's economic policies were directly influenced by the success of the Soviet economic system.
2 The Tiananmen Square massacre resulted in major economic reforms in China.
3 The success of the Cultural Revolution resulted in the increased westernization of China.
4 Communist economic policies were not meeting the needs of the society.

24 Within the past decade, the decision of the United States Government to grant China "most favored nation" status was important to China because this decision

1 allowed China to join the Southeast Asia Treaty Organization (SEATO)
2 increased China's ability to trade with the United States
3 helped protect China from a possible Japanese invasion
4 eliminated Russian influence in East Asia

25 The ancient civilizations of Mesopotamia and Egypt were similar in that both cultures

1 developed along rivers
2 used the ziggurat form for their temples
3 established trade routes to China
4 used a hieroglyphic writing system

Base your answer to question 26 on the passage below and on your knowledge of social studies.

> The Canal was dug by Egypt's sons and 120,000 of them died while working. The Suez Canal Company in Paris is an imposter company. It usurped our concessions. . . .
>
> Therefore, I have signed today the following law which has been approved by the Cabinet: Article 1 of the decree reads, "The Universal Company of the Suez Maritime Canal — Egyptian Joint-Stock Company — is hereby nationalized. All its assets, rights and obligations are hereby transferred to the Nation."
>
> Source: *World History*, Prentice Hall

26 This passage describes the decision of the Egyptian Government to

1 end trade with Mediterranean countries
2 stop building canals
3 take control of the Suez Canal
4 sell the Suez Canal to France

---

27 Jewish religious and cultural identity has been greatly influenced by

1 Ramadan and the concept of reincarnation
2 the Torah and the Diaspora
3 the New Testament and the Four Noble Truths
4 the Koran and the code of bushido

28 The major goal of many minority groups, such as the Kurds, Tamils, and Sikhs, is to

1 obtain self-rule and economic control of a homeland
2 establish a multicultural state
3 install Christianity as the state religion
4 acquire economic aid from the World Bank

29 A major effect of the decline of the Roman Empire was that western Europe

1 came under the control of the Muslims
2 was absorbed by the Byzantine Empire
3 returned to a republican form of government
4 entered a period of chaos and disorder

30 In Europe, the Crusades resulted in

1 a greater isolation of the region from the world
2 an increased demand for goods from the Middle East and Asia
3 the adoption of Islam as the official religion of many European nations
4 the strengthening of the feudal system

31 Which characteristic was common to the Golden Age of Greece and the Italian Renaissance?

1 A strong military led to national unity.
2 Written constitutions led to the establishment of democratic governments.
3 Prosperity led to the creation of many works of art.
4 Political instability led directly to the formation of unified nation-states.

32 Which system developed as a result of the Commercial Revolution in Europe?

1 manorialism
2 communism
3 bartering
4 market economy

33 According to the theory of mercantilism, colonies should be

1 acquired as markets and sources of raw materials
2 considered an economic burden for the colonial power
3 granted independence as soon as possible
4 encouraged to develop their own industries

Base your answers to questions 34 and 35 on the map below and on your knowledge of social studies.

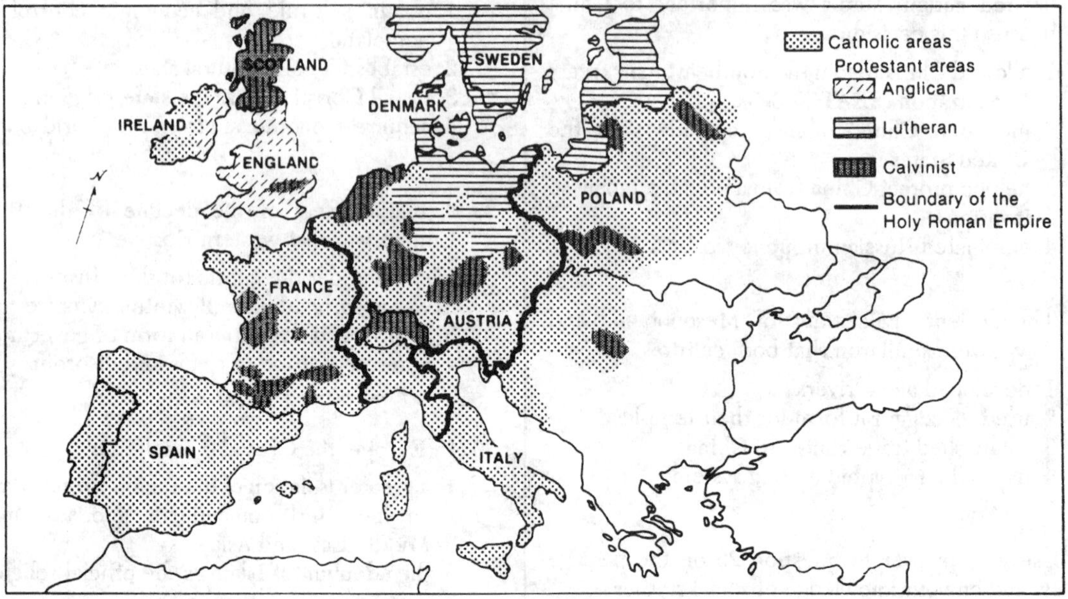

34 Which statement about the Holy Roman Empire is supported by the map?

1 The religion of the people in the Holy Roman Empire was either Lutheran or Catholic.
2 The Holy Roman Empire had fewer Protestant areas than the rest of Europe did.
3 Calvinism was dominant throughout the Holy Roman Empire.
4 Protestant influences were strongest in the northern areas of the Holy Roman Empire.

35 Which title would be the most appropriate for this map?

1 "The Impact of the Protestant Reformation"
2 "The Catholic Counter-Reformation"
3 "The Fall of the Holy Roman Empire"
4 "European Religious Unity"

36 "Revolution will occur more and more frequently in the industrialized nations as the proletariat struggles to overcome the abuses of the capitalist system."

This quotation reflects the ideas of

1 Charles Darwin
2 Karl Marx
3 Niccolò Machiavelli
4 John Locke

37 During the 1930's, the Nazi (National Socialist) Party received support from the German people because it promised to

1 abide by the Versailles Treaty
2 improve economic conditions in Germany
3 promote policies that insured ethnic equality
4 utilize international organizations to solve Germany's problems

Base your answer to question 38 on the cartoon below and on your knowledge of social studies.

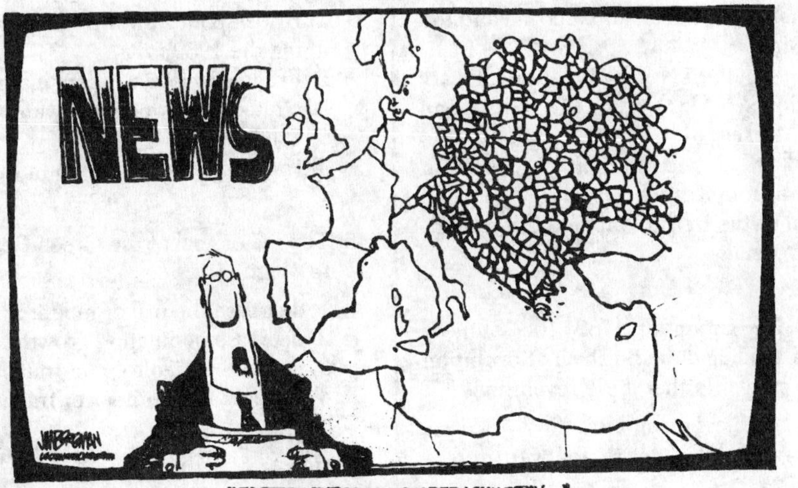

"EASTERN EUROPE SUBDIVIDED AGAIN TODAY..."

38 What is the main theme of this cartoon from the early 1990's?

1 The fragmentation of Eastern Europe continues.
2 Western Europe is investing heavily in Eastern Europe.
3 Free-enterprise zones continue to be created throughout Eastern Europe.
4 Nation-states no longer exist in Eastern Europe.

---

39 "Germany Recognizes the Independence of Slovenia"
"United States Establishes Diplomatic Relations with Croatia"
"Latvia Joins the United Nations"

These headlines illustrate the

1 collapse of the governments of these nations
2 strength of the Russian Empire
3 beginning of a united Europe
4 increase in international support for self-determination

40 Since the dissolution of the Soviet Union, the major problems in Eastern Europe and Russia have primarily resulted from the

1 high rate of illiteracy found in most of these nations
2 refusal of government leaders to allow foreign investments
3 switch from a command economy to a free-market economy
4 unwillingness of the industrialized nations to provide advisors

Base your answer to question 41 on the list below and on your knowledge of social studies.

Selected Cold War Events

Berlin blockade (1948–1949)
Premier Khrushchev's visit to the United States (1959)
Cuban missile crisis (1962)
Nuclear Test Ban Treaty (1963)
Joint Apollo-Soyuz space mission (1975)
Russian invasion of Afghanistan (1979)

41 What does this list of events suggest about the Cold War Era?

1 Throughout the period, the United States and the Soviet Union were reluctant to solve conflicts.
2 The level of tension between the United States and the Soviet Union varied.
3 Economics played a key role in causing conflict between the United States and the Soviet Union.
4 The United Nations was instrumental in reducing tensions between the United States and the Soviet Union.

42 The end of the Cold War is best symbolized by the

1 establishment of the Truman Doctrine and the Marshall Plan
2 formation of the North Atlantic Treaty Organization (NATO) and the European Common Market
3 withdrawal of United Nations forces from Somalia and from Kuwait
4 destruction of the Berlin Wall and the reunification of Germany

43 The French Revolution of 1789, the Chinese Revolution of 1911, and the Bolshevik Revolution of 1917 were similar in that these revolutions

1 were led by ruthless dictators
2 were motivated by a desire to overthrow a monarch
3 led directly to the establishment of communism
4 established a higher standard of living for the middle class

44 The amount of carbon dioxide in the atmosphere has increased in recent years. Environmentalists suggest this change is a direct result of the

1 improper storage of solid and nuclear waste
2 overcutting of forests and the increased use of fossil fuels
3 dumping of inorganic material into lakes and rivers
4 use of herbicides and toxic substances such as asbestos and DDT

45 Which policy shows that appeasement does not always prevent war?

1 British policy toward Germany in Munich during the 1930's
2 French policy in Indochina in the 1950's
3 United States policy toward Cuba in the early 1960's
4 Iraqi policy toward Iran in the 1980's

46 The major goal of the Green Revolution has been to

1 decrease the use of modern farm machinery
2 decrease population growth
3 increase agricultural output
4 increase the number of traditional farms

47 Which factor has most limited the development of national unity in India, Lebanon, and Bosnia-Herzegovina?

1 lack of natural resources
2 inability to end colonialism
3 religious and ethnic differences
4 rapid growth of industry

48
- Japan buys oil from the Middle East.
- Colombia sells coffee to the United States.
- Great Britain joins the European Community.
- Poland buys natural gas from Russia.

These statements all relate to the concept of

1 balance of power
2 interdependence
3 isolationism
4 imperialism

Answers to the following questions are to be written on paper provided by the school.

Students Please Note:

In developing your answers to Part II, be sure to

(1) include specific factual information and evidence whenever possible
(2) keep to the questions asked; do not go off on tangents
(3) avoid overgeneralizations or sweeping statements without sufficient proof; do not overstate your case
(4) keep these general definitions in mind:
(a) discuss means "to make observations about something using facts, reasoning, and argument; to present in some detail"
(b) describe means "to illustrate something in words or tell about it"
(c) show means "to point out; to set forth clearly a position or idea by stating it and giving data which support it"
(d) explain means "to make plain or understandable; to give reasons for or causes of; to show the logical development or relationships of"

Part II

ANSWER THREE QUESTIONS FROM THIS PART. [45]

1 In today's world, various global problems affect nations and regions in many different ways.

Problems

Environmental pollution
Terrorism
Human rights violations
Refugees
Overpopulation
Religious conflict

Select *three* problems from the list and for *each* one selected:

- Identify a nation or region in which this problem exists today [You must identify a different nation or region for each problem selected. Do *not* use the United States in your answer.]
- Explain *one* specific political, economic, cultural, *or* historical cause of this problem in that nation or region
- Describe *one* action that this nation *or* region *or* the international community has taken to deal with this problem [5,5,5]

2 Nationalism has played an important role throughout world history. The quotations below express various views about nationalism.

> The young men shall go forth to battle; the married men will make arms and transport food; the women will make tents, uniforms, and will serve in the hospitals; the children will prepare lint from old linen; the old men will gather in public places to rouse the courage of the warriors, to excite hatred of kings and to preach the unity of the Republic.
>
> ***Levee en Masse*, French Revolution, 1793**

> We ardently wish to free Italy from foreign rule. We agree that we must put aside all petty differences in order to gain this most important goal. We wish to drive out the foreigners not only because we want to see our country powerful and glorious, but because we want to elevate the Italian people in intelligence and moral development.
>
> **Count Camillo di Cavour, 1810–1861**

> . . . For the most part . . . the people of China can be spoken of as completely . . . Chinese. With common customs and habits, we are completely of one race . . . But the Chinese people have only family and clan solidarity; they do not have national spirit. Therefore even though we have . . . people gathered together in one China, in reality they are just a heap of loose sand.
>
> **Sun Yat-sen, 1911**

> . . . the main motive which guided me in my deed was the avenging of the Serbian people. . . . I am a nationalist. I aimed to free the Yugoslavs. For I am a Yugoslav. . . . As far as Serbia is concerned, it is her duty to free us.
>
> **Gavrilo Princip, 1914**

> . . . we insist that in Ghana . . . there should be no reference to Fantis, Ashantis, Ewes, Gas, Dagombas [all names of tribes], "strangers," and so forth but that we should call ourselves Ghanaians — all brothers and sisters, members of the same community — the state of Ghana.
>
> **Kwame Nkrumah, 1961**

> Palestine, the homeland of the Palestinian Arab people, is an inseparable part of the greater Arab homeland, and the Palestinian people are a part of the Arab Nation. . . . The Palestinian Arab people alone have legitimate rights to their homeland, and shall exercise the right of self-determination after the liberation of their homeland . . .
>
> **The Palestinian National Charter, 1968**

Select *three* of the quotations above and for *each* one selected:

- Explain the point of view toward nationalism that is expressed in the quotation
- Discuss *one* way that the attitude expressed affected the history of the society referred to in the quotation [5,5,5]

3 Religions and/or philosophies greatly influence how people live.

Religion/Philosophy

Animism
Buddhism
Christianity
Confucianism
Hinduism
Islam
Judaism

Select *three* of the religions or philosophies listed and for *each* one selected:

- Identify a region or nation other than the United States in which the religion or philosophy is practiced by a large number of people
- Explain *one* belief of the religion or philosophy [You must provide a different belief for each religion selected.]
- Describe *one* way the belief has affected the lives of its followers [5,5,5]

4 The European Industrial Revolution had positive and negative effects on certain groups. Several effects of the Industrial Revolution in Europe are shown in the diagram below.

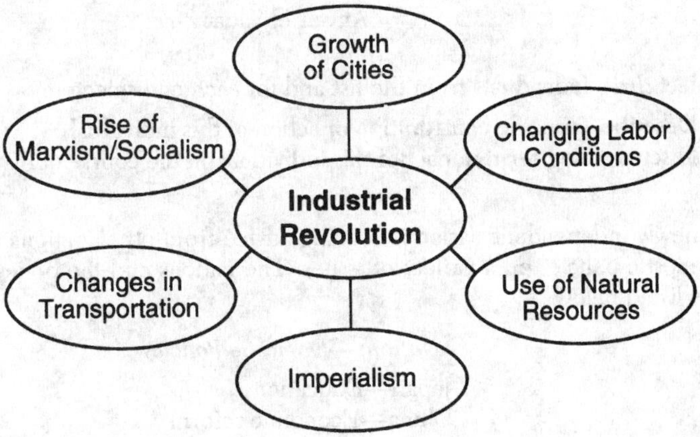

Select *three* of the effects of the European Industrial Revolution shown and for *each* one selected:

- Explain how the Industrial Revolution caused this effect
- Identify *one* specific group that was helped or harmed by this effect of the Industrial Revolution in Europe [You must choose a different group for each effect selected.]
- Describe how this group was helped or harmed by this effect [5,5,5]

5 Geography has affected civilizations and nations in many ways.

Geographic Features

Arctic Ocean
Gulf Stream/North Atlantic Drift
Himalaya Mountains
Mediterranean Sea
Monsoon
Sahara Desert
Yangtze River

Select *three* of the geographic features listed and for *each* one selected:

- Describe the specific characteristics of the geographic feature
- Explain the effect of that feature on a particular civilization or nation [5,5,5]

6 Certain individuals have had a major influence on history.

Individuals

Elizabeth I
Galileo Galilei
Adam Smith
Napoleon Bonaparte
Joseph Stalin
Ho Chi Minh
Anwar el Sadat

Select *three* individuals from the list and for *each* one selected:

- Describe a specific contribution or action of this individual
- Discuss a long-term impact of this individual on the course of history [5,5,5]

7 A newly independent nation is seeking advice from other nations as it establishes its domestic policies on a variety of issues. The nations and the policy being considered are listed below.

Nations—Domestic Policies

Japan—Education
China—Economic reform
Israel—Rights of women
United Kingdom—Health care
Brazil—Land use
India—Population policy

Select *three* nations and the domestic policy with which they are paired. For *each* one selected:

- Explain how that domestic policy was or is being implemented in that nation
- Discuss specific reasons the newly independent nation should *or* should not follow the example of that nation [5,5,5]

Part I (55 credits)

Answer all 48 questions in this part.

Directions (1–48): For each statement or question, write on the separate answer sheet the *number* of the word or expression that, of those given, best completes the statement or answers the question.

1 In most societies, works of art and architecture generally serve to
1 satisfy the needs of the leaders
2 limit the influence of religion
3 reflect the values of that society
4 express opposition to the government in power

2 Before West African civilizations had contact with Europeans, these civilizations developed
1 art that included bronze, gold, and clay sculptures
2 economies that did not rely on trade
3 one system of government for the entire region
4 social systems that emphasized the nuclear family

Base your answer to question 3 on the cartoon below.

3 Which conclusion about South Africa can be drawn from this cartoon?
1 Racial equality has been achieved in that nation.
2 In an election, most white South Africans would vote to maintain apartheid.
3 South Africans will soon vote on the issue of apartheid.
4 The majority of people favor an end to the policies of apartheid.

4 The most significant occurrence in Africa since 1950 has been the
1 decrease in the birthrate in most nations
2 decline of European colonialism
3 unification of East African nations
4 establishment of communist regimes in most nations

5 The Himalaya Mountains, the Ghat Mountains, the Deccan Plateau, and the Thar Desert are similar in that they contribute to South Asia's
1 national unity
2 cultural diversity
3 political stability
4 rapid population growth

6 The caste system influenced traditional rural Indian society by
1 limiting social and economic progress
2 promoting political instability
3 reducing the power of landowners
4 contributing to greater social mobility

7 As British rule in India came to an end, the conflict between Hindus and Muslims resulted in
1 the decision of India to allow only Hinduism to be practiced within its borders
2 Muslims becoming the dominant religious force
3 the creation of Pakistan as a separate nation
4 a large increase in converts to Sikhism

8 A lasting effect of British colonial rule in India has been the establishment of
1 racial equality in housing, education, and government
2 widespread transportation and communication systems
3 a Christian-dominated government
4 a one-crop economy

9 In India, Mohandas Gandhi's support for the rights of women and Harijans (untouchables) illustrates Gandhi's
1 ability to reach agreement with Muslim leaders
2 rejection of Western values
3 commitment to a policy of nonalignment in world affairs
4 willingness to break caste rules in the pursuit of justice

10 During the 1960's and 1970's, the primary reason for United States involvement in Southeast Asia was to
1 gain new markets for exports
2 search for new sources of oil
3 look for new colonies
4 stop the spread of communism

Base your answers to questions 11 and 12 on the statements below and on your knowledge of social studies.

Speaker A: Nationalism, democracy, and socialism are the goals of my party.

Speaker B: We must rid our country of all foreign influences and return to the true principles of communism.

Speaker C: A good ruler will rule by example, not by decree.

Speaker D: The laws of nature, not government, should rule society.

11 Which speaker's statement best reflects the ideas of China's Cultural Revolution?
(1) *A*
(2) *B*
(3) *C*
(4) *D*

12 The speaker's statement that best reflects an ideal of Confucianism is
(1) *A*
(2) *B*
(3) *C*
(4) *D*

---

13 In the Chinese Civil War (1945–1949), support for Mao Zedong's Communist forces came primarily from the
1 peasants
2 landowners
3 industrialists
4 Confucian scholars

14 In China during the 1980's, government efforts to adapt Western economic ideas resulted in
1 increased dependence on the Soviet Union
2 a slowdown of economic growth
3 increased trade with many industrialized nations
4 military confrontations with other Asian nations

15 A unique aspect of religion in Japan is that
1 most major religions have no formal priesthood
2 many Japanese practice both Buddhism and Shinto
3 all Japanese religions are theocratic
4 the current Emperor is regarded as a god

16 During the Meiji Restoration, the Japanese began to modernize their country primarily to
1 compete with Western powers
2 isolate their people from foreign influences
3 reemphasize traditional values
4 introduce Eastern religions to Japan

17 During the 1930's, Japan's foreign policy was based on the strategy of
1 territorial expansion
2 economic isolation
3 rapid consumer growth
4 democratic alliances

18 Japan's economic success during the 1980's and the early 1990's has been attributed in part to
1 the laissez-faire approach of its government
2 its policy of free trade
3 its abundant natural resources
4 the quality of its educational system

19 A lasting impact of the pre-Columbian civilizations of Latin America was that these cultures
1 influenced art and architecture of later societies
2 encouraged social mobility through education
3 developed a complex system of trade with Europe
4 developed the first representative democracies in Latin America

Base your answer to question 20 on the cartoon below and on your knowledge of social studies.

BY BABIN FOR THE TIMES UNION, ALBANY, N.Y.

20 What is the main idea of the cartoon?
1 Cuba's fishing industry is suffering a decline.
2 Cuba is isolated without Soviet economic support.
3 Castro rode the wave of world communism to a successful conclusion.
4 Castro bears responsibility for the failure of communism in Eastern Europe.

21 The primary ideas that were the basis of the 19th-century independence movements in Latin America came from the
1 Russian Revolution
2 French Revolution
3 Spanish monarchy
4 Reformation

22 A major problem that has slowed the economic development of Latin America has been
1 few good harbors
2 the abundance of resources
3 the shortage of unskilled labor
4 the lack of investment capital

23 Which situation followed both the Cuban Revolution (1959) and the Nicaraguan Revolution (1979)?
1 The role of religion was reemphasized.
2 Individual rights were guaranteed under constitutional democracies.
3 A Marxist government assumed power and promised to improve the living standards of the people.
4 Relations with the United States improved immediately.

24 Which issue currently facing Brazil has the most significant global impact?
1 the impeachment of the President
2 immigration from European nations
3 a surplus of skilled labor
4 the destruction of rain forests in the Amazon basin

25 One way in which the Seljuk Turks, Mongols, and Crusaders were similar is that they all
1 invaded the Middle East and affected its culture
2 succeeded in bringing democracy to the Middle East
3 moved through the Middle East as nomadic groups
4 established permanent empires in the Middle East

26 Since World War II, the reason the Persian Gulf region has become increasingly important to many industrialized nations is that
1 Egypt has undergone rapid modernization
2 Israel has given economic assistance to Syria and Saudi Arabia
3 Western nations have refused to trade with the Middle East
4 the economic strength of the oil-producing nations has increased

27 The primary goal of the Palestine Liberation Organization (PLO) has been to
1 establish an independent state for Palestinian Arabs
2 settle disputes between Shiite and Sunni Muslims
3 control the Organization of Petroleum Exporting Countries (OPEC)
4 seize control of the Suez Canal

28 The Hejira, Mohammed's journey from Mecca to Medina in A.D. 622, is important to Muslims because the journey
1 resulted in Mohammed's early death
2 ended Mohammed's attempts to spread Islam throughout Arabia
3 established Byzantine rule throughout the region
4 signified the establishment of the Islamic faith

29 During the Middle Ages, Europeans did not eat potatoes or corn because these vegetables
1 were forbidden by the Catholic Church for religious reasons
2 had not yet been introduced to Europe from the New World
3 were believed to be poisonous
4 were too expensive to import from China

30 In English history, the Magna Carta (1215), the Petition of Right (1628), and the Bill of Rights (1689) all reinforced the concept of
1 a limited monarchy
2 religious toleration
3 a laissez-faire economy
4 universal suffrage

31 Which was a major characteristic of the Renaissance?
1 conformity
2 humanism
3 mysticism
4 obedience

32 The best example of the success of nationalism in Europe is the
1 development of socialism in France
2 Industrial Revolution in Great Britain
3 establishment of the Common Market
4 unification of Germany

33 Which economic enterprise would Adam Smith most favor?
1 privately owned factory in France
2 government-run railroad in Africa
3 medieval manor in Europe
4 commune in Communist China

34 The primary purpose of the European Union (European Community) is to
1 create a central location for the distribution of goods
2 force Eastern European nations to change their trading partners
3 establish a tariff-free flow of goods between member nations
4 reduce European dependence on foreign oil reserves

Base your answer to question 35 on the time line below and on your knowledge of social studies.

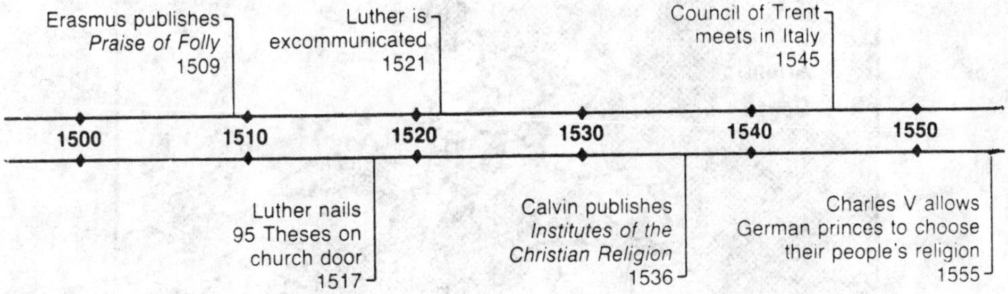

35 Which period of European history is represented by this time line?
1 Enlightenment
2 Middle Ages
3 Reformation
4 Commercial Revolution

---

36 Karl Marx and Friedrich Engels developed a theory that economic conditions would significantly improve for the working class only when
1 governments accepted the capitalist system
2 workers negotiated with the capitalists
3 the bourgeoisie became the ruling class
4 workers controlled the means of production

37 One similarity between Otto von Bismarck and Adolf Hitler was that each
1 formed an alliance with Japan during a world war
2 used warfare as an instrument of national policy
3 followed a policy of nonalignment in foreign affairs
4 supported communist ideals

38 The revolt in Hungary (1956), the demonstrations in Czechoslovakia (1968), and the formation of Solidarity in Poland (1980's) are similar in that they
1 were movements to restore the power of the aristocracy
2 were tolerated by the Communist leaders, who accepted the need for change
3 represented a challenge to Communist leadership
4 represented attempts to rid these countries of Western ideas and influence

39 Under Joseph Stalin, the Soviet Union emphasized centralized economic planning and five-year plans primarily to
1 produce more consumer goods
2 expand exports
3 create a demand for high-quality imports
4 develop heavy industry

40 During the late 1980's in the Soviet Union, the policy of perestroika was an attempt to solve economic problems by
1 introducing elements of capitalism into the Soviet economy
2 limiting imports into the Soviet Union
3 relying more heavily on central planning of the Soviet economy
4 cutting back the amount of credit given to small businesses

41 One result of the collapse of the Soviet Union has been that
1 some former republics have reorganized the Warsaw Pact
2 ethnic violence has broken out in some regions
3 an era of peace and stability has emerged in most of the former republics
4 the republics have made an easy transition to a market economy

Base your answer to question 42 on the map below and on your knowledge of social studies.

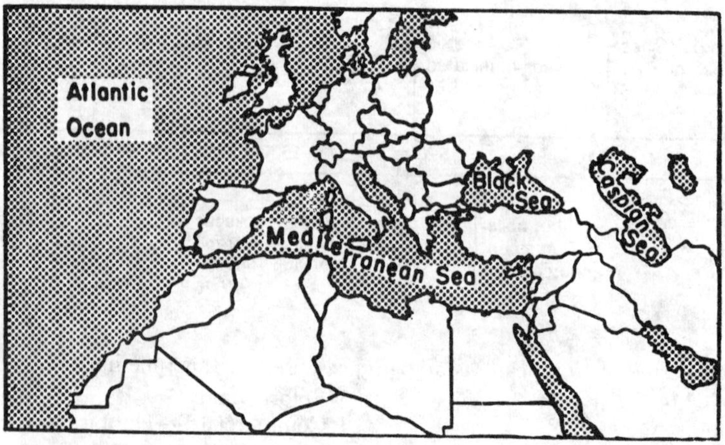

42 One way to update this map to the present day would be to
1 indicate the European colonies in North Africa
2 show the annexation of Austria and Poland by Germany
3 remove all political boundaries in the Middle East
4 draw in national boundaries for the new nations in Eastern Europe

43 The societies of traditional China, feudal Japan, and czarist Russia were all characterized by
1 a rigid class structure
2 much interaction with other cultures
3 great economic change
4 rapidly changing social values

44 Peter the Great of Russia, Kemal Atatürk of Turkey, and Shah Pahlavi of Iran were similar in that in their nations they
1 restored feudalism
2 established programs of westernization
3 instituted democratic governments
4 allowed foreign occupation

45 The location of seaports and the abundance of natural resources such as hardwoods, rubber, and spices were factors that led to
1 the use of trans-Saharan trade routes by early African empires
2 the invasion of Korea and Manchuria by Japan
3 European imperialism in Southeast Asia
4 Russian expansion into Siberia

46 Which idea did Napoleon Bonaparte, Sun Yat-sen, and Simón Bolívar have in common?
1 divine right
2 nationalism
3 totalitarianism
4 nonviolence

47 **"Russia Takes Soviet Union Seat"**
"Taiwan (R.O.C.) Ousted in Favor of People's Republic"
"Baltic Republics Join as Full Members"

These headlines best illustrate that the United Nations
1 is usually dominated by industrialized countries
2 generally relies on the use of force to enforce its decisions
3 responds to changing political conditions
4 permits developing nations to block the proposals of Western nations

48 The treatment of intellectuals under the rule of the Khmer Rouge, of the Jews in Europe during World War II, and of the Armenians in the Ottoman Empire are examples of
1 cultural diffusion
2 fundamentalism
3 modernization
4 genocide

Answers to the following questions are to be written on paper provided by the school.

Students Please Note:

In developing your answers to Part II, be sure to

(1) include specific factual information and evidence whenever possible
(2) keep to the questions asked; do not go off on tangents
(3) avoid overgeneralizations or sweeping statements without sufficient proof; do not overstate your case
(4) keep these general definitions in mind:

(a) discuss means "to make observations about something using facts, reasoning, and argument; to present in some detail"
(b) describe means "to illustrate something in words or tell about it"
(c) show means "to point out; to set forth clearly a position or idea by stating it and giving data which support it"
(d) explain means "to make plain or understandable; to give reasons for or causes of; to show the logical development or relationships of"

Part II

ANSWER THREE QUESTIONS FROM THIS PART. [45]

1 Geographic factors have had both positive and negative influences on specific nations and regions.

Geographic Factors

Mountains
Rivers
Deserts
Island location
Monsoons
Coastlines
Mineral resources

Choose *three* geographic factors from the list and for *each* one chosen, identify by name a specific factor in a nation or region and discuss *one* positive *or one* negative effect this factor has had on the nation or region. [Use a different nation or region for each geographic factor identified, and state whether the effect is positive *or* negative. Do *not* use the United States in your answer.] [5,5,5]

2 Groups throughout history have experienced violations of their human rights.

Groups

Christians in the Roman Empire
Serfs in medieval Europe
Native Americans in Latin America
Jews in Russia
Blacks in South Africa
Student demonstrators in China
Kurds in Iraq

Select *three* groups from the list and for *each* group selected:

- Describe *one* specific way the group's rights have been violated
- Discuss a social, political, *or* economic effect these violations had on the group [5,5,5]

3 Individuals have played important leadership roles throughout history.

Leaders

Elizabeth I
Louis XIV
Catherine the Great
Ho Chi Minh
Deng Xiaoping
Nelson Mandela

Select *three* leaders from the list and for *each* one selected:

- Identify the nation with which each leader is associated
- Explain *one* important political, economic, *or* social impact the leader had on that nation
- Discuss the way in which this impact affected another nation or region [5,5,5]

4 Religious beliefs affect the lives of the followers of that religion.

Religions

Buddhism
Christianity
Hinduism
Islam
Judaism
Taoism

Choose *three* religions from the list and for *each* one chosen:

- Explain *two* major beliefs of the religion
- Discuss how this religion has affected the political, economic, *or* social life of its followers [5,5,5]

5 Since the end of World War II, changes have taken place within various nations or regions. These changes have affected many aspects of life in those nations or regions.

Changes — Nations/Regions

Urbanization — Latin America
Agricultural technology — India
Family life — Japan
Role of women — Iran
Political loyalties — Africa
Family planning — China
Ownership of property — Russia

Choose *three* changes from the list and for *each* one chosen:

- Describe the change that has occurred in the nation or region with which it is paired
- Explain *one* reason for this change [5,5,5]

6 In the 1990's, conflicts have threatened peace in many nations or areas of the world.

Nations/Areas

Haiti
Korea
Nigeria
Northern Ireland
Persian Gulf
Former Soviet Union

Select *three* of the nations or areas from the list and for *each* one selected:

- Identify a major cause of the conflict in that nation or area in the 1990's [Use a different cause for each conflict.]
- Identify *two* opposing groups involved in the conflict and discuss the positions of these groups [5,5,5]

7 Nations today continue to face various problems.

Problems

Pollution
One-crop economy
Government instability
Foreign intervention
Foreign debt
Health care

a Choose *three* problems from the list and for *each* problem chosen, identify a nation that is facing this problem and describe a specific cause of this problem in that nation. [Use a different nation when discussing each problem. Do *not* use the United States.] [4,4,4]

b For *one* of the problems chosen in part *a*, discuss *one* specific way nations and/or groups have cooperated to try to solve the problem. [3]

Glossary

absolute monarch: ruler who has complete authority over the government and the lives of the people

absolutism: the belief that monarchs hold supreme power and are responsible only to God

acropolis: (uh KRAPH uhl ihs) hilltop fortress in a city-state of ancient Greece

agrarian: pertaining to land and the agricultural interests of farmers

alliance: any union, coalition, or formal agreement between nations in their common interest

annexation: to add to existing possessions/territory

anthropologist: (AN thruh PAHL uh jihst) scientist who studies the ways people organize societies

apartheid: policy of racial segregation in the Repulic of South Africa

appeasement: making concessions to an aggressor in order to preserve the peace

apprentice: (uh PREHN tihs) young person who learns a trade from a master craftsman

archaeologist: (AHR kee AHL uh jihst) scientist who studies the lives of early peoples by analyzing objects they left behind

archipelago: (AHR kuh PEHL uh GOH) chain of islands

aristocracy: (AR uh STAH kruh see) government headed by a privileged minority or upper class

armistice: (AHR muh stihs) end to fighting in a war

artifact: (AHR tuh FAKT) object made by human beings

artisan: (AHR tuh zuhn) skilled craftsperson

assimilation: (uh SIHM uh LAY shuhn) policy whereby an imperial power tries to absorb a colony politically and culturally

astrolabe: (AS truh LAYB) instrument used to calculate a ship's latitude by measuring the positions of the stars

autocracy: (aw TAH kruh see) government in which the ruler has unlimited power

autonomy: (aw TAHN uh mee) self-government

barter economy: sytem in which one set of goods is exchanged for another

blitzkrieg: (BLIHTS kreeg) German for lightning warfare; swift, massive attack, practiced by the armies of Nazi Germany

bourgeoisie: in Marxism, the social class opposed to the proletariat or working class

brahma: (BRAH muh) in Hinduism, the single, supreme force uniting everything in the universe

bushido: (BOO shee DOH) the way of the warrior; during the feudal period in Japan, a code of conduct for samurai, stressing obedience to one's lord

caliph: (KAY lihf) successor to the prophet Muhammad who acted as both religious and political leader

capital: money that can be invested in business

capitalist: a person who invests in business in order to make a profit

cash crop: crop that can be sold on the world market for money

caste: social group based on birth; in India, caste determined the jobs people could hold

caudillo: (kow DEE yoh) during the 1800s in Latin America, a military dictator

chivalry: (SHIHV'l ree) code of conduct during the Middle Ages that combined Christian values with the values of a warrior

city-state: independent town or city and the surrounding countryside

civil disobedience: refusal to comply with certain laws by means of passive resistance

clan: family group that traces its origin to a common ancestor

coalition: temporary alliance between parties in government

cold war: state of tension and hostility among nations without armed conflict

collective farm: large government-run farm; created in the Soviet Union in the 1930s

collective security: group of nations acting together to preserve peace

collectivization: a system in which the state owns and controls the means of production and distribution

colony: territory that an outside power controls directly

command economy: state controlled economic system

common law: system of law in England based on decisions of royal courts that became accepted legal principles

communism: form of complete socialism in which there is public ownership of all land and all the means of production

conquistador: (kohn KEES tah DOHR) conqueror; person given the right by rulers of Spain to establish outposts in the Americas

containment: policy whereby the United States tried to prevent the Soviet Union from expanding beyond its borders; first applied in the late 1940s

corporation: business owned by many investors who buy shares of stock and risk only the amount of their investment

coup d'état: (koo day tah) revolt by military leaders to overthrow a government

covenant: binding agreement

creole: (KREE ohl) descendant of Spanish settlers born in the Americas

crusades: series of wars launched by Christians against Muslims who controlled the Holy Land

cultural bias: the way a person's culture shapes his or her attitude toward an event

cultural diffusion: when a custom or item of a culture moves from one part of the world to another

cultural diversity: variety of customs, ideas, and ways of living among the people within a region or nation

culture: customs, ideas, and way of life of a group of people

Cyrillic alphabet: (suh RIHL ihk) alphabet devised in the ninth century by Greek monks, Cyril and Methodius

czar: (zahr) Russian word for Caesar; title of the ruler of the Russian Empire

daimyo: (DImyoh) powerful warrior knights directly below the shogun, in Japan during the feudal period

decentralization: to break down into smaller units

deforestation: to clear land of forests and trees

democracy: government in which citizens have ruling power; first developed in ancient Athens

denazification: removal of all traces of Nazism in Germany after World War II

desertification: the spread of desert into semi-arid regions nearby

détente: easing of the international tension between the Soviet Union and the United States

developed countries: countries that have established agriculture, industries, advanced technology, and strong education systems

developing countries: countries that have limited resources and face obstacles, such as, overpopulation, natural disasters, and indebtedness in achieving modern industrial economies

dissident: (DIHS uh duhnt) person who speaks out against a government

dictator: ruler with absolute power; in ancient Rome, a dictator could hold power for only six months

dynastic cycle: rise and fall of Chinese dynasties according to the Mandate of Heaven

dynasty: (DI nuhs tee) ruling family that passes the right to rule from one member to another

empire: group of territories or peoples controlled by one ruler

encomienda: (ehn koh mee EHN dah) right the Spanish government granted settlers in the Americas to demand taxes or labor services from Indians living on the land

Enlightenment: a period in the 1700s, when philosophers emphasized the use of reason, which they believed would free people from ignorance, and lead to a perfect society

entrepreneur: (AHN truh pruh NER) merchant willing to take financial risks in the hope of making large profits

extended family: large family group usually made up of a husband and wife, their unmarried children, their married sons, and the sons' wives and children

extraterritoriality: (EHKS truh TEHR uh TAWR ee AL uh tee) the right of foreigners to be protected by the laws of their own nations

federation: the joining together of two or more states into a union

federal republic: a country that has a representative democracy with a centralized government

feudalism: (FYOOD 'l ihzm) system of rule by local lords who were bound to a king by ties of loyalty; developed in western Europe during the Middle Ages

fief: (feef) during the Middles Ages, an estate that a lord provided a vassal

genocide: the systematic extermination or destruction of an entire people or national group

glasnost: policy of openness domestically and towards the West initiated by Soviet leader Mikhail Gorbachev

Green Revolution: scientific efforts to increase the amount of food produced on the same amount of land

gross national product: total value of goods and services produced by a nation in a year; abbreviated GNP

guerrilla warfare: (guh RIHL uh WAHR fahr) Spanish word for little war; fighting comprised of hit-and-run attacks

guild: association of merchants or artisans that governed a town or craft in the Middle Ages

haiku: (HI koo) short Japanese poem with 17 syllables that creates a mood or describes a scene

hejira: (hih JI ruh) Muhammad's journey from Mecca to Medina in 622

Hellenistic civilization: culture blending eastern and western influences that emerged in Greece and other lands conquered by Alexander the Great

Holocaust: (HAHL uh KAWST) the systematic murder of over 6 million Jews by the Nazis before and during World War II

humanism: the intellectual and literary movement during the Renaissance characterized by an emphasis on human interests and a study of the Greek-Roman classics

illiteracy: inability to read and write

imperialism: domination by one country of the political, economic, or cultural life of another country or region

indulgence: reduction of the punishment a sinner would suffer in purgatory; often granted by medieval and Renaissance popes

industrialization: the process of establishing large-scale industries

inflation: economic cycle in which an increase in the money supply results in an increase in prices

interdependence: countries in the world being dependent upon each other for various resources and products for their mutual benefit

isolationism: a policy of having little to do with foreign nations

kami: (KAH mee) spirits that early Japanese believed controlled the forces of nature

karma: (KAHR muh) in Hinduism, all the actions in a person's life that affect his or her fate in the next life

kibbutz: (kih BOOTS) Israeli settlement in which people live in community housing projects, work together, and share the profits of their labor

knight: in the Middles Ages, lesser noble who served as a mounted warrior for a lord

kulak: (koo LAHK) prosperous peasant in the Soviet Union who opposed collectivization during the 1930s

laissez-faire: an economic system in which the government does not interfere with the economy

liberation theology: doctrine supported by many Catholic priests, calling for the Church to take an active role in changing the conditions that contribute to poverty

life expectancy: the probable length of life for an individual

literacy: the ability to read and write

lord: in the Middle Ages, powerful noble who maintained his own land but owed allegiance to the king

mandate: after World War I, an order to a League of Nations member to establish a responsible government in conquered territory

manor: during the Middle Ages, the lands, including a village and surrounding lands, administered by a lord

manorial: during the Middle Ages the system in which land, the manor, was administered by a lord

market economy: an economy based on the buying and selling of goods and services

materialism: the belief that the accumulation of possessions is what is necessary for a good life

matrilineal: (MAT ruh LIHN ee uhl) describes a family in which children trace their family line through their mother

mercantilism: economnic theory that stated that a nation's economic strength depends on the importation of gold and silver and the establishment of colonies to serve the needs of the mother country

mestizo: (mehs TEE zoh) person in Spain's colonies in the Americas who was of mixed European and Indian parentage

Middle Ages: period of history in Europe following the fall of the Roman Empire and lasting from about 500 to 1350

militarism: glorification of the military and readiness for war

militarize: to train, prepare, or equip for war

minaret: slender tower from which Muslims are called to prayer

modernization: creation of a stable society capable of producing a high level of goods and services

monarchy: government headed by a king or queen

monopoly: (muh NAPH uh lee) total control of the market for a particular product by one corporation

monotheism: (MAHN uh thee ihzm) worship of a single god

monsoon: (mahn SOON) seasonal wind; in India, the summer monsoon brings rain and the winter monsoon brings hot, dry weather

mosque: meeting place where Muslims assemble to pray

nationalize: (NASH uh nuh LIZ) to bring a part of the economy under government control

nationalism: feeling of pride and devotion to one's country

nativism: to favor people born in a particular country over those who live in that country but are foreign born

natural resources: a source of wealth provided by nature, as forests, minerals, and water supply

Neolithic: the period of human culture characterized by the development of a system of settled agriculture

neutral: not taking part for either side in a dispute

nirvana: (nihr VAH nuh) in Hinduism and Buddhism, the ultimate goal of life; the condition of wanting nothing

nomad: person who travels in search of food

non-alignment: foreign policy of many developing countries to remain neutral with respect to the positions of the United States and the Soviet Union

nuclear family: family made up of parents, children, and occasionally grandparents

pacifist: one who is opposed to war and to serving in the military

Pan-Africanism: movement whose goal is to create a politically and economically unified Africa

passive resistance: nonviolent opposition and refusal to cooperate

patrician: (puh TRIHSH uhn) member of the class of wealthy landowners in ancient Rome

patrilineal: (PAT ruh LIHN ee uhl) describes a family in which children trace their family line through their father

peninsulare: (peh NIHN suh LAHR ay) official sent by Spain to rule Spanish colonies in the Americas

per-capita: for each person

perestroika: (pehr uh STROI kuh) restructuring of the Soviet economy and society, instituted by Mikhail Gorbachev

philosophe: (fee loh ZOHF) French word meaning philosopher; person during the Enlightenment who believed that the use of science and reason would lead to human progress

philosopher: in ancient Greece, person seeking wisdom and knowledge through systematic study and logic

plantation: large estate operated by the owner or overseer and farmed by workers living on it

plebeian: (plih BEE uhn) member of the class of common people in ancient Rome, including farmers, artisans, small merchants, and traders

pogrom: (poh GRAHM) violent raid on a Jewish community, often conducted by government troops

polytheism: (PAHL ih thee ihzm) belief in many gods

prime minister: head of the cabinet in parliamentary governments, usually the leader of the largest party in the legislature

proletariat: (PROH luh TAIR ee uht) the working class

proliferation: to grow rapidly

propaganda: (PRAHP uh GAN duh) spread of ideas to further a cause or damage an opposing cause

purdah: (PER duh) practice of secluding women; probably originated in northern India and spread to Islamic lands

quotas: a part or a share required for each person, group, or state

regionalism: loyalty to a small geographic area

reincarnation: (REE ihn kahr NAY shuhn) rebirth of the soul in another bodily form; a belief of Hinduism and Buddhism

Renaissance: (REHN uh SAHNS) period from about 1350 to 1600 in which European scholars revived the learning of ancient Greece and Rome

republic: system of government in which citizens who have the right to vote choose their leaders

revolution: the overthrow or replacement of a government or political system

Russification: the policy of the czars to have the people they conquered be forced to learn the Russian language and culture, and convert to the Eastern Orthodox religion

samurai: (SAM uh rī) warrior knights of Japan during the feudal period

satrapy: province in the Persian Empire ruled by a governor responsible to the king

savanna: (suh VAN uh) grasslands dotted with scattered trees in which rainfall is often unreliable

scarcity: inadequate supply

self-sufficiency: able to support oneself without aid or co-operation from others

serf: peasant who was tied to the lord's land

shogun: (SHOH guhn) after 1192, the chief general in Japan, who held more political power than the emperor

silt: a soil rich in minerals deposited by flooding rivers

simony: in the Middle Ages, buying and selling of religious offices

social mobility: the ability to move up or down in the social class system

socialism: economic and political system in which society as a whole, rather than private individuals, owns all property and operates all businesses

Socratic method: in ancient Greece, question-and-answer technique, developed by Socrates, that used reasoning in the search for truth

status quo: (STAYT uhs KWOH) existing state of affairs

suffrage: the right to vote

tao: (DOW) in Taoism, a universal force that can only be felt; also the way a person achieves harmony with that force

tariff: a price on imported or exported items

technology: (tehk NAHL uh jee) tools and skills people use

terrorism: unlawful acts of violence by a political group, such as bombings, hijackings, arson, etc. to publicize and achieve their causes

theocracy: (thee AHK ruh see) form of government in which priests serve as kings

Third World: in the late twentieth century, developing nations that share common economic goals and problems

tithe: (tīth) payment to the Church of 10 percent of a person's income

topography: the physical features of a region

totalitarian state: (toh TAL uh TAIR ee uhn) country in which the government is a single-party dictatorship that controls every aspect of citizens' lives

totalitarianism: political system in which the government has a single-party dictatorship and controls every aspect of citizens' lives

tribe: group of related families who recognize a common ancestor, speak the same language, and share common traditions and beliefs

tribalism: loyalty and devotion to one's tribe, as opposed to one's nation (nationalism)

tyranny: (TIR uh nee) government headed by a single individual who seizes power by force

universal suffrage: the right or privilege of voting extended to all

urbanization: the quality or state of changing over from rural villages to cities

usury: (YOO zhoo ree) during the Middle Ages, practice of lending money for interest

welfare state: state in which the government assumes responsibility for people's social and economic well-being

westernization: adoption of western ideas and customs by nonwestern nations

zaibatsu: (ZI baht SOO) wealthy Japanese families who bought the chief industries of the country in the 1880s and came to dominate the Japanese economy

Index

Absolute monarchy, 134–135
Acid rain, 335–338
Africa, 33–38, 75–80, 187–190, 237–241, 285–289
Agricultural economy, 237–241, 245, 256, 271
AIDS, 340
Albania, 67
Animism, 188
Apartheid, 80, 286, 287, 341
Aquino, Corazon, 90
Argentina, 54, 55, 111, 160, 258, 301–302, 318
Arts, 129–130, 189–190, 194–195, 201–202, 205, 208–209, 213–214, 218–221, 225–226
Austria, 153
Authoritarianism, 319
Autocracy, 312

Bangladesh, 84–85, 291, 334
Bolivia, 54, 57
Brazil, 54, 105, 208, 209, 303, 334, 335
Brunei, 43, 45, 91
Buddhism, 193, 196–197, 199, 205
Bulgaria, 67
Burma, 43, 45
Byzantine Empire, 117, 126, 162, 306

Cambodia, 43, 86, 89, 90, 159, 196, 246, 294
Capitalism, 136, 145, 146, 243, 265–266, 267–268, 271
Cash crops, 42, 57, 237–239, 245, 255
Caste system, 81, 191–192
Caudillos, 107, 301
Chile, 57, 304
China, 46–48, 92–97, 198–202, 247–250, 296–298, 334, 335
Christianity, 117, 125, 189, 194, 211, 216, 225
Climate, 37, 41, 43, 47, 50, 54, 60, 65, 69, 240
Cold War, 156–160, 173–175, 269–270, 310, 322–323
Collectivization, 172, 272–273
Colombia, 54, 57, 257
Colonialism, 77, 87–88, 105–106, 133–134, 242–243, 255
Commonwealth of Independent States, 67, 176, 321
Communism, 95, 146, 201, 223, 248–250, 269–270, 271–277, 296–297, 319–321
Confucianism, 198–199, 201
Counter Reformation, 132
Cuba, 111–112, 174, 257, 301, 304, 323
Cultural diffusion, 74, 76, 186
Cultural Revolution, 96, 249, 296
Czechoslovakia, 67, 153, 172, 174, 225, 226, 323, 324–325

Deforestation, 54–55, 335
Democracy, 123, 135, 146, 291, 312
Deng Xiaoping, 96–97, 201, 249–250, 291
Desertification, 33–35, 338–339
Dynasties, 82, 92–93

Economic imperialism, 256
Ecuador, 54
Eygpt, 59, 116, 159, 213, 261, 263, 307, 310
El Salvador, 302–303
Encomienda system, 105, 255
England, 65, 105, 118, 134, 135, 144, 153, 155, 159, 267, 270, 285, 306, 312–313, 318
Enlightenment, 136–138
Ethnic groups, 187
European Economic Community, 156–157, 160, 270, 317–318
Exploration, 104–105, 133–134, 146

Family, 187–188, 191, 200, 204, 207, 210–211, 215, 222
Fascism, 269, 314
Feudalism, 98–99, 126–127, 128, 203–204, 215–216, 257, 264, 271
Foreign investment, 109, 249–250
France, 65, 105, 118, 134, 136, 138–141, 148, 153, 154, 155, 159, 285, 306, 313, 318
Gandhi, Mohandas K., 83–84, 159, 290
Geographic setting, 32, 284
Germany, 65, 67, 143, 148–150, 152–155, 157, 158, 172–173, 269, 276, 313, 314, 315, 335
Ghana, 286
Global economy, 253–254, 300
Global regions, review, 346–347
Good Neighbor Policy, 113, 304
Gorbachev, Mikhail, 158, 175–176, 274–276, 315, 320, 323, 324, 341
Great Britain. *See* England
Greece, 65; ancient, 121–122, 218–219, 312
Greenhouse effect, 339
Grenada, 304

Hinduism, 81, 192–193
Hitler, Adolf, 152–153, 172, 314
Ho Chi Minh, 89, 293
Human resources, 51
Hungary, 67, 172, 225, 324

Imperialism, 77, 83–84, 94–95, 100, 109, 118–119, 146–148, 149, 200–201, 237–239, 252
Impressionism, 200
Independence, 83–84, 88–89, 106–107, 243, 256
India, 39–42, 81–85, 118, 159, 191–195, 242–244, 290–292, 334
Indochina, 43, 89, 159
Indonesia, 43, 45, 87, 89, 196, 245, 246, 294–295, 334
Industrialization, 194
Industrial Revolution, 143–146, 216, 267–269
Interdependence, 74, 260
Iran, 60, 119, 212, 213, 261, 263, 308–310
Iraq, 118, 119, 212, 261, 263, 306, 307, 310, 316
Islam, 81, 87, 117–118, 189, 194, 212, 224, 225
Islamic jihad, 212, 341
Israel, 119, 159, 261, 262, 307–308, 310
Italy, 65, 129, 142, 148, 152, 153, 154, 269, 313, 314

Japan, 49–51, 98, 154, 203–205, 251–254, 261, 299–300
Jordan, 306, 307
Judaism, 116, 211, 224, 225

Kenya, 240
Kenyatta, Jomo, 79, 286
Korean War, 297, 316
Kuwait, 119, 261, 263, 310, 316

Laos, 43, 89, 90, 159, 196, 246, 293
Latin America, 52–57, 103–114, 206–209, 255–259, 301–305
Lebanon, 118, 119, 306, 307, 308
Lenin, Nikolai, 169, 170–171, 271, 272, 319
Libya, 261, 263

Maastricht Treaty, 160, 270, 318
Malaysia, 43, 45, 87, 196, 245, 246
Manorialism, 264–265
Mao Zedong, 95–96, 201, 248–249, 296
Marxism, 146, 170, 223, 268–269
Mejii Restoration, 99–100, 252
Mercantilism, 105, 136, 255, 266
Mexico, 52, 57, 111, 209, 256, 258, 334
Middle Ages, 125–128, 216–218, 219, 264
Middle East, 58, 115, 210, 260, 306
Mixed economy, 242, 243, 261, 270
Monroe Doctrine, 108, 303
Morocco, 60

Namibia, 79, 286
Nationalism, 75, 77, 83, 95, 118–119, 131, 141–143, 147, 148, 160, 171, 201, 284, 286, 290, 307, 314
Nationalist groups, 348–349
Nationalist leaders, 350–360
Nationalization, 170, 257
Natural resources, 37, 41, 45, 47, 51, 55, 61, 65, 70
Nazism, 152–156, 314, 341
Netherlands, 65, 105
Nicaragua, 112–113, 302
Nkrumah, Kwame, 79, 286
Nonalignment, 79, 288–289, 291, 324
North Atlantic Treaty Organization, 158, 315, 317, 322
Northern Eurasia and Eastern Europe, 67–70, 156, 162–171, 222–227, 271–276, 319–325
Northern Ireland, 218, 341
Norway, 65
Nuclear weapons, 101, 158, 340–341

Oil politics, 261–263
Organization of African Unity, 79, 288
Organization of American States, 114, 303
Organization of Petroleum Exporting Countries, 261–262, 308
Ottoman Empire, 118, 306

Pakistan, 84–85, 285, 290, 291, 334
Palestine, 118, 306
Palestine Liberation Organization, 119, 308, 310, 341
Pan-Africanism, 79, 285, 288
Panama, 304
Panama Canal, 109, 303–304
Pan-Arabism, 306, 310
Patriarchal society, 191, 199, 204, 207, 210, 215, 222
Perestroika, 175, 274, 320–321
Peru, 54
Philippines, 43, 88, 90, 196, 293, 295
Poland, 67, 153, 154, 172, 173, 174–175, 225, 276, 323, 324
Pollution, 339–340
Population, 41, 57, 60, 146, 188, 240, 244, 257, 334–335
Portugal, 105, 133, 255
Protestant Reformation, 130–132, 218

Racism, 76
Regents exams, 361–403
Renaissance, 129–130, 219–220
Revolution, 111–112, 135, 136, 138–140, 141, 143–145, 168–170, 201, 216, 271–272, 301, 308–309, 313
Roman Catholic Church, 105, 108, 207–208, 216, 225
Romania, 67, 172, 325
Rome, ancient, 117–118, 123–125, 218–219, 264, 312
Russian Orthodoxy, 167, 224
Saudi Arabia, 261, 263
Self-determination, 79, 285
Shinto, 204
Singapore, 43, 91, 246
Socialism, 146, 261, 268
South Africa, 80, 286–287
Southeast Asia, 43, 86, 196, 245, 293
Spain, 65, 104, 105, 133, 255, 269, 314
Spanish-American War, 109, 303
Stalin, Josef, 156, 171–173, 222, 272–273, 320
Subsistence farming, 166, 200, 239, 245, 251, 256
Sudan, 59
Syria, 118, 306, 307

Taoism, 199
Technology, 74, 273
Test strategies, 14–26
Thailand, 43, 45, 87, 196, 245
Thatcher, Margaret, 160, 318
Topography, 33, 39, 43, 46, 49, 52, 58, 63, 67
Totalitarianism, 152–153, 171–172, 226, 314, 320
Tribalism, 75, 187, 188, 286
Turkey, 60, 61, 214, 263, 306

United Nations, 155, 159, 263, 307, 310, 315–317, 341
Urbanization, 188, 194, 222, 257
Uruguay, 54

Venezuela, 54, 57, 208, 257
Vietnam, 43, 89, 90, 159, 197, 245, 246, 293–294
Vietnam War, 293–294
Vocabulary, 27–28, 30

Warsaw Pact, 158, 322
Western Europe, 63, 120, 215, 264, 312
Women, 210–211
World problems, review, 344–345
World War I, 100, 148–152, 168–169, 269
World War II, 79, 88, 95, 100–101, 154–156, 172–173, 252, 269

Yeltsin, Boris, 175, 275, 360
Yugoslavia, 67, 173, 225